Property Management

Joseph W. DeCarlo, CCIM, CPM, GRI

Professor of Real Estate
Coastline Community College

Prentice Hall
Upper Saddle River, NJ 07458

Library of Congress Cataloging-in-Publication Data

DeCarlo, Joseph W.
    Property management / Joseph W. DeCarlo.
      p.   cm.
    Includes bibliographical references (p.) and index.
    ISBN 0-13-257262-1
    1. Real estate management.   2. Real estate management—United
States.   I. Title.
HD1394.D429   1997
333.3'068—dc20
                                                96-41969
                                                        CIP

Acquisitions Editor: Elizabeth Sugg
Director of Production and Manufacturing: Bruce Johnson
Managing Editor: Mary Carnis
Production Liaison: Eileen O'Sullivan
*Editorial/Production Supervision and
  Interior Design:* Tally Morgan, WordCrafters Editorial Services, Inc.
Cover Design: Marianne Frasco
Manufacturing Manager: Ed O'Dougherty
Associate Production Manager: Marc Bove
Marketing Manager: Danny Hoyt
Creative Director: Marianne Frasco
Editorial Assistant: Emily Jones
Printer/Binder: Courier/Westford

 © 1997 by Prentice-Hall, Inc.
A Division of Simon & Schuster
Upper Saddle River, New Jersey 07458

Printed in the United States of America

10 9 8 7 6 5 4 3 2 1

ISBN 0-13-257262-1

Prentice Hall International (UK) Limited, *London*
Prentice Hall of Australia Pty. Limited, *Sydney*
Prentice Hall Canada Inc., *Toronto*
Prentice Hall Hispanoamericana, S.A., *Mexico*
Prentice Hall of India Private Limited, *New Delhi*
Prentice Hall of Japan, Inc., *Tokyo*
Prentice Hall of Southeast Asia Pte. Ltd., *Singapore*
Editoria Prentice Hall do Brasil, Ltda., *Rio de Janeiro*

Contents

Appendices

List of Figures

Chapter 4

Chapter 5

Chapter 6

Chapter 7

Chapter 8

Chapter 9

Chapter 10

Chapter 11

Chapter 12

Chapter 13

Chapter 14

Chapter 15

Preface

Property Management is written for students and practitioners of property management. Over 150 illustrations and forms are used, along with examples, to provide the reader with both theory and a practical understanding of property management. This book is intended to be a basic text, not a comprehensive reference book. It does, however, contain an extensive list of further reference sources, books, and publications.

The book is divided into chapters covering areas such as leases, residential management, shopping centers, office buildings, maintenance, and landlord/tenant law, to name a few. At the end of each chapter are 15 multiple choice review questions to help the reader better understand the chapter. Answers to these questions are contained in Appendix B.

This book also contains a case study beginning with Chapter 5 and continuing throughout the book. The reader is given background information and facts about a 20-unit apartment building that has serious problems. At the end of selected chapters, questions are asked directing the reader to use the material in the chapter to help solve some of these problems. Suggested answers will be found in Appendix C. Appendix A includes an extensive list of frequently used property management terms.

Acknowledgments

I want to express my appreciation to all the people who encouraged me and helped me to write this book. Advice was solicited and received from real estate professionals (CPMs), property management instructors at other colleges, attorneys, the California Apartment Association, California Association of Realtors, the California Department of Real Estate, the Institute of Real Estate Management, the Buildings Owners and Managers Association International, and the International Council of Shopping Centers. The list of reviewers for individual chapters includes Ph.D.s, CPMs, CSMs, RPAs, attorneys, and MBAs. My Coastline Community College, fall 1995 and spring 1996 property management classes were also of great assistance in reviewing the individual chapters.

For their assistance I give special thanks to illustrator Bill Hankla; typist Cathie Carey, who transcribed the manuscript; publication coordinator Julie Shafii, who spent countless hours editing and tying the loose ends together; fellow real estate professional Dennis McKenzie, who promoted the idea of a national version of this property management book; and Carla McLelland, CPM, whose help in writing, researching, editing and reviewing was invaluable.

Last, but certainly not least, my sincere gratitude to my wonderful wife Susan and three children Christine, David and Joey, whose support and encouragement enabled me to finish this challenging book.

ADDITIONAL ACKNOWLEDGMENTS

Lowell Anderson
Real Estate Coordinator
Cerritos College
Norwalk, CA

James Ashcraft, Jr., B.S.
Ashcraft Electric Co.
Long Beach, CA

Ray Baca, CPM
Monterey Properties
El Paso, TX

Hitesh Barot, Student
Coastline Community College
Fountain Valley, CA

John Bennett, CPM
Tomlinson Black Management
Spokane, WA

Russell W. Berry
Executive Vice President
Woodmont Companies
Belmont, CA

Rick Burnett, CPM
Los Angeles, CA

Gary Conkey, B.A.
United Insurance Agencies
Pasadena, CA

Mike Cook, Broker
Windward Investments
Huntington Beach, CA

Evelyn Daniel, Attorney
Real Estate Coordinator
Rancho Santiago College
Santa Ana, CA

Tony Diana, CPM
Diana Management
Bel Air, MD

Mike Dunn, Attorney
Dunn & Associates
Costa Mesa, CA

Steve Duringer, Attorney
Duringer & Associates
Newport Beach, CA

Michael Easton
Easton Pacific Co.
Irvine, CA

Walt Edwards, CPM
Capital Area Development Authority
Sacramento, CA

Susan Fassnacht, CPM
Santa Ana, CA

Frank Fowler
Torrance, CA

Glenn French, CPM
Raleigh, NC

Thomas Gille, CPM, RPA
San Francisco, CA

Gene Harrison
Victor Valley College
Apple Valley, CA

Barbara L. Holland, CPM
H&L Realty and Management
Las Vegas, NV

Cecilia Hopkins, Ph.D., Retired
College of San Mateo
San Mateo, CA

Judy Jenks, ARM
Simi Valley, CA

Audrey King, RECI
Real Estate Broker
Tustin, CA

Peter Kroosz, CPM, MBA
Peter Kroosz Realty Management
Newport Beach, CA

Mike Lango, RPA
San Luis Obispo, CA

Carla McLelland, CPM
JD Property Management, Inc.
Costa Mesa, CA

John Phelps, CPM, CSM
Fullerton, CA

Chet Platt, Ph.D.
Associate Dean
Coastline Community College
Fountain Valley, CA

Judith C. Ricker, CPM
Cortland-Dane Management Group
Santa Barbara, CA

Trudy Rideout
Coastline Community College
Fountain Valley, CA

Carey Roth, CPM
UCLA
Los Angeles, CA

Donald Smith, CPM, CSM
DWA Smith & Co.
Newport Beach, CA

Lainy Steinberg
Irvine, CA

Rocky Tarantello, Ph.D., Professor
University of Southern California
Los Angeles, CA

Robert Taylor, CPM, MBA
Real Estate Marketing/Management
Anaheim Hills, CA

Gene Trowbridge, Attorney, CCIM
Trowbridge & Associates
Newport Beach, CA

Terence Tom, CPM
Optima Management Group
Oakland, CA

Dennis White, CPM
Port of Oakland
Oakland, CA

Chapter 1

Property Management as a Profession

Key terms

AMO	CSM	Regional manager
ARM	FIABCI-USA	Resident manager
Asset manager	ICSC	RPA
BOMI	IREM	Property manager
CPM	Mixed-use complexes	

Food for thought

"A journey of 1,000 miles begins with a single step."

INTRODUCTION

During the twentieth century, the United States moved into an era of urbanization and rapid development. The real estate profession has responded to this revolutionary trend with increased specialization and a higher and more sophisticated level of service to its clients.

Many professional designations originated to coincide with increased levels of professional service and specialization. The appraisal area developed specialists called MAI (Member Appraisal Institute) appraisers. Commercial real estate brokers designate their specialists as CCIMs (Certified Commercial Investment Member).

One of the fastest-growing areas of specialization to arise as long-term real estate investments increased was that of property manager. The highest designation bestowed on this new professional field was that of CPM® (Certified Property Manager®). This special recognition is bestowed only after intensive study, including completion of classes, seminars, testing, demonstration reports, and several years of experience in the field while abiding by a strict code of ethics.

CERTIFIED PROPERTY MANAGER®

EVOLUTION OF PROPERTY MANAGEMENT

The profession of property management is both an evolving and a rapidly expanding field. The role of being just a rent collector is disappearing. Instead, property management has emerged as a highly technical and specialized managerial science. The property manager of today must possess communications skills and be a dynamic and effective decision maker. He or she must act as a market analyst, an advertising executive, a diplomat, and a maintenance engineer as he or she associates with property owners, prospective tenants and investors, tenants, employees, attorneys, accountants, and others involved in the real estate field.

History

During colonial times, the development of American cities occurred at seaports and along major waterways. These early cities—New York, Boston, and Philadelphia—served as living, trading, and shopping areas. During the 1800s, the population of the United States profoundly increased in the downtown centers of cities, and office and commercial buildings soon developed.

In the early 1900s, significant changes were starting to take place. Three important technological advances occurred:

1. Steel-framed buildings

2. The perfection of high-speed elevators

3. The popularization of the automobile

The first two technological advances brought about taller buildings, thereby increasing the density of office, commercial, and apartment buildings. The central business district (CBD) was created. The advent of the automobile permitted both business owners and residents to move away from the congested downtown areas into a newly developing phenomenon—"suburbia."

After World War II, assisted by VA and FHA loans, returning soldiers were able to purchase their own homes. Many of these new homes were located away from the CBD in suburbia. Following this migration, developers built office and shopping centers convenient to the growing suburban population.

Initially, these suburban shopping centers tended to be small and convenience oriented, made up mostly of grocers and small retailers. From the 1960s through the 1980s, as the population migration continued, commercial developers became increasingly interested in serving the shopping needs of suburbia. Larger centers were soon built, offering one-stop shopping, free parking, and climate-controlled malls to meet the needs of the burgeoning "Baby Boomers." Today, over 600 major regional malls plus 35,000 shopping centers exist throughout the United States.

Projections for the Future

Present trends indicate a reversal of this migration pattern. Many areas of the country are now saturated with large shopping centers. As a result, those under construction are frequently smaller in size. The population is growing at a slower rate and moving back to smaller rural towns in significant numbers. America is changing from a nation of producers to one that supplies information and services. The property manager, therefore, must keep abreast of changing demographics regarding location, family size, age, and consumer buying habits.

CLASSIFICATION OF PROPERTIES

The real estate industry is large and diversified, with many types of properties that need to be managed. Properties are defined according to their uses.

Retail—properties where things are sold; i.e., regional shopping centers to strip centers (Chapter 8).

Office—properties where services are rendered; i.e., skyscrapers to garden offices (Chapter 9).

Industrial—properties where things are made; i.e., large manufacturing plants to small industrial parks (Chapter 11).

Agricultural—properties where food is grown; i.e., large farms to strawberry fields in urban areas.

Residential—properties where people live; i.e., apartments, condos, single-family homes (Chapter 7).

Special Purpose—properties where the use dictates the design; i.e., motels, mobile home parks, ministorage (Chapter 11).

Within these general classifications are many subdivisions.

PROPERTY MANAGEMENT DESIGNATIONS

The term *professional property manager* has been misunderstood, misused, and abused in the past. Presently, there is no degree or major in property management in four-year colleges. However, property management courses are becoming more common in community colleges throughout the nation, some of which now offer a two-year associates degree in property management. Several professional designations exist in the field of property management, the three major ones being certified property manager (CPM), real property administrator (RPA), and certified shopping center manager (CSM).

The CPM designation is conferred by the Institute of Real Estate Management (IREM), a branch of the National Association of Realtors (NAR). The organization was formed in 1933 by a group of property managers concerned with establishing ethical standards and professionalism in the property management field. To qualify for this designation, already earned by over 14,000 property managers in the United States, the property manager must meet stringent qualifying standards in areas of education, experience, and ethical conduct. In addition to passing three exams in these areas, a candidate must satisfactorily complete a management plan (minithesis). The candidate must also currently manage a set minimum management portfolio (for example, over 300 apartment units or 100 single-family homes, or 120,000 square feet of retail space), and have five years of experience as a property manager. If directly supervised by a CPM, the time element may be reduced to three years. Additional information concerning this professional designation can be obtained by writing to:

IREM Institute of Real Estate Management

of the NATIONAL ASSOCIATION OF REALTORS®
National Headquarters: 430 North Michigan Avenue, Chicago, IL 60611-4090
(312) 661-1930   Telex (312) 025-3742

The RPA designation is bestowed by the Building Owners and Managers Institute International (BOMI). BOMI has had experience (three years) and portfolio (40,000 square feet) requirements since January 1, 1990. They also have a code of ethics. Each candidate must successfully complete a seven-course educational program. Additional information can be obtained by writing to:

Building Owners and Managers Institute International
1201 New York Ave., N.W., Suite 300
Washington, D.C. 20005
(202) 408-2662

The CSM designation is conferred by the International Council of Shopping Centers. At the present time, no management courses are required, but courses are available to help the candidate pass the required examination. Additional information can be obtained by writing to:

International Council of Shopping Centers
665 Fifth Ave., New York, N.Y. 10022
(212) 421-8181

The AMO® designation (accredited management organization) is also awarded by IREM to firms engaged in property management which have met the high standards IREM has established in areas of education, experience, integrity, and financial stability.

The ARM® (accredited resident manager) designation is awarded by IREM to residential on-site managers who have met experience and educational standards after passing a test at the end of a one-week course.

The terms CPM®, ARM®, and AMO® are registered trademarks of the Institute of Real Estate Management.

The Urban Land Institute (ULI) is an independent, nonprofit education and research organization whose stated purpose is to improve the quality standards for land-use planning and development. ULI was founded in 1936 and has published hundreds of publications and held numerous seminars and on-site study projects. These items range from office handbooks, rental housing, and dollars and cents of shopping centers to shared-parking computer programs. A complete list can be obtained by writing to:

 THE URBAN LAND INSTITUTE
625 Indiana Ave., N.W., Ste. 400
Washington, D.C. 20004
(202) 624-7000

Another very useful source of information is the National Apartment Association (NAA). Legal briefs and updates are sent to the organization members along with red alerts concerning unfavorable legislation, whether it be taxes, rental control, and so on. Local and state apartment associations have developed an extensive list of forms such as rental applications and security deposit return forms and hold monthly meetings, print monthly newsletters, and offer tenant credit-checking services to their members. The names and addresses of local chapters near you can be obtained by writing the NAA. One such chapter, the Apartment Association of Orange County in California publishes a 100-page monthly magazine and has over 3,000 members. They also have a designation called the certified apartment manager (CAM), which is issued after completion of two courses, preparation of an apartment community-analysis report, an additional 40 hours of optional credits, two years of management experience, and successfully passing a national examination. Additional information can be obtained by writing to:

NATIONAL APARTMENT ASSOCIATION
1111 14th N.W., 9th Floor
Washington, D.C. 20005

INTERNATIONAL MANAGEMENT ORGANIZATIONS

The International Real Estate Institute has a designation of registered property manager (RPM), which has a code of ethics, although no courses or tests are required to earn the designation. They also published the International Real Estate Journal.

The most widely recognized international real estate organization is FIABCI, which was founded in 1949. It is also a National Association of Realtors affiliate. It has registered over 6,000 international real estate specialists and operates in more than 44 countries. The name is derived from its French origins and stands for Federation Internationale des Administrateurs de Biens Conseils Immobiliers. FIABCI publishes a world directory and a professional newsletter

International Real Estate Institute

8383 E. Evans Rd.
Scottsdale, AZ 85281 USA
(602) 998-8267

and holds educational seminars. It has a professional designation called certified international property specialist (CIPS). Candidates must fulfill criteria in three main categories: education, participation in FIABCI, and work experience.

FIABCI-USA
777 14th Street N.W.
Washington, D.C. 20005
(202) 383-1000

TRENDS IN PROPERTY MANAGEMENT
Multifamily Housing (Apartments)

At the present time there are approximately 35 million rental units in the United States, 9 million of which are single-family homes. The rental ownership is well diversified, with the top 50 largest owners controlling just a little over 4 percent of the total. This percentage will increase in the future as large investors and syndicators move into the industry with even larger complexes in many locations throughout the country. Approximately 34 percent of all housing units are rentals with the remaining 66 percent owner occupied.

Government Participation

Participation by the federal government in rental housing is slowing as funding for rent subsidies and low-cost government housing has been reduced. The use of tax-free bond financing, which in the past helped the development of new projects by lowering debt financing costs, has been curtailed. Under the current tax code, the depreciation schedule was increased to $27\frac{1}{2}$ years for residential (apartments) and 39 years for commercial buildings. This change reduces the tax shelter benefits—a form of government participation—that real estate enjoyed in the past.

Increase in Condominiums and Smaller Single-Family Homes

As the number of people per household declines (presently 2.5), there is less need for the large four- and five-bedroom homes preferred by the larger families of the past. Houses are getting smaller as high land costs spur the development of condominiums and PUDs (planned unit developments).

Mixed-Use Complexes

These complexes usually include offices, retail stores, and apartments or condos. By using shared parking, land costs are lowered while providing convenience and aesthetics to the development. Examples are Tricorp Towers in New York and Water Towers in Chicago.

Complexity of Management

The increasing costs, risks, and sophistication of real estate development—leasing, financing, and government regulations—have created a need for professional property management. Landlord/tenant laws and court cases have thrust a considerable amount of liability on the shoulders of managers and owners.

In addition, there are different types of interactions with tenants. Residential residents are more emotional about their apartments, while commercial tenants are more business minded and not as sentimental concerning their rented space.

Most professional property managers work for either the individual owner, institutions, banks or syndications, or as an independent contractor for a fee for several owners. These "fee managers" are often large management companies, called third-party managers, and the property manager is employed by the management company, not by the owner of the property.

CAREER OPPORTUNITIES

Steps in achieving the position of property manager have traditionally followed the career path of assistant resident manager, then resident manager, and finally, property manager. This is no longer the case, however, as a person who excels at running one building (on-site resident manager) may not have the temperament, skills, or ability to manage several properties (property manager). The old adage "The best salesperson does not always make the best sales manager" may apply here.

Many different types of businesses and organizations employ property managers. Some of these include property management companies, full-service real estate firms, development companies, real estate investment trusts (REITs), banks, insurance companies, and government agencies.

Resident Manager

The terms *on-site manager* and *resident manager* (Figure 1–1) are interchangeable. The main duties of a resident manager are:

1. Renting units

2. Collecting rents

3. Responsibility for tenant relations

Figure 1–1. Resident Manager

4. Maintenance

5. Supervision

6. Keeping records

7. Completing proper paperwork

Personality traits usually found in good resident managers or assistant resident managers include:

1. Conscientiousness

2. Congenial personality

3. Accuracy

4. Salesmanship

5. Tact

6. Honesty

Property Manager

The terms *property manager* and *property supervisor* are also interchangeable. These persons differ from the on-site manager in that they deal with several properties and supervise the on-site manager. They usually interface directly with the owner. In addition to being problems solvers, they must also be planners, directors, delegators, and have the ability to organize and implement comprehensive control of the properties they manage.

The main duties of a property manager or property supervisor include:

1. Budgeting, reports, and monthly statements

2. On-site inspections

3. Supervision

4. Controlling expenditures

5. Establishing rental rates

6. Establishing standard operating procedures

7. Maximizing income stream and value

A property manager, in addition to having the personality traits of a resident manager, should also be:

1. Analytical and detail-oriented

2. Personable

3. Self-starting, motivated, enthusiastic

4. Assertive and ambitious

5. Able to be firm and say no

6. Able to represent both owner and tenant

Regional Manager

This job description relates to larger property management companies in which a manager supervises several property managers or property supervisors. The regional manager must have especially good communication skills and be able to delegate, motivate, and accomplish objectives through the efforts of subordinates (see Figure 1–2).

EMPLOYMENT OPPORTUNITIES
IN
PROPERTY MANAGEMENT

- **Executive Manager**
- **Asset Manager**
- **Property Supervisor — Residential**
- **Property Supervisor — Commercial**
- **Property Supervisor — Condominiums**
- **Onsite Manager — Residential**
- **Onsite Manager — Commercial**
- **Leasing Agent — Offsite**
- **Leasing Agent — Onsite**
- **Accounts Supervisor — Bookkeeping**
- **Controller**
- **Administrative Assistant**
- **Maintenance Supervisor**
- **Building Engineer**
- **General Maintenance**

Figure 1–2.   Employment Opportunities

Asset Manager

The most ill-defined job title in property management is that of asset manager. An asset manager may be responsible for a multimillion-dollar portfolio at one company or simply work on site at another. The correctly defined asset manager is normally an employee of a large investment-holding company with little or no responsibility for the day-to-day activity of the portfolio properties. The asset manager is usually responsible for the investment and financial-planning aspects of the entire portfolio.

Executive Manager

The executive manager is responsible for the overall property management performance of the company or business. This responsibility includes supervision of property supervisors, accounting divisions, and maintenance departments. The executive manager is usually a certified property manager (CPM) and in smaller companies typically is the owner-operator.

SPECIALIZATIONS WITHIN PROPERTY MANAGEMENT

Just as different types of properties exist, different management companies specialize in specific types of properties. As an example, some management companies specialize in residential units and would therefore be a poor choice to manage a medical building, which has unique individual problems and specific needs. Another example would be a management company that manages large complexes (over 100 units). The supervisor might be qualified to manage this size complex, but probably would not be able to manage smaller complexes that have no on-site manager. The systems and procedures geared toward larger properties require more experienced on-site managers. Conversely, a management company that handles single-family houses probably does not have the computerized system necessary to manage larger operations. A fully computerized full-service company, however, may have divisions capable of handling the entire management spectrum.

TYPES OF PROPERTY MANAGEMENT OPERATIONS

Large Insurance and Pension Corporations

These firms usually have salaried asset managers to handle the property portfolio in-house, but may subcontract the day-to-day property management to outside third-party fee managers.

"Ma and Pa" Owners

This type of owner is usually someone who owns single-family houses or a few multi-unit complexes. He or she usually self-manages, which requires minimal training and experience. The professional qualifications usually come from the "school of hard knocks." Local apartment associations would be beneficial to these owners to keep abreast of new laws and trends pertaining to vacancies and rental rates in the their local markets.

Local Real Estate Office

Suppose a real estate agent sells a fourplex to an investor and tells him about all the benefits of ownership (appreciation and tax benefits), but forgets to mention evictions, stopped-up toilets, and tenant phone calls at all hours of the night. The investor can tell the real estate agent that if he wants the listing when the property is to be sold, he must mange the property until the sale. This is called "management by default". (A real estate office is shown in Figure 1–3.)

Figure 1–3. Local Real Estate Office

Professional Fee Management Company

Investors (owners) who need a manager in order to bring to their operation diversified talents, experience, and controls, including computer operation, all in one package, will hire a professional property management company. The compensation for this service is usually based on a percentage of the collected income. These companies usually have one or more certified property managers (CPMs) on staff.

GROWTH OF WOMEN IN THE FIELD

In the past several years, the number of women entering the field has increased significantly (see Figure 1–4). Many firms are now headed by women who have risen to top positions based on their performance. The reasons for this are many, but include the following considerations:

1. It is a comparatively new area (nontraditional).
2. Promotions are based on merit and hard work (no glass ceilings).
3. Traits attributed to most successful property managers, such as even temperament, patience, and good decision-making ability, are commonly traits attributed to women.

FUTURE TRENDS

1. More specialization as the property management field becomes more complex, technical, and sophisticated.
2. More formal education (a college degree) may be required along with accounting and financial courses.
3. More reliance on the computer, including systems, procedures, and on-site terminals.
4. Standardization of the industry relative to terms, methods, procedures, and reports.
5. More government regulations, including regulation of requirements for property mangers beyond the present real estate licensing requirements.
6. More team play in which the property manager will be involved from conception in consulting projects with attorneys, architects, builders, and so on.

Figure 1–4. Women in Property Management

7. Greater need for professional management as tax benefits are reduced and investors are increasingly pressured to manage real estate as a full-time business. Investors will want to hire the best managers to maximize investment income and property appreciation.

8. Increased salary compensation along with the increased importance of property management.

SUMMARY

With the advent of urbanization during the twentieth century, the real estate industry became more specialized and sophisticated. The specialized designation of certified property manager (CPM) was instituted in 1933. This designation necessitated taking three educational courses and having five years of experience. The evolution of the property manager was from the role of rent collector to that of sophisticated professional manager who must possess communication skills, technical knowledge, and be a rational decision maker. The advent of important technological advances (steel framing, high-speed elevators, etc.) in the early 1900s enabled the erection of taller buildings and thus increased density. The increased use of the automobile helped create a migration from the city to the suburbs. The major classifications of properties that emerged were retail, office, industrial, agricultural, residential, and special-purpose. The property manager must keep abreast of changing trends in demographics, consumer buying habits, and the economic consequences of a society shifting from manufacturing to service industries.

Professional organizations that have emerged in the property management field of specialization (followed in parentheses by the titles they confer) include IREM (CPM), BOMI (RPA), ICSC (CSM), NAA (CAM), and FIABCI-USA (CIPS).

Positions in property management are many and varied and include asset manager, property manager, leasing agent, controller, maintenance supervisor, building engineer, and others.

The resident manager or on-site manager is the person who usually resides on the property and is responsible for day-to-day activities such as rentals, rent collection, tenant relations, maintenance, supervision, keeping records, and related paperwork. This person should be conscientious, congenial, accurate, tactful, honest, and possess sales ability.

The property manager is the person who usually supervises the resident managers of several properties. Duties include budgeting, inspection, supervision, controlling expenditures, establishing rental rates and operating procedures, and maximizing the cash flow and appreciation for the property. The property manager needs to be analytical, personable, self-starting, assertive, and logical.

Types of management operations range from small "Ma and Pa" owners to large insurance and pension corporations, local real estate offices and professional fee management companies. Future trends in property management include growth and opportunities for women, more specialization and standardization, more government regulations, and higher salary levels.

We conclude from our analysis that the property management profession is an art and not a science. It has neither an empirical nor an exact body of knowledge, no standard code of ethics to which all must adhere, and no specific educational requirements. Property management is a mixture of the theories of the management process (getting things done with and through people), empirical theory (the use of past experience), and decision theory (the rational approach to decision making).

Most property managers don't choose their career in high school like attorneys and doctors, but grow into the field. Carla McLelland is no exception. As a young mother, Carla hired on as an on-site manager for a 45-unit apartment building. "I hadn't graduated from college and I always joke that I couldn't type and didn't like waiting tables. At 25, it was a rare opportunity when my employer offered to pay for my school to get my real estate license." For two years Carla sold homes through the same old established firm for whom she was an on-site manager. "Sales were excellent, but I needed more challenge." Her broker asked her if she would consider becoming a property supervisor. Within a year she was promoted to head up the firm's entire income property management division. "Property management was fun, but I realized I needed more education to be really effective." Attending the local community college and taking real estate and property management classes were the first step. Later, Carla took the three required courses by the Institute of Real Estate Management (IREM), wrote her management plan, and thus received the prestigious certified property manager (CPM) designation.

Carla's specialty was the management of medical office associations and the leasing of medical office space. Carla says, "Dealing with doctors takes a special type of person. You must be strong and knowledgeable to gain their trust and approval." Her career progressed and she became a partner in a medium-size property management firm as well as an astute real estate investor herself.

REVIEW QUESTIONS

1. A designation for a property manager is

   a. MAI.   c. CPM.
   b. REEA.   d. CCIM.

2. Property management developed as a profession around

   a. the early 1980s.   c. the early 1900s.
   b. the Middle Ages.   d. the early 1850s.

3. High-speed elevators, structural steel, and reinforced concrete made possible

   a. high-rise buildings.   c. single-story industrial buildings.
   b. strip shopping centers.   d. both a and c

4. Regional (large) shopping centers were developed

   a. in the early 1900s.   c. after World War II.
   b. before World War II.   d. after 1990.

5. Major factors affecting real estate management include

   a. high-rise buildings.   c. neither a nor b
   b. cities becoming more concentrated.   d. both a and b

6. The CSM designation means

   a. commercial skyscraper manager.   c. commercial slum manager.
   b. certified shopping center manager. d. commercial shopping center manager.

7. The on-site manager designation for apartments is

   a. ARM.   c. CSM.
   b. RPA.   d. CPM.

8. BOMI is an educational organization primarily for

    a. shopping center managers.   c. appraisers.
    b. office managers and owners.   d. apartment managers and owners.

9. Which position is usually higher on an organizational chart?

    a. on-site manager   c. property supervisor
    b. maintenance manager   d. apartment manager

10. The Institute of Real Estate Management bestows which designation?

    a. CPM   c. RPA
    b. REEA   d. CSM

11. The RPA designation is awarded by

    a. IREM.   c. ICSC.
    b. BOMI.   d. NAA.

12. The CSM designation is awarded by

    a. IREM.   c. ICSC.
    b. BOMI.   d. NAA.

13. The CAM designation is awarded by

    a. IREM.   c. ICSC.
    b. BOMI.   d. NAA.

14. The central business district (CBD) is shrinking due to

    a. the expansion of suburbs.   c. both a and b
    b. the expansion of shopping centers.   d. neither a nor b

15. Third-party fee managers work directly for the

    a. owner of the property.   c. on-site manager.
    b. management company.   d. maintenance company.

ADDITIONAL READING AND REFERENCES

Accredited Resident Manager Profile, Institute of Real Estate Management, Chicago, IL, 1994.

Cushman, Robert, and Neal Rodin, *Property Management Handbook*, John Wiley & Sons, Somerset, NJ, 1985.

DeCarlo, Joseph W., CPM, *Real Estate Adventures, Principles & Practices*, JD Seminars & Publications, Inc., P.O. Box 1230, Costa Mesa, CA 92626, 1994.

Downs, Anthony, *Rental Housing in the 1980's*, The Brookings Institution, Washington, DC, 1983.

Downs, James Jr., *Principles of Real Estate Management*, Institute of Real Estate Management, 12th Edition, Chicago, IL, 1980.

Institute of Real Estate Management, *The Certified Manager Profile*, Chicago, IL, 1984.

Journal of Property Management (Bimonthly), Institute of Real Estate Management, 430 N. Michigan Ave., Chicago, IL 60611.

Professional Apartment Manager, Brownstone Publishers, Inc., 149 Fifth Ave, 16th Fl., New York, N.Y. 10010.

Walter, William Jr., CPM, *The Practice of Real Estate Management*, Institute of Real Estate Management, Chicago, IL, 1983.

Chapter 2

Real Estate Economics

Key terms

Capitalization	Gross multiplier	Real depreciation
Cash flow	Income approach	Reproduction
Economic	Market approach	approach
obsolescence	Net operating income	Supply and demand
Economic oversupply	(NOI)	Tax depreciation
Family formations	Nuisance increase	Technical oversupply
Functional	Physical obsolescence	
obsolescence	Population growth	

Food for thought

"There is always time for the things you put first."

SIZE OF THE MARKET

In order to maximize real estate income and value, the property manager/owner must understand the real estate market. The market, due to its large size, has a significant influence representing approximately 3 percent of the total Gross Domestic Product (GDP), or almost 200 billion dollars per year in rental income. According to the United States Department of Commerce, rental households make up 35 percent of a total of 108 million U.S. households, or 39 million nationwide. The total number of rental housing units is approximately 35 million in the United States. The medial residential rent is projected at $475 nationwide. Arthur Anderson and Co. estimated U.S. real estate values at 9 trillion dollars, 2.7 trillion of which is commercial real estate. Clearly, the rental real estate market needs capable, trained professional property managers to shepherd these vast assets.

BUSINESS CYCLES

With the coming of the Industrial Revolution and the development of sophisticated banking and financial markets, the various sectors of the U.S. economy became interdependent, which has led to cyclical economic fluctuations. These cycles are constantly changing. However, the makeup, severity, and duration differs from cycle to cycle. Cycles can last from one to fifteen years and usually occur in three phases.

Phase I   Expansion—Recovery
Phase II   Prosperity—Peak
Phase III   Recession (possible depression)—Decline

Business cycles are measured using an artificial index made up of individual indicators, such as unemployment, industrial production, and gross domestic product. The causes of these cycles are not known, but four theories exist.

1. *Monetary theories*—changes in money supply; i.e., interest rates and credit.

2. *Savings and investments theories*—savings that are used for expanded production will eventually lead to overproduction and recession. In other words, increasing levels of investment cannot be maintained indefinitely, and lead to decline as a "normal" business activity.

3. *Business economy theories*—which were championed by John Maynard Keynes, say that business cycles are a self-generating phenomenon, inherent in industrial society.

4. *Social cycles*—society determines the cyclical pattern. In his best seller, *The Great Depression of 1990*, Dr. Ravi Batra states that society is composed of four types of people, each endowed with a different frame of mind.

   a) *Warrior mentality*—soldiers, policemen, athletes, etc.
   b) *Intellectual mentality*—writers, lawyers, physicians, white-collar workers, etc.
   c) *Acquisitors' mentality*—merchants, bankers, landlords, etc.
   d) *Physical labor mentality*—unskilled workers.

Dr. Batra's theory states that cycles of prosperity and depression are a result of broad economic and social forces rather than unique events caused by individuals.

Government Efforts to Control Cycles

Since the Great Depression, the United States government has sought to stimulate orderly economic growth while cushioning the adverse effects of cyclical fluctuations. Some of these control mechanisms and devices include:

1. Margin requirements on stocks to reduce speculation.

2. The Federal Reserve Bond, which can increase the money supply (print more money) or reduce the rate it charges member banks to borrow funds (discount rate).

3. Government programs such as unemployment insurance, welfare, price supports for farmers, social security, food stamps, public works projects, and road building.

In summary, forecasts of the real estate market and business cycles are based on monitoring and analyzing four major classes of data.

Demand factors—population, effective buying income of families, family formations, etc.

Supply factors—existing inventory and new construction starts, demolitions, etc.

Catalyst factors—mortgage interest rates, unemployment rates, etc.

Psychological factors—perception by consumers of economic changes such as inflation.

CAUSES OF REAL ESTATE FLUCTUATIONS
Money

As a general rule, real estate values increase during inflationary times and decrease during times of recession or depression. Inflationary conditions are frequently due to behavior rather than to economic causes. For example, if Americans believe the value of the dollar will decrease due to the government printing more money (monetizing) to pay its debts, they will purchase real estate, gold, and items that increase in inflationary times. This action may have little relationship to supply and demand, but rather to a perceived future demand. Money is simply the medium of exchange of goods and services. In today's market, credit has enhanced and expanded the use of money.

Supply and Demand

If demand (tenants) is greater than supply (units), rents will generally increase. This will, in theory, cause developers to build more units to meet the increased demand caused by the low vacancy rate (see Figure 2–1).

In the perfect market in which property is homogenous and complete information is available to all buyers and sellers in their negotiations, supply and demand will fluctuate to find the market equilibrium point. This striving for the equilibrium causes fluctuations in supply and demand. Real estate, however, operates in an imperfect marketplace in which the product is unique due to location, terms, financing, timing, size, amenities, and so forth. The striving for the equilibrium point by supply and demand is still responsible for the fluctuation in selling prices and rent levels. Supply is defined as properties for sale or rent and demand is the amount of square footage of units available.

1. *Vacancy rates* are often incorrectly calculated. Local apartment associations are a good source for vacancy rates. Also, the *IREM Experience Exchange Apartments* for major cities is a good reference.

2. *Excess demand* can lead to overcrowding and doubling up of tenants in existing units. It may also result in rent control.

3. *Technical oversupply* occurs in areas where there are more units than tenants. It frequently occurs in boomtowns or where major sources of employment have moved out (e.g., energy boomtowns or military base closure towns).

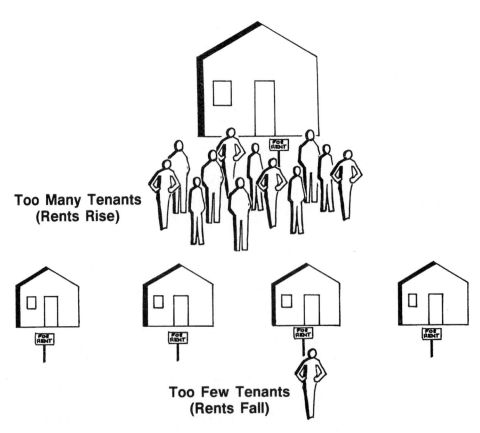

**Too Many Tenants
(Rents Rise)**

**Too Few Tenants
(Rents Fall)**

Figure 2–1. Supply and Demand

4. *Economic oversupply* occurs when tenants cannot afford the existing rent levels for housing. This happens often in depressed areas where two or more families or nonrelated parties share an apartment, thereby reducing their housing costs. It frequently leads to accelerated wear and tear on the housing unit and excessive demands for water, gas, and electricity. In addition, these types of arrangements often lead to unsanitary living conditions.

Employment Levels During periods of high unemployment, tenants may not have money to pay rent, resulting in delinquencies and evictions (Figure 2–2).

Government Policies These include public assistance in the form of

1. Welfare

2. Unemployment compensation

3. Social security

4. Tax or mortgage (loan) benefits to investors or developers for additional housing

5. HUD Section 8 payments to subsidize rents of low-income tenants

Rental Rates The real estate industry produces a fixed product (building) that lasts for 50 years or longer. The manager or owner has no power to reduce the supply by manufacturing fewer products.

Market conditions affect rates. If rents are at market level or higher, you might consider advertising in areas with even higher rents in an attempt to draw those people accustomed to paying higher rents to your building.

Rent increases are general divided into four parts.

1. *Nuisance.* Usually $10 or less; tenants will pay a nuisance increase rather than incur the cost and hassle of moving.

Economic Indicators

Dow Jones Average
Balance of Trade
T-Bill Rate
Employment Figures
Bond Prices and Yield
Corporate Earnings
Consumer Price Index
Gold Prices
U.S. Government Borrowing
Federal Reserve Discount Rate
Gross Domestic Product
Housing Starts
Retail Sales
Industrial Production
Wholesale Price Index

Figure 2–2. Economic Indicators

2. *Economic*. Usually based on what the traffic will bear and usually needed to keep pace with rising costs of operation such as insurance, utilities, etc.

3. *New tenants*. New tenant rents should be increased, if market permits, as the unit changes tenancy. This accomplishes two goals. First, existing tenants feel they are getting a better deal (a bargain) because of their longevity. Second, it helps establish a new, higher market level for future increases.

4. *Rent control*. If your units are under some form of rent control, your ability to increase rents to existing and new tenants may be restricted. Local ordinances must be consulted prior to any rent increases.

Home Prices and Affordability

The cost of an existing single-family home increased dramatically from 1977 to 1993 on a national basis by 145 percent. Between 1993 and 1996, the values increased to approximately $109,000 nationwide. The range went from the San Francisco Bay area at $263,000 to Ocala, Florida, and Beaumont, Texas, at $64,000. Cleveland, Ohio; Richmond, Virginia; and Minneapolis/St. Paul, Minnesota, were around the median of $109,000. The qualifying income with a 20 percent down payment was $32,000, excluding FHA loans, in 1995.

Demand Analysis

A local region's commercial and manufacturing sectors are either basic (export) or nonbasic (local customers). In other words, basic industries sell to nonlocal customers and nonbasic industries recirculate dollars within the community. By identifying local base industries and their expansion plans, which will employ more people, a forecast of general population increase and increase in local buying power can be prepared.

Forecasted Total Employment

Let's forecast total employment in the following market of Littlesburg, Pennsylvania, in five years.

Total population in Littlesburg	50,000
Total employment in Littlesburg	25,000
Total basic employment in Littlesburg	11,900
Forecast (five years) basic employment	15,000

The economic base (EB) multiplier is the ratio of total employment to basic employment.

$$\text{EB multiplier} = \frac{\text{total employment}}{\text{basic employment}} = \frac{25,000}{11,900} = 2.1 \text{ EB}$$

Formula

Forecasted basic employment	=	Forecasted basic employment	×	EB multiplier

Forecasted
total employment = 15,000 × 2.1

Forecasted
total employment
(in 5 yrs.) = 31,513

Supply Analysis

The calculation of the total existing supply tells how many units or square feet are in our local market. In order to project (forecast) what the supply will be in the future, we need to know the existing supply, "pipeline" (new units planned), "drain" (units being demolished) to find the absorption.

For example, in Littlesburg, Pennsylvania, we find the following absorption analysis:

BOY last year (beginning of year)	
Total number of units	20,000
Vacancy	4,000
Total occupied	16,000
EOY last year (end of year)	
Total number of units	20,480
Vacancy	4,100
Occupied	16,380
EOY occupied units	16,380
BOY occupied units	16,000
Absorbed units	380
Present vacant units	4,100
Amount vacant for 10% vacancy	2,048
Required absorption to get 10% vacancy	2,052
Projected future absorption per year	400
Time to reach 10% vacancy:	
2,052 ÷ 400 per year =	5.13 years

In summary, we discover that, provided there are no future changes, it will take our market 5.13 years to have the vacancy rate drop to 10% at present absorption. This would not be a good market in which to expand, buy, or rehab units.

Population Trends

1. *Increasing supply of renters*—due to fewer people being able to afford their own homes.

2. *Mobility*—as people move to other parts of the country.

3. *Sun Belt*—these states have the highest growth rate, but are more service oriented.

4. *Frost Belt*—areas in the Northeast are showing renewed growth.

5. *Rust Belt*—areas of large industries such as steel are being hurt by foreign imports, but are adapting to new technology industries.

6. *Grain Belt*—farming areas have little projected growth.

Family Formation

The average size of households (2.62 persons) is decreasing and will continue to decrease in the future. The traditional family has a male head of household. Single parents—mostly women—now head 17 percent of U.S. households and number over 10.7 million according to a recent Census Bureau study. The female household heads outnumber the male by a three to one margin in single-parent households. Over 8.8 million households are headed by people over the age of 65 and that number is growing. The Census Bureau projects that by the year 2010 over 40 million people, representing 10.3 percent of our total projected population of 300 million, will be over the age of 65. These trends mean that the property manager must reexamine screening and selection methods for rental housing units.

Shifts in Ethnic Groups

The population in 1995 was 82.9 percent White, 12.6 percent Black, and 3.7 percent Asian. By the year 2010, the White percentage is projected to drop to 80 percent, Black to increase to 13.4 percent, and Asian to increase to 5.6 percent. In some states, such as California, the majority of the population is of minority status considering the Hispanic population which is not a separate race. The Hispanic population in the 1990 census was 9 percent and is projected to increase dramatically to 14 percent by 2010.

First-Time Homebuyers

In 1995, the median first-time homebuyer house was $94,000 with a 10 percent downpayment. The loan payment was $640 per month which would increase $100–150 when taxes and insurance were added. The median income was approximately $25,000. This equates out to approximately 35 percent of new homebuyers' income being spent on housing. The property manager needs to do an analysis of the local market to see at what level it is cheaper to rent than to buy. With homeowners' costs going up, there will be pressure to increase rents and renters may stay for longer periods. The census bureau found that only 10 percent of renters nationwide could afford to buy a home.

Business Environment

The United States is changing from a producer of goods to a provider of services. Manufacturing jobs are decreasing and service-oriented jobs will, by the year 2000, comprise almost 75 percent of the workforce. The property manager must be aware of how these changes will affect properties now and in the future. For example, a property manager should not submit a plan to upgrade an apartment building next to a steel mill or military base that might be closing, as the tenants would be unable to afford the upgraded amenities.

APPRAISAL

When conducting studies on rehabilitation, refinancing, or possible sale of a property, the property manager must be aware of how to estimate value. Three approaches to value will be examined here, with emphasis on the income approach. The goal is to estimate the property's value at its highest and best use.

Reproduction (Cost) Approach

To determine the reproduction cost, it is necessary to calculate the cost of constructing a similar building at today's construction costs. The steps are shown in Figure 2–3.

Cost statistics can be obtained from Marshall & Swift Valuation Service and are usually based on square footage. The disadvantage of this method is that it ignores cash flow and comparable prices. This method is used mostly for special-purpose buildings (churches, post offices) or in areas where there have been few recent market sales.

Market Approach

This method is valid only if there have been numerous recent similar sales in the property market area. Basically, one compares current selling prices of similar properties and adjusts those prices for differences in amenities such as pool, size of units, and so on, and the method of financing. This method works best with single-family homes. A variation is used in apartment sales by comparing the price per unit or square footage. For example, a 20-unit building with 22,000 square feet sold for $787,000. Thus:

Price per unit	$39,350.00
Price per square foot	$35.77
Cap rate	9.0

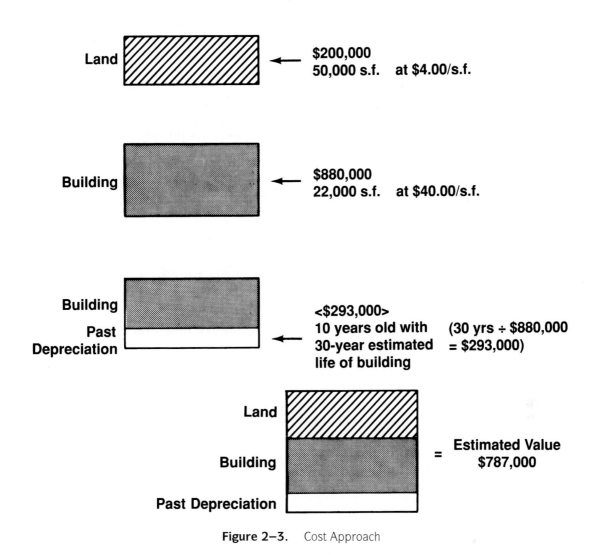

Figure 2–3. Cost Approach

A similar 20-unit building with 20,000 square feet sold for $784,000. Thus:

Price per unit	$39,200.00
Price per square foot	$39.20
Cap rate	9.1

One must be careful to remember not to compare one-bedroom units with two- or three-bedroom units when using the price-per-unit method.

Income Approach This method basically derives the value based on income generated by the property. Within the income approach, there are several methods used to arrive at value. The most commonly used methods are examined here.

1. *Capitalization, IRV (Income, Rate, and Value).* The net income at the time of sale is divided by the purchase price paid, which results in a yield called the capitalization (cap) rate. This approach works best where there have been some recent sales and reliable data on rents and expenses can be obtained. Cap rates from different properties can be compared and allowances made for varying conditions and the location of the property.

Less desirable locations and conditions, such as "fixer-uppers" in poor neighborhoods, result in higher cap rates as investors want higher yields for greater risks (see Figure 2–4).

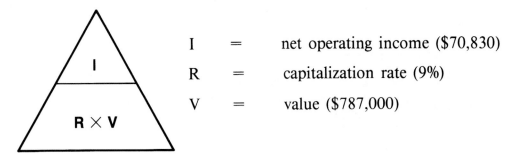

I   =   net operating income ($70,830)

R   =   capitalization rate (9%)

V   =   value ($787,000)

With two of the three factors, the third can be easily found by covering up the desired factor (R or V or I).

To find *net operating income* (NOI), just multiply rate times value.

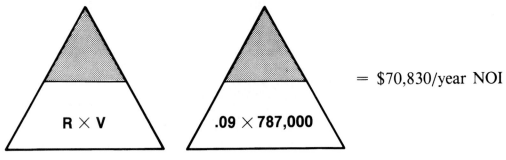

= $70,830/year NOI

To find value, just divide NOI by the cap rate.

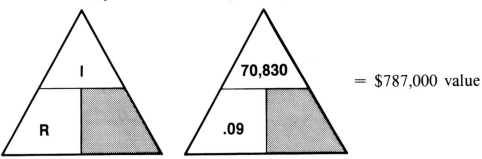

= $787,000 value

To find rate, divide NOI by the value.

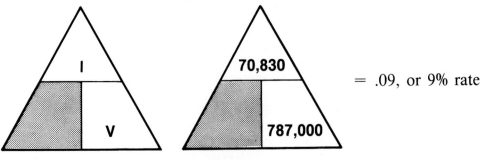

= .09, or 9% rate

Figure 2–4. Capitalization

The historical built-up method of determining the cap rate an investor wants to receive is composed of several factors based on subjective assumptions such as

Bank rate	6.0%
Risk rate	2.0%
Nonliquidity	1.0%
Cap rate	9.0%

A more sophisticated method of determining the investor's cap rate would be the band of investment. It is sometimes referred to as the debt/equity band of investment. It relies, only on interest rates, however, and does not take into account the risk or location factors.

25% down payment

75% first trust deed 10% – 30-year loan constant

Loan constant	0.1053	
	$(0.1053 \times 75\%) =$	7.89
25% equity (owner wants 12% return)		
	$12\% \times 25\% =$	3.00
	Cap rate =	10.89 or 10.9%

2. *Cash flow.* See Figure 2–5. Net operating income (NOI) can be calculated simply by using the following format:

Scheduled gross income	$ 120,000
Less vacancy (5%)	($ 6,000)
Plus misc. income (washer, dryer)	$ 2,000
Effective gross income	$ 116,000
Less operating expenses (taxes, insurance, utilities, maintenance, management fees, etc.)	($ 45,170)
Net operating income (NOI)	$ 70,830
Less debt service	($ 79,850)
Cash flow	($ 9,020)

Figure 2–5. Cash Flow

It can be seen from the above example that the disadvantage of the capitalization rate analysis is that it does not consider debt service (the high loan payment) which may be the result of overleveraging. Therefore, the 20-unit apartment building in our case study has a negative cash flow. Investors are becoming interested in cash flow as well as NOI when analyzing real estate investments.

3. *Gross rent multiplier*. The gross rent multiplier is a rule-of-thumb method of determining value. The gross rent multiplier method recognizes the ratio between the gross rent roll and the sales price. The sales price is divided by the gross rent roll at the time of the sale. The resulting number is then multiplied by the rent roll of the subject property to establish estimated value. For example:

$$\text{Gross rents} \times \text{gross multiplier} = \text{value}$$

$$\$120,000 \times 6.56 = \$787,000$$

To find the gross multiplier:

$$\text{Sales price} \div \text{gross rents (gross scheduled income)} = \text{gross rent multiplier}$$

$$\$787,000 \text{ value} \div \$120,000 \text{ gross scheduled income} = 6.56 \text{ gross rent multiplier}$$

The disadvantage of this method is that it does not take into consideration financing costs or whether a building has separate or master-metered utilities. For example, if a building has master-metered gas representing 7 percent of gross annual income ($8,400), subtracting this figure which inflates the rent would result in:

$$\$120,000 - \$8,400 = \$111,600$$

$$\$787,000 \div \$111,600 = 7.05 \text{ gross rent multiplier}$$

We have examined the three main methods of income approach (capitalization rate, cash flow, and gross rent multiplier) and concluded that cash flow is the most critical to the owner. Other methods of valuation are available, but an understanding of the above three will enable the property manager to discuss the proposed rehabilitation, refinancing, or sale and its effects with the owner and other interested parties.

DEPRECIATION

Depreciation is of two basic types: tax and real (physical). Depreciation is defined as a reduction in value of the property as it wears out through age or other causes.

Real Depreciation

1. *Physical obsolescence*. Physical obsolescence is the loss of value by wear and tear from use and decay. Proper repair and maintenance can defer such physical depreciation which is thus, in most cases, curable (Figure 2–6).

2. *Economic and social obsolescence*. Economic and social obsolescence is the adverse influence on the property by changes in zoning, noise, nuisance, population, and industry shifts. For example, if the neighborhood in which your apartment building is located has turned into a "ghetto," the value of your property may decrease.

3. *Functional obsolescence*. Functional obsolescence is the loss of value due to outdated or poor architectural design or layout and lack of necessary

Physical

Economic

Functional

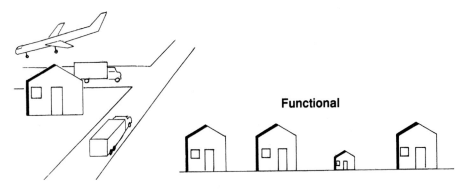

Figure 2–6.   Depreciation

amenities. This type of depreciation is difficult to cure. An example would be an office building with few windows, lots of columns, and inadequate elevator capacity for peak periods. The cost to cure may not be economically feasible.

Tax Depreciation   This form of depreciation calculates a loss in book value, not real value, based on a scheduled number of years. Tax depreciation is sometimes referred to as "phantom depreciation" as the building can, in fact, be appreciating in real value while the government allows you to lower its value by providing a deduction of this prorated depreciation from your taxes each year. Under the Tax Reform Act of 1986, and the Omnibus Budget Reconciliation Act of 1993, the minimum recovery period that can be used is:

Residential rental property	27½ years
Nonresidential rental property	39 years

Straight-line depreciation, however, is for 40 years for the alternative minimum tax. Using the above schedule results in a tax preference item for the difference between 27½ years and 40 years, which is one of the items used to calculate the alternative minimum tax (AMT) that a taxpayer may owe. The taxpayer will owe the regular tax or the alternative minimum tax, whichever is higher.

One can depreciate only improvements, not the land. Breakdown as to land value can be obtained from sources such as property tax bills or appraisals.

Value of property when purchased	$787,000
Less land value	–$196,750
Value of improvements (apt. building)	$590,250

Improvements = $590,250 = $21,464 depreciation per year

Depreciated life 27½ years

TAX LAW CHANGES   In contrast to the Tax Reform Act of 1986, which affected nearly every taxpayer, the Omnibus Budget Reconciliation Act (OBRA) of 1993 directs new tax increases toward wealthier taxpayers. According to the *Wall Street Journal*, people earning more than $200,000 annually will pay an average of 17.4 percent more in taxes. These tax law changes affect the purchase and operation of real estate rental properties and need to be understood in order to better meet the client's investment goals (see Figure 2–7).

Treatment of Income   The Tax Reform Act of 1986 divided income into three basic categories.

1. *Active*—income actually earned, including wages, tips, salaries, bonuses, etc.

2. *Portfolio*—includes interest, annuities, dividends, and royalty income.

3. *Passive*—The Omnibus Budget Reconciliation Act (OBRA) of 1993 eased the passive activity loss (PAL) rules for those in the real property business for tax years beginning January 1, 1994. All rental activity is now always classified as passive, even if it's the investor's sole business activity. These passive losses are suspended and carried forward until disposition of the property. Under new rules (OBRA), a taxpayer can deduct losses from rental activities against nonpassive as well as passive income if the taxpayer is in one or more real property businesses and the taxpayer materially participates. The term *real property business* includes most real property "trades or businesses" such as construction, rental, management, leasing, brokerage, acquisition, conversion, etc. The requirements for material participation include

   a) *Regular participation*—spending more than 500 hours, or at least 100 hours, and taxpayer participation is not less than the participation of any other person.
   b) *The 50% rule*—taxpayer must spend more than half of his or her personal-services time in the real property business or businesses in which there is material participation.
   c) *More than 750 hours spent in the business*—taxpayers must spend more than 750 hours in total for the year in real property businesses in which there is material participation. If the taxpayer is married, either spouse can qualify. For example, if the wife is a doctor and the husband is a property manager, the taxpayer (couple) would qualify, as the husband would be a "desirable spouse."

Joint Returns: 1996		**Single Returns: 1996**	
Taxable Income	Marginal Tax Rate	Taxable Income	Marginal Tax Rate
$0–40,100	15%	$0–24,000	15%
Over $40,100	28%	$24,000–58,150	28%
Over $96,900	31%	$58,150–121,300	31%
Over $147,700	36%	$121,300–263,700	36%
Over $263,750	39.6%	Over $263,750	39.6%

Figure 2–7.   Tax Brackets

Other Tax Changes (1993)

1. *Capital gains*—on assets held more than one year, the tax rate remains unchanged at 28 percent. With the top individual rate at 39.5 percent, a capital gains rate of 28 percent can now represent considerable tax savings.

2. *Debt restructuring*—the Omnibus Budget Reconciliation Act of 1993 gives borrowers the option of reducing the depreciable basis of real property by the amount of discharged debt to avoid taxable income in year of discharge. This provides incentive for workouts on delinquent mortgages and depressed properties.

3. *Alternative minimum tax*—the rate increased January 1, 1994, to 26 percent on the first $175,000 and 28 percent on the balance of alternative minimum taxable income.

4. *Club dues*—dues for country clubs and business clubs will no longer be a tax-deductible expense.

5. *Business meals and entertainment*—now only 50 percent tax deductible.

6. *Business travel*—spouse travel costs are deductible only if the spouse is also an employee and there is a valid business purpose.

7. *Corporate tax rate*–increased from 34 percent to 35 percent on income over $410 million.

8. *Compensation limits*—the maximum compensation taken into account for qualified plan contributions is reduced to $150,000.

9. *1031 tax-deferred exchange rules*—were left in their existing format. This will result in more sellers considering exchanges rather than selling in the future.

10. *Small business expensing allowance*—increased the deduction for otherwise depreciable property to $17,500.

How Does the Tax Reform Act Affect the Property Manager?

Owners in the future will not be granted as favorable tax benefits and will tend to view the property as a business which should generate a monthly profit (positive cash flow). They will need professional help to achieve this goal. The demand for certified property managers (CPMs) will increase, as will their compensation levels.

Owners who do not qualify for the new passive loss rules for real estate professionals may still qualify for the old provision under the 1986 Tax Reform Act. The owner must have an "active role" in the management of the property in order to qualify for a passive loss deduction of up to $25,000 per year. This does not mean the owner cannot retain the services of a property manager. The Senate Finance Committee set forth the following definitions of "active role":

1. Must own at least 10 percent of the investment.

2. Must participate in management decisions.

   a) Guidelines for approval of tenants; e.g., income criteria.
   b) Guidelines on rental terms; e.g., pet policy.
   c) Approval of capital and repair budgets; e.g., repaving driveway, reroofing, etc.

In order to satisfy this active role requirement, a written plan of action should be obtained from the owner (Mini Management Plan, Figure 4–7).

When the property manager is involved with depreciation and tax issues, the owner should be advised to seek counsel from a certified public accountant as the laws and regulations are constantly changing. The property manager is not licensed to practice law or accounting. Some of the forms can be found in Figures 2–8 through 2–11.

Department of the Treasury
Internal Revenue Service

Passive Activity Loss Limitations

▶ See separate instructions.

▶ Attach to Forms 1040, 1041, or 1120 (Personal service corporation and closely held C corporations).

OMB No. 1545 1008

Attachment Sequence No. **88**

Name(s) as shown on return   *Paul and Paige Jones*

Social security or employer identification number   *123-00-4567*

Part I	Computation of 1987 Passive Activity Loss

Caution: See the worksheets on page 4 of the instructions before completing Part I.

Rental Real Estate Activities With Active Participation (See the definition of active participation under **Rental Activities** on page 2 of the instructions.)

Activities acquired before 10-23-86:

1a	Activities with net income	1a	
1b	Activities with net loss	1b	(3,000)
1c	Combine lines 1a and 1b	1c	(3,000)

Activities acquired after 10-22-86:

1d	Activities with net income	1d	100
1e	Activities with net loss	1e	(3,100)
1f	Combine lines 1d and 1e	1f	(3,000)
1g	Net income or (loss). Combine lines 1c and 1f.	1g	(6,000)

All Other Passive Activities (See Lines 2a through 2g on page 4 of the instructions.)

Activities acquired before 10-23-86:

2a	Activities with net income	2a	
2b	Activities with net loss	2b	(3,231)
2c	Combine lines 2a and 2b	2c	(3,231)

Activities acquired after 10-22-86:

2d	Activities with net income	2d	
2e	Activities with net loss	2e	
2f	Combine lines 2d and 2e	2f	
2g	Net income or (loss). Combine lines 2c and 2f.	2g	(3,231)
3	Combine lines 1g and 2g. If the result is net income, see the instructions for line 3. If this line and line 1g are both losses, go to line 4. Otherwise, enter -0- on line 9 and go to line 10.	3	(9,231)

Part II	Computation of the Special Allowance for Rental Real Estate With Active Participation

Note: *Before completing Parts II and III, see page 4 of the instructions for how to treat numbers as if they were all positive.*

4	Enter the smaller of the loss on line 1g or the loss on line 3		4	6,000
5	Enter $150,000 ($75,000 if married filing separately and you lived apart for the entire year)	5	150,000	
6	Enter modified adjusted gross income, but not less than -0- (see instructions). If line 6 is equal to or greater than line 5, skip lines 7 and 8, enter -0- on line 9, and then go to line 10. Otherwise, go to line 7. . .	6	147,000	
7	Subtract line 6 from line 5	7	3,000	
8	Multiply line 7 by 50% (.5). Do not enter more than $25,000 ($12,500 if married filing separately and you lived apart for the entire year)		8	1,500
9	Enter the smaller of line 4 or line 8		9	1,500

Part III	Computation of Passive Activity Loss Allowed

10	Combine lines 1c and 2c and enter the result. If the result is -0- or net income, skip to line 16. (See instructions.)	10	6,231
11a	If line 9 is -0-, enter -0- on line 11 and go to line 12.		
11b	If line 1c shows income, has no entry, or shows -0-, enter -0- on line 11. Otherwise, enter the smaller of line 1c or line 8.	11	1,500
12	Subtract line 11 from line 10. If line 11 is equal to or greater than line 10, enter -0-.	12	4,731
13	Subtract line 9 from line 3	13	7,731
14	Enter the smaller of line 12 or line 13	14	4,731
15	Multiply line 14 by 65% (.65) and enter the result	15	3,075
16	Enter the amount from line 9	16	1,500
17	**Passive Activity Loss Allowed for 1987.** Add lines 15 and 16	17	4,575
18	Add the income, if any, on lines 1a, 1d, 2a, and 2d and enter the result	18	100
19	**Total losses allowed from all passive activities for 1987.** Add lines 17 and 18. See page 5 of the instructions to see how to report the losses on your tax return	19	4,675

For Paperwork Reduction Act Notice, see separate instructions.

Form **8582** (1987)

Figure 2–8. Form 8582 Passive Activity Loss Limitations

Form 4562

Form 4562

Department of the Treasury
Internal Revenue Service

Depreciation and Amortization

▶ See separate instructions.
▶ Attach this form to your return.

OMB No. 1545-0172

Attachment
Sequence No. **67**

Name(s) as shown on return

Identifying number

Business or activity to which this form relates

Part I **Depreciation** (Do not use this part for automobiles, certain other vehicles, computers, and property used for entertainment, recreation, or amusement. Instead, use Part III.)

Section A.—Election To Expense Depreciable Assets Placed in Service During This Tax Year (Section 179)

(a) Description of property	(b) Date placed in service	(c) Cost	(d) Expense deduction
1			

2 Listed property—Enter total from Part III, Section A, column (h) . . . .

3 Total (add lines 1 and 2, but do not enter more than $10,000) . . . .

4 Enter the amount, if any, by which the cost of all section 179 property placed in service during this tax year is more than $200,000 . . . .

5 Subtract line 4 from line 3. If result is less than zero, enter zero. (See instructions for other limitations) . .

Section B.—Depreciation

(a) Class of property	(b) Date placed in service	(c) Basis for depreciation (Business use only—see instructions)	(d) Recovery period	(e) Method of figuring depreciation	(f) Deduction
6 Accelerated Cost Recovery System (ACRS) (see instructions): *For assets placed in service ONLY during tax year beginning in 1987*					
a 3-year property					
b 5-year property					
c 7-year property					
d 10-year property					
e 15-year property					
f 20-year property					
g Residential rental property					
h Nonresidential real property					

7 Listed property—Enter total from Part III, Section A, column (g) . . . .

8 ACRS deduction for assets placed in service prior to 1987 (see instructions) . . . .

Section C.—Other Depreciation

9 Property subject to section 168(f)(1) election (see instructions) . . . .

10 Other depreciation (see instructions) . . . .

Section D.—Summary

11 Total (add deductions on lines 5 through 10). Enter here and on the Depreciation line of your return (Partnerships and S corporations—Do NOT include any amounts entered on line 5.) . . . . .

12 For assets above placed in service during the current year, enter the portion of the basis attributable to additional section 263A costs. (See instructions for who must use.) . .

Part II **Amortization**

(a) Description of property	(b) Date acquired	(c) Cost or other basis	(d) Code section	(e) Amortization period or percentage	(f) Amortization for this year
1 Amortization for property placed in service only during tax year beginning in 1987					
2 Amortization for property placed in service prior to 1987 .					
3 Total. Enter here and on Other Deductions or Other Expenses line of your return					

See Paperwork Reduction Act Notice on page 1 of the separate instructions.

Form **4562** (1987)

Figure 2–9. Form 4562 Depreciation and Amortization

Supplemental Income Schedule

(From rents, royalties, partnerships, estates, trusts, REMICs, etc.)
► Attach to Form 1040, Form 1041, or Form 1041S.
► See Instructions for Schedule E (Form 1040).

OMB No. 1545-0074

Attachment
Sequence No. 13

Name(s) as shown on Form 1040	Your social security number
Paul and Paige Jones	123 : 00 : 4567

Part I Rental and Royalty Income or (Loss)   Caution: Your rental loss may be limited. See Instructions.

1 In the space provided below, show the kind and location of each rental property.	2 For each property listed, did you or a member of your family use for personal purposes any of the properties for more than the greater of 14 days or 10% of the total days rented at fair rental value during the tax year?			3 For each rental real estate property listed, did you actively participate in the operation of the activity during the tax year? (See Instructions.)		
		Yes	No		Yes	No
Property A House, Somewhere, U.S.A.	Post ►		×	. . . . ►	×	
Property B Duplex, Somewhere, U.S.A.	Pre ►		×	. . . . ►	×	
Property C Boat Dock, Somewhere, U.S.A.	Post ►		×	. . . . ►	×	

Rental and Royalty Income		Properties			Totals (Add columns A, B, and C)	
		A	B	C		
4 Rents received		7,200	6,000	2,400	4	14,400
5 Royalties received					5	
Rental and Royalty Expenses						
6 Advertising.	6					
7 Auto and travel	7					
8 Cleaning and maintenance . . .	8					
9 Commissions	9					
10 Insurance	10	400	300	100		
11 Legal and other professional fees .	11					
12 Mortgage interest paid to financial institutions (see Instructions) . . .	12	5,500	6,000	1,200	12	12,700
13 Other interest	13					
14 Repairs	14	150		300		
15 Supplies	15					
16 Taxes (Do **not** include windfall profit tax here. See Part V, line 40.). . .	16	1,200	700	200		
17 Utilities	17					
18 Wages and salaries	18					
19 Other (list) ►						
....						
....						
....						
20 Total expenses other than depreciation and depletion. Add lines 6 through 19.	20	7,250	7,000	1,800	20	12,850
21 Depreciation expense (see Instructions), or depletion (see Publication 535). .	21	3,050	2,000	500	21	5,550
22 Total. Add lines 20 and 21	22	10,300	9,000	2,300		
23 Income or (loss) from rental or royalty properties. Subtract line 22 from line 4 (rents) or 5 (royalties) . .	23	(3,100)	(3,000)	100		
24 Deductible rental loss. **Caution:** Your rental loss on line 23 may be limited. See Instructions to determine if you must file **Form 8582,** Passive Activity Loss Limitations	24	(1,725)	(1,666)	—		

25 **Profits.** Add rental and royalty profits from line 23, and enter the total profits here	25	100
26 **Losses.** Add royalty losses from line 23 and rental losses from line 24, and enter the total (losses) here .	26 (	3,880)
27 Combine amounts on lines 25 and 26, and enter the net profit or (loss) here	27 (	3,780)
28 Net farm rental profit or (loss) from Form 4835. (Also complete Part VI, line 43.)	28	
29 Total rental or royalty income or (loss). Combine amounts on lines 27 and 28, and enter the total here. If Parts II, III, IV, and V on page 2 do not apply to you, enter the amount from line 29 on Form 1040, line 17. Otherwise, include the amount from line 29 in line 42 on page 2 of Schedule E	29 (	3,780)

For Paperwork Reduction Act Notice, see Form 1040 Instructions.

Schedule E (Form 1040) 1987

Figure 2–10.   Schedule E, Form 1040

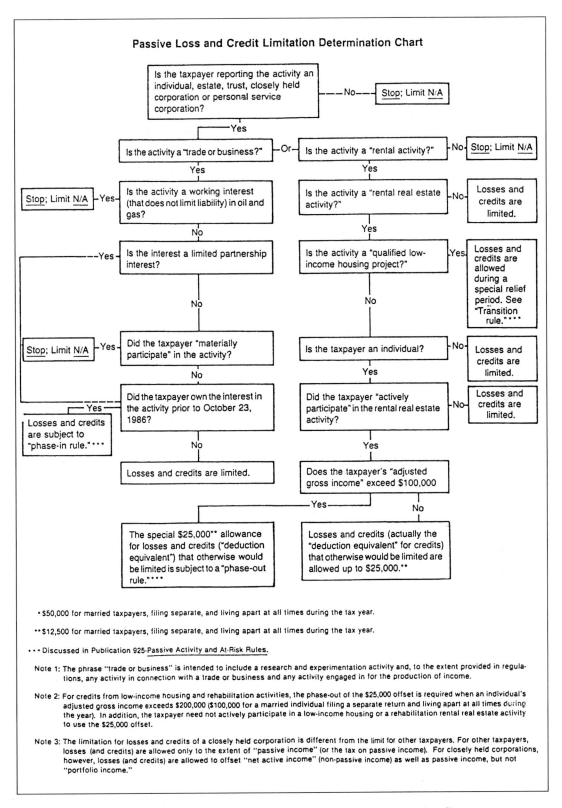

Passive Loss and Credit Limitation Determination Chart

Is the taxpayer reporting the activity an individual, estate, trust, closely held corporation or personal service corporation? —No— Stop; Limit N/A

Yes

Is the activity a "trade or business?" —Or— Is the activity a "rental activity?" —No— Stop; Limit N/A

Yes — Yes

Stop; Limit N/A —Yes— Is the activity a working interest (that does not limit liability) in oil and gas? | Is the activity a "rental real estate activity?" —No— Losses and credits are limited.

No — Yes

—Yes— Is the interest a limited partnership interest? | Is the activity a "qualified low-income housing project?" —Yes— Losses and credits are allowed during a special relief period. See "Transition rule."****

No — No

Stop; Limit N/A —Yes— Did the taxpayer "materially participate" in the activity? | Is the taxpayer an individual? —No— Losses and credits are limited.

No — Yes

—Yes— Did the taxpayer own the interest in the activity prior to October 23, 1986? | Did the taxpayer "actively participate" in the rental real estate activity? —No— Losses and credits are limited.

Losses and credits are subject to "phase-in rule."****

No — Yes

Losses and credits are limited. | Does the taxpayer's "adjusted gross income" exceed $100,000

—Yes— No

The special $25,000** allowance for losses and credits ("deduction equivalent") that otherwise would be limited is subject to a "phase-out rule."**** | Losses and credits (actually the "deduction equivalent" for credits) that otherwise would be limited are allowed up to $25,000.**

* $50,000 for married taxpayers, filing separate, and living apart at all times during the tax year.

** $12,500 for married taxpayers, filing separate, and living apart at all times during the tax year.

*** Discussed in Publication 925-Passive Activity and At-Risk Rules.

Note 1: The phrase "trade or business" is intended to include a research and experimentation activity and, to the extent provided in regulations, any activity in connection with a trade or business and any activity engaged in for the production of income.

Note 2: For credits from low-income housing and rehabilitation activities, the phase-out of the $25,000 offset is required when an individual's adjusted gross income exceeds $200,000 ($100,000 for a married individual filing a separate return and living apart at all times during the year). In addition, the taxpayer need not actively participate in a low-income housing or a rehabilitation rental real estate activity to use the $25,000 offset.

Note 3: The limitation for losses and credits of a closely held corporation is different from the limit for other taxpayers. For other taxpayers, losses (and credits) are allowed only to the extent of "passive income" (or the tax on passive income). For closely held corporations, however, losses (and credits) are allowed to offset "net active income" (non-passive income) as well as passive income, but not "portfolio income."

Figure 2–11. Passive Loss and Credit Limitation Determination Chart

In order to understand real estate economics, we examined the size of a market that contains over 35 million residential rental units nationwide and over 39 million households. The real estate cycles analysis showed that we still cannot predict the occurrence or length of the cycles. Two of the causes were money and supply and demand. The best sources for information on vacancies are local apartment associations or IREM Experience Exchange books. We differentiated between technical oversupply and economic oversupply. Boomtowns such as Houston have a temporary oversupply called technical oversupply. Economic oversupply occurs when tenants cannot afford the rental rates. We analyzed how we can determine supply and demand for our local real estate market.

Four types of rental increases were discussed: nuisance ($10 or less), economic (market rent), new tenants (top of market), and rent control (restricted). Government policies such as welfare, unemployment compensation, Social Security, and Section 8 housing were identified as having an effect on real estate economics. The size of the average household is decreasing and is projected to continue to decrease in the future, with one out of four families having only one adult. Different population trends such as mobility were reviewed; the Sun Belt, Frost Belt, Rust Belt, and Grain Belt were analyzed, with the Sun Belt having the highest projected growth rate.

In order to value a real estate investment, an estimate of value must be prepared. Whether it be for refinance, rehabilitation, or sale, the estimated value needs to be known. The three approaches to value were discussed— cost approach, used mostly for special-purpose buildings; the market approach, comparing recent sales; and the income approach, using the cap rate and gross multiplier. The two types of depreciation, real and tax, were discussed. Under real depreciation, we have physical, economic, social, and functional obsolescence.

The Tax Reform Act of 1986 specified a minimum residential depreciation rate at $27\frac{1}{2}$ years and 39 years for commercial properties. Three methods of treating income exist: active (wages), portfolio (interest and dividends), and passive (rental income property). The property manager must know the client's tax bracket and its effects on the property managed.

The purpose of this chapter was to familiarize the property manager with the real estate environment. The basic purpose of property management is to increase the income stream by increasing revenues while minimizing expenses. This subsequently leads to an increase in real estate values.

PERSONALITY PROFILE

Some property managers work for institutions or government agencies in handling the management and leasing of their real property. One such individual is Dennis White who works for the Port of Oakland, which also includes airport facilities. Its annual budget exceeds $130 million. This agency is non-tax supported and Dennis is involved in leasing as well as development and management.

Dennis is a certified property manager (CPM) and on the National Faculty for the Institute of Real Estate Management (IREM). He graduated from St. Mary's College and has been in the property management business for over 20 years.

Upon returning to his office one day, Dennis picked up his voice mail to hear two callers who had earlier tried to link him into a conference call. It was obvious that they did not pay attention to his voice mail message informing them that he was away from his office and inviting them to press "0" to speak with his secretary or leave a recorded message. Dennis's recorder picked up their conversation. At first, one of the callers said to the other, "I think it said please hold and a secretary would be right with us." The pair of callers continued to discuss (privately, they thought) their position on deal issues of a proposed lease and their strategy on how to make the deal. Needless to say, it was one of the few times Dennis knew exactly where he stood.

REVIEW QUESTIONS

1. How many residential rental units are there in the United States?

   a. approximately 1 million
   b. approximately 10 million
   c. approximately 35 million
   d. approximately 90 million

2. During a recession, real estate values usually

   a. increase.
   b. remain the same.
   c. decrease.

3. If the money supply is abundant, interest rates usually

   a. decrease.
   b. remain the same.
   c. increase.

4. If the number of renters increases faster than the supply of new apartments, rents will usually

   a. increase.
   b. remain the same.
   c. decrease.

5. The rental population is affected by

   a. the Department of Real Estate.
   b. earning power.
   c. mobility.
   d. both a and b
   e. both b and c

6. Which of the following is an appraisal method?

   a. cost approach
   b. market survey
   c. income approach
   d. only a and b
   e. all of the above

7. Net operating income (NOI) does *not* include

   a. debt service.
   b. property taxes.
   c. management fees.
   d. maintenance.

8. Depreciation of a property for income tax purposes

   a. reduces value.
   b. increases value.
   c. has no effect on physical assets.

9. "Sun Belt" refers to

   a. warmer-climate areas.
   b. only the orange-growing areas.
   c. apartment buildings that face east.
   d. properties laid out in a circular manner.

10. Cash flow is calculated by

    a. subtracting NOI from effective rents.
    b. subtracting operating expenses from effective rents.
    c. subtracting loan payments from NOI.
    d. adding loan payments to NOI.

11. If the cap rate goes up and the NOI stays the same, the price will

    a. increase.   c. remain the same.
    b. decrease.

12. If the cap rate is 10 percent and the NOI is $200,000 what is the value of the property?

    a. $200,000   c. $1,000,000
    b. $2,000,000   d. $2,100,000

13. If the gross rent multiplier is 7 and the gross rents are $300,000, what is the value?

    a. $200,000   c. $1,000,000
    b. $2,000,000   d. $2,100,000

14. What is the number of years to depreciate a residential income property?

    a. 19 years   c. $31\frac{1}{2}$ years
    b. $27\frac{1}{2}$ years   d. 39 years

15. Rental real estate falls into what basic income category?

    a. active   c. passive
    b. portfolio

ADDITIONAL READING AND REFERENCES

Batra, Ravi, *The Great Depression of 1990*, Simon and Schuster, New York, NY, 1987.

Callaghan's Federal Tax Guide, Clark Boardman Callaghan, 155 Pfingsten Rd., Deerfield, IL 60015.

Commercial Investment Journal (Bimonthly), 430 N. Michigan Ave., Chicago, IL 60611.

DeCarlo, Joseph, *Essential Facts: Real Estate Management*, Warren, Gorham & Lamont, 31 James Ave, Boston, MA 02116, 1995.

Gaddy, Wade Jr., *Real Estate Fundamentals*, Real Estate Education Co., Chicago, IL, 1994.

The Journal of Real Estate Taxation (Quarterly), Warren, Gorham & Lamont, Inc., 31 St. James Ave., Boston, MA 02116.

Real Estate Economics (Quarterly), University of Michigan, P.O. Box 3588, Ann Arbor, Michigan 48106.

Real Estate Financing Update (Monthly), Warren, Gorham & Lamont, Inc., 31 St. James Ave., Boston, MA 02116.

Sirota, David, *Essentials of Real Estate Investment*, Real Estate Education Co., Chicago, IL, 1995.

U.S. Housing Market Conditions (Quarterly), HUD User, P.O. Box 6091, Rockville, MD 20849.

U.S. Master Tax Guide, Commerce Clearing House, Inc., Chicago, IL, 1996.

U.S. Real Estate Week (Weekly), Warren, Gorham & Lamont, Inc., 31 St. James, Boston, MA 02116.

Chapter 3

The Management Plan

Key terms

Alteration	Measurement of	Operating history
Areas of analysis	market	Pro forma analysis
Comparable analysis	Modernize	Property analysis
Infrastructure	Neighborhood analysis	Regional analysis
IRR		

Food for thought

"There are two things to aim at in life: First, to get what you want; and after that to enjoy it. Only the wisest of mankind achieve the second."

Logan Pearsall Smith

INTRODUCTION

One of the most important property management tools is the management plan. It establishes management objectives for the property and the blueprint by which to achieve these objectives. The management plan is formulated by gathering, analyzing, and interpreting all information pertaining to the property. It is important that the owner, property manager, and on-site manager understand the game plan the property manager uses to manage and operate the building.

The management plan format is divided into six sections. Each section will be analyzed separately to simplify the subject matter. After identifying trends and factors in the regional, neighborhood, property, and market analysis, the manager analyzes and organizes the material to help determine the strengths and weaknesses of the property. A recommended plan is then prepared with financing and return on investments projected along with final recommendations for the operation and management of the property.

SCOPE OF THE PLAN

The scope of the management plan should include financing, staffing, occupancy, tenant mix, marketing and leasing policies, income and expenses of the property, physical inspections, and policies and procedures. Some of these areas will be interrelated. For example, deferred maintenance will affect the vacancy factor which affects net operating income on the subject property. Basic assumptions, limitations, terminology, and time frame should be outlined along with the qualifications of the preparer. The plan cost and payment schedule for the client should also be referenced.

FORMAT OF THE PLAN The plan should start with a title page (Figure 3–1), including an identification of the property, the address, and a description of the project. The page should also contain the owner's name and address as well as that of the preparer of the plan. The proposed completion date and a photograph of the property should be included. A table of contents that outlines the format of the plan

---

Management Plan

For

Whiskey Manor

1000 Civic Center Drive

Garden Grove, CA

This is a 20-unit, garden-style (two-story) apartment building

picture

Prepared For: Prepared By:

Peter and Mary Ross   JD Property Management, Inc.
200 Highland   3520 Cadillac Ave., Ste. B
Los Angeles, CA 92712   Costa Mesa, CA 92626
                                                                       (714) 751-2787

Date: January 15, 19 ___

Figure 3–1. Title Page

```
                    TABLE OF CONTENTS
                         FOR
              WHISKEY MANOR MANAGEMENT PLAN


                                                        Page


STATEMENT OF LIMITING CONDITIONS                         v

WARRANTY                                                 vi


CHAPTER I    -  REGIONAL ANALYSIS                        1

CHAPTER II   -  NEIGHBORHOOD ANALYSIS                    6

CHAPTER III  -  SUBJECT PROPERTY ANALYSIS               10

CHAPTER IV   -  MARKET ANALYSIS                         30

CHAPTER V    -  RECOMMENDED OPERATING PLAN              40

CHAPTER VI   -  FINANCIAL ANALYSIS                      45

CHAPTER VII  -  RECOMMENDATIONS AND CONCLUSIONS         53

CHAPTER VIII -  QUALIFICATIONS OF ANALYST              56


APPENDIX
```

Figure 3–2. Table of Contents

and provides page references should be the second page (Figure 3–2). The third page should be a letter of transmittal including a summary of observations, conclusions, and recommendations (Figure 3–3). The plan should contain pictures, charts, graphs, references of the sources of data.

REGIONAL ANALYSIS

The region encompasses the metropolitan area in which the property is located. The property manager should try to use one of the 64 Standard Metropolitan Statistical Areas (SMSA) compiled by the Bureau of the Census. This makes it easier to obtain statistical data for

1. Population characteristics and growth, past and projected trends

2. Demographics of the area

3. Industrial base

4. Transportation facilities

5. Educational facilities

6. Real estate market

JD PROPERTY MANAGEMENT INCORPORATED 3520 Cadillac Avenue / Suite B
Costa Mesa, California / 92626
714 751-2787 / Fax 714 751-0126

January 10, 19—

Peter and Mary Ross
200 Highland
Los Angeles, CA 92712

RE: Management Plan for Whiskey Manor

Dear Peter and Mary:

Pursuant to your assignment in your letter of December 12th, I have prepared a comprehensive management survey of your subject property located at 1000 Civic Center Drive, Garden Grove, CA.

After three personal inspections of the subject property and three selected properties in the rental area, plus analyzing the immediate neighborhood and region, and analyzing your financial data, I am prepared to answer your specific questions and make the following recommendations.

The management plan to be implemented calls for correction of deferred maintenance, both exterior and interior, replacing the present on-site manager, and increasing the rental rates through a planned marketing approach. The present operation functions with a $6,000 negative cash flow and a decline in value of the property due to deteriorated condition and poor management policies. The proposed improvements and operational plan will produce a positive cash flow—and increase the value almost $200,000.

The estimated costs of the improvements are $50,000. A detailed analysis with cost breakdown is located in this report. Our survey of the region indicates that growth will increase over 17% by 2000, creating a need for housing. An analysis of the neighborhood shows that it is a lower-income, blue-collar area with a large contingent of immigrants from Southeast Asia that will continue to grow. The income level of the area is also rising and is sufficient to afford the proposed new rental rates of the operational plan. In other words, the demand is already present for upgrading Whiskey Manor.

Sincerely,

BRANCH OFFICES
2105 W. GENESEE ST., SUITE 210, SYRACUSE, NY 13219 (315) 468-0556
LICENSED REAL ESTATE BROKER CALIFORNIA AND NEW YORK

Figure 3–3. Letter of Transmittal

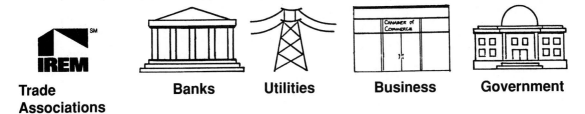

Figure 3–4. Sources of Information

7. Political and social climate and trends

8. Employment levels

   Additional sources of data are given in Figure 3–4.

1. Trade associations
   a) Institute of Real Estate Management (IREM)
   b) International Council of Shopping Centers (ICSC)
   c) Building Owners and Managers Institute International (BOMI)

2. Local and state governments
   a) Redevelopment agencies

3. Local chambers of commerce

4. Local banks and savings and loans

5. Local utility companies

NEIGHBORHOOD ANALYSIS

Under the regional analysis, we were looking to measure the market to see if trends were positive. In the neighborhood analysis, we are looking for positive trends in the three- to five-mile area around the subject property.

1. Property characteristics and trends
   a) Family size
   b) Neighborhood life cycle (improving, static, deteriorating)
   c) Age level
   d) Population increasing or decreasing

2. Economic characteristics
   a) Employment levels going up or down
   b) Types of industry or business
   c) Rental rates and sales prices

3. Infrastructure
   a) Transportation
      (1) Bus lines
      (2) Freeways
   b) Government and political attributes (favorable or unfavorable)
   c) Amenities
      (1) Schools
      (2) Shopping

4. Measurement of neighborhood market
   a) Square miles
   b) Major streets or freeways
   c) Natural boundaries (e.g., rivers, mountains)

PROPERTY ANALYSIS

1. Physical
   - *a*) Age
   - *b*) Number of units and unit mix
   - *c*) Layout of complex, e.g., can alterations be made?
   - *d*) Condition
     - (1) Roof
     - (2) Elevators
     - (3) Plumbing and electrical
     - (4) Mechanical (e.g., air-conditioning)
   - *e*) Obsolescence
     - (1) Functional, e.g., can we modernize?
     - (2) Economic

2. Desirability of property
   - *a*) Curb appeal
   - *b*) Tenant mix
   - *c*) Attractiveness of units
     - (1) Layout and size
     - (2) View
     - (3) Fixtures and appliances
   - *d*) Condition of public areas
     - (1) Laundry facilities
     - (2) Halls
     - (3) Parking lot
   - *e*) Amenities and their condition

3. Management of property
   - *a*) Vacancy rate (Figure 3–5)
   - *b*) On-site staff
   - *c*) Records and files

RESIDENTIAL INCOME PROPERTY
(MULTI-FAMILY UNITS)
VACANCY RATE SURVEY

		TOTAL UNITS	VACANT USED Number	VACANT USED Percent	VACANT NEW Number	VACANT NEW Percent	VACANT TOTAL Number	VACANT TOTAL Percent	UNDER CONSTRUCTION Number	UNDER CONSTRUCTION Percent
Anaheim	92801	9,519	243	2.6%	0	0.0%	243	2.6%	84	0.9%
	92802	5,733	138	2.4%	0	0.0%	138	2.4%	0	0.0%
	92804	11,505	428	3.7%	0	0.0%	428	3.7%	82	0.7%
	92805	5,320	104	2.0%	24	0.5%	128	2.4%	49	0.9%
	92806	5,563	288	5.2%	0	0.0%	288	5.2%	48	0.9%
	92807	2,143	34	1.6%	0	0.0%	34	1.6%	93	4.3%
Total Anaheim		39,783	1,235	3.1%	24	0.1%	1,259	3.2%	356	0.9%
Costa Mesa	92626	6,845	217	3.2%	130	1.9%	347	5.1%	148	2.2%
	92627	9,213	89	1.0%	20	0.2%	109	1.2%	24	0.3%
Total Costa Mesa		16,058	306	1.9%	150	0.9%	456	2.8%	172	1.1%
Garden Grove	92640	4,616	217	4.7%	78	1.7%	295	6.4%	78	1.7%
	92641	2,811	49	1.7%	0	0.0%	49	1.7%	0	0.0%
	92643	3,687	42	1.1%	11	0.3%	53	1.4%	0	0.0%
	92644	3,111	80	2.6%	0	0.0%	80	2.6%	28	0.9%
	92645	362	0	0.0%	0	0.0%	0	0.0%	0	0.0%
Total Garden Grove		14,587	388	2.7%	89	0.6%	477	3.3%	106	0.7%
Huntington Beach	92646	4,198	104	2.5%	35	0.8%	139	3.3%	0	0.0%
	92647	8,274	296	3.6%	16	0.2%	312	3.8%	4	0.0%
	92648	6,597	109	1.7%	0	0.0%	109	1.7%	4	0.1%
	92649	4,818	193	4.0%	35	0.7%	228	4.7%	60	1.2%
Total Hunt. Beach		23,887	702	2.9%	86	0.4%	788	3.3%	68	0.3%

Source: Federal Home Load Bank of San Francisco

Figure 3–5.   Vacancy Survey

d) Screening procedures
e) Tenant relations
f) New building checklist (Figure 3–6)

4. Financial data
   a) Debt service
   b) Real estate taxes
   c) Insurance
   d) Operating history—expenses and income

NEW BUILDING CHECKLIST   Managed by _____

STREET & NUMBER _____
MANAGEMENT COMMISSION RATE _____ STARTING DATE _____
OWNER'S SOC. SEC. # OR I.D. # _____
WHO GETS A COPY OF THE MONTHLY STATEMENT:
   Name _____ Address _____
   Phone _____
If more than one owner, or add'l copies needed, use reverse side.
WHO GETS PAID BILLS WITH MONTHLY STATEMENT? _____
DISTRIBUTE FUNDS MONTHLY OR KEEP A BALANCE? _____
IF TITLE TO BUILDING IS IN TRUST, WHO HOLDS TITLE? (Bank & Trust #)
_____

PREVIOUS AGENT
   Company _____ Person _____
   Address _____ Phone _____
   Copy of previous month's statement _____

PAYROLL
   Do we handle? _____ Employer name

   Employer I.D. # _____ (as listed with gov't) _____
   If new, do we file? _____
   If previous employer, collect prior quarter returns.

JANITOR
   Name _____ Address _____
   Phone _____ Date began on bldg. _____
   Monthly Salary _____ Married or single? _____
   Number of dependents _____ Anything extra w/h from salary? _____

LEASES
   Collect current leases _____ Show how many rooms on lease.
   Last decorated? _____ Security deposits _____
Units   Apartments _____ Stores _____ Office _____
   Garages _____ Total number of units _____

REAL ESTATE TAXES & MORTGAGE
   Permanent Index No. _____ Volume _____
   Do we handle payment or do we handle direct? _____
   Do we charge a monthly reserve? _____ Amount _____
   Attorney for tax protest _____
   Is there a mortgage? _____ With whom? _____
   Loan # _____
   Does mortgage have a tax reserve? _____

INSURANCE
   Current agent? _____ Phone _____
   OLT, AMOUNT _____ WC, AMOUNT _____ FIRE & EC AMT, _____
   Endorsement needed to add our name _____
   Copy of policies needed for our files _____
   Upon expiration, shall we write? _____

MAINTENANCE
   Fuel _____ Type _____
   Exterminator _____ Scavenger _____
   Hardware _____ Decorator _____
   Plumber _____ Electrician _____

GUARANTEES:
   Roof _____
   Boiler _____

Figure 3–6. New Building Checklist

PROCEDURES MANUAL

TABLE OF CONTENTS

SUBJECT	PAGE
Application to Rent..............................	1
Form	2
Discrimination Policy...........................	3
Credit Checking..................................	4
Tenant Qualifier.................................	5
Form	6
Before Move-In Responsibilities...............	7
Move-In and Move-Out Check Sheet.............	8
Form	9
Contract to Rent (Completion of).............	10
Form	11
Rules & Regulations Form	12
Rental Agreement Changes......................	14
Vacating Residents............................	15
Form	16
Form	17
Onsite Files	18
Security Deposit Refund Statement............	19
Form	20
Housekeeping/Maintenance......................	21
Pool Maintenance................................	22
Occupancy Reporting............................	23
Form	24
Vacancy & Notice Status.......................	25
Form	26
Serving of Legal Notices......................	27
Form	28
Declaration of Service.........................	29
Incident Report.................................	30
Form	31
Bookkeeping - Cash Journals...................	32
Form	33
Traffic Reports.................................	34
Form	35
New Maintenance Procedure.....................	36
Form	37
Marketing Window................................	38
Leasing Presentation...........................	40
Telephone Leasing Techniques..................	45
Overcoming Objections..........................	46

Figure 3–7. SOP Manual

5. Policies and procedures—A policies and procedures manual should be compiled into one body of records. The "standard operating procedures" manual is the plan of operation for the property. It is a guideline for both on-site managers and supervisors. It details the objectives of operating the property and describes the jobs and skills needed to carry out the plan. The manual spells out

a) What is to be done
b) Who is to do it
c) How it is to be done
d) When it is to be done
e) Why it is to be done

A proper manual describes every activity that could, would, or should happen at a property (Figure 3–7).

APPRAISAL REPORTS

Although the property manager does not usually prepare appraisal reports, he or she should be familiar with the format. The property manager is often involved in the refinancing, selling, or purchasing of property, which involves appraisal reports. States have enacted appraisal standards systems to comply with federal appraisal requirements for most institutional real estate loans. The Appraiser Qualifications Board (AQB) of the Appraisal Foundation sets forth minimum criteria guidelines for licensed appraisers by states.

Certified Residential Criteria

This category is for appraisers whose practice entails one- to four-family residential units. Appraisers with this license cannot do complex nonresidential appraisals. The requirements as of January 1, 1994, include:

Category	Education	Experience
Licensed	75 hours	2,000 hours over any time period
		Noncomplex, one to four units residential, less than $1 million transaction value; complex, one to four units residential, less than $250,000 transaction value.
Certified Residential	105 hours	2,000 hours with no more than 1,000 in any 12-month period
		All one- to four-unit residential without regard to transaction value or complexity.
Certified General	165 hours	2,000 hours with 50% in nonresidential (more than four units experience)
		All real estate transactions without regard to value or complexity.

PROPERTY TAXES

Property taxes are called ad valorem taxes which is derived from the Latin, meaning "according to value." In other words, the higher the value of the property assessed, the higher the property tax bill.

Assessed Valuation

The local municipality will usually put a value on the property for real estate purposes. Some states and localities use 100 percent assessment, which means the property is taxed at fair market value. Some municipalities and states will only assess at a certain percentage of value such as 30 percent. For example, if a property value was $500,000, the assessment roll would show a value of

$150,000. Some states have a split assessment in which owner-occupied residences are assessed lower than investment residential and commercial properties. In other words, investment properties pay higher taxes.

Effective Tax Rates

The bottom line to the investor is the effective tax rate, which is calculated by combining the tax rate and the assessment. For example, if the assessed valuation is $150,000 and the tax rate is $5.00 per hundred dollars of valuation, the taxes owed would be $150,000 × $5.00, or $7,500.

State Comparisons

Some states, such as New York, Oregon, Maine, Arizona, and Illinois, have high effective tax rates. States with lower tax burdens include Arkansas, Kentucky, and Alabama. Some states, such as California, tax at 100 percent of the purchase price and the tax rate is 1 percent. Maximum annual increases are thereafter a maximum of 2 percent unless a property is sold or a bond measure is passed.

Property Tax Appeal

Most assessment agencies allow for appeal during a certain period each year. They also have detailed and specific rules and guidelines for the appeal process. The property manager may at times handle appeals for the client who feels the assessment is unfair. An hourly or flat additional fee is usually charged for the appeal as it is not usually considered part of the property manager's normal duties.

Payment of Taxes

Payment schedules differ for each state. For example, California property taxes are due on December 10 and April 10; Alabama on October 1; Florida and Connecticut on November 1; New York on January 31; and Texas on November 30 and June 30.

MARKET ANALYSIS

The market analysis determines the rental, leasing, and vacancy rates in the market served by the subject building.

1. Measurement of the market
    a) Submarket (apartment buildings)
        (1) Multistory (high-rise)
        (2) Mid-rise (four-story)
        (3) Low-rise (two-story)
        (4) Garden apartments
    b) Size and characteristics of the market
        (1) Age of units in the area
        (2) Number of units in the area
        (3) Size of units (e.g., one bedroom, 650 square feet)
        (4) Rental rates
            (a) Monthly rent (residential)
            (b) Cost per square foot (commercial)
        (5) Vacancy level

2. Comparable analysis
    a) Conduct market survey (Figure 3–8). Compare and contrast to subject property—is your building better or worse? (See Chapter 7.) (Complete the comparison worksheet, Figure 3–9.)
    b) Location analysis
        (1) Freeways and transportation
        (2) Prestige area

MARKET SURVEY WORKSHEET

Complex Name: _____ Cross Streets: _____

Address: _____ Map Page: _____

City: _____ State: _____ Zip: _____

Manager Name: _____ Phone: _____

Owner Name: _____ Phone: _____

Description of Complex

_____ one-story   _____ two-story   _____ three-story   _____ other

No. of one-bedrooms: _____   No. of baths: _____

No. of two-bedrooms: _____   No. of baths: _____

No. of three-bedrooms: _____   No. of baths: _____

No. other: _____   No. of baths: _____

Total Units: _____

Location of Complex

_____ Superior   _____ Equal   _____ Inferior   _____ Other: _____

Curb Appeal

_____ Superior   _____ Equal   _____ Inferior   _____ Other: _____

Special Features (i.e., Ocean View)

_____ Superior   _____ Equal   _____ Inferior   _____ Other: _____

Age of Project

_____ Newer   _____ Equal   _____ Inferior   _____ Year Built

Amenities in Complex

_____ A/C	_____ Exercise Room	_____ Refrigerator
_____ Cable TV	_____ Fireplace (wood/gas)	_____ Sauna
_____ Carpeting	_____ Garages	_____ Security gate
_____ Covered Carports	_____ Microwave	_____ Stove
_____ Dishwashers	_____ Laundry Facilities	_____ Trash comp.
_____ Disposals	_____ Parking spaces	_____ Util. incl.
_____ Drapes	_____ Pool	_____ gas
_____ Elevators	_____ Recreation Room	_____ electric

RENTAL ANALYSIS

Type	No. Baths	Sq.Ft.	Mo. Rent	Vacancy	Price per Sq. Ft.
Bachelor	_____	_____	_____	_____	_____
1 bedroom	_____	_____	_____	_____	_____
2 bedroom	_____	_____	_____	_____	_____
3 bedroom	_____	_____	_____	_____	_____
Other	_____	_____	_____	_____	_____

Prepared by: _____   Date: _____

Figure 3–8. Market Survey Worksheet

COMPARISON WORKSHEET

<u>Subject Property</u>   <u>Comparison Property</u>

Complex Name: _____   Complex Name: _____

Address: _____   Address: _____

No. Units: _____   No. Units: _____

	<u>Subject</u>		<u>Comparable</u>	
	Present Condition	After Rehabilitation	Present Condition	After Rehabilitation

<u>Exterior</u>

Accessibility	_____	_____	_____	_____
Age	_____	_____	_____	_____
Curb appeal	_____	_____	_____	_____
Exterior	_____	_____	_____	_____
Grounds	_____	_____	_____	_____
Laundry	_____	_____	_____	_____
Location	_____	_____	_____	_____
Parking (gar.)	_____	_____	_____	_____
Pool	_____	_____	_____	_____
Rec room	_____	_____	_____	_____
Other:	_____	_____	_____	_____

<u>Interior</u>

Carpet	_____	_____	_____	_____
Closets	_____	_____	_____	_____
Dishwasher	_____	_____	_____	_____
Disposal	_____	_____	_____	_____
Drapes	_____	_____	_____	_____
Fireplace	_____	_____	_____	_____
Range	_____	_____	_____	_____
Refrigerator	_____	_____	_____	_____
Size of units	_____	_____	_____	_____
Utilities				
Gas	_____	_____	_____	_____
Electric	_____	_____	_____	_____
Other:	_____	_____	_____	_____

<u>Area Amenities</u>

Access roads	_____	_____	_____	_____
Churches	_____	_____	_____	_____
Image	_____	_____	_____	_____
Public trans.	_____	_____	_____	_____
Schools	_____	_____	_____	_____
Shopping	_____	_____	_____	_____
Other:	_____	_____	_____	_____

Present Rents:	_____	_____	_____	_____
Rents per s.f.:	_____	_____	_____	_____
Rent change:	_____	_____	_____	_____
New rents:	_____	_____	_____	_____
New rent per s.f.	_____	_____	_____	_____

Figure 3–9.   Comparison Worksheet

3. Obtain cost data for rehab
   a) `Local contractors and vendors should be contacted for cost estimates; e.g., carpet is usually quoted by price per yard plus padding, plus installation. Cost may range from $8–10 per yard.
   b) Consult annual reference books that contain cost data broken down by item such as a garbage disposal. One such reference is *Mean Repairs and Remodeling Cost Data—Commercial Residential*, published by the R. S. Means Co. Another reference is Marshall Valuation Service, Marshall & Swift Publication Co., Los Angeles, CA.
   c) Cost of supervision, usually 10–15 percent, should be added to these estimates. In some cases the property manager will be the rehab supervisor and will be paid the fee. At other times a general contractor will be hired.

ANALYSIS OF ALTERNATIVES

In the alternatives analysis, the building is reviewed not only for its present use "as is," but also for the "highest and best use" of the property. A pro forma budget analysis (Figure 3–10), showing projected rents, expenses, and increased net return to the owner, should be prepared for each alternative scenario being considered (see Figure 3–10).

PRO FORMA BUDGET

	Last Year	Current year	Projected As Is	Projected After Rehab.
Gross Potential Income				
Laundry				
Other income				
Vacancy loss				
Effective Gross Income				
Operating Expense				
Repair				
Painting				
Plumbing				
Electrical				
Building				
Supplies				
Utilities				
Water				
Electric				
Gas				
Trash				
Management				
Onsite				
Offsite				
Legal & Accounting				
Taxes				
Insurance				
Capital Improvements				
Roof				
Appliances				
Other:				
Subtotal Expenses				
Net Operating Income				

Figure 3–10. Pro Forma Budget

Selected Metropolitan Areas—U.S.A.　　Median Income And Operating Costs　　By Building Type

Raleigh-Durham, NC
Garden-Type Buildings
38 Buildings　6,416 Apartments
5,854,603 Rentable Square Feet

	Bldgs.	% of GPI Med	Low	High	$/Sq. Ft. Med	Low	High	$/Unit Med
INCOME								
RENTS—APARTMENTS	(38)	97.2%	96.6%	98.6%	6.64	6.01	7.82	6020
RENTS—GARAGE/PARKING	( )							
RENTS—STORES/OFFICES	( )							
GROSS POSSIBLE RENTS	(38)	97.2%	96.6%	98.6%	6.64	6.01	7.82	6020
VACANCIES/RENT LOSS	(38)	4.7	3.5	6.0	.32	.23	.46	256
TOTAL RENTS COLLECTED	(38)	92.7	91.3	93.9	6.49	5.77	7.47	5721
OTHER INCOME	(37)	2.8	1.4	3.4	.19	.11	.28	182
GROSS POSSIBLE INCOME	(38)	100.0%	100.0%	100.0%	7.03	6.17	8.02	6160
TOTAL COLLECTIONS	(38)	95.4	94.0	96.5	6.83	5.86	7.62	5910
EXPENSES								
MANAGEMENT FEE	(36)	4.7	3.9	5.1	.34	.27	.38	277
OTHER ADMINISTRATIVE**	(34)	6.7	5.7	8.8	.52	.40	.63	485
SUBTOTAL ADMINISTR.	(38)	11.0%	8.9%	12.9%	.78	.64	.96	706
SUPPLIES	(33)	.2	.1	.6	.02	.01	.05	14
HEATING FUEL—CA ONLY*	(22)	.3	.1	.5	.02	.01	.04	19
CA & APTS.*	(2)	10.3			.60			633
ELECTRICITY—CA ONLY*	(35)	1.4	.9	1.7	.10	.06	.13	96
CA & APTS.*	(3)	1.3			.11			101
WATER/SEWER—CA ONLY*	(4)	1.3			.10			79
CA & APTS.*	(33)	2.6	2.1	3.4	.18	.14	.25	173
GAS　CA ONLY*	(15)	.1	.1	.2	.01	.00	.02	11
CA & APTS.*	(2)	1.6			.10			100
BUILDING SERVICES	(31)	.5	.3	.8	.04	.02	.06	36
OTHER OPERATING	(16)	.5	.3	.7	.04	.02	.06	27
SUBTOTAL OPERATING	(38)	5.5%	4.3%	6.8%	.40	.31	.50	336
SECURITY**	(6)	.1			.00			4
GROUNDS MAINTENANCE**	(38)	2.5	2.1	3.1	.18	.15	.22	155
MAINTENANCE—REPAIRS	(38)	3.4	2.2	6.1	.24	.15	.41	220
PAINTING/DECORATING**	(38)	2.4	1.7	2.7	.15	.12	.20	128
SUBTOTAL MAINTENANCE	(38)	8.3%	6.7%	11.3%	.59	.50	.76	539
REAL ESTATE TAXES	(37)	6.4	5.6	7.5	.48	.35	.57	395
OTHER TAX/FEE/PERMIT	(15)	.0	.0	.0	.00	.00	.00	2
INSURANCE	(37)	1.6	1.0	2.0	.11	.08	.15	91
SUBTOTAL TAX—INSURANCE	(37)	8.0%	7.2%	8.8%	.57	.49	.69	468
RECREATIONAL/AMENITIES**	(24)	.4	.3	.6	.03	.01	.05	29
OTHER PAYROLL**	(29)	5.5	3.3	7.9	.40	.27	.53	349
TOTAL ALL EXPENSES	(38)	39.5%	35.2%	45.0%	2.95	2.42	3.19	2545
NET OPERATING INCOME	(38)	55.4%	50.5%	59.2%	3.75	3.20	4.61	3271
*PAYROLL RECAP**	(25)	11.1%	8.4%	13.5%	.81	.66	.94	706

Richmond, VA
Garden-Type Buildings
32 Buildings　7,783 Apartments
6,629,166 Rentable Square Feet

	Bldgs.	% of GPI Med	Low	High	$/Sq. Ft. Med	Low	High	$/Unit Med
RENTS—APARTMENTS	(32)	97.9%	96.3%	98.6%	6.10	5.56	7.21	5297
RENTS—GARAGE/PARKING	(2)	.3			.03			25
RENTS—STORES/OFFICES	(2)	5.3			.33			255
GROSS POSSIBLE RENTS	(32)	97.9%	96.4%	98.6%	6.10	5.67	7.21	5297
VACANCIES/RENT LOSS	(32)	8.0	6.4	20.5	.56	.48	1.22	475
TOTAL RENTS COLLECTED	(32)	89.1	76.9	90.5	5.65	4.24	6.76	4736
OTHER INCOME	(32)	2.1	1.4	3.6	.15	.08	.25	134
GROSS POSSIBLE INCOME	(32)	100.0%	100.0%	100.0%	6.19	5.78	7.49	5414
TOTAL COLLECTIONS	(32)	92.1	79.5	93.6	5.90	4.32	6.98	4913
MANAGEMENT FEE	(32)	4.7	3.9	4.8	.31	.24	.37	243
OTHER ADMINISTRATIVE**	(32)	6.1	4.9	7.6	.42	.29	.52	317
SUBTOTAL ADMINISTR.	(32)	10.9%	9.1%	12.4%	.76	.53	.89	597
SUPPLIES	(30)	.3	.1	.4	.02	.01	.02	14
HEATING FUEL—CA ONLY*	(20)	1.0	.5	1.1	.05	.04	.07	49
CA & APTS.*	(6)	8.2			.46			386
ELECTRICITY—CA ONLY*	(28)	1.4	1.0	1.9	.08	.06	.13	73
CA & APTS.*	(3)	1.8			.11			86
WATER/SEWER—CA ONLY*	(3)	4.2			.27			242
CA & APTS.*	(29)	3.9	3.3	5.3	.31	.21	.34	267
GAS　CA ONLY*	(10)	.4			.02			19
CA & APTS.*	(6)	2.3			.16			132
BUILDING SERVICES	(30)	1.3	1.1	1.5	.08	.06	.11	72
OTHER OPERATING	(20)	.2	.1	.3	.01	.01	.02	10
SUBTOTAL OPERATING	(32)	8.4%	7.0%	11.8%	.61	.48	.72	482
SECURITY**	(17)	.2	.1	.2	.01	.01	.02	9
GROUNDS MAINTENANCE**	(32)	2.6	2.1	2.8	.15	.13	.18	135
MAINTENANCE—REPAIRS	(32)	3.0	2.0	4.3	.19	.12	.23	170
PAINTING/DECORATING**	(32)	3.0	2.0	3.6	.19	.13	.20	174
SUBTOTAL MAINTENANCE	(32)	9.3%	7.0%	10.3%	.51	.47	.62	456
REAL ESTATE TAXES	(32)	5.1	4.6	5.7	.32	.28	.41	286
OTHER TAX/FEE/PERMIT	(27)	.5	.1	.9	.04	.00	.05	36
INSURANCE	(32)	1.7	1.4	2.4	.11	.09	.17	86
SUBTOTAL TAX—INSURANCE	(32)	7.4%	6.6%	8.7%	.47	.43	.55	396
RECREATIONAL/AMENITIES**	(25)	.5	.3	.6	.03	.02	.04	26
OTHER PAYROLL**	(30)	5.7	4.3	6.9	.35	.24	.49	285
TOTAL ALL EXPENSES	(32)	43.7%	36.8%	47.6%	2.72	2.37	3.34	2252
NET OPERATING INCOME	(32)	44.9%	29.3%	52.5%	2.55	1.86	4.07	2336
*PAYROLL RECAP**	(31)	11.0%	9.9%	13.6%	.72	.61	.86	617

Figure 3–11.
Medium Income & Operating Expenses
Published annually, © Institute of Real Estate Management,
430 N. Michigan Avenue, Chicago, IL 60611

1. Alteration
   a) Change of use
      (1) Condominium conversion
      (2) Convert to retail or office use (consider city zoning and use ordinances)
   b) Change of unit mix
      (1) Converting bachelor and one-bedroom units to two- or three-bedroom units; converting two- or three-bedroom units to one-bedroom or bachelor units
   c) Convert units to furnished units

2. Modernize and rehabilitate
   a) Replace original equipment (e.g., air-conditioning, carpets)
   b) Upgrade or replace building facade
   c) Correct deferred maintenance

After analyzing the projected income and expense (Figure 3–11) of the proposed property upgrade alternatives, an investment analysis of the property from the client's perspective must be made (Figure 3–12). This may be time consuming and the property manager may not have the expertise or background to provide an investment analysis. Consultation with a certified public accountant (CPA) or attorney may be required.

1. Areas of analysis
   a) Cash flow calculations (five-year IRR [Internal Rate of Return])
      (1) Presently existing operation
      (2) After improvements
   b) Depreciation benefits
   c) Valuation of building (capitalization rate)
      (1) Presently existing operation
      (2) After improvements
   d) Financing costs, sources, and methods
   e) Tax ramifications
      (1) Income tax
      (2) Property tax

Cash Flow

Financing

Depreciation
Depreciation
Depreciation
Depreciation

Taxes

Figure 3–12.
Investment Analysis

RECOMMENDATIONS AND CONCLUSIONS

The property manager should have supporting documentation for the recommendations. A five-year pro forma cash flow projection must be devised based on the internal rate of return (IRR) both before and after taxes, considering:

1. Complete cost estimates as supplied by contractors

2. A method to finance and cost thereof

3. A market study to support the increased rental income

Be prepared to defend your recommendations, but remember that it is the client's property and money and the client will make the final decision.

FINANCIAL CALCULATIONS

In order to determine whether an investor should proceed with the rehabilitation of a property, an analysis of the present operating income and expenses must be made. These figures must be projected on a pro forma basis into the future. The same process must take place on projected income and expenses for the proposed rehabilitation alternative. If the investor can get a higher return and greater cash flow, he or she will probably decide to proceed. The property manager should be familiar with how to make the necessary calculations.

HP12C Calculator

The Hewlett-Packard 12C financial calculator (Figure 3–13) is commonly used in the real estate industry. This small, hand-held calculator has four registers and is programmable.

HP19BII Calculator

The Hewlett-Packard 19BII business calculator, faster than the HP12C and menu driven, is now used exclusively in CPM courses. It is advisable to take a one-day class on how to operate both calculators. If students would like solutions to the problems that follow using the HP19BII, please send a self-addressed envelope to JD Seminars, 3520-C Cadillac Ave., Costa Mesa, CA 92626.

For the examples in this book we utilize the HP12C.

Loan Constants

In order to compare which loan is more advantageous when the interest rates and lengths of the loan differ, we need to convert to a loan constant (Figure 3–14). For example, which is the best loan for an investor?

The HP-12C Keyboard and Continuous Memory

Figure 3–13. HP12C Calculator

Keystrokes				Display
f	4		=	0.0000
1	CHS	PV	=	−1.000
10.5	g	i	=	0.8750 interest rate per month
25	g	n	=	300 months
PMT			=	0.0094 monthly constant
12	×		=	0.1133 annual constant

Figure 3–14. Loan Constant Calculation

Loan information	Loan constant
10.5% for 25 years	0.1133
11% for 30 years	0.1143
9.5% for 20 years	0.1119 ← Best Loan

The loan with the lowest loan constant, which is comprised of the interest and principal, is usually the best loan. If there were a balloon payment (all due and payable) after the fifth year on the 9.5 percent loan, the investor might choose a loan with a longer life.

Calculation of Loan Payments

It used to be necessary to use tables to calculate loan payments, which is time consuming; also, the tables are not always readily available. Using the HP12C, it is relatively easy (Figure 3–15). For example, what are the monthly and annual loan payments for the following loan?

25 years—term of the loan

10.5%—25 years

$650,000—amount of the loan

Loan Balance

It is necessary to know the loan balance during the term of the loan in order to determine logically the financial implications of the rehabilitation project (Figure 3–16). The process starts with determining the loan payment as previously shown. We now add some steps to determine the loan balance at the end of five years.

Keystrokes				Display
f	2		=	0.00
10.5	g	i	=	0.88 interest rate per month
25	g	n	=	300 months
650,000		PV	=	$650,000 amount of loan
PMT			=	$6,137.18 payment per month
12	×		=	$73,646.17 payment per year

Figure 3–15. Loan Payment Calculation

Keystrokes				Display
10.5	g	i	=	0.88 interest rate per month
25	g	n	=	300 months
650,000		PV	=	$650,000 amount of loan
PMT			=	$6,137.18 payment per month
60	f	h	=	$332,944.88 interest—5 years
	x><y		=	$35,285.92 principal—5 years
RCL		PV	=	$614,714.08 loan balance— end of fifth year

Figure 3–16.   Loan Balance Calculation

Loan amount—$650,000

Term—25 years

Interest—10.5%

Rate of Return

The investor, when comparing the proposed solutions, needs to know the return on investment (ROI), payback period (how many years to get the extended funds back), and the internal rate of return (IRR) (Figure 3–17). We use the IRR when the amount of the cash flow is not the same from period to period. The IRR is used to determine the return rate. This formula is complex and not used very often by the property manager. We could figure either before or after income tax. We will outline the basic keystrokes for those who want to do the calculations.

As an example, suppose you purchased a building for $650,000 and sold it for $1,100,000 five years later. You had cash flows as follows:

Initial cost	(650,000)
1st year	(25,000)
2nd year	(10,000)
3rd year	5,000
4th year	20,000
5th year	20,000 + 1,100,000

What is the IRR before income tax for the five years?

Keystrokes					Display	Remarks
f	CLX			=	0.00	
650,000	CHS	g	CFo	=	−650,000	cost of building
25,000	CHS	g	CFj	=	−25,000	1st year cash flow
10,000	CHS	g	CFj	=	−10,000	2nd year cash flow
5,000	g	CFj		=	5,000	3rd year cash flow
20,000	g	CFj		=	20,000	4th year cash flow
20,000 + 1,100,000	g	CFj		=	1,100,000	5th year cash flow plus sales proceeds
f	IRR			=	11.03	

Figure 3–17.   IRR Calculation

FOLLOW-UP AND IMPLEMENTATION

When the management plan finally emerges, one of three things can happen to it.

1. The owner, property manager, and on-site manager breathe a sigh of relief, put the plan in a binder, and let it collect dust.

2. The management plan becomes sacred—and adjusting it becomes impossible; i.e., it is etched in stone.

3. The management plan emerges as a working tool. Assumptions and projections are monitored and changed when necessary.

The development of the management plan should result in the third scenario. It is the "game plan" for how the property is to be managed.

SUMMARY

In this chapter, the management plan, sometimes called the blueprint to manage the property, was discussed and outlined. The actual format of a plan, starting with the title page and followed by the table of contents and the letter of transmittal, was explained and examples were provided. The actual plan was divided into six sections: regional analysis, neighborhood analysis, property analysis, marketing analysis, analysis of alternatives, and recommendations and conclusions.

Under regional analysis, the areas covered were population characteristics and growth, demographics, industrial base, transportation and educational facilities, and political and social trends. This data can be obtained from trade associations, chambers of commerce, banks, and utility companies, as well as government agencies, such as the Census Bureau. The next step in developing the management plan is to analyze the neighborhood in which the subject property is located, usually comprised of three to five miles. As in the regional analysis, we are looking for characteristics and trends in population, employment, types of businesses in the neighborhood, rental rates and sales prices, adequate transportation systems, and controlled government attitudes (it may not be desirable to do a rehabilitation in a rent-controlled community that looks unfavorably on landlords, such as New York City or Santa Monica, California).

The next step is to analyze the subject property. Questions that need to be answered include: What is the physical condition, age, number of units, layout, and both functional and economic obsolescence? What is the desirability of the property (which would include curb appeal, tenant mix, amenities, vacancy, tenant relations, management, and financial data such as taxes, insurance, repair costs, and debt)? Does the property have a standard operating procedure (SOP) manual? Do deficiencies exist in any of the above areas? Can these problems be corrected and at what cost?

The next area we turn to is the market analysis, in which a rental survey is done on similar properties. The subject property is compared and contrasted to comparable properties and an indicated rent is determined both before and after rehabilitation. Cost estimates are obtained from contractors and reference books such as R. S. Means and Marshal and Swift, in order to prepare pro forma budgets, valuations, and cash-flow projections. The next step is recommendations and conclusions in which the property manager will point out the rehabilitation benefits of increased cash flow, higher resale value, and payback period of the rehabilitation costs to the owner. In some cases, the regional or neighborhood analysis will bring to the surface factors that may not make rehabilitation a viable alternative. The rate of return, payback period, and increase in value may also be insufficient to warrant a recommendation to proceed.

The last step is follow-up and implementation of the management plan. It should be used as a working tool or the "game plan" for management of the property.

Management plans should be prepared for all types of properties: apartments, offices, retail, or industrial. The length and depth of the plan depend on property size, financial condition, owner goals, and so forth. Most property managers charge an extra fee on an hourly basis for anything other than a short, simple plan. A full-scale management plan can run up to 150 pages, including pictures, charts, illustrations, references, and supporting data.

PERSONALITY PROFILE

The property manager can come from many different backgrounds and be involved in specialized areas of property management. Walt Edwards, a CPM from Sacramento, is an example of such an individual. He is a graduate of Hastings College of Law in San Francisco, and holds a B.A. in Psychology from California State University, San Francisco.

Walt is now involved in market rate and subsidized housing. He has been an executive property manager for 18 years, responsible for a staff of 40 people and a $1.6–2 million annual budget. In managing 400,000 square feet of retail commercial space, Walt develops management and marketing plans and strategies for the properties. His experience range also includes commercial office and residential space.

Walt shared that his first major mistake was entering an apartment through a window during an eviction. He was told by a deputy sheriff that if he intended on having a long career, he'd better not ever do that again. You can bet he has not repeated that mistake.

Walt has served as IREM chapter president and regional vice president, as well as being a member of the IREM national executive committee and secretary of the Urban League.

REVIEW QUESTIONS

1. The management plan
   a. establishes objectives and goals for the property.
   b. is used for tax assessments.
   c. is used for tax depreciation.
   d. establishes the value of the property.

2. The management plan is sometimes called a
   a. management agreement.
   b. blueprint.
   c. depreciation schedule.
   d. demographics profile.

3. Sources of regional information include
   a. trade associations.
   b. country clubs.
   c. the local PTA.
   d. comparable property.

4. Neighborhood analysis considers
   a. employment levels.
   b. rental rates.
   c. both a and b
   d. neither a nor b

5. Boundaries for the neighborhood include
   a. major streets or freeways.
   b. natural boundaries such as rivers.
   c. both a and b
   d. neither a nor b

6. Property analysis considers
   a. the unemployment rate.
   b. physical condition.
   c. family size.
   d. demographics.

7. Financial data in the property analysis include
   a. debt service.   c. curb appeal.
   b. income taxes.   d. both a and b

8. Considerations under the physical profile of the property include
   a. age of the units.   c. tenant mix.
   b. debt service.   d. policies and procedures.

9. Modernization includes
   a. replacing the resident manager.   c. correcting deferred maintenance.
   b. replacing the property manager.   d. writing a standard operating
                                           procedures (SOP) manual.

10. Pro forma cash flow projections are used for
    a. real estate tax assessors.   c. projecting profits before and after
    b. federal income tax returns.   improvements.
                                        d. calculating management fees.

11. The management plan is
    a. a contract.   c. an agreement to manage the property.
    b. a management tool.   d. required by the Department of Real Estate.

12. A regional analysis in the management plan covers
    a. the subject building.   c. management policies.
    b. the financial plan.   d. demographic trends.

13. A standard operating procedures (SOP) manual is a(n)
    a. financial plan.   c. legal document.
    b. guideline for operations.   d. agreement to manage the property.

14. The best loan is usually the one with the
    a. highest loan constant.   b. lowest loan constant.

15. Who should make the final decision for major rehabs?
    a. the property management   c. the client
    b. the resident manager   d. a CPA

ADDITIONAL READING AND REFERENCES

American Institute of Real Estate Appraisers, *Directory of Members*, Chicago, IL, 1996.

American Institute of Real Estate Appraisers, *The Uniform Residential Appraisal Report*, Chicago, IL, 1996.

California Real Estate Journal (Monthly), 915 E. First St., Los Angeles, CA 90012.

Coffin, Chris, and Ted Wadman, *An Easy Course in Using the HP12C Calculator*, Grapevine Publications, Corvallis, OR, 1984.

Commercial Property News (Bimonthly), One Penn Plaza, New York, NY 10119.

Crane, Eric, *The HP12C Made Easy*, Eric Crane Seminars, La Canada, CA, 1990.

Demographic Profiles Service, Donnelly Marketing Information Systems, 70 Seaview Ave., Stamford, CT 06904.

Downs, James, *Principles of Real Estate Management*, Institute of Real Estate Management, Chicago, IL, 1991.

Institute of Real Estate Management, *Expense Analysis: Apartments*, Chicago, IL, 1996.

Kyle, Donald, and Frank Baird, *Property Management*, 5th Edition, Real Estate Education Company, Chicago, IL, 1995.

Means Co., *Means Repair and Remodeling Cost Data—Commercial and Residential*, Chicago, IL, 1995.

Today's Realtor, National Association of Realtors, 430 N. Michigan Ave., Chicago, IL 60611.

United States Bureau of the Census, *Statistical Abstract of the United States*, 1995, U.S. Government Printing Office, 1995.

Chapter 4

The Management Client

Key terms

Cash flow	Management	Sole proprietorship
Corporation	agreement	Tax benefits
Fee management	Partnership	Trust account
Leverage	REIT	

Food for thought

"Be sure you love people and use things. Don't use people and love things."

Will Rogers

INTRODUCTION

The property manager must manage the property according to the owner's objectives and goals. A feeling of mutual understanding, requiring a coordinated effort between agent and owner, should develop. This chapter will deal with types of ownership, owners' goals and objectives, the management agreement, fiduciary responsibility, and the establishment of management fees.

PRINCIPAL/AGENT RELATIONSHIPS

In the principal/agent relationship, the property manager acts as the go-between for the owner in relation to other parties. The property manager has the power to represent the owner for the purpose of making decisions and contracts on the owner's behalf. This agency arrangement, if it is for over one year, must be governed by a written agreement (See Figure 4–4, Management Agreement). Under most states' agency laws, the property manager, as the agent for the owner, discloses this fact to other parties, such as tenants and vendors.

The property manager may need a real estate license if he or she acts as an agent for an owner. This is commonly known as fee management. Some states, such as Idaho, Illinois, Indiana, Maine, North Dakota, and Vermont, among others, do not require a state real estate license. Some states, including Oregon and Montana, require a separate license for the management of rental property. Some other exceptions to licensing include

1. Managing one's own property

2. Property managers working for banks or trust companies, etc.

3. Working directly as an employee for an owner

Requirements and exemptions vary according to states and are constantly changing. You should check with the real estate commission office of the state in which you operate for the most current requirements.

If the property manager is licensed, the employing broker is held responsible for his or her activities. All trust fund records and other important documents and agreements must be kept on file for usually three or more years, depending on state law, and will be subject to audit by the Department of Real Estate. Any violations of real estate law or regulations could result in the revocation or suspension of the agent's or broker's license, or both.

Employer/Employee

The employer/employee situation exists when the property manager works directly for the owner and is on salary. Examples are property managers working for banks, insurance companies, and corporations.

FORMS OF OWNERSHIP
Sole Proprietorship

A sole proprietorship investor usually owns properties as investments and has other businesses (e.g., a medical practice) or employment. Since the investor or owner does not have the time or expertise to collect rents, lease, and handle management, a professional property manager is hired. Title of this type of ownership is usually held in the form of joint tenants, tenants in common, severalty, or as community property.

Advantages

1. Simplicity and ease of establishing and dissolving.

2. Fewer organizational and legal restrictions.

3. Lowest cost to organize and operate.

4. Less disclosure and more secrecy.

5. More self-satisfaction and ego gratification for owners.

Disadvantages

1. Unlimited liability.

2. Less counsel and professional input on decisions.

3. Lack of survivorship—depends on health of owner.

4. More difficult to raise funds.

General Partnership

Advantages

1. Capital contributions and loans easier to obtain than for sole proprietorship.

2. Spreads risk and liabilities among more individuals.

3. Ease of formation and operation.

Disadvantages

1. Death, insanity, or bankruptcy of one partner may affect the partnership.

2. Needs mutual agreement (divided authority).

3. Unlimited liability of partners.

4. Transferring of ownership interest is difficult.

Limited Partnership   **Advantages**

1. Limited liability to limited partners.

2. No personal involvement or effort by limited partners.

3. Taxed at taxpayer level only (K-1).

Disadvantages

1. Unlimited liability of general partner.

2. Transferring of ownership interest is difficult.

3. Success depends mainly on performance of general partner.

4. Passive tax loss.

Corporation   A corporation has perpetual life and operates under a charter granted by the State Department of Corporations. It is a legal entity and may enter into contracts, leases, sales, and so on. The stock (ownership) is held by its shareholders who are limited in liability to the cost of their stock. A board of directors is elected to run the company and appoint its officers (president, treasurer, secretary, etc.). Most large businesses are corporations, except in real estate due to double taxation of profits. Corporate profits are taxed at the company level and then the dividends distributed to the stockholders are taxed as personal (portfolio) income. If managing for a corporation, the property manager should make sure there is a corporate resolution and that authorized corporate officers have signed the management agreement.

Advantages

1. Ease of transfer and marketability—sell stock on exchange.

2. Limited liability.

3. Perpetual life.

4. Easier to raise money by selling more stock or bonds.

Disadvantages

1. Formation and operation of corporation is costly.

2. Security laws and regulations are cumbersome.

3. Double taxation.

Real Estate Investment Trust (REIT)   A real estate investment trust allows investors to share in ownership and profits without being involved in the management or operations of the property. The trust issues shares of ownership to investors that can be bought and sold much like mutual funds. This allows for quick liquidity, which is usually not found in real estate investments.

   The REIT is allowed to avoid corporate income tax, but must invest in real estate or mortgages. It must meet criteria such as minimum number of shareholders, widely disbursed ownership, asset and income tests. If criteria are met and the REIT distributes 90 percent of its income to shareholders, it is not taxed on that income. Shareholders must report the income on their personal tax return.

Limited Liability Company (LLC)

This is a hybrid between a partnership and a corporation, having features of both. It provides limited liability like corporations, but is taxed at a taxpayer level (K-1) like a partnership. The test for material participation for partners in real estate rentals is more stringent than in a partnership.

We will discuss forms of ownership for the management company in Chapter 13.

Government Agencies

Several local, state, and federal agencies hire professional property managers to manage and lease their facilities. Contracts are usually let on a bid basis with stiff requirements for both insurance and reporting by the manager. Examples would be right-of-way lands, Veterans Administration foreclosures, HUD properties, and so on.

OWNERS' GOALS AND OBJECTIVES

While it is true that owner goals vary, it is possible for the property manager to categorize these goals and then set priorities to meet the requirements of the client (Figure 4–1).

Cash Flows

Most investors prefer a positive cash flow, but often they will purchase property at too high a price or with too low a down payment, resulting in expenses and mortgage payments exceeding rental income. This is called a negative cash flow or an "alligator" since it needs to be constantly fed by additional owner funds. Investors who are retired and/or on a fixed income are necessarily very concerned with cash flow. Astute investors today are insisting on reasonable cash flow, at least comparable to other investments such as stocks and bonds.

Tax Benefits

Through depreciation (phantom loss), the owner can reduce the profit on property for income tax purposes. This write-off may reduce personal income tax up to a maximum of $25,000 per year, if the taxpayer makes less than $100,000 annually and is active in its management. If the owner meets the desirable spouse requirements, he or she may be able to write off all passive

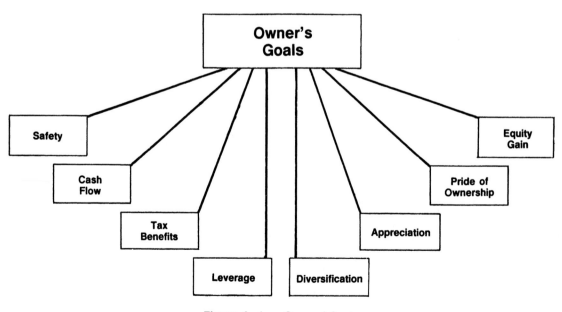

Figure 4–1. Owners' Goals

losses in the year in which they occur. These losses are described as passive income under the Tax Reform Act of 1986, as discussed in Chapter 2. In other words, large losses from real estate may not be deductible in the year of loss, but may have to be carried over to the year of sale. As tax laws change, tax benefits for real estate seem to be on a trend toward curtailment with fewer depreciation write-offs likely in the future.

The Omnibus Budget Reconciliation Act of 1993 was of mixed benefit to real estate. It lengthened the commercial depreciation schedule while easing the rules on passive losses.

Leverage

Most investments (stocks, bonds, etc.) require that the investor pay in full or at least 70 percent for their purchase. In real estate, one can make a 10–30 percent down payment and purchase property by borrowing the balance. This is known as leverage (Figure 4–2). In other words, others' funds are used to acquire a larger investment than is possible with an "all cash" purchase. This strategy works well in times of rising real estate values, but may result in foreclosures during hard times. For example:

Sales price	$1,000,000
Down payment	100,000
Loan (first trust deed)	900,000

If the inflation rate is 10 percent, the investor's profit (10 percent of $1 million) would be $100,000. If the same investor put the same funds (down payment) of $100,000 in a bank at 10 percent simple interest, the return would be only $10,000. In this case, the investor's additional gain is $90,000 the first year in real estate.

Appreciation

All investors want the property to increase in value during the ownership period. Some investors'—sometimes referred to as speculators—primary motivation is to buy, hold, and sell the property, making a profit through appreciation. Speculators usually have a short holding period of one to three years and are willing to incur a negative cash flow. In periods of high inflation, speculators have seen the sales price more than double in a few years, and many investors easily become millionaires. As in most high-stakes investment strategies, however, the risks are considerable. The property manager should ensure that sufficient funds are available to cover expenses, especially those

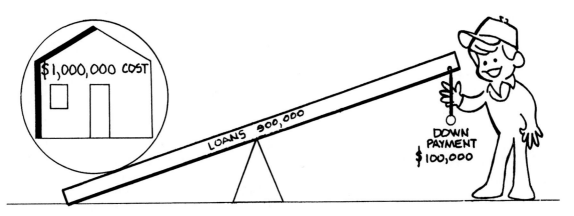

Figure 4–2. Leverage

relating to habitability of the property. Government agencies have gone to court and have named the management company as defendant in some cases in which repairs could not be made due to lack of funds.

Pride of Ownership

Pride of ownership is an important factor for investors who want to drive by their property with relatives, friends, and associates to show it off. The curb appeal should be high on the property management priority list when managing this type of property. People like to see, feel, and touch their investment. A well-manicured strip center on a busy street in a prestigious area would be an example of a site that would elicit pride of ownership.

Safety and Sense of Security

Investors who purchase high-grade bonds, blue chip stocks, or have money in federally insured certificates of deposit have more liquidity and safety than they would with a real estate investment. An office building in Houston, Texas, with its high vacancy rate and depressed value, is not as secure as high-grade bonds. A conservative investor would feel uncomfortable with the risky office building, preferring a safer investment at a lower yield.

Equity Buildup

Equity buildup is really the power of loan pay-down. At some point, the loan will be paid off and the NOI (net operating income) will equal the cash flow. The most basic example is the purchase of a single-family rental house each year for ten years, starting at the investor's age of 25. If at the time of purchase the rents of $1,000 per month equal the mortgage payment on a 30-year loan, when the investor is 65 he could retire with $10,000 per month income assuming all other factors remain constant. With just 3 percent appreciation per year for the 30 years, the monthly income would be $24,273.

Diversification

The goal of some real estate investors is diversification of their investment portfolio. A balance of investments—stocks, bonds, real estate, etc.—is desirable to protect the value in total during times of decreasing value of one investment.

NET WORTH STATEMENT

In order to better understand and assist your client, it is helpful to examine the net worth statement, a snapshot of the client's financial position (Figure 4–3). The difference between assets and liabilities (net worth) is a measure of the client's wealth. This statement will reveal existing loans, equity, and cash on hand. If your client's loan to equity is 80 percent (high) and few cash assets are on hand, you, as the property manager, will probably have a difficult time obtaining more funds from the owner for major rehabilitation projects and must prepare the owner for major capital expenditures, such as a new roof, well in advance of the expenditure.

THE MANAGEMENT AGREEMENT

Statute of Frauds law requires agreements of more than one year to be in writing. The professional property manager will insist on a contract that spells out his or her responsibilities, duties, authority, and fees. Figure 4–4 is an example of such an agreement. The management agreement is a legally binding contract.

SAMPLE
NET WORTH STATEMENT

Assets			Liabilities & Net Worth		
Liquid Assets			**Short-Term Liabilities**		
Cash in bank	$	10,000	Credit cards	$	5,000
CD certificate		40,000	Installment loans		6,000
Money market fund		10,000	Personal loans		10,000
Total liquid assets	$	60,000	Borrowing — life insurance		4,000
			Accrued income tax		
Investment Assets			Total short-term liabilities	$	25,000
Notes receivable	$	50,000			
Stocks and bonds		10,000	**Long-Term Obligations**		
IRA/retirement		15,000	Mortgage loans — R.E.	$	600,000
Real estate (Market Value)		950,000	Mortgage — residence		100,000
Total investment assets	$1,025,000		Loans — personal assets		5,000
			Loans — investments		8,000
			Other		
			Total long-term obligations	$	713,000
Personal Assets					
Residence	$	250,000	**Total Liabilities**	$	738,000
Furnishings		50,000			
Vehicle		20,000			
Other		10,000	**Net Worth**	$	677,000
Total personal assets	$	330,000			
Total Assets	$1,415,000		**Total Liabilities & Net Worth**	$1,415,000	

Assets	$1,415,000	
Liabilities	−738,000	
Net Worth	$ 677,000	

Figure 4–3. Net Worth Statement

Essential Clauses

1. Description of property, i.e., address.

2. Term, usually one year.

3. Fees and special costs, i.e., percentage of gross rents.

4. Authority to operate, i.e., collect rent, pay bills, etc.

5. Spending limit by property manager without owner approval other than normal operating expenses, e.g., a new roof.

6. Hold-harmless clause (indemnification).

7. Additionally insured, when the client's insurance company covers the agent along with the owner. Cost is usually negligible and protects the interests of the property manager.

JD PROPERTY   3520 Cadillac Avenue / Suite B
MANAGEMENT   Costa Mesa, California / 92626
INCORPORATED   714 751-2787 / Fax 714 751-0126

MANAGEMENT AGREEMENT

PARTIES:

In consideration of the covenants hereto contained,_____

_____(owner), and

_____(agent).

EXCLUSIVE AGENCY:

The owner hereby employs the Agent exclusively to rent, lease, operate and manage the property whose address is:_____

upon the terms hereinafter set forth, beginning _____19____

and continuing until either party gives a thirty (30) day written notice of cancellation in writing. Said agreement shall be for a minimum of one year.

RENTING OF PREMISES:

The Agent accepts the employment and agrees:

> To use diligence in the management of the premises for the period and upon the terms herein provided, and agrees to furnish the services of its organization for the renting, leasing, operating and managing of the herein described premises.

MONTHLY STATEMENTS:

> To render monthly statements of receipts, expenses, and charges. In the event the disbursements shall be in excess of the rents collected by the Agent, the Owner hereby agrees to pay such excess promptly upon demand of the Agent.

SEPARATE OWNER'S FUNDS:

> To deposit all receipts collected for Owner (less any sums properly deducted as otherwise provided herein), in an Account, separate from Agent's personal account. However, Agent will not be held liable in the event of bankruptcy or failure of a depository.

ADVERTISING AND SIGNS:

> The Owner hereby gives the Agent the following authority and powers and agrees to assume the expenses in connection herewith:

Licensed Real Estate Broker in California and New York.
Branch Offices: 10485 Magnolia Ave., Ste. 4-334 / Riverside, CA 92505 / Phone & Fax 909 734-6252
2105 W. Genesee St. Suite 210 / Syracuse, NY 13219 / 315 468-0556

Figure 4-4.   Management Agreement

COLLECTION OF RENT:

To advertise the availability for rental of the herein described premises, and to display signs thereon, to sign, renew and/or cancel leases for the premises; to collect rents due or to become due and give receipts therefore; to terminate tenancies and to sign and serve in the name of the Owner, notices as are deemed needful by Agent; to institute and prosecute actions, to evict tenants and to recover possession of said premises; to sue for in the name of the Owner and recover rents and other sums due; and when expedient, to settle, compromise, and release such actions or suits or reinstate such tenancies.

REPAIRS:

To make or cause to be made, and supervise repairs, alterations, and to do decorating on said premises; to purchase supplies and pay all bills. The Agent agrees to secure the approval of the Owner on all expenditures in excess of $1,000.00 for any item, except monthly or recurring operating charges and/or emergency repairs in excess of the maximum, if in the opinion of the Agents such repairs are necessary to protect the property from damage or to maintain services to the tenant as called for by their tenancy.

EMPLOYEES:

To hire, discharge and supervise all labor and employees required for the operation and maintenance of the premises; it being agreed that all employees shall be deemed employees of the Owner and not the Agent, and the owner is advised to obtain fidelity bonding. Agent shall, however, administer and pay for payroll of said employees including appropriate payroll taxes, out of funds of property and be entitled to a 10% surcharge for said administration. The Agent may perform any of its duties through its attorneys, agents or employees and shall not be responsible for their acts, default or negligence, if reasonable care has been exercised in their appointment and retention. The Agent shall not be liable for any error in judgment or for any mistake of fact of law, or for anything which it may do or refrain from doing, hereafter, except in cases of willful misconduct or gross negligence.

SERVICE CONTRACTS:

a) To make contracts for utilities, and other services as the Agent shall deem advisable; the Owner to assume the obligation of any contract so entered into at the termination of this agreement.

b) Owner is aware and acknowledges that all repairs and services of the building are performed at the then current hourly rate by independent maintenance subcontractors. JD charges 10% of subcontractors and advertising bills.

INSURANCE:

To save the Agent harmless from all damage suits in connection with the management of the herein described property and from liability from injury suffered by any employee or other person whomsoever, and to carry, at his own expense, necessary public liability and worker's compensation insurance adequate to protect the interests of the parties hereto, which policies shall be so written as to protect the Agent in the same manner and to the same extent they protect the owner. The Agent shall be added as additional insured to his policy.

INTEREST AND TAX PAYMENTS, INSURANCE:

To advise the Agent in writing if payment of mortgage indebtedness, property or employee taxes or special assessments, or the placing of fire, liability, steam boiler, pressure vessel, or any other insurance is desired.

Figure 4–4.   Continued

AGENT'S COMPENSATION:

    a.   To pay the Agent each month:

For Management: _____

For rental of each vacancy: _____

Owner responsible for all fees incurred for resident manager (to include salary, payroll taxes, etc.).

    b)   Owner agrees to deposit with Agent _____ per unit to open Owner's bank account.

    c)   Account will be charged $1.50 per unit per month for postage and copying. If late charges or fees for NSF checks are collected on said property, they shall become property of Agent for additional bookkeeping.

    d)   In the event that Owner sells or cancels the building while managed by JD Property Management, Inc., Owner shall pay a three (3) month management fee penalty based on the last month's fee. The Management Company is authorized to withdraw said penalty funds from the Owner's account prior to closing account. This condition is waived if new Owner retains JD Property Management, Inc. as managing Agent.

    e)   Managing Agent will be responsible for all lease renewals at one half of the existing new leasing lease commission rates.

    f)   Account will be charged $10.00 per unit with a $100.00 minimum as a one time computer set up fee.

This Agreement shall be binding upon, the successors and assigns of the Agent and the heirs, administrators, executors, successors, and assigns of the Owner. Any disputes will be submitted to binding arbitration.

_____   _____
Owner's Name   Agent

_____   JD Property Management, Inc.
Signature   3520 Cadillac Ave., Suite B
                                                          Costa Mesa, CA. 92626
_____   (714) 751-2787   Fax (714) 751-0126
Signature

_____   _____
Address   Date

_____
City, State, Zip

(_____)_____
Business Phone

(_____)_____
Home Phone

TIN or SS#_____

Figure 4–4.   Continued

FIDUCIARY RESPONSIBILITY
Trust Accounts

Most states require that funds collected by the property manager be deposited into a trust account. People often question whether a separate trust account is needed for each owner. The answer is usually no, but a separate accounting of each owner's funds must be maintained. Interest collected, however, should be passed on to the owner. Brokers' personal real property cannot be kept in the trust account. Usually only real estate agents can sign on the account unless other designated individuals are bonded for an amount in excess of the entire trust account.

Trust Account Procedures

1. All trust accounts must be maintained in accordance with standard accounting procedures.
   a) Clients' accounts must be balanced daily.
   b) Dates and amounts of funds deposited must be recorded.
   c) Dates, amounts, and check numbers of checks written must be recorded.

2. Trust account records usually must be kept for three years.

3. Trust funds must be kept in a federally insured bank, savings and loan, or thrift. The amount for any one client cannot exceed $100,000, which is the maximum amount of the federal insurance. The master trust account balance may exceed the $100,000 limit in total.

4. The account should be opened and labeled as a trust account with the broker named as trustee.

5. Funds must be deposited the next working day after receipt. (This requirement is sometimes difficult for the property manager to meet.)

6. Bank reconciliation should be done at least on a monthly basis and will be checked by the Department of Real Estate during spot audits of property management firms.

7. The owner or property name and address, or code, should identify each transaction.

8. The broker is only allowed to have small amount of his or her own money as "slush funds" in the account for extra bank charges or miscellaneous items. The broker or his or her salespersons cannot deposit rents on their personal (principal) properties into the trust account, but must open a separate account even if a management fee is charged for their own properties' management. This also applies to any limited partnerships a broker or agent may be involved in.

Master Trust Account (All Funds Collected)

Advantages

1. Easier and faster to record and deposit funds.

2. Computerized check writing and statements.

Disadvantages

1. More difficult to reconcile bank balances.

2. More complicated.

3. Checks for owner who has no funds could clear and cause commingling.

Separate Trust Accounts (Individual Checking Accounts)

Advantages

1. Mistakes limited to one checkbook.

2. Gives a greater sense of security to owner.

3. Less likely to commingle funds.

Disadvantages

1. More difficult for computerization.
2. More time-consuming paperwork.

Secret Profit

Secret profit by the management company could occur if the management company owning a part of the landscaping or maintenance company doing work on the property fails to inform the owner of this relationship. Ownership of such entities is permissible and may be advantageous to the owner, but must be disclosed before the fact.

Commingling

Commingling occurs when one client's funds are used to pay another client's bills. Daily balance reconciliation must be part of any utilized computer program in order to avoid inadvertent commingling. It also occurs when the broker has mixed client funds with his or her own funds. The computer system should have a fail-safe device so checks can't be written without first searching client's bank account to insure a positive balance in the account after a check is written.

Conversion

Conversion is illegally using or misappropriating client funds for the property manager's own interests (e.g., payment of rent on the management office).

Offset of Monies Due

Even if the licensee has a valid civil claim, trust funds held may not be used as an offset to pay debts, unless written authorization is given by the owner of the funds.

ESTABLISHING THE MANAGEMENT FEE

The management company, like the owner, wants to make a profit. If the property manager prices services too low, the firm will go out of business. This is an area of weakness with many good property managers. The real estate law in most states says that management fees are negotiable. The property manager should know his or her costs and bid services accordingly.

Kinds of Fees

1. *Flat amount.* A flat amount per month for management services provided to the property; e.g., $500 per month.
2. *Per door.* A unit fee which is a certain dollar figure for each unit managed; e.g., a 36-unit apartment building at $14 per unit would equal $504 per month.
3. *Percentage of collected income.* This is the method most commonly used (e.g., if rents are $15,500 per month and your management percentage is 5 percent of gross income collected, the management company's income would be $775 per month). Sometimes, firms charge a flat-fee minimum or percentage, whichever is greater. Owners and managers prefer this method as it gives incentives to collect and increase rents. Fees are usually based on collected income and not on security deposits which must be returned and thus are not considered income.
4. *Lease or re-rent fees.* Extra charges that would be made to the owner when performing special specified rental services.
5. *Special fees.*
   a) Tax assessment appeal
   b) Refinance preparation
   c) Supervision of contractors
   d) Leasing fees
   e) Payroll surcharges
   f) Extra meetings
   g) Extra reports
   h) Telephone, postage, copying charges

Determining the Cost of Management

In order for the property manager to intelligently bid services, a monthly profit and loss statement should be prepared for the management company. From this statement, using percentages, it will be seen that salary is the largest expense, consuming over 40 percent of the fee income. A standard bid sheet should be prepared so that, when asked to quote, the property manager need only fill in the appropriate blanks and total the figures (see Figure 4–5). Additional management company expenses are discussed in Chapter 13.

```
                          MANAGEMENT FEE
                            BID SHEET


     Property address_____ City_____
     Date_____ Miles from office_____ No. of units_____
     Sq. ft._____ Age_____ Condition_____ Gross rents_____


     Owner's name_____ Phone no. (___)_____
     Address_____ City_____ State_____

                                                      Total
     MANAGEMENT SERVICES      No.     Hours    Rate    Hours      Cost

     Inspections:
       Property supervisor   _____  _____  _____  _____    _____
       CPM                   _____  _____  _____  _____    _____

     Association meetings:
       Property supervisor   _____  _____  _____  _____    _____
       CPM                   _____  _____  _____  _____    _____

     Improvement supervision:
       Property supervisor   _____  _____  _____  _____    _____
       CPM                   _____  _____  _____  _____    _____

     Management review:
       Property supervisor   _____  _____  _____  _____    _____
       CPM                   _____  _____  _____  _____    _____

     Travel expense:
       Property supervisor   _____ miles x _____¢ per mile  =  _____
       CPM                   _____ miles x _____¢ per mile  =  _____

     ADMINISTRATION AND ACCOUNTING                    SUBTOTAL   _____

     Computer input          _____  _____  _____  _____    _____
     Disbursements           _____  _____  _____  _____    _____
     Payroll                 _____  _____  _____  _____    _____
     Monthly statements      _____  _____  _____  _____    _____
     Computer expense        _____  _____  _____  _____    _____
     Extra reports           _____  _____  _____  _____    _____

                                                      SUBTOTAL   _____


     OVERHEAD ON PERSONNEL                            _____%
     OVERHEAD FOR POSTAGE, COPYING, RENT, ETC.        _____%
     PROFIT & CONTINGENCIES                           _____%
                                                      SUBTOTAL   _____

     TOTAL MONTHLY FEE                                           _____

     Fee per unit: $_____ fee ÷ no. of units $_____ = $_____ per unit
     % management fee: $_____ fee ÷ gross rents $_____ = _____%
     Received management at _____%   Competitor_____ bid %_____

     Prepared by_____
```

Figure 4–5. Management Fee Bid Sheet

Ethics Ethics is an important aspect of the property manager's daily activity. The owner must have trust and confidence in the property manager in order to have a successful relationship. The definitions of ethics are many and varied. Webster's Collegiate Dictionary defines ethics as, "Principles of conduct governing an individual or group." Dr. Albert Schweitzer, the Nobel Prize humanitarian, said, "Ethics is the name we give to our concern for good behavior. We feel an obligation to consider not only our own personal well-being, but also that of others and of human society as a whole."

Unethical acts by the property manger include cash or expensive gifts from vendors, billing for work not performed, not reporting all the rents, and so on. The Institute of Real Estate Management (IREM) has a code of ethics (Figure 4–6) to which all certified property managers (CPMs) must adhere. The National Association of Realtors has a code of ethics for its Realtors.

The mini management plan shown in Figure 4–7 is a good tool for facilitating discussions on goals and objectives.

REAL ESTATE OWNERSHIP FACTS AND FIGURES

1. Total U.S. real estate stock as estimated by an Arthur Anderson Real Estate Services Group study in 1990 was $8.777 trillion.

   Individuals own $5,088 trillion.

   Corporations own $1,699 trillion.

   Partnerships own $1,011 trillion.

   Nonprofit organizations and the government own $.965 trillion.

2. Foreign ownership is relatively small at $35.8 billion, even though it gets a disproportionate amount of attention.

3. Commercial properties account for $2,655 trillion, or 30 percent of total inventory.

   Retail value is $1.115 trillion (13%).

   Office value is $1.009 trillion (11%).

   Manufacturing is $308 billion (3.5%).

   Warehouse is $223 billion (2.5%).

4. Residential properties account for $6,122 trillion or 70 percent of total, with $107.6 million housing units.

Single family homes	67.3 million units (63%), $3.857 trillion
Multifamily conventional	24.9 million units (23%), $1.4 trillion
Other (HUD, condo, mobile home)	15.4 million units (14%), $86 billion

5. Size of U.S. residential properties is small. Only 14 percent of housing structures have 50 or more units. Most units, therefore, are located in small complexes.

SUMMARY

The property manager should manage the property according to the owner's goals and objectives. The property manager may be an agent for the owner, acting as an intermediary between the owner and other parties. The property manager, if he or she manages for more than one owner, may need a real estate license. A written management agreement outlining the duties

Institute of Real Estate Management

Code of Professional Ethics of the CERTIFIED PROPERTY MANAGER®

Introduction

To establish and maintain public confidence in the honesty, integrity, professionalism, and ability of the professional property manager is fundamental to the future success of the Institute of Real Estate Management and its members. This Code and performance pursuant to its provisions will be beneficial to the general public and contribute to the continued development of a mutually beneficial relationship among CERTIFIED PROPERTY MANAGER®s, Candidates, REALTORS®, clients, employers, and the public.

The Institute of Real Estate Management, as the professional society of property managers, seeks to work closely with all other segments of the real estate industry to protect and enhance the interests of the public. To this end, members of the Institute have adopted and, as a condition of membership, subscribe to this Code of Professional Ethics. By doing so, they give notice that they clearly recognize the vital need to preserve and encourage fair and equitable practices and competition among all who are engaged in the profession of property management.

Those who are members of the Institute are dedicated individuals who are sincerely concerned with the protection and interests of those who come in contact with the industry. To this end, members of the Institute have subscribed to this Professional Pledge:

I pledge myself to the advancement of professional property management through the mutual efforts of members of the Institute of Real Estate Management and by any other proper means available to me.

I pledge myself to seek and maintain an equitable, honorable, and cooperative association with fellow members of the Institute and with all others who may become a part of my business and professional life.

I pledge myself to place honesty, integrity, and industriousness above all else; to pursue my gainful efforts with diligent study and dedication to the end that service to my clients shall always be maintained at the highest possible level.

I pledge myself to comply with the principles and declarations of the Institute of Real Estate Management as set forth in its bylaws and regulations and the CPM® Code of Professional Ethics.

1. Fiduciary Obligation to Clients

A CERTIFIED PROPERTY MANAGER® shall at all times exercise the utmost business loyalty to the interests of his or her clients and shall be diligent in the maintenance and protection of the clients' properties. In order to achieve this goal, a CERTIFIED PROPERTY MANAGER® shall not engage in any activity which could be reasonably construed as contrary to the best interests of the client or the client's property. The CERTIFIED PROPERTY MANAGER® shall not represent personal interests divergent or conflicting with those of the client, unless the client has been previously notified in writing of the actual or potential conflict of interest, and has also in writing assented to such representation. A CERTIFIED PROPERTY MANAGER®, as a fiduciary for the client, shall not receive, directly or indirectly, any rebate, fee, commission, discount or other benefit, whether monetary or otherwise, which has not been fully disclosed to and approved by the client.

2. Disclosure

A CERTIFIED PROPERTY MANAGER® shall not disclose to a third party confidential information which would be injurious or damaging concerning the business or personal affairs of a client without prior written consent of the client, except as may otherwise be required or compelled by applicable law or regulation.

3. Accounting and Reporting

A CERTIFIED PROPERTY MANAGER® shall at all times keep and maintain accurate accounting records concerning the properties managed for the client, and such records shall be available for inspection at all reasonable times by each client. A CERTIFIED PROPERTY MANAGER® shall cause to be furnished to the client, at intervals to be agreed upon with the client, a regular report in respect to that client's properties.

4. Protection of Funds and Property

A CERTIFIED PROPERTY MANAGER® shall at all times exert due diligence for the protection of client's funds and property in the possession or control of the CERTIFIED PROPERTY MANAGER® against all reasonably foreseeable contingencies or losses.

5. Relations with Other Members of the Profession

A CERTIFIED PROPERTY MANAGER® shall not make, authorize, or otherwise encourage any unfounded derogatory or disparaging comments concerning the practices of another CERTIFIED PROPERTY MANAGER®. CERTIFIED PROPERTY MANAGER®'s subscribing to this Code shall not exaggerate or misrepresent the services offered by him or her as compared with competing CERTIFIED PROPERTY MANAGER®'s. Nothing in this Code, however, shall restrict legal and reasonable business competition by and among CERTIFIED PROPERTY MANAGER®'s.

6. Contract

The contract, if any, between a CERTIFIED PROPERTY MANAGER® and his or her client shall provide for the specific terms agreed upon between the parties and shall be in clear and understandable terms, including a general description of the services to be provided by and responsibilities of the CERTIFIED PROPERTY MANAGER®.

7. Duty to Firm or Employer

A CERTIFIED PROPERTY MANAGER® shall at all times exercise the utmost loyalty to his or her employer or firm and shall be diligent in the maintenance and protection of the interests and property of the employer or firm. The CERTIFIED PROPERTY MANAGER® shall not engage in any activity or undertake any obligation which could reasonably be seen as contrary to the obligation of loyalty and diligence owed to his or her employer or firm, and shall not receive, directly or indirectly, any rebate, fee, commission, discount or other benefit, whether monetary or otherwise, which could reasonably be seen as producing a conflict with the interests of his or her employer or firm. A CERTIFIED PROPERTY MANAGER® shall at all times exercise due diligence for the protection of the funds of his or her employer or firm against all reasonably foreseeable contingencies or losses and shall as agent of his or her employer or firm exercise the highest degree of responsibility for the safekeeping and preservation of these funds.

8. Preserving and Protecting Property of the Client

It shall be the duty of the CERTIFIED PROPERTY MANAGER®, as a skilled and highly trained professional, to competently manage the property of the client with due regard for the rights, responsibilities and benefits of the tenant. A CERTIFIED PROPERTY MANAGER® shall manage the property of his or her client in a manner which takes due regard for his or her obligations to conserve natural resources and to maximize the preservation of the environment.

9. Duty to Former Clients and Former Firms or Employers

All obligations and duties of the CERTIFIED PROPERTY MANAGER® to clients, firms, and employers as specified in this Code shall also apply to relationships with former clients and former firms and employers. The CERTIFIED PROPERTY MANAGER® shall conduct himself or herself in the highest professional manner when, for whatever reason, relationships are terminated between the CERTIFIED PROPERTY MANAGER® and clients and firm or employer. Nothing in this section, however, shall be construed to cause a CERTIFIED PROPERTY MANAGER® to breach obligations and duties to current clients and firm or employer.

10. Compliance with Laws and Regulations

A CERTIFIED PROPERTY MANAGER® shall at all times conduct his or her business and personal activities with knowledge of and in compliance with applicable federal, state, and local laws and regulations, and shall maintain the highest moral and ethical standards consistent with membership in and the purposes of the Institute of Real Estate Management

11. Continuing Professional Education

A CERTIFIED PROPERTY MANAGER®, in order to assure the continued retention and further growth and development of his or her skills as a professional, shall utilize to the highest extent possible the facilities offered to him or her for continuing professional education and refinement of his or her management skills

12. Incorporation of NATIONAL ASSOCIATION OF REALTORS® Code of Ethics

The Code of Ethics of the NATIONAL ASSOCIATION OF REALTORS® as in effect from time to time, is incorporated by reference into this Code and in relevant parts shall be binding on CERTIFIED PROPERTY MANAGER®'s as other articles of this Code

13. Enforcement

Any violation by a CERTIFIED PROPERTY MANAGER® of the obligations of this Code shall be determined in accordance with and pursuant to the terms of the Bylaws and Rules and Regulations of the Institute of Real Estate Management. Disciplinary action for violation of any portion of this Code shall be instituted by the Institute of Real Estate Management in accordance with the Bylaws and Rules and Regulations established by the Governing Council of the Institute. The result of such disciplinary action shall be final and binding upon the affected CERTIFIED PROPERTY MANAGER® and without recourse to the Institute, its officers, councillors, members, employees or agents

Figure 4–6. Code of Ethics

MINI MANAGEMENT PLAN

Owner: _____   Date: _____

Building Address: _____   Type: _____

_____   Units: _____

Owner Goals: _____   Holding Period: _____

_____

Prepared By: _____

1. Regional Analysis:

2. Neighborhood Analysis:

3. Property Analysis:
   a. Physical:

   b. Fiscal (Budget):

   c. Operational (Policies & Procedures):

4. Market Analysis:
   a. Rent Survey Summary:

   b. Vacancy Rate:

5. Analysis of Alternatives:

6. Proposed Plan Performance:
   a. Physical:

   b. Implementation & Timing:

   c. Fiscal:

   d. Operational:

7. Financing Needed:
   a. Capital Budget Needed in Dollars $ _____
   b. Expenses to Rental Income Ratio: _____%

8. Valuation Comparison:
   a. Present Status:
      (1.) Dollar Value _____
      (2.) Cap Rate _____
      (3.) Gross Multiplier _____ _____

   b. Projected Status:
      (1.) Dollar Value _____
      (2.) Cap Rate _____
      (3.) Gross Multiplier _____ _____

9. Recommendations & Conclusion:

Approved By: _____

Figure 4–7. Mini Management Plan

and responsibilities should also be signed. In some instances, the property manager works as an employee of the owner, or may be the owner of the building. Forms of ownership include sole proprietorship, which is the most popular due to the ease of establishing and dissolving; partnerships, which can be either general or limited (corporations offer limited liability but incur double taxation); and REITs, which are usually large in size and distribute 95 percent of their income each year to stockholders, but avoid double taxation.

The goals of the owner are varied and differ from owner to owner. Cash flow is a goal that owners with fixed incomes frequently favor. Tax benefits are a goal that has been diminished by the 1986 Tax Reform Act. Leverage is a goal used by investors who foresee high inflation. Appreciation is another goal of most investors, while pride of ownership, safety and security, and diversification are additional goals of some owners.

The management agreement spells out the responsibilities, duties, authority, and fees of the property manager. Some essential clauses include a description of the property, term, fees, authority, spending limits, hold-harmless, and additional insured.

The property manager, if managing for others, probably needs a real estate license and must establish and maintain a trust account. The client's account must be balanced daily and the trust account reconciled on a monthly basis with the bank balance. These funds must be kept in a federally insured institution and money must be deposited by the next working day after receipt. The files must be kept for a minimum of three years in most states. Management fees are negotiable and vary according to the type, size, and location of the property. The four basic kinds of fees are flat amount, per door, percentage of collected income, and lease or re-rent fees. The property manager should determine the company costs so that a profit can be achieved on each property managed.

The property manager should view the property as a business entity and run it in accordance with the goals and objectives of the owner. The main function of the property manager is to increase the income stream, thereby increasing the NOI and the value of the property. Rapport and feedback should exist between the owner and the property manager in order to develop a long-term business relationship.

PERSONALITY PROFILE

Property managers may work for large corporations, third-party fee companies, banks, or insurance or pension firms. However, a property manager may also work for one individual owner as is the case of Ray Bacca of El Paso, Texas. Ray works for an investor who recognized that having an in-house property manager was desirable.

Ray earned his CPM designation and also teaches on the National Faculty for the Institute of Real Estate Management. Ray used his bilingual talents to become the first instructor to teach the IREM courses in Spain.

REVIEW QUESTIONS

1. In a principal/agent relationship, the property manager would probably
   a. need a real estate license.
   b. need to be an attorney.
   c. not need a license.
   d. need to be a CPA.

2. The type of real estate ownership that mandates 95 percent of profits to be distributed is a
   a. corporation.
   b. REIT.
   c. partnership.
   d. sole proprietorship.

3. A prudent property manager insists on
   a. a written management agreement.
   b. a free company car.
   c. a large office.
   d. an oral agreement.

4. An increase in value over time refers to which benefit of ownership?
   a. tax benefits
   b. pride of ownership
   c. appreciation
   d. leverage

5. A management agreement for longer than what period of time needs to be in writing?
   a. six months
   b. one year
   c. three months
   d. five months

6. The management agreement should include
   a. the term.
   b. fees.
   c. both a and b
   d. the management company's profit projection.

7. Which of the following is required for trust accounts?
   a. a separate bank account for each client
   b. a separate accounting for each owner
   c. to be held only in large banks
   d. to only be balanced once a year

8. Commingling is
   a. one client's funds used to pay the bills of another.
   b. failure to have a real estate license.
   c. failure to have CPM designation.
   d. failure to use an attorney.

9. What is the management fee in dollars if the gross collected rents equal $20,000 and the management fee is 6 percent?
   a. $1,000
   b. $1,200
   c. $1,500
   d. none of the above

10. Which of the following is usually the most desirable fee structure?
    a. minimum and/or percentage fee, whichever is higher
    b. fixed amount
    c. percentage
    d. per door

11. Using other people's money refers to which benefit of ownership?
    a. tax benefits
    b. pride of ownership
    c. appreciation
    d. leverage

12. Depreciation would refer to which benefit of ownership?
    a. tax benefits
    b. pride of ownership
    c. appreciation
    d. leverage

13. The management agreement is a
    a. preliminary proposal.
    b. legally binding agreement.
    c. form of ownership.
    d. form of a mini management plan.

14. A per-door fee of $10 per door per month for 20 units would equal an annual fee of
    a. $100.
    b. $200.
    c. $2,000.
    d. $2,400.

15. What form is helpful in determining the management fee?
    a. management agreement
    b. net worth statement
    c. code of ethics
    d. management bid sheet

ADDITIONAL READING AND REFERENCES

California Department of Real Estate, *Real Estate Law*, Sacramento, CA, 1996.

California Department of Real Estate, *Reference Book; A Real Estate Guide*, Sacramento, CA, 1996.

Commercial Investment Real Estate Journal (Bimonthly), 430 N. Michigan Ave., Chicago, IL 60611.

Hallman, Victor, and Jerry Rosenbloom, *Personal Financing Planning*, 3rd Edition, McGraw-Hill, New York, NY, 1983.

Jarchow, Steven, *Real Estate Investment Trusts*, John Wiley & Sons, Somerset, NJ, 1988.

O'Connell, Daniel, *Apartment Building Valuation, Finance and Investment Analysis*, John Wiley & Sons, Somerset, NJ, 1982.

The Real Estate Briefing (Quarterly), Arthur Young and Company, One Post Street, Ste. 3100, San Francisco, CA 94104.

Real Estate Investment Journal (Bimonthly), P.O. Box 19564, Irvine, CA 92713.

Real Estate Review (Bimonthly), Touche Ross & Company, 1 Maritime Plaza, San Francisco, CA 94111.

Realtor (Monthly), National Association of Realtors, 430 N. Michigan Ave., Chicago, IL 60611.

The REIT Report (Bimonthly), National Association of Real Estate Investment Trusts, Inc., 1101 Seventeenth St., N.W., Ste. 700, Washington, DC 20036.

Chapter 5

Performance Objectives of the Property Manager

Key terms

Appearance	Location	Security deposit report
Check register	Marketing survey	Tenant mix
Demographics	Minimize expenses	Vacancy report
Increase revenue	Rent roll	

Food for thought

"The difference between crazy and eccentric is net worth."

DEFINITION OF PROPERTY MANAGEMENT

Property management has been described and defined in many different ways over the years. The Department of Real Estate describes it as "a branch of the real estate business involving the marketing, operation, maintenance, and day-to-day financing of rental properties." Our definition is "the management, by an independent agent, of a property to maximize net operating income (NOI) while protecting and enhancing appreciation." NOI can be increased by three basic methods or a combination of these methods.

1. Increase revenues (rents)
   a) Rental surveys, i.e., comp grids
   b) Addition of amenities; e.g., ceiling fans, etc.
   c) Good curb appeal; i.e., landscaping, facade
   d) Good on-site management; i.e., ARM designation
   e) Rental contracts; e.g., laundry, soda machines

2. Minimize expenses

   a) Budgeting of expenses; e.g., utilities
   b) Centralized and volume purchasing; e.g., paint
   c) Energy-saving techniques
      (1) Insulation of water pipes
      (2) Insulation in attic area
      (3) Hot water heater blanket
      (4) Solar power
   d) An effective preventative maintenance program

3. Protect the asset
    a) Proper insurance coverage; e.g., million-dollar liability
    b) Adequate lighting for safety; e.g., parking lot

REPORTING TO THE OWNER

The property manager, like any other type of manager, must give status reports to the client or boss. In property management these not only have to be accurate, since they concern other people's money, but they must be timely as well. Nothing is more distressing than getting a statement or report too late to address the issue. See Figure 5–1.

TYPES OF REPORTS
Income and Expense Reports

This type of report (Figure 5–2) shows a summary of rents collected and operating expenses by category (plumbing, insurance, etc.). The difference between the two is called net operating income (NOI). If a loan payment is included, as in Figure 5–2, it becomes a cash-flow statement. Only the interest and not the principal of a mortgage payment is deductible on income taxes, so a "thirteenth month" adjustment must be made after the December statement, breaking down loan expense into principal and interest. Cash flow is "pocket income," money that can be sent to the owner each month. This report also includes year-to-date summaries and comparison percentages of expense items to income collected.

Rent Roll

The rent roll (Figure 5–3) is part of the cash-flow statement and is also sent to the client. A rent roll shows the unit numbers as well as receipts and disbursements for each unit. In our example, which is for a 12-unit building, it's easy to see whether all tenants paid their rent and the amounts of their individual rents. In Figure 5–3, we see one vacancy in unit 914-4. When all the

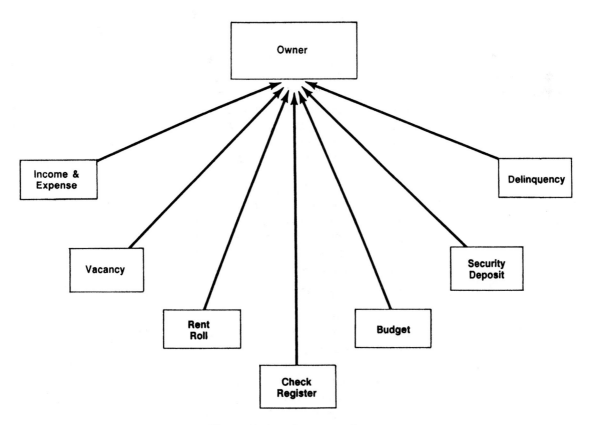

Figure 5–1. Reports to Owner

STATEMENT OF INCOME & EXPENSE
FOR THE 12 MONTH(S) ENDED DECEMBER 31
3341

INCOME	CURRENT MONTH	%	YEAR TO DATE	%
OPERATING INCOME				
RENTAL INCOME	5,300.00	97.54	67,481.63	97.89
WASHER/DRYER INCOME	133.50	2.46	1,551.70	2.25
PREVIOUS RENT	0.00	0.00	(99.04)	(0.14)
TOTAL OPERATING INCOME	5,433.50	100.00	68,934.29	100.00
TOTAL INCOME	5,433.50	100.00	68,934.29	100.00
OPERATING EXPENSES				
G&A EXPENSE				
APPLIANCES	0.00	0.00	460.00	0.67
BUILDING REPAIRS	(1.83)	(0.03)	3,253.93	4.72
CARPETS/CARPET CLEANING	0.00	0.00	245.00	0.36
CLEANING	(40.00)	(0.74)	65.00	0.09
DRAPES	196.10	3.61	285.25	0.41
ELECTRIC	101.43	1.87	919.32	1.33
ELECTRICAL REPAIRS	0.00	0.00	97.95	0.14
FLOOR REPAIRS	0.00	0.00	417.37	0.61
GAS	296.89	5.46	3,545.95	5.14
GLASS/SCREENS	40.78	0.75	187.45	0.27
HEATING/COOLING	0.00	0.00	492.12	0.71
INSURANCE	0.00	0.00	899.00	1.30
LANDSCAPE MAINTENANCE	75.00	1.38	1,081.03	1.57
LEGAL	0.00	0.00	(8.00)	(0.01)
LICENSES	0.00	0.00	25.00	0.04
LIGHTING REPAIRS	0.00	0.00	184.81	0.27
LOCKS/KEYS	40.00	0.74	143.16	0.21
LOAN PAYMENT	1,696.00	31.21	20,352.00	29.53
MANAGEMENT FEES	265.00	4.88	3,369.14	4.89
MANAGER'S SALARY	243.43	4.48	1,576.77	2.29
MISCELLANEOUS	0.00	0.00	150.00	0.22
PAINTING	(56.50)	(1.04)	913.17	1.32
PAYROLL TAXES	0.00	0.00	194.52	0.28
PEST CONTROL	54.00	0.99	450.00	0.65
PLUMBING	84.71	1.56	3,203.29	4.65
PROPERTY TAXES	1,593.87	29.33	3,143.21	4.56
ROOFING	0.00	0.00	975.00	1.41
RUBBISH COLLECTION	140.50	2.59	1,407.13	2.04
SUPPLIES	0.00	0.00	45.09	0.07
WATER	280.50	5.16	2,074.55	3.01
TOTAL OPERATING EXPENSES	5,009.88	92.20	50,148.20	72.75
NET PROFIT OR LOSS	423.62	7.80	18,786.09	27.25
OPENING TRUST BALANCE	4,025.00			
MONIES TO/FROM OWNER	0.00		(18,122.47)	
CLOSING TRUST BALANCE	4,448.62			
SECURITY DEPOSITS	3,905.00			
TOTAL BANK BALANCE	8,353.62			

Figure 5–2. Statement of Income and Expense

J. D. PROPERTY MANAGEMENT
P.O. Box 1438, Costa Mesa, CA 92626
(714) 751-2787

PROPERTY MANAGEMENT STATEMENT

IMPORTANT: RETAIN FOR
INCOME TAX RETURNS

FOR:

3341.1

DATE: 31 DEC

PROPERTY:

SANTA ANA, CA. 92703

DATE	CHECK NO OR DATE PAID TO	RECEIPTS	DISBURSEMENTS	TRANSACTION DESCRIPTION	UNIT DESIGNATION
13 DEC 85	01 JAN 86	475.00		RENT	908-1
13 DEC 85		55.00		SD RECEIPT/REFUND	908-2
13 DEC 85	01 JAN 86	475.00		RENT	908-2
13 DEC 85	01 JAN 86	475.00		RENT	908-3
13 DEC 85	01 JAN 86	475.00		RENT	908-4
13 DEC 85	01 JAN 86	475.00		RENT	914-1
13 DEC 85	01 JAN 86	475.00		RENT	914-2
13 DEC 85	01 JAN 86	475.00		RENT	914-3
12 DEC 85	21336.1		338.50	SD RECEIPT/REFUND SD	914-4
12 DEC 85		40.00		CLEANING 6430	914-4
12 DEC 85		76.50		PAINTING	914-4
12 DEC 85		10.00		LOCKS/KEYS	914-4
12 DEC 85		10.00		BUILDING REPAIRS	914-4
12 DEC 85			136.50	SD RECEIPT/REFUND SD	914-4
13 DEC 85	01 JAN 86	475.00		RENT	920-1
13 DEC 85	01 JAN 86	465.00		RENT	920-2
13 DEC 85	01 JAN 86	475.00		RENT	920-3
13 DEC 85	01 DEC 85	560.00		RENT	920-4
01 DEC 85	M3708		20.00	PAINTING	
10 DEC 85	21279.1		1593.87	PROPERTY TAXES-REAL	
13 DEC 85	21346.1		243.43	MANAGERS SALARY	
16 DEC 85	21379.1		1696.00	LOAN PAYMENT	
17 DEC 85		119.50		WASHER/DRYER INCOME	
17 DEC 85		14.00		WASHER/DRYER INCOME	
18 DEC 85	21498.1		39.30	ELECTRIC	
18 DEC 85	21498.1		32.27	ELECTRIC	
18 DEC 85	21498.1		29.86	ELECTRIC	
18 DEC 85	21454.1		107.50	RUBBISH COLLECTION	
18 DEC 85	21491.1		84.71	PLUMBING	

DEPOSIT BALANCE				CLIENTS BALANCE			
PREVIOUS BALANCE	RECEIPTS	DISBURSED	CLOSING BALANCE	PREVIOUS BALANCE	RECEIPTS	DISBURSEMENTS	CLOSING BALANCE

HERITAGE BUSINESS FORMS—(714) 859-1667   584333

Figure 5–3.   Rent Roll

rents are added up, they equal the amount under the rental-income category of cash-flow statement.

Check Register

The check register (Figure 5–4) is also part of the cash-flow statement. It allows the client to see the amount of each check, date written, check number, and purpose. If each payment under "electrical" is totaled, that total would equal the electrical expense category in the cash-flow statement shown in Figure 5–2. This is not only an invaluable control tool for the client, but also a security check that allows the client to easily see how the money was spent.

Security Deposit Balance

The security deposit balance is also shown on the check register. For accounting purposes, only the security deposit balance is reported separately from the client's balance (see Figure 5–4). In some states, these funds may have to be put into a separate bank account. Also, in some states and communities, interest may have to be paid to the tenant on the amount of the security deposit.

J. D. PROPERTY MANAGEMENT
P.O. Box 1438, Costa Mesa, CA 92626
(714) 751-2787

PROPERTY MANAGEMENT STATEMENT

FOR:

3341.1

DATE: 31 DEC

PROPERTY:

SANTA ANA, CA. 92703

DATE	CHECK NO. OR DATE PAID TO	RECEIPTS	DISBURSEMENTS	TRANSACTION DESCRIPTION	UNIT DESIGNATION
18 DEC 85	21451.1		8.17	BUILDING REPAIRS	
18 DEC 85	21451.1		50.00	LOCKS/KEYS	
19 DEC 85	21524.1		27.00	PEST CONTROL	
19 DEC 85	21524.1		40.78	GLASS/SCREENS	
20 DEC 85	21690.1		27.00	PEST CONTROL	
23 DEC 85	21696.1		75.00	LANDSCAPE MAINTENANC	
23 DEC 85	21562.1		280.50	WATER	
23 DEC 85	21562.1		33.00	RUBBISH COLLECTION	
23 DEC 85	21574.1		196.10	DRAPES	
23 DEC 85	21595.1		94.74	GAS	
23 DEC 85	21595.1		145.33	GAS	
23 DEC 85	21595.1		56.82	GAS	
31 DEC 85	18197		265.00	MANAGEMENT FEES MGMT	

DEPOSIT BALANCE				CLIENTS BALANCE			
PREVIOUS BALANCE	RECEIPTS	DISBURSED	CLOSING BALANCE	PREVIOUS BALANCE	RECEIPTS	DISBURSEMENTS	CLOSING BALANCE
4325.00	55.00	475.00	3905.00	4025.00	5570.00	5146.38	-4448.62

Figure 5–4. Check Register

Total Cash Balance

The total cash balance in Figure 5–2 is the sum of the closing security-deposit balance and the closing client balance, which in our illustration is $8,353.62.

Budget Comparison Statement

This type of report is an expanded cash-flow report that includes a budget and variances from the budget (see Chapter 10, Figure 10–2). This is used when more sophisticated reports are needed, such as for banks, institutions, and larger properties.

Vacancy Report

The vacancy report can be generated for each property on a weekly basis, or daily, for problem properties. In many cases, a project marketing summary report is prepared.

Delinquency Report

Delinquency reports (Figure 5–6) are usually generated by the fifth of the month to begin the eviction process on tenants who have not paid their rent.

RESIDENT ...... NAME .... ADDRESS .... DEP-AMT........

RESIDENT	NAME	ADDRESS	RENT	SECURITY DEPOSIT
3920.1.1	MANUEL CORTEZ MARTINEZ	1141 POPLAR SO. #1	400.00	375.00
3920.1.10	G. CHAVEZ/D. ARMAS	1143 POPLAR SO. #2	430.00	375.00
3920.1.11	MARIO DE JESUS GUARDADO	1143 POPLAR SO. #3	430.00	390.00
3920.1.12	CONSUELA ALCARAZ	1143 POPLAR SO. #4	430.00	75.00
3920.1.13	B. ALBERTO/G. BELMONTES	1143 POPLAR SO. #5	430.00	290.00
3920.1.14	ANGEL GUZMAN	1143 POPLAR SO. #6	450.00	425.00
3920.1.15	MARY IBARRA	1143 POPLAR SO. #7	430.00	380.00
3920.1.16	VACANT	1143 POPLAR SO. #8		
3920.1.2	MARTHA HERNANDEZ	1141 POPLAR SO. #2	390.00	390.00
3920.1.3	IRMA CASTRO/SIMON D'CAMPO	1141 POPLAR SO. #3	430.00	380.00
3920.1.4	EFREN CORTEZ	1141 POPLAR SO. #4	430.00	380.00
3920.1.5	ARMANDO GARCIA	1141 POPLAR SO. #5	430.00	360.00
3920.1.6	MARIA RUIZ	1141 POPLAR SO. #6	430.00	290.00
3920.1.7	ARTURO DIAZ/RACINDO AMBRIZ	1141 POPLAR SO. #7	400.00	495.00
3920.1.8	HECTOR AGUSTO	1141 POPLAR SO. #8	430.00	340.00
3920.1.9	JOSE OTIZ	1143 POPLAR SO. #1	430.00	250.00

[405] 16 ITEMS LISTED

Figure 5–5.   Security Deposit Report

J.D. PROPERTY MANAGEMENT
COMMERCIAL DELINQUENCY STATUS REPORT
28 FEB

RES NO	SURNAME	UNIT DESIG	CHARGE	PRIOR BALANCE	AMOUNT BILLED	AMOUNT RECEIVED	CURRENT BALANCE	TOTAL DUE	PAID TO DATE
1 3		8916	EST CAM		71.73	71.73			03-01
			RENT		974.81	974.81			
			CAM	20.03			20.03	20.03	
1 5		8920	EST CAM		52.00	52.00			03-01
			RENT		660.00	660.00			
				287.21			287.21	287.21	
1 11		8932	EST CAM		105.00	105.00			03-01
			RENT		800.00	800.00			
			CAM	586.80			586.80	586.80	
1 12		8944	EST CAM		148.00		148.00		02-26
			RENT		1650.00	1650.00			
			CAM	818.27			818.27	966.27	
1 13		8948	EST CAM		540.00		540.00		02-26
			RENT		5265.00	5265.00			
			CAM	999.84		999.84		540.00	
1 15		8956	EST CAM		346.00		346.00		02-01
			RENT		4025.00		4025.00		
			CAM	1902.12			1902.12	6273.12	
1 16		8960	EST CAM		904.80	904.80			03-01
			RENT		7062.30	7062.30			
			CAM	283.05			283.05	283.05	
1 17		8962	EST CAM		233.36	233.36	233.36		02-01
			RENT	2865.64	2806.97	2865.64	2806.97	3040.33	
1 21		8976	EST CAM		110.00		110.00		02-01
			RENT		1212.75		1212.75		
			CAM	599.36		96.32	503.04	1825.79	
1 22		8978	RENT	740.00	1617.00	2280.00	77.00		02-25
			EST CAM		148.00		148.00		
			CAM	926.99			926.99	1151.99	
1 25		8988	RENT	2950.00	1840.90	1519.73	3271.17		01-07

Figure 5–6. Delinquency Status Report

Some computer programs print out 3-Day Pay Rent or Quit notices from the delinquency list in a matter of minutes.

Monthly Summary   The monthly summary (Figure 5–7) is a narrative report that goes along with the cash-flow report and summarizes the events of the past month. It comments on vacancies, delinquencies, major expenditures, budget variances, and any major problems occurring on the property.

JD PROPERTY   3520 Cadillac Avenue / Suite B
MANAGEMENT   Costa Mesa, California / 92626
INCORPORATED 714 751-2787 / Fax 714 751-0126

Shelton Terrace Monthly Summary—December

   Vacancies—one
   Delinquencies—none

1. <u>Property Taxes</u> of $1,593 were paid this month which is the main reason for the low profit margin this month.

2. <u>Rental</u> of apartment 914-4 was at $560.00. It was completed after statement was run and doesn't show this month.

3. <u>Repairs</u> were minor replacements with no major problems.

4. <u>Year-End Comments:</u>
   A. The rental income increased 8.2% this year vs. last year. We hope to achieve at least 7% in the coming year.
   B. Repairs were down 1% over last years and we don't anticipate any major projects in the coming year.

<u>BRANCH OFFICE</u>
2105 W. GENESEE ST., SUITE 210, SYRACUSE, NY 13219 (315) 468-0556

LICENSED REAL ESTATE BROKER CALIFORNIA AND NEW YORK

Figure 5–7.   Monthly Summary

Bills to Owner   In many cases, the property manager sends the client the paid bills each month. This relieves the property manager of the responsibility for storage and the ensuing costs. Most states require that the property manager keep records for up to four years. The property manager should never give accounting advice, but should refer the client to a certified public accountant.

THE MARKETING SURVEY   The success of a property in meeting the goals and objectives set forth by either the property manager or owner depends primarily on the quality of the tenants occupying the building. Each building is unique and will attract different types of tenants. The property manager must examine the property to determine its strengths and weaknesses, and highest and best use, before a management plan can be written for operating the building (Figure 5–8).

Location   Location is always paramount in real estate. If an office building is near the courthouse, it will attract attorneys as clients. A hospital-proximate medical building has a distinct advantage in attracting physician tenants. An apartment building in a high-crime area will have trouble attracting affluent renters.

Appearance   Appearance, or curb appeal, is important as people like to live and work in nice surroundings. Banks and institutions like to be located in prestigious, high-image buildings. An apartment building that has weeds and no landscaping will not attract renters who can afford to pay more for a "nice" place to live.

Government   Restrictive zoning or stiff parking requirements for office/retail use could deter potential tenants. On the other hand, being next to a well-used bus line or in a city which has good police, fire protection, and schools is a plus.

Demographics   Where are your tenants coming from? If near a freeway interchange, your office building will attract sales-oriented businesses or companies that need easy transportation access for their employees. If an apartment building is located in a depressed area, it will be difficult to attract good tenants.

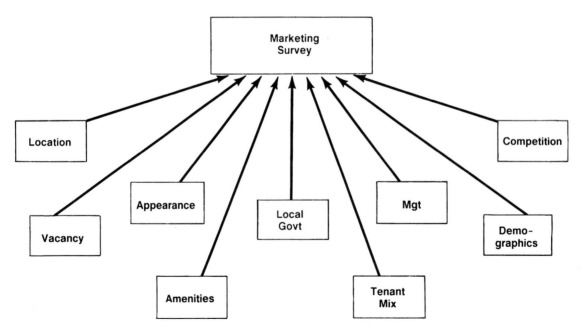

Figure 5–8.   Project Marketing Survey

Competition Who and where is your competition? What are their rental rates and giveaway programs (e.g., free rent, free parking)? We will examine how to use the comp grid in Chapter 7 (Figure 7–7).

Vacancy Rate What is the vacancy rate in your area? The local apartment association and investment brokers for both commercial and residential are good sources of information.

Amenities Does your apartment building provide drapes or miniblinds? Does it have garages, fireplaces, extra bathrooms? Rental rates cannot be compared without taking a survey to determine how your amenities stack up compared to those of the competition. Refer back to Figure 5–8.

Tenant Mix The tenant mix is important in retaining and attracting new tenants. Renting to a veterinarian, for example, in a medical building could hurt the building's image and the existing tenants' (the medical doctors) business could suffer. In this instance, the veterinarian's application could be denied as economic discrimination (see Chapters 8–11). The property manager must be careful, however, not to discriminate on the basis of race, age, religion, color, creed, national origin, or handicap.

Management Potential tenants are attracted to a well-managed building. Are the lobbies, elevators, and restrooms clean? Is management responsive to tenant questions and problems and maintenance reports?

TAKEOVER OF NEW CLIENT After negotiations between the owner and management company have been completed, terms must be agreed to in the form of a signed management agreement (Figure 4–4). You will have to have a takeover plan. The owner needs to provide the management agent with information such as rent roll, security deposit roll, list of vendors, utilities, and mortgage lender. Often the information comes in at different times and incomplete and therefore a management takeover checklist should be used (Figure 5–9). You will need the name, address, and phone number of the owners as well as their tax identification number, the name of the insurance agent and a copy of the policy, a statement on when and how the property taxes are to be paid, and copies of the tax bills. Are there any existing outstanding bills? Who will do the payroll for the managers?

The management agent will make up a rough budget to determine income and expenses and if any additional funds will be needed as working capital from the owners. Without adequate working capital to pay bills, the property management agent will be hamstrung and unable to operate effectively. The property manger will arrange the changeover and give notice to vendors and utilities of the new billing address. Normally, bills are billed to the property or the owner in care of the property manager. For example:

Terrance View Apartments
c/o JD Property Management, Inc.
3520-B Cadillac Ave.
Costa Mesa, CA 92626

It is important to insert "c/o" so the property management agent is not responsible if the owner does not provide sufficient funds. Some exceptions are owners who insist on paying the taxes or mortgage payments directly themselves.

Commercial Property Management Take-over Checklist

Building Information   **Date**_____

Address of Building: _____

City:_____State:_____Zip:_____

Type of Building:_____Class: A   B   C   D

Number of Stories:_____Windows:_____

Total Square Feet:_____Rentable Square Feet:_____

Number of Units:_____Age:_____Type of Construction:_____

Type of HVAC:_____Sprinklers: Yes   No   Parking Spaces:_____

Elevator: Yes   No   Serviced By:_____

Other Features:_____

Insurance Carrier:_____

Policy Number:_____Amount of Insurance: _____

1ˢᵗ Mortgage Holder:_____Amount of Loan:_____

Monthly Payment:_____Loan Due Date:_____

Rental Incentives

Free Rent:_____months   Tenant Improvement Allowance:_____

Parking Spaces:_____Moving Allowance:_____

Signage:_____

Owner/Manager Information

Owner Name:_____Phone:_____

Owner Address:_____

City:_____State:_____Zip:_____

Property Manager:_____Phone:_____

City:_____State:_____Zip:_____

On-site Contact:_____Phone:_____

Other:_____

Tenant Information

Unit #	Tenant Name	Sq. Ft.	Rate per s.f.	Total Rent	Lease Expiration

Figure 5–9.   Management Takeover Checklist

Meeting with the Owner

After the takeover is complete, how often should the management agent meet with the owners? It depends on the type of property, problems on the property, requirements of the owner, and geographical distance. Meeting annually with an owner may be sufficient, as in the case of a single-family rental or a property that is running smoothly. Monthly reports are being sent and telephone contact will usually clear up any questions. If the property has deferred maintenance, such as leaky roofs, it may be a good idea to have the owner meet the management agent for a physical inspection to focus on the problems. Some owners schedule quarterly or semiannual regular visits. Some owners live in foreign countries and may not visit the property for years at a time.

SUMMARY

No one definition of property management is widely accepted. This book defines the role of the property manager as being threefold.

1. Increase net operating income
   a) Increase rents; e.g., offer amenities, good management
   b) Minimize expenses; e.g., use energy-saving techniques

2. Enhance value; i.e., increase curb appeal, sales price

3. Protect the asset; i.e., adequate insurance, inspections

The property manager needs to give adequate and timely reports to the owner on the operation of the building. Typical reports include income and expense, vacancy, rent roll, check register, budgets (operating and pro forma), security deposit, and delinquency. These reports may be weekly or monthly depending on owner reporting requirements. In many instances, the client also receives the paid bills each month to keep for his or her files.

The property manager should conduct a market survey of the property to determine its strengths and weaknesses. This is very important for determining how the property manager will meet the owner's goals and objectives. Areas to examine in the marketing survey include location, vacancy, appearance, government, demographics, competition, amenities, tenant mix, and management.

PERSONALITY PROFILE

The property manager has to be able to provide reports in the manner and time frame that the client requires. Managing properties for the Housing and Urban Affairs Department (HUD) requires accurate and timely reporting procedures. Terence Tom and his company, Optima Management, in the San Francisco Bay area has managed HUD properties for many years. Terry has his certified property manager (CPM) designation from the Institute of Real Estate Management as well as an ARM designation. He worked his way up to the top through education and by adapting to change and seizing opportunities.

Terry began in the real estate industry as a leasing agent and later became a resident manager. He quickly progressed up the ladder, ultimately becoming the vice president of marketing for a local San Francisco firm. Terry's success contributed to the growth of the company as it expanded to numerous states across the nation and eventually gave him the experience he needed to venture out on his own. Terry cofounded Optima Property Management Group, a real estate management corporation in Oakland, California, of which he is the principal.

Terence Tom is a professional in the industry. Being a professional involves more than the successful work that he does and has done in the past. It also includes being an active member and volunteer in the business community, giving back to the industry that supports us all. Terry has shown that he is a leader in both of these capacities.

Terry has been active in the Bay Area business community and many of its professional organizations, meanwhile pursuing career professionalism through continuing education. In all, Terry is an asset to the community and the industry he serves. He freely admits, "What I am today, I owe to IREM."

1. The property manager can increase revenues by
   a. adding amenities.
   b. good curb appeal.
   c. neither a nor b
   d. both a and b

2. The property manager can minimize expenses by
   a. installing energy-saving devices.
   b. raising rents.
   c. adding washers and dryers.
   d. painting the building.

3. The goal of the property manager is to
   a. increase revenues.
   b. minimize expenses.
   c. protect future value.
   d. all of the above
   e. only increase revenues.

4. Rent roll statements should be prepared
   a. weekly.
   b. monthly.
   c. annually.
   d. bimonthly.

5. Security deposit records should be kept
   a. only when the tenant vacates.
   b. only when the tenant rents.
   c. at all times during the tenant's residency.
   d. only if the tenant requests that they be kept.

6. Reports to the owner
   a. should be timely and accurate.
   b. should be submitted only once a year.
   c. should include tax returns prepared by the property manager.
   d. none of the above

7. Location is important for which type of real estate?
   a. apartments
   b. office buildings
   c. neither a nor b
   d. both a and b

8. Local government controls
   a. interest rates.
   b. zoning and parking.
   c. tenant selection.
   d. population and income characteristics.

9. Demographics deals with
   a. interest rates.
   b. zoning and parking.
   c. population and income characteristics.
   d. agency issues.
   e. landlord/tenant laws.

10. Tenant mix allows the property manager to discriminate on the basis of
    a. color.
    b. race.
    c. national origin.
    d. none of the above
    e. only b and c

11. Protection of assets includes
    a. adding washers and dryers.
    b. adding amenities.
    c. adequate lighting.
    d. raising rents four times a year.

12. A check register would show
    a. monthly income.
    b. delinquencies.
    c. vacancy.
    d. the date and number of each check.

13. A management takeover checklist should include
    a. insurance information.
    b. mortgage information.
    c. the preparation of the client's tax return.
    d. the client's tax identification number.

14. Vendors should invoice property bills to
    a. the owner.
    b. the property in care of the management company.
    c. the management company.
    d. the owner's CPA's name.

15. How often the management agent meets with the owner depends on
    a. the net worth of the client.
    b. when reports are due.
    c. only on the anniversary date of the management contract.
    d. problems associated with the property.

CASE STUDY

Introduction

To enhance your understanding of property management while learning to apply in practice the principles discussed in this book, we have developed a case study to complement the practical application of each chapter. This somewhat humorous case study concerns a 20-unit apartment building called Whiskey Manor, located in Orange County, California. The study will address rental rates, vacancy, maintenance and repair, and property performance improvement techniques. The student will be asked to develop solutions and management strategies. Since property management is both an art and a science, there are no absolute answers. The answers to the case study problems in the back of the book will offer possible solutions to help guide the student. Case study questions are located at the end of several chapters.

Whiskey Manor Fact Sheet

Whiskey Manor is located in Orange County, California, which has a rapidly growing population, now over two million people. Most of the employment in the county is moving from manufacturing toward the service industry. Wages are $6–12 per hour with low unemployment (less than 4 percent). The area has several minority groups comprising in total nearly 50 percent of the population. These minorities tend to earn lower wages. The climate is one of the world's best, with moderately warm summers and mild winters (no snow). The area has a major regional shopping center (five miles away), several colleges, and cultural and recreational facilities within a 30-mile radius. The area is served by several newspapers, but the main ones are the *Los Angeles Times* and the *Register*. The *Register* is best for advertising vacant apartments because of its "local paper" reputation.

Neighborhood Information

The property is located in a central city of the county with a population of approximately 80,000 (Figure 5–10). A large contingent of immigrants from Southeast Asia has settled in the area. Most employment in the immediate area is service related, with an average wage of $6–9 per hour. Shopping, schools, parks, and churches are all available nearby. The most immediate neighbor is a Catholic church. A bus stop is four blocks away. The apartment building overlooks the city civic center, administration building, and police station. The area vacancy rate is 3–4 percent.

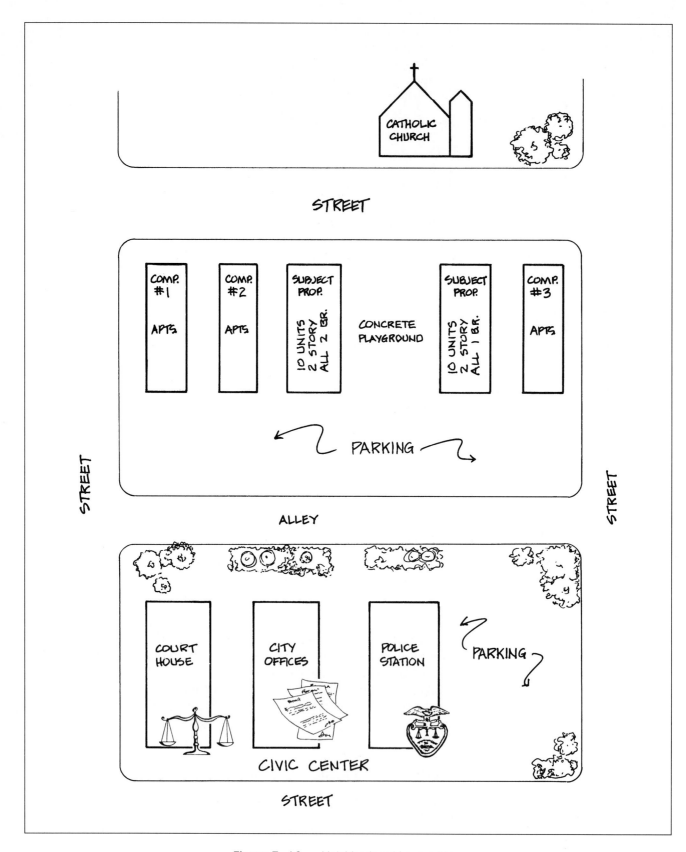

Figure 5–10. Neighborhood Layout Map

Amenities	Subject Property	Comp. #1	Comp. #2	Comp. #3
1 bedroom	$450	$530	$525	$535
2 bedrooms	$500	$570	$575	$565
Fireplace	No	No	No	Yes
Utilities	Partial	No	Yes	Partial
Pool	No	No	Yes	Yes
Garage	No	Yes	Yes	No
Spa	No	No	Yes	No
Age	20 years	15 years	New	10 years
Condition	Fair	Good	Good	Good
Location	Good	Fair	Good	Good
Play area	Yes	No	No	No

The Property

1. Age: 20 years

2. Construction: Two-story wood frame with stucco

3. Number of units: 10 one-bedroom, approx. 650 sq. ft..
   10 two-bedroom, approx. 750 sq. ft..

4. Heating: Gas wall units; gas stoves

5. Utilities: Electricity paid by tenant; gas and water paid by owner (see Figure 5–11)

6. Amenities: No pool, but large concrete play area; coin laundry facilities; no air-conditioning

7. Parking: One space per apartment

8. Landscaping: Nonexistent

9. Condition of units: Fair, but has plumbing problems; has new roof

10. Layout: Two buildings facing each other across a courtyard which is part parking and part play area

History of Units

The complex was formerly owned for several years by "Big Bertha," a neighborhood "madam," who had a red light on at the manager's apartment for her clients. She was shot and killed by a dissatisfied customer. The present owners, Pete and Mary Scrooge, purchased the units at an estate sale.

ADDITIONAL READING AND REFERENCES

Boardroom Reports (Biweekly), 330 W. 42nd St., New York, NY 10036.

Crittenden Bulletin (Monthly), Crittenden Research, Inc., P.O. Box 1150, Novato, CA 94948.

Institutional Investor (Monthly), Institutional Investor, Inc., 488 Madison Avenue, New York, NY 10022.

Klink, James, *Real Estate Accounting and Reporting*, John Wiley & Sons, Somerset, NH, 1985.

```
Scheduled income                                          $9,500

   Vacancies and delinquencies      ($2,700)

   Actual income                                $6,800
   Washer/dryer                                    110
   Total income                                              6,910

Operating expenses:

   Advertising                               $     0
   Building repairs                              385
   Carpets/carpet cleaning                        24
   Electricity                                    82
   Gas                                           282
   Insurance                                      76
   Landscaping                                     0
   Legal                                          24
   Loan payment                                4,900
   Management fees                                 0
   Manager's salary                              400
   Property taxes                                623
   Repairs:
     Painting                                     77
     Plumbing                                     79
     Electrical                                    0
   Rubbish                                       154
   Water                                         231
   Miscellaneous                                  13
   Total operating expenses                                  7,350

Cash flow (negative)                                      ($   440)
```

Figure 5–11. Whiskey Manor Income and Expense

McKenzie, Dennis, Lowell Anderson, Frank Battino, and Cecilia Hopkins, *California Real Estate Principles*, 4th Edition, John Wiley & Sons, New York, NY, 1994.

National Real Estate Investor, 6151 Powers Ferry Rd., Atlanta, GA 30399.

Transition—Taking Over a Management Account, Institute of Real Estate Management, Chicago, IL, 1992.

Real Estate Issues (Semiannual), 430 N. Michigan Ave., Chicago, IL 60611.

Chapter 6

Leases

Key terms

Assignment	Gross lease	Periodic tenancy
CAM	Late charges	Radius clause
Commercial lease	Month-to-month	Residential lease
Estate for years	Net lease	Sublet

Food for thought

"Frustration is not having anyone to blame but yourself."

INTRODUCTION

One of the major functions of a property manager is to rent and lease the property for the owner. One must then be familiar with the duties, rights, and terminology involved in leasing. Successful leasing creates the income that the property manager, increasing net operating income while enhancing appreciation and value, strives to protect. The property manager may be involved either directly, as the leasing agent, or supervisorally when independent leasing agents are used. In either case, a firm knowledge of leases and their effect on the property is mandatory.

Historically, leases have been drawn by attorneys and usually favor the owner. Many managers use the same "boiler plate" lease and rental agreement over and over again. These documents should be reviewed periodically by legal counsel to be sure they reflect updates and changes in the law and business practice. The property manager is given authority through the management agreement and can usually sign leases and rental agreements as an agent on behalf of the owner. In so doing, the property manager is responsible for the contents of the agreements.

TYPES OF LEASEHOLD ESTATES
Estate for Years

An estate for years is an agreement between a lessor (owner) and lessee (tenant) for a fixed period of time. The estate for years has a specific beginning and ending date. If the term is for more than one year, the lease agreement must be in writing. As the length of time on a commercial lease may be for several years, a very detailed lease agreement frequently is used.

Estate at Sufferance

An estate at sufferance occurs when a tenant holds over (stays) on the premises after the lease has expired or after the tenant has given notice to vacate. If the landlord or manager accepts rental payments, the lease will revert to a periodic tenancy. The period of such tenancy will usually be month to month, or in some cases for the period of time between rental payments that is specified in the original lease.

Estate from Period to Period

A periodic tenancy (sometimes called an estate from period to period) is most commonly referred to as a month-to-month rental agreement and is used primarily for residential properties or for small commercial spaces (see Figure 7–11 in Chapter 7). The periodic tenancy has no specific ending date and can be terminated by either party giving notice usually equal to the period of time between rental payments. A written rental agreement is not required by the Statute of Frauds if the period of tenancy is under one year, but is highly advisable. In order to collect attorney's fees, as under any lease, a specific clause must be written indicating that "the prevailing party will be entitled to attorney's fees" in the event of a dispute.

Estate at Will

An estate at will can be terminated by either the tenant or the owner at will as it has no fixed time period. In some states this would not be a valid lease.

TYPES OF LEASES
Gross Lease

Under a gross lease, the tenant pays the owner a fixed monthly rental sum that may include the landlord's taxes, as well as the costs of maintenance, insurance, and utilities in the gross fee. This is the common form of residential lease as maintenance and repairs are part of habitability which cannot be delegated to the tenant by the owner. It also is frequently used for small commercial sites when the lease term is for short periods of time and the lessor and lessee desire a simpler form of rental payment. A definite advantage accrues to the tenant in that the predetermined rent can be budgeted without worrying about increases in building maintenance costs.

Net Lease

Under a net lease, the tenant pays a minimum rental rate and then pays a pro-rated share of taxes, insurance, and maintenance. A single net lease refers to the tenant paying one of the above-mentioned items; a double net, two; and a triple net, three. Frequently the lease will specify that the tenant pay for professional management or at least a percentage for supervision of the billings in addition to the common area charges. This supervision fee can accrue to the property management firm as part of its management fee. Sometimes this additional fee is referred to as a quadruple net lease. Because of the residential habitability issue, net leases refer to commercial leases and are not used in residential management.

Percentage Lease

Under a percentage lease, the tenant pays the higher of either a minimum base rent or a percentage of total sales each month. Used in shopping centers, especially larger ones, it is primarily a retail lease. Nowhere else is the partnership relationship between the owner and tenant more evident than in a percentage lease. The more successful the tenant, the more successful the center and vice versa.

While the percentage lease is used primarily with large, national tenants, it is helpful in charting the success of small tenants. The required percentage sales reports help the manager chart the success of the tenant. Are sales going up or down? What effect does a particular tenant have on the others? What sort of rental increase can be effected? Should the lease be renewed?

Another major consideration when writing a percentage lease should be the assignable use. The expected rent from a major supermarket could be adversely affected if assignment is made to a cafeteria chain or another use that produces lower monthly sales and does not draw in large numbers of shoppers to the center.

Acceleration Lease

In an acceleration lease, the rental rate is accelerated to predetermined amounts at fixed dates during the term of the lease. It protects the landlord against inflation and keeps the base rent closer to market so the rental increase at the time of renewal isn't large. Its use is also very appropriate for a tenant just starting out, but with good potential. The rate may start at lower than market, but end, when the tenant is more financially strong, at a rate higher than expected. The acceleration lease also exemplifies the partnership of the landlord and tenant. The landlord defers a return until the tenant succeeds, thereby increasing the expected return at a later date. Here is an example:

Standard Lease	Accelerated Lease
1,000 s.f. at $1.00/s.f.	$0.75 1st year—$9,000
5-year term	$1.00 2nd year—$12,000
$12,000 per year	$1.25 thereafter—$45,000
$60,000 per term	$66,000 per term

Requirements of a Valid Lease

Lease and rental agreements vary in size and content. No agreement is perfect. A good suggestion is to use one that has been drawn by a competent attorney who specializes in real estate law. Although the lease must be updated periodically to conform with changing laws and business practices, one should resist change for change's sake alone or using different agreements from tenant to tenant. A standard agreement, such as that shown in Figure 7–11 will become familiar and comfortable. Standardization of lease clauses makes implementation easier than when each tenant operates under separate rules. A local real estate attorney should review any standard lease to make sure it complies with local and state laws.

The requirements for a valid lease are similar to those for a valid contract. Both parties must have legal capacity to enter into a mutual agreement that is legal in nature. The items listed below outline the specifics with which the property manager should be familiar.

1. *Description of property.* Use the address, a plot plan, and a layout diagram as necessary to adequately describe the space.

2. *Names of parties.* Both lessor and lessee must be named. If a corporation is a party to the lease, a corporate resolution may be necessary to validate the lease. As lessor, it may be prudent to require a "personal guarantee" from a corporate officer when dealing with small or individually owned corporations.

3. *Signature.* The signature of all parties should be obtained. Payment of rent and taking possession is sometimes considered sufficient acceptance. Common sense dictates, however, that all parties sign and be knowledgeable of the lease contents.

4. *Written agreement.* Required for terms of over one year, but a property manager would be prudent to have all rental and lease agreements in writing.

5. *Term of lease.* The term of the lease should specify the duration. Automatic renewal options, if any, should be in bold type.

6. *Rental rate.* The rental rate and accelerations thereof should be specified along with payment dates and the location where the rent should be paid.

7. *Legal purpose.* The "use" of the lease must be legal in nature (no bookie operations).

8. *Competence of parties.* Contracting parties must be over 18 years of age and competent to negotiate.

COMMERCIAL LEASE CLAUSES

Rent Increases

Periodic rent accelerations may be based on an increase in the local or national Consumer Price Index (CPI) (published monthly by the U.S. Department of Labor) (Figure 6–1), or for a stated percentage or specified amount at specific intervals. All long-term leases should have an acceleration clause.

Sample Clause

Annual CPI Adjustments—The amount of monthly Minimum Rent due hereunder shall be adjusted annually commencing with the expiration of the first full twelve (12) calendar months following the Commencement Date and every twelve (12) months thereafter on the same day of the year (the "adjustment date"). The adjustment, if any, shall be calculated on the basis of Consumer Price Index for All Urban Consumers.

Renewal Options

Renewal options usually favor the tenant. They specify notice time, future rental rate, and length of option. For example, "upon ninety (90) days' prior written notice, Lease shall be extended at tenant's option, provided tenant is not in default under this Lease, for an additional five (5) years. Rent shall be negotiated at the then current market rate with all other terms and conditions remaining the same." The landlord should always get as long a notice period as possible for the renewal option to be able to find a new tenant in the event the option is not exercised.

Sample Clause

Lessee shall, at its option, have the right to _____ successive extensions of this Lease to be exercised separately, each such extension to be for a period of _____ years and to be on the same covenants, terms, and conditions as those of this Lease.

Unless Lessee shall have given Lessor not less than _____ days' notice by certified or registered mail, return receipt requested, of his (its) intention to renew or extend this Lease at its expiration or at the expiration of any extended term or period with the exception of the last extension period, Lessee shall be deemed as having elected not to exercise option to extend or renew from term to term.

Assignment and Sublet

1. In residential leases there are no assignments, as they are of short duration (one year).

2. In commercial leases, courts have usually held that "consent cannot be unreasonably withheld." Legal interpretation of what is "reasonably withheld consent" is usually based on the financial implications of the assigned use. Is the assignee as creditworthy as the original tenant? Will the intended use conflict with other tenants' use, or be detrimental to the landlord's percentage rent potential?

3. The basic difference between an assignment and a sublet is as follows: An assignment is between the owner and tenant(s) and may relieve the original tenant of all rights and responsibilities to the lease by transferring it to the new tenant (see Figure 6–2). A sublet is between the original tenant and a new tenant or concessionaire and keeps the original tenant financially responsible. A sublet can be for less than the entire term, or for only a portion of the space covered under the "master" lease.

Sample Clause

Landlord's Consent Rule—Tenant shall not, either voluntarily or by operation of law, assign, sell, mortgage, encumber, pledge, or otherwise transfer all or any part of tenant's leasehold estate hereunder, or permit

Consumer Price Index for All Urban Consumers
U.S. Cities Average
1967=100

	Jan	Feb	Mar	Apr	May	Jun	Jul	Aug	Sep	Oct	Nov	Dec
1990	381.5	383.3	385.5	386.2	386.9	389.1	390.7	394.1	397.5	400.0	400.7	400.9
1991	403.1	403.8	404.3	405.1	406.3	407.3	408.0	409.2	411.1	411.5	412.7	413.0
1992	413.8	415.2	417.2	417.9	418.6	419.9	420.8	422.0	423.2	424.7	425.3	425.2
1993	427.0	428.7	430.1	431.2	432.0	432.4	432.6	433.9	434.7	436.4	436.9	436.8
1994	437.8	439.3	441.1	441.4	441.9	443.3	444.4	446.4	447.5	448.0	448.6	448.4
1995	450.3	452.0	453.5	455.0	455.8	456.7	457.0	458.0	459.0			

Consumer Price Index for All Urban Consumers
Los Angeles, Anaheim, Riverside
1967=100

	Jan	Feb	Mar	Apr	May	Jun	Jul	Aug	Sep	Oct	Nov	Dec
1990	390.3	394.8	397.3	396.4	397.7	399.0	400.7	402.6	402.7	409.7	410.3	411.4
1991	413.6	413.2	412.8	415.7	416.1	415.8	418.2	418.7	421.3	422.3	423.9	422.9
1992	426.2	428.1	429.8	430.9	431.5	431.8	433.3	434.1	435.5	438.4	437.8	437.7
1993	440.9	443.3	442.7	442.8	443.4	442.3	442.6	442.8	443.8	445.8	447.8	448.9
1994	449.6	449.8	450.5	448.9	447.3	446.9	448.2	449.2	451.0	453.1	451.8	453.1
1995	455.9	456.5	456.9	457.1	458.2	457.4	456.6	456.3	456.7			

Calculation of Consumer Price Index (CPI) Increase

In order to calculate the annual CPI increase we need to compare the current year's CPI to the previous year's CPI.

When writing a commercial lease it is a good idea to write the lease utilizing an index three months previous to the rent increase date so rent increases can be sent in a timely manner. You need to obtain the current month CPI report from the Bureau of Labor Statistics. The current index is divided by the previous year's index for the same month to find the new rent. For example, if the rent is $1,500 per month, the current month's index is 413.6 with last year's index at 390.3, what is the new rental rate?

$$\frac{\text{Current CPI}}{\text{Last Year CPI}} = \frac{413.6}{390.3} = \text{1.06\% CPI increase rate (or 6\% increase)}$$

Rental Rate x CPI increase rate
1,500 x 1.06 = $1,590.00 new rental amount

Figure 6–1.   CPI Index

ASSIGNMENT OF LEASE

For value received, the undersigned,_____

_____ present Lessees in that certain lease dated _____

_____, which was executed by and between _____

_____, as Lessee, and _____ as Lessor, with

respect to premises located at_____

do hereby assign all of their right, title and interest in and to said lease

together with the options and lease security as set forth therein, to_____

_____

Dated this _____ day of _____, 19___.

_____

_____

ASSUMPTION OF LEASE

For value received, and in consideration of the above assignment by the Lessee,

and in consideration of the written consent of the Lessor thereto, the under-

signed hereby assume and agree to make all payments, and to perform all of the

terms, convenants and conditions of the foregoing lease, and which the said

lessee therein had agreed to make and perform.

Dated this _____ day of _____, 19___.

_____

_____

CONSENT TO ASSIGNMENT

For value received, and in consideration of the assumption of the lease re-

ferred to heretofore by the above prior named assignee thereof, the undersigned

lessor hereby consents to the above assignment, but does not thereby waive

any of his rights under said lease or any extensions thereof, as to the lessee,

or as to any assignee. An administrative fee of $100.00 will be charged by the

management company.

Dated this _____ day of _____, 19___.

_____

_____

Figure 6–2.   Assignment of Lease

TABLE OF CONTENTS

Figure 6–3. Lease Table of Contents

the Premises to be occupied by anyone other than Tenant or Tenant's employees, or sublet the Premises or any portion thereof without written consent of the Landlord.

Sign Restriction Sign restriction controls signage by the tenants. Not only may the size and design of signage be addressed, but the content of window dressing may be also (e.g., "no more than 50 percent of the window space may be utilized for 'special' advertising at one time with content to be approved by property manager").

Permitted Use Clause

Use clauses should clearly specify the type of business activity permitted by tenants under the lease; e.g., a Mexican restaurant with an on-site beer and wine license.

Sample Clause

Permitted Use—Tenant shall use the Premises for these uses _____ and under that trade name specified in the Fundamental Lease Provisions and shall not use or permit the Premises to be used for any other purpose or under any other trade name.

Insurance

The tenant is usually required to carry fire and liability insurance on the contents and lease premises. The owner usually carries the coverage on the buildings and common areas on behalf of the tenant (one of the net charges). This usually results in a lower obligation to the tenant as the owner generally is able to secure a lower insurance cost on the property as a whole. It also ensures that the property is properly insured. The clause may go on to specify that if the tenant's business or practices increase the cost of the landlord's insurance, the tenant will be responsible to pay that increased cost. Usually the manager will want to specify minimum amounts the tenant must carry and require the tenant to name the owner and its management agent as "Additionally Insured" under the policy (see Chapter 13). The landlord should also be given notification upon cancellation.

Sample Clause

Liability Insurance—Tenant shall, at Tenant's expense, obtain and keep in force during the term of this Lease a policy of comprehensive public liability insurance insuring Landlord and Tenant in an amount of not less than $_____ for injury or death of one person in any one accident or occurrence and in the amount of no less than $_____ for injury or death of more than one person in any one accident or occurrence. Such insurance shall further insure Landlord and Tenant against liability for property damage of at lease $_____.

Property Insurance—Tenant shall, at Tenant's expense, obtain and keep in force during the term of this Lease a policy of all-risk insurance, including, but not limited to, coverage against direct physical loss such as fire, theft, burglary, structural collapse, sprinkler leakage, vandalism, and malicious mischief, in an amount sufficient to cover at least ninety percent (90%) of the replacement cost.

Insurance Policies—All insurance to be obtained by Tenant pursuant to this Article 13 shall be provided by Companies rated A-15 or better in "Best's Insurance Guide" or in the event "Best's Insurance Guide" is no longer published, any comparable rating in a similar guide selected by Landlord.

Radius Clause

A radius clause disallows a retailer from opening a new location within a certain radius of the existing store, usually three miles. The purpose of the radius clause is to prohibit the tenant, especially those with percentage rent obligations, from drawing business away from the shopping center and lowering the tenant's percentage rent potential. If the tenant does open a location within the radius, this clause may provide as a penalty that percentage rent be paid on the combined sales of both the old and new operations.

Sample Clause

So long as this Lease shall remain in effect, Lessee shall not, within a radius of _____ (_____) mile(s) straight true measurement from the shopping center, either directly or indirectly, own, operate, or be financially interested in, either by itself or with others, a business like, or similar to, or nearing the name of or selling the same goods and wares as, the business permitted to be conducted under this lease.

Exclusive Use Clause

An exclusive use clause specifies that only one merchant will be allowed to perform a particular "primary use" in a shopping center; for example, operate a donut shop. This prevents another donut shop from opening, but still allows a coffee shop to offer donuts as part of their menu. This, while in common usage, may be considered "restraint of free trade" by the courts in the event the clause is challenged and is used in smaller centers (under 200,000 square feet).

Sample Clause

Landlord covenants that it will not lease, rent, or permit to be occupied as a retail food store, any premises owned, leased, or occupied by it, its legal representatives, successors, or assigns, not presently occupied by as such a store within the center, without landlord's written consent. Without limitation of the meaning of "retail food store," such prohibition shall in particular apply at a supermarket, meat market, grocery store, fruit and vegetable store, and frozen or otherwise processed food store, but shall not apply to a delicatessen, bakery, drugstore, take-out food store, or any restaurant or lunchroom.

Continuous Operation Clause

This clause requires that the tenant continuously occupy and operate the business during prescribed business hours and "customary" days over the entire term of the lease. This clause assists the owner in preventing "ark" (closed) stores (e.g., a tax service that is open only for the tax season and closed the balance of the year, or a retail business that opens only three days a week), thus adversely affecting the curb appeal and foot traffic in the center.

Sample Clause

Hours of Business—Tenant shall continuously and uninterruptedly during the entire term hereof conduct and carry on Tenant's business in the Premises and keep the Premises open for business during all business hours customary for businesses of like character in the County in which the Premises are located; provided, however, that this provision shall not apply if the Premises should be closed and the business of Tenant temporarily discontinued therein for not more than three (3) days out of respect to the memory of any deceased corporation officer or employee of Tenant, or the relative of any such officer or employee. Tenant shall, at all times, (a) keep the Premises adequately stocked with merchandise, (b) maintain sufficient sales personnel to care for the patronage to the Premises, and (c) conduct its business in the Premises in accordance with sound business practices.

Condemnation Clause

A condemnation clause sets forth the consequences to the parties in the event the property, or a portion of the property, is taken by condemnation. This clause normally relieves the owner of any responsibility.

Sample Clause

Termination of Lease—If more than twenty-five percent (25%) of the Floor Area of the Premises shall be taken or appropriated by any public or quasi-public authority under the power of eminent domain, either party hereto shall have the right to terminate this Lease effective upon the date possession is required to be surrendered to such authority. Such rights must be exercised, if at all, by written notice to the other party hereunder within thirty (30) days after such effective date.

Recapture Clause (Triple Net Reimbursement)

Recapture clauses usually fall into four separate areas: common area maintenance (CAM), real estate taxes, insurance, and building operating expenses. CAM allows an owner to charge tenants for expenses of the common areas; that is, landscaping, common utilities, parking lot and sidewalk upkeep, and so on. Separate clauses may specify payment of property taxes, insurance, and building operating expenses (usually found in office building leases) or increases thereof. Specific attention should be given to the payment of property taxes after the sale of the property and the ensuing reassessment. Tenants will desire that increases due to sale be excluded from their tax cost, owners the opposite. The tax clause should also require the tenant to pay for any reassessment caused by his or her action; for instance, extensive remodeling. The charges may be based on a prorated share of actual cost or, on a modified basis, on an increase over a fixed base (usually the costs of a specific "base" year).

Sample Clause

Operating Expenses—Tenant agrees to pay Landlord, as additional rent for the Premises, the following costs and expenses incurred by Landlord from and after the commencement date:

1. Real Property Taxes
2. Insurance
3. Building Expense

Merchants Association Clause

The merchants association clause provides that the tenant belong to and participate in the activities of a merchants association. This clause should also spell out mandatory dues and special assessments and may include the hours and days of operation in the center.

Sample Clause

Tenant will promptly become a member of the Merchants Association and agrees fully to participate in and to remain a member in good standing of said Association. Tenant agrees to pay the Merchants Association dues, in equal monthly installments, as Tenant's contribution toward the advertising, promotion, public relations, and administrative expenses paid or incurred by the Association.

Commercial Lease Summary

We have seen by examining the various lease clauses that negotiations can be very complicated. The long time period the lease is in effect dictates that the relationship between owner and tenant be spelled out in detail to avoid adverse effects on the operation and value of the property. The lessee should be aware, however, that the owner's lease will favor the owner and should have this document reviewed by an experienced commercial real estate agent and an attorney who specializes in real estate law.

In order to understand the lease, it is advisable to review Figure 6–2, an assignment of lease form; Figure 6–3, a lease table of contents; and Figure 6–4, an actual commercial lease. The sample lease clauses are only abstracts in most cases and are not necessarily the full wording of each clause. They are used only for illustration.

SHOPPING CENTER LEASE

Address of leased space:_____

_____

1.   **PARTIES**. This lease, dated, for reference purposes only_____

_____, 19____, is made by and between_____

_____(herein called "Landlord") and

_____(herein called "Tenant").

2.   **PREMISES**. Landlord does hereby lease to Tenant and Tenant hereby leases from Landlord that certain space (herein called "Premises"), having dimensions of approximately _____ feet of frontage by _____ feet in depth and containing approximately _____ square feet of floor area. Said premises are located in the City of _____, County of _____, State of _____.

Said Lease is subject to the terms, covenants and conditions herein set forth and the Tenant covenants as a material part of the consideration for this Lease to keep and perform each and all of said terms, covenants and conditions by it to be kept and performed.

3.   **USE**. Tenant shall use the Premises for_____

_____

and shall not use or permit the Premises to be used for any other purpose without the prior written consent of Landlord.

4.   **TERM**. Lease Term_____. The term of this Lease

shall commence as of_____, 19_____.

5.   **MINIMUM RENT**. Tenant agrees to pay to Landlord as Minimum Rent, without notice or demand, the monthly sum of_____

_____Dollars.

The first month's rent shall be paid upon the execution hereof. Rent for any period during the term of hereof which is for less than one (1) month shall be prorated portion of the monthly installment herein, based upon a thirty (30) day month. Said rental shall be paid to Landlord, without deduction or offset, in lawful money of the United State of America, at such place as Landlord may from time to time designate in writing.

Figure 6–4. Shopping Center Lease

6. **SECURITY DEPOSIT.** Tenant has deposited with Landlord the sum of_____

_____($_____) Dollars.
Said sum shall be held by Landlord as security for the faithful performance by Tenant of all the terms, covenants and conditions of the Lease to be kept and performed by Tenant during the term hereof. If Tenant defaults with respect to any provision of this Lease, including but not limited to the provisions relating to the payment of rent, Landlord may (but shall not be required to) use, apply or retain all or any part of the security deposit for the payment of any rent or any other sum in default, or for the payment of any amount which Landlord may spend or become obligated to spend by reason of Tenant's default, or to compensate Landlord for any other loss or damage which Landlord may suffer by reason of Tenant's default. If any portion of said deposit is so used or applied, Tenant shall, within five (5) days after written demand therefor, deposit cash to its original amount and Tenant's failure to do so shall be a default under this Lease. Landlord shall not be required to keep this security deposit separate from its general funds, and Tenant shall not be entitled to interest on such deposit. If Tenant shall fully and faithfully perform every provision of the Lease to be performed by it, the security deposit or any balance thereof shall be return to Tenant (or, at Landlord's option, to the last assignee of Tenant's interest hereunder) within ten (10) days following expiration of the Lease term. In the event of termination of Landlord's interest in this Lease, Landlord shall transfer said deposit to Landlord's successor in interest.

7. **ADJUSTMENTS.**

I. In addition to the Minimum Rent provided in Article 5 hereinabove, and commencing at the same time as Minimum Rent commences, Tenant shall pay to Landlord the following items, herein called Adjustments:

a. All real estate taxes and insurance premiums on the Premises, including land, building, and improvements thereon. Said real estate taxes shall include all real estate taxes and assessments that are levied upon and/or assessed against the Premises. Said insurance shall include all insurance premiums for fire, extended coverage, liability, and any other insurance that Landlord deems necessary on the Premises. Said taxes and insurance premiums for purpose of this provision shall be reasonably apportioned in accordance with the total floor area of the Premises as it relates to the total rentable floor area of the building or buildings of which the Premises are a part, (provided, however, that if any tenants in said building or buildings pay taxes directly to any taxing authority or carry their own insurance, as may be provided in their leases, their square footage shall not be deemed a part of the floor area).

b. That percent of the total cost of the following items as Tenant's total floor area bears to the total floor area of the shopping Center which is from time to time completed as of the first day of each month.
(i) All real estate taxes including assessments, all insurance costs, and all costs to maintain, repair, and replace common areas, parking lots, sidewalks, driveways and other areas used in common by the tenants of the Shopping center.
(ii) All costs to supervise and administer said common areas, parking lots, sidewalks, driveways, and other areas used in common by the tenants or occupants of the Shopping Center. Said costs shall include such fees as may be paid to a third party in connection with same and shall also in any event include a fee to Landlord to supervise and administer same in an amount equal to ten (10%) percent of the total costs of (i) above.
(iii) Any parking charges, utilities surcharges, or any other costs levied, assessed or imposed by, or at the direction of, or resulting from statutes or regulations, or interpretations thereof, promulgated by any governmental authority in connection with the use or occupancy of the premises or the parking facilities serving the premises.

_____**Initial**   _____**Initial**
Page 2

Figure 6–4. Continued

II.   Upon commencement of rental, Landlord may, at landlords's option, submit to Tenant a statement of the anticipated monthly adjustments for the period between such commencement and the following January and Tenant shall pay some and all subsequent monthly payments concurrently with the payment of Minimum Rent. Tenant shall continue to make said monthly payments until notified by Landlord of a change thereof. By March 1 of each year Landlord shall endeavor to give Tenant a statement showing the total Adjustments for the Shopping Center for the prior calendar year and Tenant's allocable share thereof, prorated from the commencement of rental. In the event the total of the monthly payments which Tenant has made for the prior calendar year be less than the Tenant's actual share of such Adjustments then Tenant shall pay the difference in a lump sum within ten days after receipt of such statement from Landlord and shall concurrently pay the difference in monthly payments made in the then calendar year and the amount of monthly payments which are then calculated as monthly Adjustments based on the prior year's experience. Any over-payment by Tenant shall be credited towards the monthly Adjustments next coming due. The actual Adjustments for the prior year shall be used for purposes of calculating the anticipated monthly Adjustments for the then current year with actual determination of such Adjustments after each calendar year as above provided; excepting that in any year in which resurfacing is contemplated Landlord shall be permitted to include the anticipated cost of same as part of the estimated monthly Adjustments. Even though the term has expired and Tenant vacated the premises, when the final determination is made of Tenant's share of said Adjustments for the year in which this Lease terminated, Tenant shall immediately pay any increases due over the estimated Adjustments previously paid and conversely, any overpayment made shall be immediately rebated by Landlord to Tenant.

8.   **USES PROHIBITED.** Tenant shall not do or permit anything to be done in or about the Premises nor bring or keep anything therein which will in any way increase the existing rate of or affect any fire or other insurance upon the Building or any of its contents, or cause a cancellation of any insurance policy covering said Building or any part thereof or any of its contents. Tenant shall not do or permit anything to be done in or about the Premises which will in any way obstruct or interfere with the rights of other tenants or occupants of the Building or injure or annoy them or use or allow the Premises to be used for any improper, immoral, unlawful or objectionable purpose, nor shall Tenant cause, maintain or permit any nuisance in, on or about the Premises. Tenant shall not commit or allow to be committed any waste in or upon the Premises.

9.   **COMPLIANCE WITH LAW.** Tenant shall not use the Premises, or permit anything to be done in or about the Premises, which will in any way conflict with any law, statute, ordinance or governmental rule or regulation now in force or which may hereafter be enacted or promulgated. Tenant shall, at its sole cost and expense, promptly comply with all laws, statutes, ordinances and governmental rules, regulations or requirements now in force or which may hereafter be in force and with the requirements of any board of the underwriters or other similar bodies now or hereafter constituted relating to or affecting the condition, use or occupancy of the Premises, excluding structural changes not related to or affected by Tenant's improvements or acts. The judgment of any court of competent jurisdiction or the admission of Tenant in any action against Tenant, whether Landlord be a party thereto or not, that Tenant has violated any law, statute, ordinance or governmental rule, regulation or requirement, shall be conclusive of that fact as between the Landlord and Tenant.

10.   **ALTERATIONS AND ADDITIONS.** Tenant shall not make or allow to be made any alterations, additions or improvements to or of the Premises or any part thereof without the written consent of Landlord first had and obtained and any alterations, additions or improvements to or of said Premises, including, but not limited to, wall covering, paneling and built-in cabinet work, but excepting moveable furniture and trade fixtures, shall at once become a part of the realty and belong to the Landlord and shall be surrendered with the Premises. In the event Landlord consents to the making of any alterations, additions or improvements to the Premises by Tenant, the same shall be made by Tenant at Tenant's sole cost and expense. Upon the expiration or sooner termination of the term hereof, Tenant shall, upon written demand by Landlord, given at least thirty (30) days prior to the end of the term,

_____**Initial**   _____**Initial**

Page 3

Figure 6–4. Continued

10. Cont'd.

at Tenant's sole cost and expense, forthwith and with all due diligence, remove any alterations, additions or improvements made by Tenant, designated by Landlord to be removed, and Tenant shall, forthwith and with all due diligence, at its sole cost and expense, repair any damage to the Premises caused by such removal.

11. **REPAIRS.**

I. By entry hereunder, Tenant shall be deemed to have accepted the Premises as being in good, sanitary order, condition and repair. Tenant shall, at Tenant's sole cost and expense, keep the Premises and every part thereof in good condition and repair including without limitation the maintenance, replacement and repair of any storefront, doors, window casements, glazing, heating and air conditioning system (when there is an air conditioning system, Tenant shall obtain service contract for repairs and maintenance of said system, said maintenance contract to conform to the requirements under the warranty, if any, on said system), plumbing, pipes, electrical wiring and conduits. Tenant shall, upon the expiration or sooner termination of this Lease hereof, surrender the Premises to the Landlord in good condition, broom clean, ordinary wear and tear and damage from causes beyond reasonable control of Tenant excepted. Any damage to adjacent premises caused by Tenant's use of the Premises shall be repaired at the sole cost and expense of the Tenant.

II. Notwithstanding the provisions of Article 11.I hereinabove, Tenant shall bear the cost repairing and maintaining (through their CAM payments) the structural portions of the Building, including the exterior walls and roof; Tenant waives the right to make repairs at Landlord's expense under any law, statute or ordinance now or hereafter in effect.

12. **LIENS.** Tenant shall keep the Premises and the property in which the Premises are situated free from any liens arising out of any work performed, materials furnished or obligations incurred by Tenant.

13. **ASSIGNING, MORTGAGING, SUBLETTING.** The Tenant shall not transfer, assign, sublet, enter into license or concession agreements, change ownership or hypothecate this Lease or the Tenant's interest in and to the Premises without first procuring the written consent of the Landlord, which shall not be unreasonably withheld. Any assignment, mortgage, pledge, hypothecation, encumbrance, subletting or license of this Lease, the leasehold estate hereby created, or the Premises or any portion thereof, either voluntary or involuntary, whether by operation of law or otherwise, without the prior written consent of Landlord first had and obtained therefore, shall be null and void and shall at the option of Landlord terminate this Lease. Without in any way limiting Landlord's right to refuse to give such consent for any other reason or reasons, Landlord reserves the right to refuse to give such consent unless Tenant remains fully liable during the unexpired term of the Lease and Landlord further reserves the right to refuse to give such consent if in Landlord's sole discretion and opinion the quality of merchandising operation is or may be in any way adversely affected during the term of the Lease or the financial worth of the proposed new tenant is less than that of the Tenant executing this Lease. Tenant agrees to reimburse Landlord for Landlord's reasonable attorney fees incurred in conjunction with the processing and documentation of any such requested transfer, assignment, subletting, licensing or concession agreement, change of ownership or hypothecation of this Lease or Tenant's interest in and to the Premises.

Each transfer assignment, subletting, license, concession agreement and hypothecation to which there has been consent shall be by an instrument in writing in form satisfactory to Landlord, and shall be executed by the transferor, assignor, sublessor, licensor, concessionaire, hypothecator or mortgagor and the transferee, assignee, sublessee, licensee, concessionaire or mortgagee in each instance, as the case may be, and each transferee, assignee, sublessee, licensee, concessionaire or mortgagee shall agree in writing for the benefit of the Landlord herein to assume, to be bound by, and to perform the terms, covenants and conditions of this Lease to be done, kept and performed by the Tenant. One executed copy of such written instrument shall be delivered to the Landlord. Failure to first obtain in writing Landlord's consent or failure to comply with the provisions of the

_____Initial   _____Initial

Page 4

Figure 6–4. Continued

13. Cont'd.

Article shall operate to prevent any such transfer, assignment, subletting, license, concession agreement or hypothecation from becoming effective.

Notwithstanding anything to the contrary in the foregoing provisions, Tenant shall be entitled to assign and transfer this Lease to any corporation or affiliated firm owned or controlled by Tenant, or to the surviving corporation in the event of a consolidation or merger to which Tenant shall be a party; provided, however, that such subsidiary, affiliated firm or surviving corporation shall in writing expressly assume all of the provisions, covenants and conditions of this Lease on the part of Tenant to be kept and performed; and provided, further, that no such assignment or transfer shall act as a release of Tenant from any of the provisions, covenants and conditions of this Lease on the part of Tenant to be kept and performed. A transfer fee of $500.00 will be paid by the tenant to the management agent. Landlord has the right to increase the rent to the then current market rent which he determines at the time of assignment as a condition of this assignment.

14. **HOLD HARMLESS.** Tenant shall indemnify and hold harmless Landlord against and from the conduct of its business or from any activity, work, or other things done, permitted or suffered by the Tenant in or about the Premises, and shall further indemnify and hold harmless Landlord against and from any and all claims arising from any breach or default in the performance of any obligation on Tenant's part to be performed under the terms of this Lease, or arising from any act or negligence of the Tenant, or any officer, agent, employee, guest, or invitee of Tenant, and from all costs, attorney's fees, and liabilities incurred in or about the defense of any such claim or any action or proceeding brought against Landlord by reason of such claim. Tenant upon notice from Landlord shall defend the same at Tenant's expense by counsel reasonably satisfactory to Landlord. Tenant as a material part of the consideration to Landlord hereby assumes all risk of damage to property or injury to persons in, upon or about the Premises, from any cause other than Landlord's negligence, and Tenant hereby waives all claims in respect thereof against Landlord.

Landlord or its agents shall not be liable for any loss or damage to persons or property resulting from fire, explosion, falling plaster, steam, gas, electricity, water or rain which may leak from any part of the building or from the pipes, appliances or plumbing works therein or from the roof, street or subsurface or from any other place resulting from negligence of Landlord, its agents, servants or employees. Landlord or its agents shall not be liable for interference with the light, air, or any latent defect in the Premises. Tenant shall give prompt notice to Landlord in case of casualty or accidents in the Premises.

15. **SUBROGATION.** As long as their respective insurers so permit, Landlord and Tenant hereby mutually waive their respective rights of recovery against each other for any loss insured by fire, extended coverage and other property insurance policies existing for the benefit of the respective rights of recovery against each other for any loss insured by fire, extended coverage and other property insurance policies existing for the benefit of the respective parties. Each party shall apply to their insurers to obtain said waivers. Each party shall obtain any special endorsements, if required by their insurer to evidence compliance with the aforementioned waiver.

16. **LIABILITY INSURANCE.** Tenant shall, at Tenant's expense, obtain and keep in force during the term of this Lease a policy of comprehensive public liability insurance insuring Landlord and Tenant against any liability arising out of the ownership, use, occupancy or maintenance of the Premises and all areas appurtenant thereto. Such insurance shall be in the amount of not less than $300,000.00 for injury or death of one person in any one accident or occurrence and in the amount of not less than $500,000.00 for injury or death of more than one person in any one accident or occurrence. Such insurance shall further insure Landlord and Tenant against liability for property damage of at least $50,000.00. The limit of any such insurance shall not, however, limit the liability of the Tenant hereunder. Tenant may provide this insurance under a blanket policy, provided that said insurance shall have a Landlord's protective liability endorsement attached thereto. If Tenant shall fail to procure and maintain said insurance, Landlord may, but shall not be required to, procure and maintain same, but at the expense of Tenant. insurance required hereunder shall be in companies rated A+AAA or better in "Best's Insurance Guide".

_____Initial   _____Initial

Page 5

Figure 6–4. Continued

16. Cont'd.

Tenant shall deliver to Landlord, prior to right of entry, copies of policies of liability insurance required herein or certificates evidencing the existence and amounts of such insurance with loss payable clauses satisfactory to Landlord. No policy shall be cancellable or subject to reduction of coverage. All such policies shall be written as primary policies not contributing with and not in excess of coverage which Landlord may carry.

17. **UTILITIES.** Tenant shall pay for all water, gas, heat, light, power, sewer charges, telephone service and all other services and utilities supplied to the Premises, together with any taxes thereon. If any such services are not separately metered to Tenant, Tenant shall pay a reasonable proportion to be determined by Landlord of all charges jointly metered with other premises.

18. **PERSONAL PROPERTY TAXES.** Tenant shall pay, or cause to be paid, before delinquency any and all taxes levied or assessed and which become payable during the term hereof upon all Tenant's leasehold improvements, equipment, furniture, fixtures, and any other personal property located in the Premises. In the event any or all of the Tenant's leasehold improvements, equipment, furniture, fixtures and other personal property shall be assessed and taxed with the real property, Tenant shall pay to Landlord of a statement in writing setting forth the amount of such taxes applicable to Tenant's property.

19. **RULES AND REGULATIONS.** Tenant shall faithfully observe and comply with the rules and regulations that Landlord shall from time to time promulgate and/or modify. The rules and regulations shall be binding upon the Tenant upon delivery of a copy of them to Tenant. Landlord shall not be responsible to Tenant for the nonperformance of any said rules and regulations by any other tenants or occupants.

20. **HOLDING OVER.** If Tenant remains in possession of the Premises or any part thereof after the expiration of the term hereof with the express written consent of Landlord, such occupancy shall be a tenancy from month to month at a rental in the amount of the last Monthly Minimum Rent, plus all other charges payable hereunder, and upon all the terms hereof applicable to a month to month tenancy.

21. **ENTRY BY LANDLORD.** Landlord reserves, and shall at any and all times have, the right to enter the Premises to inspect the same, to submit said Premises to prospective purchasers or tenants, to post notices of non-responsibility, to repair the Premises and any portion of the Building of which the Premises are a part that Landlord may deem necessary or desirable, without abatement of rent, and may for the purpose erect scaffolding and other necessary structures where reasonably required by the character of the work to be performed, always providing that the entrance to the Premises shall not be blocked thereby, and further providing that the business of the Tenant shall not be interfered with unreasonably.

22. **TENANT'S DEFAULT.** The occurrence of any one or more of the following events shall constitute a default and breach of this Lease by Tenant.

22.A. The vacating or abandonment of the Premises by Tenant.

22.B. The failure by Tenant to make payment of rent or any other payment required to be made by Tenant hereunder, as and when due, where such failure shall continue for a period of three (3) days after written notice thereof by Landlord to Tenant.

22.C. The failure by Tenant to observe or perform any of the covenants, conditions or provisions of this Lease to be observed or performed by the Tenant, other than described in Article 22.B. above, where such failure shall continue for a period of thirty (30) days after written notice hereof by Landlord to Tenant; provided, however, that if the nature of Tenant's default is such that more than thirty (30) days are reasonably required for its cure, then Tenant shall not be deemed to be in default if Tenant commences such cure within said thirty (30) days period and thereafter diligently prosecutes such cure to completion.

_____Initial   _____Initial

Page 6

Figure 6–4. Continued

22.D. The making by Tenant of any general assignment or general arrangement for the benefit of creditors, or the filing by or against Tenant of a petition to have Tenant adjudged a bankrupt, or a petition or reorganization or arrangement under any law relating to bankruptcy (unless, in the case of a petition filed against Tenant, the same is dismissed within sixty (60) days); or the appointment of a trustee or a receiver to take possession of substantially all of Tenant's assets located at the Premises or of Tenant's interest in this Lease, where possession is not restored to Tenant within thirty (30) days; or the attachment, execution or other judicial seizure of substantially all of Tenant's assets located at the Premises or of Tenant's interest in this lease, where such seizure is not discharged in thirty (30) days.

23. **REMEDIES IN DEFAULT.** In the event of any such default or breach by Tenant, Landlord may at any time thereafter, with or without notice or demand and without limiting Landlord in the exercise of a right or remedy which Landlord may have by reason of such default or breach:

23.A. Terminate Tenant's right to possession of the Premises by any lawful means, in which case this Lease shall terminate and Tenant shall immediately surrender possession of the Premises to Landlord. In such event Landlord shall be entitled to recover from Tenant all damages incurred by Landlord by reason of Tenant's default including, but not limited to; the cost of recovering possession of the Premises; expenses of reletting, including necessary renovation and alteration of the Premises; reasonable attorney's fees; the worth at the time of award by the court having jurisdiction thereof of the amount by which the unpaid rent and other charges and Adjustments called for herein for the balance of the term after the time of such award exceeds the amount of such loss for the same period that Tenant proves could be reasonably avoided; and that portion of any leasing commission paid by Landlord and applicable to the unexpired term of this Lease. Unpaid installments of rent or other sums shall bear interest from the date at the rate of ten (10%) percent per annum; or,

23.B. Maintain Tenant's right to possession, in which case this Lease shall continue in effect whether or not Tenant shall have abandoned the Premises. In such event Landlord shall be entitled to enforce all of Landlord's rights and remedies under this lease, including the right to recover the rent and any other charges and Adjustments as may become due hereunder; or

23.C. Pursue any other remedy now or hereafter available to Landlord under the laws or judicial decisions of the State in which the Premises are located.

24. **RECONSTRUCTION.** In the event the Premises are damaged by fire or other perils covered by extended coverage insurance, Tenant agrees to forthwith repair same, and this Lease shall remain in full force and effect. Tenant shall carry business interruption insurance to cover rent and expenses for a minimum of three (3) month period. Landlord shall not be required to repair any injury of damage by fire or other cause, or to make any repairs or replacements of any leasehold improvements, fixtures, or other personal property of Tenant.

25. **TENANT'S STATEMENT.** Tenant shall at any time and from time to time upon not less than three days prior written notice from Landlord execute, acknowledge and deliver to Landlord a statement in writing (a) certifying that this Lease is unmodified and in full force and effect (or, if modified stating the nature of such modification and certifying that this Lease as so modified is in full force and effect), and the date to which the rental and other charges are paid in advance, if any and (b) acknowledging that there are not, to Tenant's knowledge, any uncured defaults on the part of the Landlord hereunder, or specifying such defaults if any are claimed, and (c) setting forth the date of commencement of rents and expiration of the term hereof. Any such statement may be relied upon by any prospective purchaser or encumbrancer of all or any portion of the real property of which the Premises are a part.

_____Initial   _____Initial

Figure 6–4. Continued

26.   **PARKING AND COMMON AREAS.** Landlord covenants that upon completion of the Shopping Center, an area approximately equal to the common and parking areas as shown on the Exhibit "A", if so attached, shall be at all times available for the non-exclusive use of Tenant during the full term of this Lease or any extension of the term hereof, provided that the condemnation or other taking by any public authority, or sale in lieu of condemnation, of any or all of such common and parking areas shall not constitute a violation of this covenant. Landlord reserves the right to change the entrances, exits, traffic lanes and the boundaries and locations of such parking area or areas.

26.A. Prior to the date of Tenant's opening for business in the Premises, Landlord shall cause said common and parking area or areas to be graded, surfaced, marked and landscaped at no expense to Tenant.

26.B. The Landlord shall keep said automobile parking and common areas in a neat, clean and orderly condition, and shall repair any damage to the facilities thereof, but all expenses in connection with said automobile parking and common areas shall be charged and prorated in the manner as set forth in Article 7 hereof.

26.C. Tenant, for the use and benefit of Tenant, its agents, employees, customers, licensees and sub-tenants, shall have the non-exclusive right in common with Landlord, and other present and future owners, tenants and their agents, employees, customers, licensees and sub-tenants, to use said common and parking areas during the entire term of this Lease, or any extension thereof, for ingress and egress, and automobile parking.

26.D. The Tenant, in the use of said common and parking areas, agrees to comply with such reasonable rules, regulations and charges for parking as the Landlord may adopt from time to time for the orderly and proper operation of said common and parking area. Such rules may include but shall not be limited to the following: (1) The restricting of employee parking to a limit, designated area or areas; and (2) The regulation of the removal, storage and disposal of Tenant's refuse and other rubbish at the sole cost and expense of Tenant.

26.E. Lessee shall not obstruct the sidewalk adjacent to the demised premises or any portion of the common areas by placing any item hereon, including, but without limitation to; newspaper racks, bicycle stands, weighing machines and amusement rides.

27.   **SIGNS.** The Tenant may affix and maintain upon the glass panes and supports of the show windows and within twelve (12) inches of any window and upon exterior walls of the Premises only such signs, advertising placecards, names, insignia, trademarks and descriptive material as shall have first received the written approval of the Landlord as to type, size, color, location, copy nature and display qualities. Anything to the contrary in this Lease notwithstanding. Tenant shall not affix any sign to the roof. Tenant shall, however, erect one sign on the front of the Premises not later than the date Tenant opens for business, in accordance with a design to be prepared by Tenant and approved in writing by Landlord.

28.   **DISPLAYS.** The Tenant may not display or sell merchandise or allow grocery carts or other similar devices within the control of Tenant to be stored or to remain outside the defined exterior walls and permanent doorways of the Premises. Tenant further agrees not to install any exterior lighting, amplifiers or similar devices or use in or about the Premises any advertising medium which may be heard or seen outside the Premises, such as flashing lights, searchlights, loudspeakers, phonographs or radio broadcasts.

29.   **AUCTIONS.** Tenant shall not conduct or permit to be conducted any sale by auction in, upon or from the Premises, whether said auction by voluntary, involuntary, pursuant to any assignment for the payment of creditors or pursuant to any bankruptcy or other insolvency proceeding.

_____Initial   _____Initial

Page 8

Figure 6–4. Continued

30. **GENERAL PROVISIONS.**

(i) Plats and Riders. Clauses, plats, riders and addendums, if any, affixed to this Lease are a part hereof.

(ii) Waiver. The waiver by Landlord of any term, covenant or condition herein contained shall not be deemed to be a waiver of such term, covenant or condition or any subsequent breach of the same or any other term, covenant or condition herein contained. The subsequent acceptance of rent hereunder by Landlord shall not be deemed to be a waiver of any preceding default by Tenant of any term, covenant or condition of this Lease, other than the failure of the Tenant to pay a particular rental so accepted, regardless of Landlord's knowledge of such preceding default at the time of the acceptance of such rent.

(iii) Joint Obligation. If there be more than one Tenant the obligations hereunder imposed shall be joint and several.

(iv) Marginal Headings. The marginal headings and article titles to the articles of this Lease are not a part of this Lease and shall have no effect upon the construction or interpretation of any part hereof.

(v) Time. Time is of the essence of this Lease and each and all of its provisions in which performance is a factor.

(vi) Successors and Assigns. The covenants and conditions herein contained, subject to the provisions as to assignment, apply to and bind heirs, successors, executors, administrators and assigns of the parties hereto.

(vii) Recordation. Neither Landlord not Tenant shall record this Lease, but a short form memorandum hereof may be recorded at the request of Landlord.

(viii) Quiet Possession. Upon Tenant paying the rent reserved hereunder and observing and performing all of the covenants, conditions and provisions on Tenant's part to be observed and performed hereunder, Tenant shall have quiet possession of the Premises for the entire term hereof, subject to all the provisions of this Lease.

(ix) Late Charges. Tenant hereby acknowledges that late payment by Tenant to Landlord of rent or other sums due hereunder will cause Landlord to incur costs not contemplated by this Lease, the exact amount of which will be extremely difficult to ascertain. Such costs include, but are not limited to, processing and accounting charges, and late charges which may be imposed upon Landlord by terms of any mortgage or trust deed covering the Premises. Accordingly, if any installment of rent or any sum due from Tenant, Tenant shall pay to Landlord a late charge equal to ten (10%) percent of such overdue amount, plus any attorney's fees incurred by Landlord by reason of Tenant's failure to pay rent and/or other charges when due hereunder. The parties hereby agree that such late charges represent a fair and reasonable estimate of the cost that Landlord will incur by reason of the late payment by Tenant. Acceptance of such late charges by the Landlord shall in no event constitute a waiver of Tenant's default with respect to such overdue amount nor prevent Landlord from exercising any of the other rights and remedies granted hereunder. A five (5) day grace period will be given to the tenant.

(x) Prior Agreements. This Lease contains all of the agreements of the parties hereto with respect to any matter covered or mentioned in this Lease, and no prior agreements or understanding pertaining to any such matters shall be effective for any purpose. No provision of this Lease may be amended or added to except by an agreement in writing signed by the parties hereto or their respective successors in interest. This Lease shall not be effective or binding on any party until fully executed by both parties hereto.

(xi) Inability to Perform. This Lease and the obligations of the Tenant hereunder shall not be effected or impaired because the Landlord is unable to fulfill any of its obligations hereunder or is delayed in doing so, if such inability or delay is caused by reason of strike, labor troubles, acts of God, or any other cause beyond the reasonable control of the Landlord.

_____Initial   _____Initial

Page 9

Figure 6–4. Continued

30. Cont'd.

(xii) Partial Invalidity. Any provision of this Lease which shall prove to be invalid, void, or illegal shall in no way affect, impair or invalidate any other provision hereof and such other provision shall remain in full force and effect.

(xiii) Cumulative Remedies. No remedy or election hereunder shall be deemed exclusive but shall, wherever possible, be cumulative with all other remedies at law or in equity.

(xiv) Choice of Law. This Lease shall be governed by the laws of the State in which the Premises are located.

(xv) Attorney's Fees. In the event of any action or proceeding brought by either party against the other under this Lease the prevailing party shall be entitled to recover for the fees of its attorneys in such action or proceeding, including costs of appeal, if any, in such amount as the court may adjudge reasonable as attorney's fees. In addition, should it be necessary for Landlord to employ legal counsel to enforce any of the provisions herein contained, Tenant agrees to pay all attorney's fees and court costs reasonably incurred.

(xvi) Sale of Premises by landlord. In the event of any sale of the Premises by Landlord, Landlord shall be and is hereby entirely freed and relieved of all liability under any and all of its covenants and obligations contained in or derived from this Lease arising out of any act, occurrence or omission occurring after the consummation of such sale; and the purchaser, at such sale or any subsequent sale of the Premises shall be deemed, without any further agreement between the parties or their successors in interest or between the parties and any such purchaser, to have assumed and agreed to carry out any and all of the covenants and obligations of the Landlord under this Lease.

(xvii) Subordination, Attornment. Upon request of the Landlord, Tenant will in writing subordinate its rights hereunder to the lien of any mortgage, or deed of trust, to any bank, insurance company or other lending institution, now or hereafter in force against the Premises, and to all advances made or hereafter to be made upon the security thereof.

In the event any proceedings are brought for foreclosure, or in the event of the exercise of the power of sale under any mortgage or deed of trust made by the Landlord covering the Premises, the Tenant shall attorn to the purchaser upon any such foreclosure or sale and recognize said purchaser as the Landlord under this Lease.

The provisions of this Article to the contrary notwithstanding, and so long as Tenant is not in default hereunder, this Lease shall remain in full force and effect for the full term hereof.

(xviii) Notices. All notices and demands which may or are to be required or permitted to be given by either party on the other hereunder shall be in writing. All notices and demands by the Landlord to the Tenant shall be sent by United States Mail, postage prepaid, addressed to the Tenant shall be sent by United States Mail, postage prepaid, addressed to the Tenant at the Premises, and to the address hereinbelow, or to such other place as Tenant may from time to time designated in a notice to Landlord. all notices and demands by the Tenant to the Landlord shall be sent by United States Mail, postage prepaid, addressed to the Landlord at the address set forth herein, and to such other person or place as the Landlord may from time to time designated in a notice to the Tenant.

To Landlord at:_____

To Tenant at:_____

_____Initial

Figure 6–4.   Continued

_____Initial

31.   **HAZARDOUS MATERIALS LEASE CLAUSE**

Subject to the remaining provisions of this paragraph, Leassee shall be entitled to use and store only those Hazardous Materials (defined below), that are necessary for Lessee's business, provided that such usage and storage is in full compliance with all applicable local, state and federal statutes, orders, ordinances, rules and regulations (as interpreted by judicial and administrative decisions). Lessor shall have the right at all times during the term of this Lease to (i) inspect the Premises, (ii) conduct tests and investigations to determine whether Lessee is in compliance with the provisions of this paragraph, and (iii) request lists of all Hazardous Materials used, stored or located on the Premises; the cost of all such inspections, tests and investigations to be borne by Lessee, if Lessor reasonable believes they are necessary. Lessee shall give to Lessor immediate verbal and follow-up written notice of any spills, releases or discharges of hazardous Materials on the Premises, or in any common areas or parking lots (is not considered part of the Premises), caused by the acts or omissions of Lessee, or its agents, employees, representatives, invitees, licensees, subtenants, customers or contractors. lessee covenants to investigate, clean up and otherwise remediate any spill, release or discharge of Hazardous Materials caused by the act or omissions of Lessee, or its agents, employees, representatives, invitees, licensees, subtenants, customers at Lessee's cost and expense; such investigation, clean up and remediation to be performed after Lessee has obtained Lessor's written consent, which shall not be unreasonably withheld; provided, however, that Lessee shall be entitled to respond immediately to an emergency without first obtaining Lessor's written consent. Lessee shall indemnify, defend and hold Lessor harmless from and against any and all claims, judgements, damages, penalties, fines, liabilities, losses, suits, administrative proceedings and costs (including, but not limited to attorneys and consultants fees) arising from or related to the use, presence, transportation, storage, disposal, spill, release or discharge of Hazardous Materials on or about the Premises caused by the acts or omissions of Lessee, its agents, employees, representatives, invitees, licenses, subtenants, customers or contractors. Lessee shall not be entitled to install any tanks under, on or about the Premises for the storage of hazardous Materials without the express written consent of Lessor, which may be given or withheld in Lessor's sole discretion. As used herein, the term hazardous Materials shall mean (i) any hazardous or toxic wastes, materials or substances, and other pollutants or contaminants, which are or become regulated by all applicable local, state and federal laws, including but not limited to, 42 U.S.C. 6901 et seq., 42 U.S.C. 9601 et seq., and California Health and Safety Code Sections 25100 et seq., and 25300 et seq; (ii) petroleum; (iii) asbestos; (iv) polychlorinated biphenyls; and (v) radioactive materials.

_____**Initial**   _____**Initial**

Page 11

Figure 6–4. Continued

ADDITIONS OR CHANGES

_____

_____

_____

_____

_____

_____

_____

_____

_____

_____

_____

_____   _____

_____   _____

_____   _____
(Landlord)   (Tenant)

_____   _____
Date   Date

_____Initial   _____Initial

Figure 6–4. Continued

ADDENDUM #1

RENTAL PAYMENTS AND ADJUSTMENTS

During the term of this Lease, rent for said premises shall be paid in installments as follows:

For that period of time commencing_____and ending
_____,Lessee shall pay to Lessor, at such place or places as may be
designated by Lessor, the sum of $_____ per month, due and payable on the 1st day of each and every
month. For each succeeding yearly period of this agreement, Lessee shall pay to Lessor in monthly installments the
sum of the previous year's rental adjusted on the basis of the fluctuation in the U.S. Department of Labor, Bureau
of Labor Statistics, all urban consumers, Consumer Price Index (all items) for the Los Angeles - Long Beach area
(hereinafter called the Index). For purposes of computation, the level of the Index for the previous year, on the
anniversary date of the Lease term, shall be used in arriving at the percentage increase of the level of Index for the
next succeeding period of this agreement. The formula for said computation is as follows:

FORMULA FOR COMPUTATION AND AGREEMENT OF ARBITRATION

Consumer Price Index for
    the current year
_____ x Current year's monthly rental = new monthly rental
Consumer Price Index for
    the previous year

In the event that the present Index above mentioned is discontinued, then a new Index of consumer prices for the
Los Angeles - Long Beach areas shall be used which can be mutually agreed upon between the parties hereto. If
the parties cannot mutually agree to the manner of equating to the new Index or to a new Index, then the matter of
rental evaluation as called for by this option shall be determined by arbitration. Each party hereto shall appoint
one (1) arbitrator and the two (2) arbitrators shall select a third, and the three (3) arbitrators so selected shall meet
and determine a fair method of computing the rental reevaluation and to equitably adjust the rental from the next
preceding year so as to protect both Lessor and Lessee from monetary inflation. The decision of the majority of
the arbitrators shall be binding upon the Lessor and Lessee. The fees of the arbitrator appointed by each party
shall be paid by the party appointing him, and the fees of the third arbitrator and the expenses of the arbitration
shall be divided equally between Lessor and Lessee. Maximum increase per year will be 10% and minimum
increase per year will be 7%.

In no event shall the rental rate be less than that of the next preceding year.

_____Initial   _____Initial

Page 13

Figure 6–4. Continued

Commercial Lease Clauses   **115**

RESIDENTIAL AGREEMENTS

Lease versus Month-to-Month Rental Agreement

The question of whether it is better to put a residential property on a month-to-month rental agreement or lease is frequently asked. As in most areas of property management, there is no absolute answer. It depends on the property. An expensive single-family beachfront rental house may be on a lease since the rental value depends on the season. A suburban apartment building with a low vacancy rate would probably be best with a month-to-month agreement.

With a month-to-month agreement, rent can increase with only thirty (30) days' notice, unless regulated by rent control (see Figure 6–5). A 30-day notice must be given when asking a tenant to vacate (except in areas of rent control or when the reason is based on either retaliation or discrimination by the landlord). This gives the property manager flexibility to maximize the in-

---

JD J. D. PROPERTY MANAGEMENT

3520 Cadillac Ave., Suite B, Costa Mesa, CA 92626
(714) 751-2787

Date_____

Dear Mr./Mrs./Ms. _____,

It is with genuine reluctance that we must inform you of an increase in the rent you are paying.

Although we regret the necessity of taking this step, we feel you will recognize that the value of this rental property has increased since the last rent adjustment.

Please consider this official notice that effective on _____ your rent, which is presently _____ per month, will increase to _____.

We appreciate your good tenancy and hope you will remain in residence indefinitely. However, may we remind you of each resident's responsibility to give thirty days notice when they plan to move.

Sincerely,
J.D. PROPERTY MANAGEMENT CO.

Joseph W. DeCarlo, CPM

JWD:lr

Figure 6–5. Rent Increase Letter

come and offers better salability if the owner decides to sell the property. In high-occupancy areas, the renters benefit more from a residential lease than do the landlords. In areas with high vacancy rates—where the unit might remain unoccupied for a long period of time—a lease might help prevent that vacancy.

Waiver of Tenant Rights

The residential renter cannot waive any rights in areas such as habitability, security deposits, right to sue, notice, entry, or retaliation by the owner. If the owner inserts such clauses, they are void even though the tenant may sign the agreement.

Residents have the right to be treated fairly and equally when applying for and residing in rental housing. They are entitled to quiet enjoyment of their units and the landlord needs to give notice prior to entering, inspection, showing, or repairing unless requested by the tenant or in the case of an emergency. Tenant habitability issues must be addressed; plumbing, electrical, and heating systems must be in safe and good working order. Doors and windows must be secure, roof leaks must be repaired, and the building must be free of pests and in good repair.

Uniform Residential Landlords and Tenants Act

This act is a model for states in preparing to codify landlord/tenant laws. The purpose of its creators, the National Conference on Commissioner on Uniform State Laws, was to standardize the laws of each state. The act does not have any federal enforcement or validity and therefore has been interpreted differently by each state. We do not then have any uniform national landlord/tenant laws other than the Federal Fair Housing and Americans with Disabilities Acts (ADA) (see Chapter 14). Each state has passed its own laws, which means a local real estate attorney familiar with your area should be consulted on legal matters, forms, evictions, and so on.

Sublet

Most residential agreements prohibit sublet or assignment. On a month-to-month agreement, sublet prohibition is a moot point as the owner may terminate the tenancy if the tenant sublets.

Overcrowding

A good residential agreement should list names, ages, and number of tenants occupying a unit. Families in low-income neighborhoods will often double up, with two or more families living in one apartment. This not only causes additional wear and tear, but also might be illegal in some cities.

Fair housing advocacy groups have accused owners and managers of setting low occupancy standards to keep out children and minorities. Owners on the other hand need to limit the number of occupants due to limited parking spaces, sewer and garbage capacity, and utility costs. The Department of Housing and Urban Development (HUD) in 1991 issued a memo by its General Counsel, Frank Keating, stating that two persons per bedroom was a reasonable occupancy standard. Some state agencies, such as California's Department of Fair Employment and Housing, have added "plus one" to each unit. In other words, a two-bedroom unit could house 2+2+1 or 5 people. HUD is considering revising this benchmark with the Building Official and Code Administrator (BOCA) Code, which deals with load stress maximums and has no bearing on health, safety and habitability conditions. This code classifies living and dining rooms as sleeping rooms, allowing a higher number of residents per unit.

The property manager should keep up to date on these changing regulations and not rely on the preceding paragraph.

In the event the tenant increases occupancy after the rental agreement is signed, the owner may waive the right to terminate the rental agreement in the future by accepting rent while knowing of the additional occupants. (See Chapter 14.)

Roommates

When renting to roommates, the agreement should read that they are severally responsible. This means that if one roommate does not pay, the other(s) must pay the balance or face eviction. The roommates are thus treated as one entity.

Late Charges

Referred to as late fees, service charges, or administrative fees, some landlords charge a penalty to encourage the tenants to pay rent in a timely manner. Different states have different interpretations as to whether late fees may be charged. You must have a provision in your rental agreement, however, in order to collect any late charges.

When preparing a "Notice to Pay Rent or Quit" when a tenant is delinquent in the rental payment, do not include the late charge. The notice must state the exact amount of rent (and only rent) due, or the notice may be ruled invalid at the time of trial. This would necessitate starting the process over. Again, this increases the possibility of rent loss. In many cases, the hassle of the late charge is not worth the effort. Another more effective method may be to send a month-to-month tenant who is frequently late on the rent a 30-day change-of-terms notice, raising the rent 6 percent for each month thereafter, telling the tenant the rent increase was caused by continued late payments. The tenant will either move or pay on time thereafter. Another method is to offer promptness discounts for rent paid by the first of the month. For example, if the rent is $530 and the tenant pays on time, they would pay only $500, thereby receiving a promptness discount of $30. In areas of low vacancy, this could reduce the income to the owner by $30 per month times the number of units (20 units × $30 = $600 per month). The apartments, when advertised for rent, would have to be advertised at $530. However, another school of thought is, why pay the tenant for paying on time when they are legally obligated to do so anyway?

How much should the landlord charge? The typical late charge on a residential home loan is 6 percent of a monthly payment. If the monthly rent is $500, using this rationale, you would charge a $30 late fee. Some landlords charge a flat $20 or $25, regardless of the rental amount.

House Rules

A clause is usually contained in most rental agreement that the tenant agrees to comply with all reasonable rules and regulations. These rules should be given to the tenant before signing the agreement and made an addendum to the rental agreement.

RESIDENTIAL CREDIT APPLICATIONS
Filled Out and Signed

Prior to checking credit, the application must be filled out and signed by the prospective tenant (see Chapter 7, Figure 7–8) giving permission to run a credit check by the landlord or his or her management agent.

Residence Information

Applications should include present and past residences and previous managers' phone numbers. Call and check housing references, especially the one prior to where the tenant is now living. Unfortunately, sometimes the present landlord will give a favorable reference to get rid of a bad tenant. Previous landlords are more likely to give a truthful response as they do not benefit from the renter's vacancy.

Employment History

The application should include an employment history and Social Security number, which is needed to do a credit check. As time is of the essence, it is difficult to check with large employers who respond only to written requests. A quick shortcut is to have the prospect show a recent paycheck stub. If a listed employer is a small firm, the manager should check the phone book to see if such a business exists. This eliminates the ruse of the friend or relative who answers the phone, "Joe's Carpet Shop."

Vehicle and Driver's License Number

What kind of car is the prospect driving? Does it look clean and well cared for? Compare the name, signature, address, and picture on the driver's license to the information the tenant wrote on the credit application.

Credit Reporting Agencies

Agencies such as TRW can give the manager a verbal credit report in a matter of a few hours for less than $15. Additional reports are available that will reveal if the tenant has ever been evicted. Many times, local apartment associations offer these services at low rates to their members, and reports can be done within hours using a phone and fax.

Bank Account Verification

It is easy to verify a bank balance by using a little subterfuge. Call the bank branch at which the account is held and ask if a check for the amount the tenant says is in the account is good. The property manager may also request a rating on the account at this time. Landlords do not accept personal checks for the first month's rent, and usually ask the prospect for a blank deposit slip which has the bank address and account number imprinted. This prevents errors when transcribing account numbers onto the printed application and also double-verifies the existence of the account and the prospect's address.

In Case of Emergency

Emergency names and phone numbers from applications can be used to track down tenants to collect judgments after eviction.

Permission to Check Credit

The permission to check credit clause on the residential application allows the manager to check the prospect's credit. It is an invasion of privacy and against the law to do so without written permission. The manager cannot discriminate on the basis of race, religion, creed, national origin, marital status, sex, age, or handicap. The manager can discriminate on the basis of the prospective tenant's financial ability to pay rent. The same questions should be asked of all tenants, not just those to whom the manager does not want to rent. Credit criteria must be applied equally.

Consumer Credit Reporting Law

In some states, such as California, if the manager or the landlord relies on information from a credit report to deny rental, the manager must

1. Provide the prospective renter with a written notice of denial.

2. Provide the prospective renter with the name, address, and phone number of the credit reporting agency.

3. Provide notice to the prospective renter of the right to a free credit report within 60 days and that information given may be disputed by the prospective renter.

If information for rental denial is from a former employer, landlord, or creditor, then the prospective renter must be advised of the right of full disclosure from that party, and the name, address, and phone number of the source must be given to the prospective renter.

SUMMARY

The property manager is often involved in the leasing function either as the leasing agent or by supervising the leasing agent. The types of leases, lease clauses, and terms are items the property manager should be familiar with and have a working knowledge of.

Four basic types of leasehold estates exist: estate for years (specific termination date), estate at sufferance (holdover), estate from period to period (month to month), and estate at will. The most common is periodic tenancy (estate from period to period) which is the basic residential month-to-month agreement.

The three basic types of leases are gross lease (tenant pays one fixed amount), net lease (tenant pays minimum rent plus share of taxes, insurance, and maintenance), and percentage rent (tenant pays percentage of gross sales each month). Lease and rental agreement vary, but valid leases should contain at least the following: a description of the property, the name of the parties, a signature, the term of duration, the rental rate, legal purpose, and competent parties.

Commercial lease clauses are numerous and very detailed due to the fact that these leases are for long periods and must specify what happens under certain conditions in order to protect both parties. Rent acceleration (CPI index increases) is a very common clause. Renewal options by the tenant should specify the time to exercise, rental rate, and length of option. The assignment and sublet clause has usually been held by the courts to restrict the owner/manager from "unreasonable withholding" of permission. The use clause specifies the particular use allowed the tenant under the lease. Other common clauses include radius, exclusive use, condemnation, common-area maintenance, sign restrictions, and merchants association.

Residential agreements cannot waive rights or deprive tenants of their rights. Applications should be filled out and signed, with information verified before renting. Credit reporting agencies can provide fast, inexpensive credit reports for the owner/manager.

In conclusion, the property manager should review the lease and leasing procedures as to their effects on the subject property. On legal questions, consult a competent attorney who specializes in real estate law.

PERSONALITY PROFILE

Leasing is unique and distinct from property management and the traits that make a good property manager may not lend themselves to being a successful leasing manager. Anthony Diana of Baltimore, Maryland, is an example of a person who was successful at both property management and leasing. To quote Tony, "No one is more qualified to do leasing than an experienced property manager. After all, who knows the property more intimately than the person who manages it?"

Tony earned his CPM designation and became a member of the Institute of Real Estate Management's National Faculty. He has toured the United States giving two-day leasing lectures for the Northwest Education Center. Tony has also started his own real estate school in Maryland.

REVIEW QUESTIONS

1. The most common type of commercial lease is an
   a. estate for years.
   b. estate at sufferance.
   c. estate from period to period (periodic tenancy).
   d. estate at will.

2. The most common type of residential lease is an
   a. estate for years.
   b. estate at sufferance.
   c. estate from period to period (periodic tenancy).
   d. estate at will.

3. Basic types of commercial leases include
   a. gross.
   b. net.
   c. percentage.
   d. only a and b
   e. a, b, and c

4. Percentage leases are most often used in the leasing of
   a. offices.
   b. retail stores.
   c. residential units.
   d. industrial spaces.

5. Requirements of a valid lease include
   a. term.
   b. rental rate.
   c. names of parties.
   d. a, b, and c
   e. only a and c

6. In an assignment, the former lessee
   a. may no longer be responsible.
   b. is still responsible.
   c. is responsible only in the event of default.
   d. is responsible only in the event of bankruptcy.

7. The radius clause protects the
   a. lessee.
   b. lessor.
   c. lender.
   d. property manager.

8. The condemnation clause protects the
   a. lessee.
   b. lessor.
   c. city.
   d. property manager.

9. Waiver of residential tenant rights
   a. is permissible if the tenant signs the lease.
   b. is permissible if the tenant verbally agrees.
   c. is permissible if the tenant is over 18 years of age.
   d. is never permissible.

10. Lease terms should be reviewed by
    a. a real estate agent.
    b. a CPA.
    c. an attorney.
    d. a maintenance foreman.

11. If monthly retail sales equal $30,000, and the tenant has a percentage rent clause of 6 percent or a $1,500 minimum rent, what is the rent this month?
    a. $1,500
    b. $1,600
    c. $1,800
    d. $3,300

12. If a tenant pays $12 per year, per square foot, and she has 1,000 sq. ft., what is her monthly rent?
    a. $12,000
    b. $41,000
    c. $6,000
    d. $2,000

13. Why is the use clause necessary?
    a. for higher rent
    b. to protect the merchant
    c. to protect the landlord
    d. to protect the lender

14. The Uniform Residential Landlord/Tenant Act is a
    a. federal law.
    b. state law.
    c. local law.
    d. model, but not a law.

15. The rental application form should also have a clause
    a. giving permission to check credit.
    b. giving the owner unlimited right of entry to a unit.
    c. allowing entry of a landlord not making repairs.
    d. allowing for immediate shutoff of utilities if rent is delinquent.

ADDITIONAL READING AND REFERENCES

Advertising Age, 740 Rush St., Chicago, IL 60611.

Black's Office Leasing Guide (Annual), 818 W. Diamond Ave., 3rd Floor, Gaithersburg, MD 20878.

Gale, Jack L., *Commercial Investment Brokerage*, National Association of Realtors, Chicago, IL, 1979.

Kusnet, J., and R. Lepatin, *Modern Real Estate Leasing Forms*, Warren, Gorham & Lamont, Inc., Boston, MA, 1986.

Lease Clause Escalators and Other Pass-Through Clauses, Institute of Real Estate Management, Chicago, IL, 1991.

Real Estate Leasing Report (Monthly), Federal Reserve Press, 210 Lincoln St., Boston, MA.

Real Estate Record and Builder's Guide (Weekly), 475 Fifth Ave., New York, NY 10017.

Real Estate Times (Twice Monthly), Commercial Property News, One Penn Plaza, New York, NY 10119.

Zankel, Martin, *Negotiating Commercial Real Estate Leases*, Dearborn Financial Publishing, Chicago, IL, 1991.

Chapter 7

Residential Management

Key terms

Base rent	Deliquency rate	Pricing apartments
Break-even vacancy	Garden apartments	Rental agreement
SBA	Last month's rent	Security deposit
SPS	Mid-rise	"Shopping"
Curb appeal	Normal wear and tear	Signage

Food for thought

"He who is always right may be left."

INTRODUCTION

In this chapter we will examine the largest area of property management—residential property management. We will interweave the case study of Whiskey Manor which was outlined in Chapter 5. During this case study you will be acting as the property manager and will be expected to make decisions on the operation of the property. Possible answers to the problems at the end of the chapter can be found in Appendix B.

The property manager must take into consideration that local and state laws may vary and are constantly changing and being revised (rent control and eviction, for example). Discussion, then, will be in general terms based on present laws within the state. The property manager should routinely consult with local attorneys, apartment associations, and government officials to fully understand the laws in his or her geographic area.

CLASSIFICATIONS OF MULTIFAMILY BUILDINGS
Garden Apartments

Garden apartments are usually spread-out, low-rise (two–three story), walk-up apartments containing one- and two-bedroom units. They are of low density (25 units per acre) and located mostly in the suburbs due to lower land costs. The main characteristics of garden apartments include amenities such as pools, tennis courts, ample parking, recreation rooms, extensive landscaping, central laundries, and individual air-conditioning. Garden apartments are usually individually metered.

Mid-Rise

Mid-rise apartments are usually found on the edge of urban areas and are of medium density. These apartments usually have elevators and can be four to nine stories in height. More often, these buildings are now being developed in the suburbs, increasing in density as land costs rise. The main characteristics of the mid-rise include parking structures, central lobby areas, pools, recreation or exercise rooms, and central air-conditioning.

High-Rise High-rise apartments are usually found in major metropolitan areas where land costs are very high and high density is a resulting necessity. They have the highest density per acre. The main characteristics of the high-rise include elevators, central air-conditioning, security, pools, and so forth. The size can exceed 25 stories. Prestigious locations and views are extremely important as many of these buildings are marketed as luxury apartments.

Other Types Other types of residential buildings include duplexes, triplexes, walk-up apartments, and single-family rental houses. On these types of properties typically there is no on-site manager due to cost considerations. Management is therefore difficult and time consuming.

Classifications of Apartment Buildings Investors and lenders are now classifying apartment buildings into four basic types.

Class A—Large newer buildings in prime area with amenities such as garages, in-unit washer/dryers, pools, spas, exercise gyms, etc. Usually owned by institutions.

Class B—Buildings in good areas with many amenities, but not as nice as Class A buildings and over 10 years old.

Class C—Older buildings, well maintained, in blue-collar areas. Square footage in units may be smaller; have fewer amenities than Class B buildings.

Class D—Older buildings in marginal areas with higher vacancies, deferred maintenance; unit mix has more efficiency units; few, if any, amenities.

Government-Assisted Housing This requires specialized training of the property manager due to special demands such as verification of eligibility, rental increases, evictions, and government reports (see Chapter 11 for further discussion).

MARKET ANALYSIS The property manager and on-site manager must know geographic area, competition, schools, transportation, population, and income statistics. We discussed these under the management plan in Chapter 3. Rental value—except in areas of rent control—is determined by supply and demand. Supply and demand is determined by ascertaining the vacancy rate within the market area. The vacancy factor can be obtained through the Federal Home Loan Bank which compiles rates broken down by zip code (Figure 7–1), or through your local apartment association. Under uninfluenced supply and demand, rents will increase until prospective renters can find a cheaper form of housing (e.g., purchase, doubling up with family or friends, etc.). Shopping competitive properties is one of the best methods of analyzing the market.

APARTMENT MARKETING STRATEGIES The property manager and on-site manager can help create demand and desirability for their units, resulting in increased rental rates.

	ZIP CODE	TOTAL UNITS	VACANT						UNDER CONSTRUCTION	
			-----USED-----		-----NEW-----		-----TOTAL-----			
			Number	Percent	Number	Percent	Number	Percent	Number	Percent
Newport Beach	92660	3,006	187	6.2%	0	0.0%	187	6.2%	0	0.0%
	92661	436	20	4.6%	0	0.0%	20	4.6%	0	0.0%
	92662	391	16	4.1%	0	0.0%	16	4.1%	0	0.0%
	92663	4,452	165	3.7%	0	0.0%	165	3.7%	46	1.0%
Total Newport Beach		8,285	288	3.5%	0	0.0%	388	4.7%	46	0.6%
Orange	92665	1,572	26	1.7%	0	0.0%	26	1.7%	0	0.0%
	92666	1,800	33	1.8%	0	0.0%	33	1.8%	100	5.6%
	92776	3,030	42	1.4%	0	0.0%	42	1.4%	0	0.0%
	92668	3,914	112	2.9%	0	0.0%	112	2.9%	0	0.0%
	92669	1,818	41	2.3%	24	1.3%	65	3.6%	0	0.0%
Total Orange		12,134	254	2.1%	24	0.2%	278	2.3%	100	0.8%
Santa Ana	92701	6,928	163	2.4%	122	1.8%	285	4.1%	199	2.9%
	92703	1,770	44	2.5%	22	1.2%	66	3.7%	451	25.5%
	92704	6,746	211	3.1%	0	0.0%	211	3.1%	0	0.0%
	92705	2,454	31	1.3%	0	0.0%	31	1.3%	0	0.0%
	92706	3,106	78	2.5%	0	0.0%	78	2.5%	90	2.9%
	92707	5,236	170	3.2%	0	0.0%	170	3.2%	2	0.0%
	92708	3,097	82	2.6%	0	0.0%	82	2.6%	184	5.9%
	92709	293	0	0.0%	0	0.0%	0	0.0%	0	0.0%
	92714	6,313	72	1.1%	324	5.1%	396	6.3%	0	0.0%
	92715	5,137	0	0.0%	0	0.0%	0	0.0%	67	1.3%
	92720	1,324	20	1.5%	0	0.0%	20	1.5%	0	0.0%
Total Santa Ana		42,404	871	2.1%	468	1.1%	1,339	3.2%	993	2.3%

Definition of terms: *Multi-Family Units* — housing units in the same building, attached to each other along the side(s), floor, and/or ceiling; includes apartment buildings and high rise condominiums.

Figure 7–1. Vacancy Survey

Merchandising   There is an old adage, "Merchandise well displayed is half sold." What is the appearance (curb appeal) of your building? Is it well landscaped? Are grounds neat and clean? Are old junk cars parked in the parking lot? Have the vacancies been cleaned and made ready to show to prospects?

A model apartment should be cheerful and tastefully decorated, but not so fancy that a prospective tenant will not be able to identify with it. (Hint: Mirrors on walls make units seem larger.)

Signage and Graphics   The signage, building graphics, letterhead, and brochures should be coordinated in type style, color, theme, and logo. Signage should always look crisp, clean, and new and be simple to read. Colors should be warm and friendly. Flowers and landscaping around the posts will enhance the signage (Figures 7–2, 7–3, and 7–4).

The name of the complex should reflect the area. If there is a mountain in view, the complex could be called Mountain View Terrace. A name such as Whiskey Manor for a complex located across from a church is offensive. Residential units should post ownership/management signs including an emergency phone number in two separate and conspicuous locations. Examples of locations are next to mailboxes, the laundry room, or entrances to the complex.

Advertising   Advertising creates traffic and brings prospects to your complex. An ad should answer three questions.

1. *What am I going to get?* One- or two-bedroom apartment and amenities. Can I have a pet? Do I pay for utilities?

2. *What is it going to cost?* Placing the rental rate in the ad eliminates wasted calls from residents who cannot afford the unit. A converse opinion, for times of poor rental, is that deleting the rate from the ad broadens your market to those tenants who have set a figure in mind while being able, in actuality, to pay more.

Figure 7–2.   Good Signage

Figure 7–3. Billboard

Figure 7–4. Poor Signage

3. *How can I find you?* Telephone number and/or address. In display ads, a simple map to the property may be appropriate.

Newspapers are the most common form of media. Frequently, smaller (local) newspapers with a good circulation in the market area will pull in more prospects than larger, more expensive, and prestigious papers.

1. *Classified ads* (Figure 7–5) usually produce the best results per dollar of advertising cost.

2. *Display ads* (Figure 7–6) are more expensive and require artwork. Display ads are frequently used for large complexes, new projects, or in times of high vacancy.

3. *Magazines* are good for institutional ads, but, due to long lead time prior to printing, are not timely. They are a useful medium mostly for large, prestigious complexes.

4. *News releases* on unique features of your complex or tenants may be helpful. For example, a child-care center in an apartment complex would be newsworthy.

5. *Apartment guides* are magazines listing apartment communities, their amenities, rental ranges, addresses, and phone numbers, and showing pictures of the communities. The publications are distributed through a variety of conventional outlets including supermarkets, convenience stores, banks and savings associations, restaurants, newsstands, hotels and motels, airports, car rental agencies, corporate personnel departments, chambers of commerce, and high-traffic retail locations. Depending on local market conditions, these guides are published annually, quarterly, or monthly. Some are very high-quality publications featuring full-color pictures on glossy paper.

Marshall's apartment *Map and Video*™ is a pioneer in both the directory format and more recently the large fold-out map format, which pinpoints apartment location, lists outstanding features, and includes full-color pictures of each apartment. Their company also produces and distributes videotaped tours of local apartments (short showings of several apartments on a single videotape) so prospective tenants can review several communities at once (in the comfort of their own homes or offices) before deciding which to actually visit. These services are not only time saving, but a major advantage to those relocating into the area from other parts of the nation or world. The *Map*™ publication and *Video Tours*™ are available at major hotels/motels, corporate personnel offices, retail outlets, relocation companies, and video rental stores.

Advertising Guidelines   It is now unlawful to print or publish, with respect to rental, leasing, or sale, any advertisement that indicates a preference, limitation, or discrimination be-

---

CIVIC CENTER TERRACE

Lg., spacious 1 bdrm., newly decorated, ready for immediate occupancy, only $595. Pets OK. 20 Civic Center Dr., (714) 751-2787. Ask for Sue.

Figure 7–5.   Classified Ad

OPEN HOUSE

1 & 2 Bedroom Apartments

Beautiful new townhomes, now available for rent.

$595 +UTILITIES

- Underground Heated Garage
- Wall to Wall Carpet
- Storage/Laundry Facilities in Building
- Heat and Hot Water Included
- $300 Security Deposit
- 1st Month Rent Free
- Health Club Facilities Available

SATURDAY DECEMBER 14 10am–4pm
SUNDAY DECEMBER 15 11am–4pm

THE
VILLAGE HIGHLANDS 451-7142
5-1 Avon Parkway, Liverpool (Off Morgan Rd.)

Figure 7–6. Display Ads

cause of race, color, religion, national origin, sex, familial status, or handicap. The publisher as well as advertiser may be prosecuted. For example, an apartment complex ad that reads "walking distance to St. Michael's church" may be considered discriminatory due to religion and handicap (implies everyone can walk). Eliminate the use of phrases such as *adult building*, and words such as *preferred* or *desired*. Also, avoid using human models in ads as some minority may not be represented. Place ads in different ethnic newspapers and not in the same newspapers each time, for example, Hispanic or Korean papers as well as English.

Sales Presentation The on-site manager's appearance should be neat, clean, and businesslike. First impressions are very important. The manager should know the product and the community. (Is there a church nearby? Schools?) A good on-site manager will develop a rapport with the prospect, helping the prospect relax. Care should be exercised in prequalifying the tenant to avoid actual or perceived discrimination. A traffic list is usually kept on prospects coming through the complex. A rule of thumb is for the manager to close (rent) one out of every three prospects.

On-site managers are not usually born good salespeople; in many cases they have to be properly trained. Training firms such as Dorothy Gourly & Associates in Irvine, California, will visit (shop) the complex, grading the manager's sales presentation for the property manager. Such firms will then set up a training session to correct the manager's weak areas, followed by another "shop" to see if the manager is following through on learned skills. A good property manager will spot-check managers through phone calls to ascertain that on-site personnel are following procedures regarding sales presentation and avoiding discrimination.

A good salesperson helps the prospect make decisions by asking positive questions: "Would you prefer the brown carpet or the gray?" "Would you like to move in on the first or the fifteenth?" The key is to ask questions that elicit responses, not just yes or no answers. What is the prospect's hot button? By learning the prospect's objections, a good salesperson can overcome them by emphasizing other positive amenities. To overcome objections, the manager should never argue, but switch to a positive benefit. For example, if the tenant complains that the bathtub is too small, the manager might say, "Most of our residents like this model, and we do have a spa next to the pool." If, however, the prospect insists on a large bathtub, a manager should never promise something that cannot be delivered, as an owner normally will not bear this unnecessary cost. In the same vein, selling does not stop when the renter moves in. Renewals and referrals by existing residents are the best way to achieve a high occupancy rate. Be courteous and responsive to tenant requests. Sometimes the manager forgets that the renter is the customer. Without the renter, the property manager would not have a job and the owner would not have a business.

Marketing training can take place in a variety of ways. Mitch Cazier developed a day-long seminar in which he brings together 20 or 30 of his on-site managers at a particular complex. The morning session is devoted to role-playing with some managers acting as prospective tenants while others act as monitors and still others attempt to rent an apartment. Objects such as smelly, half-eaten sandwiches are left in a cupboard to create a problem to which the manager must respond. Discussion of these responses is held during a round table session at the end of the role-playing. The afternoon session is devoted to policies and procedures and their implementation. An example is keeping rental tools available in one packet prior to the prospect's arrival. These tools include credit application, rental agreement, brochures, and so on.

PRICING AN APARTMENT

Some property managers think all similar units in a complex need to have the same rental rate. Astute managers charge higher prices based on amenities (view and desirability) and usually charge existing renters slightly less than incoming renters, the rate for new tenants being constantly increased with each vacancy. Annual or semiannual increases are given existing residents to keep them at market. Increasing the rents for new tenants also tests the market.

Aggressive Rents versus Vacancies

If vacancies never occur, rents are probably too low. Conversely, if the rents are too high, a serious vacancy problem will occur. For example, let's examine a 50-unit building with no vacancies with the idea of raising rents. The property manager needs to determine how high the vacancy factor can increase before vacancy losses exceed additional rental income. In the following example, while increasing the vacancy factor, we show the ensuing income and valuation increase after an appropriate rent increase.

No Increase	*Rent Increase*
Before increase: 50 units at $550/month = $27,500/month	After increase ($50/month, or a 9% increase): 50 units at $600/month = $30,000/month
Zero vacancy: monthly income: $27,500	5% vacancy: monthly income: $28,500 Additional income: $1,000/month
Annual income: $330,000	Annual income: $342,000
Assume 30% operating expense: $99,000	Assume 30% operating expense: $102,600
NOI: $231,000	NOI: $239,400
Assume cap rate of 10%	Assume cap rate of 10%
Valuation: $2,310,000	Valuation: $2,394,000
	Increased value: $84,000

The break-even vacancy rate in this example would be approximately 8.5 percent.

The example shows that by raising rent approximately 9 percent ($50 per month), the monthly income will increase by $1,000 per month with the vacancy rate increasing from zero to 5 percent. The vacancy rate must increase to 8.5 percent before losses from vacancy would exceed the additional income. The property manager has also increased the value of the complex by $84,000, as exemplified by a 10 percent cap rate. This value increase is over four times more than the typical management fee. "Good management doesn't cost, it pays" should be the motto of the property manager.

Determining Base Rent

Since all apartments are not alike, a property manager has to compare apples with apples. This can be done through the use of a comparison guide. Information is collected by using the rental survey form discussed in Chapter 5. By combining the property manager's knowledge of the market area, including factors such as neighborhood vacancy rate and income data, an indicated rent is determined. This is accomplished by comparing, by grid (Figure 7–7), properties similar to the subject property after making adjustments for differences such as amenities, age, unit size, and so on. The grid sometimes makes it confusing as to whether to add or subtract. If the property manager remembers the following formula, he or she should have no problem.

Subject property better = add (+) to comparable rent (SBA)

Subject property poorer = subtract (–) from comparable rent (SPS)

Using this formula, rents can be adjusted on the comparable properties. In the example in Figure 7–7 of two-bedroom, one-bath units, comparable 1 does not have a fireplace and it is determined that renters would pay $5.00 per month in rent for this amenity. Thus we add $5.00 to the comparable's rent to determine rent comparison for the subject property.

Many times students are confused when to add or subtract on the comparable. Remember that all the additions (+) and subtractions (–) are made to the comparable property and not to the subject property. A formula to help you remember is comparable 2 has a fireplace, as does the subject property, thus there is no advantage and the grid is marked 0, which indicates equal comparison.

If the adjustments are added to and subtracted from present rents, the rent of comparable 1 is $525 per month, and that of comparable 2 is $520 per month compared to only $475 per month for the subject property. The property manager should consider raising the rent to the $515–520 rental range.

Amenities	Subject (Your Property)	Comparable #1 (Competition)		Comparable #2 (Competition)	
Pool	Yes	No	+ 10	No	+ 10
Fireplace	Yes	No	+ 5	Yes	0
Garage	No	Yes	− 10	No	0
Utilities	No	No	0	Yes	− 30
		Total:	+ 5	Total:	− 20
Current Rents	$475	$520		$530	
			+ 5		− 20
Adjusted indicated rents:		$525		$510	
Proposed rental rates: $515 for subject building					

Figure 7–7. Comparison Grid

RESIDENT SELECTION

Prudent property managers know that poor selection is the root of most tenant problems. If the vacancy rate is 5 percent and the delinquency rate is 7 percent, the loss rate is 12 percent per month (financial vacancy loss). Eviction cases are in many instances more costly than having the unit vacant as the tenant uses utilities, creates wear and tear, and causes legal costs to be incurred by the owner. Winning in court, if the tenant is indigent or unemployed, is a hollow victory as the property manager seldom collects the judgment. Remember, the primary purpose of an eviction proceeding is to regain control of the unit.

No car dealer would give the keys to a new $50,000 Mercedes without thoroughly checking the buyer's credit. Likewise, a prudent manager should not give the keys to a $50,000 apartment unit to a prospective tenant without doing a proper credit check.

In Chapter 6 (Leases), we reviewed residential credit-checking procedures to ensure proper tenant screening. The tenant application form (Figure 7–8) should be completed and signed by each residential prospect. Standard forms should be reviewed by a real estate attorney in your community to make sure they are in compliance with local and state laws.

Questions to Ask Prospects

Gleaning information from the tenant application (Figure 7–8), the property manager should try to spot "red flags" of inconsistency. Sample questions follow:

1. *"Our company policy is to thoroughly check references with past landlords and employers as well as TRW and UDR credit reports. Is there anything you would like to tell me that might show up as unfavorable?"* Many prospects find an excuse to leave, ("My wife needs to fill out the application") when this question is asked. It is a great screening technique to eliminate the professional "deadbeat." (See Figure 7–9)

2. *"Do you have your own telephone? What is the number?"* A telephone is no longer a luxury but a necessity. Prospects without a phone frequently have been cut off by "Ma Bell."

3. *"Our company policy is that rent should not exceed 30 percent of the prospect's gross income."* FHA and VA lenders use similar qualifying criteria. Using this basic criterion, a person who earns $2,000 per month could rent a $600 apartment. If this person rented a $1,000 apartment, only 50 percent of

RESIDENTIAL APPLICATION TO RENT

Property Address_____Unit #_____Rental Rate_____

Name of Applicant_____

Present Address_____How Long_____

City_____State_____Zip_____Phone #_____

Date of Birth_____CDL#_____Soc. Sec. #_____

Landlord Name_____Phone #_____

Reason for Moving_____

Previous Address (if less than three years at present)_____

City_____State_____Zip_____How Long_____

Landlord Name_____Phone #_____

Reason for Moving_____

Names of Proposed Occupants_____

_____

Liquid Filled Bed? Yes or No / Pets? Yes or No, What Kind?_____

Present Employer_____How Long_____

Address_____City_____State_____Zip_____

Position_____Supervisor_____Gross Mo. Income_____

Previous Employer (if less than one year)_____

Address_____City_____State_____Zip_____

How Long_____Supervisor_____Phone #_____

Position_____Gross Mo. Income_____

Other Income $_____Source_____

Name of Bank_____ Branch_____Acct. #_____

Address_____City_____State_____Zip_____

Names of Creditors	Acct. #	Mo. Pymt.	Balance
_____/_____		$_____	$_____
_____/_____		$_____	$_____
_____/_____		$_____	$_____
_____/_____		$_____	$_____

In Case of Emergency please notify:

Name	Address	Phone #	Relationship
1._____			
2._____			

Auto Make_____Model_____Yr._____Lic. Plate #_____

Have you been party to an eviction or bankruptcy in the past 7 years? Yes or No

If Yes, explain_____

Applicant represents that all the above statements are true, correct and complete and hereby authorizes verification of the above information provided including, but not limited to obtaining a credit report and agrees to furnish additional credit information upon request. The cost of this credit processing is $_____ to be paid by the applicant. This cost is not rent or deposit and will not be refunded or applied to future rent event if this application is denied.

Applicant's Signature_____Date_____

EQUAL HOUSING OPPORTUNITY

J.D. PROPERTY MGT. INC.
P.O. Box 1230
Costa Mesa, CA 92628

Figure 7–8. Tenant Application

The Updated Credit Profile Report

TRW

TRW's Credit Profile report is designed to display information in a standard, objective, easy-to-read manner. An illustration and description of a sample Profile report for a fictitious person follows.

1. Name and address as recorded on automated subscriber tapes, including date of most recent update.

2. Employment name and address as reported by a subscriber through an inquiry on the date shown.

3. A code designating the TRW or Credit Bureau office nearest the consumer's current address, for your use in consumer referrals.

4. Consumer's social security number.

5. Three columns indicating positive, nonevaluated, and negative status comments.

6. A (Automated) and M (Instant Update or Manual Form) indicate the method by which the credit grantor reports information to TRW.

7. Name and number of reporting subscriber.

8. Association code describing the legal relationship to the account.

9. Account or docket number.

10. Status comment reflecting the payment condition of the account as of the status date.

11. Date the account was opened.

12. Scheduled monthly payment amount.

13. Estimated monthly payment amount.

14. Date last payment was made.

15. Type and terms of the account.

16. The original loan amount (ORIGL), credit limit (LIMIT), historical high balance (HIBAL), or original amount charged to loss (C/OAM), represented in dollar amounts.

17. Balance owing, balance date, and amount past due, if applicable.

18. The applicant's payment history during the past 24 months. The code reflects the status of the account for each month, displayed for balance reporting subscribers only.

C	—	Current
N	—	Zero balance reported/current account
1	—	30 days past due
2	—	60 days past due
3	—	90 days past due
4	—	120 days past due
5	—	150 days past due
6	—	180 days past due
— (Dash)	—	No history reported for that month
Blank	—	No history maintained; see status comment

19. Inquiries indicate a request for the applicant's credit information — inquiring subscriber; date of inquiry; and type, terms and amount, if available.

20. Public Record: Court name, court code, docket number, type of public record, filing date, amount, and judgment creditor. This information may include bankruptcies, liens and/or judgments against the applicant.

21. Profile report messages alert the subscriber about a credit applicant's social security number, name, address, generation, or year of birth. See back of page for further explanation.

Figure 7–9. Credit Profile

his or her income would be left for food, clothing, transportation, medical expenses, and so forth. The prospect would probably be a poor credit risk or would have to bring in friends to share the rent, thus overcrowding the apartment. Recurring expenses also have to be taken into consideration. Even if the rent does not exceed 30 percent of the prospect's income, the rent might be too high if the prospect has a substantial car loan or other installment payments.

4. *"Your credit history does not qualify you for this apartment. Can you get a parent or relative to cosign the lease and sign a personal guarantee?"* This allows

younger renters, single heads of household, and welfare families who otherwise would not qualify because of credit history or low income to rent, if so desired. The credit of the "personal guarantor" should also be checked.

These are only a few questions to ask. Points can be given for each question with a cutoff level determined to help rank prospective tenants. Credit criteria must be applied equally to all prospects to avoid actual or perceived discrimination.

This author has the philosophy that 95 percent of renters are good and will pay their rent. That leaves only 5 percent who are "deadbeats." (This 5 percent is usually evicted every three months, or four times a year, so that 5 percent multiplied by four equals 20 percent.) These deadbeats will often gravitate to property managers and owners who do not properly check credit or have not been properly trained.

Skip-Tracing

"Skip-tracing" is the art of tracking down deadbeat tenants who leave owing unpaid rent. Start the process with the information contained in the rental application. Some additional hints include

1. DMV—If you have a driver's license number, a copy of a person's Department of Motor Vehicle file can be ordered which may contain a current address in most states.

2. Post office—Send a blank letter and write on the envelope the phrase "do not forward—address correction requested." For a small fee, the new address can be obtained at the post office.

3. Tax assessor's office—If the tenant owns real property, check the assessor's records for a listed address.

4. Voter registration—Call the county registrar's office to obtain the registered address.

5. Credit bureau checks—You have the tenant's social security number and an authorization for a credit check on the rental application the tenant signed when initially applying to rent. Run another check to find a current address.

6. Hanes-Polk XX Directories—These list phone numbers, addresses, and sometimes place of employment, and are updated regularly. They are available at public libraries.

7. State agencies—Was the tenant a real estate licensee, beautician, contractor, etc.? These professions require a state license.

8. Employer—Ask for the tenant's new address or new work number.

Additionally, several collection bureaus will accept tenant delinquency for collection. Credit bureau collection charges are about 15 percent to 50 percent of the amount collected, depending on the difficulty of the case.

SECURITY DEPOSITS

The most common dispute between property managers and renters is the handling of security deposits. In many cases the manager/owner does not realize that the "deposit" is rightfully the resident's if all the conditions (such as proper notice and cleaning of the apartment) are met.

What Is the Law? Each state has laws covering the handling of security deposits that include:

1. *Maximum amount of deposit*—for example, two months.

2. *Refundability*—for example, a $100 nonrefundable move-in fee.

3. *Returning of deposits*—for example, 14, 21, or 30 days.

4. *Interest on deposits*—for example, 5 percent annual interest paid to tenant.

5. *Penalties*—for example, if owner does not comply with the law.

6. *What is deductible?* "Normal wear and tear" is not deductible. Nonpayment of rent, tenant-caused holes in walls, unreturned keys, or a dirty apartment are just a few of the items that can be charged to the renter. Deductibility is, however, a gray area that judges interpret differently. The prudent property manager should resolve these deposit disputes before he or she goes to court in order to reduce hassle and save time. Strict interpretation of the deductibility law could lead to a resident's grapevine passing the word that the property manager will always find a speck of dust on a windowsill and charge for full cleanup. If the residents have no hope of getting back their security deposit, they may automatically leave the apartment a mess, resulting in a longer turnaround time and an increased vacancy rate. This author's best advice is to use the Golden Rule: Treat the tenant as you yourself would want to be treated.

Move-In/Move-Out Form In order to reduce conflicts and misunderstanding, the property manager should use a move-in/move-out form (Figure 7–10). This is similar to the walk-through form Realtors use when selling a house. When the apartment is first rented, the on-site manager and tenant go through the move-in checklist and mark down any problems, for example, a hole in the master bedroom door. The form is dated, signed by both the resident and the manager, and a copy is given to the resident. The manager puts the original in the resident's file.

Upon move-out, the apartment is reinspected by both parties and the form is again dated and signed. Without this form, especially if the renting manager is no longer with the complex, there is no way to disprove the renter's claim of existing damage when he or she moved in.

Deposit Return Form The manager prepares the resident refund and liability statement, or deposit return form (Figure 7–11), from the move-in/move-out form. This disposition must be prepared and mailed within the time prescribed by law, to the forwarding address given by the renter. If no forwarding address was left, the disposition may be mailed to the renter's last known address (i.e., the apartment itself). A check for any monies to be returned should accompany the form.

Security Deposit versus Last Month's Rent These terms are often confusing to both property managers and renters. The prudent manager should use only the term *security deposit* as it is more inclusive and can be used for unpaid rent, cleaning, damage, improper notice, and so on. If the property manager collects the last month's rent, it can be used only for the last month's rent. The amount of the security deposit should be different from the monthly rent to avoid confusion. For example, if the rent is $500, the security deposit should be $475. This also avoids the problem of having to increase the "last month's rent" each time there is a rental increase. In addition, it helps the tenant understand the difference between "last month's rent" and a security deposit. When determining the maximum security deposit, the last month's rent is included in the calculation of legal maximum deposit.

RESIDENCE CONDITION CHECK LIST

Residence_____ Apt. #_____

	MOVE-IN	MOVE-OUT		MOVE-IN	MOVE-OUT
LIVING & DINING ROOMS			**BEDROOMS**		
Carpets			Closet		
Drapes			Doors		
Windows			Carpet		
Screens			Drapes		
Light fixtures			Windows		
Walls/Ceilings			Screens		
Doors			Misc.		
Misc.					
KITCHEN			**PATIO/BALCONY**		
Cabinets			Weed Free		
Sink			Fence/Rails		
Counter Tops			Patio doors		
Drawers			Screens		
Floors			Clean		
Dishwasher			Misc.		
Garbage Disposal			**HALL**		
Refrigerator			Closets		
Range/oven/burners			Carpets		
Hood/fan/filters			Misc.		
Misc.			**SMOKE DETECTOR**		
BATHROOM(s)			**LOCKS & HINGES**		
Tub					
Track			MOVE-IN REMARKS:_____		
Shower door					
Medicine Cabinet					
Toilet					
Sinks					
Towel Racks			MOVE-OUT REMARKS:_____		
Counter					
Floor					
Drains					
Misc.					

MOVE-IN DATE _____

                    MANAGER   RESIDENT

MOVE-OUT DATE _____

                    MANAGER   RESIDENT

FORWARDING ADDRESS _____

J.D. PROPERTY MANAGEMENT, INC.
P. O. BOX 1438
COSTA MESA, CA. 92626

Figure 7–10. Move-in/Move-out Form

Interest on Security Deposits	Some states and/or cities require the landlord/manager to pay interest on tenant security deposits. This could be a fixed rate such as 5 percent or an adjustable rate. Local apartment associations are a good source for information in this area. Commercial security deposits are not usually covered, and interest, if any, is negotiable between the tenant and the owner.

RESIDENT REFUND AND LIABILITY STATEMENT

NAME: _____   RESIDENT ADDRESS: _____

FORWARDING ADDRESS: _____   _____

_____   RESIDENT NUMBER: _____

_____   RESIDENT NAME: _____

TODAY'S DATE: _____   MOVE OUT DATE: _____

INITAL SECURITY DEPOSIT PAID $ _____

CHARGES TO TENANT:

Apartment cleaning (_____)
Carpet cleaning   (_____)
Drapery cleaning   (_____)
Painting   (_____)
Carpet   (_____)
Drapery   (_____)
Exterminating   (_____)
Glass/screens   (_____)
Other   (_____)
Legal   (_____)
_____   (_____)
_____   (_____)
Utilities   (_____)

TOTAL CHARGES   ($ _____)

TOTAL DEPOSIT REFUND OR
  BALANCE DUE (circle one) $ _____

LESS RENT DUE: (insufficient
  30 day notice) $ _____

_____ days @ _____ $ _____

PLUS RENT REFUND:

_____ days @ _____ $ _____
(rent paid through _____)

TOTAL CHECK OR BALANCE DUE: $ _____
(circle correct item) Ck. No. _____

REMARKS: _____
_____
_____
_____

J.D. PROPERTY MANAGEMENT, INC.
P. O. BOX 1438
COSTA MESA, CA. 92626

COMPUTER INPUT ONLY:

PORTION TO REFUND TO TENANT WITH CHECK

A. Debit Ck-Amt   Credit Ck-Amt
        2003   1103

PORTION TO REDISTRIBUTE TO CLIENT

B. Debit Tot.Dist.Amt.Credit Tot.Dist.
        2003   1103

DISTRIBUTION AGAINST EXPENSES

C. Debit Exp. Amt.   Credit Exp. Amt.
        1002

COMPUTER INPUT NOTES:

A + B must equal amount of total S.D.
The total distribution of C must equal
the amount of B.
If manual check has been written for
S.D. refund use B & C only and in C
credit 6540 for amount that was refunded
(Manual check should Dr. 6540)

Figure 7–11. Deposit Return

THE RENTAL AGREEMENT

As with credit applications, we recommend a standard form for the rental agreement (Figure 7–12). Both credit application and rental agreement should be signed and dated.

The rental agreement lists the parties, terms, and conditions of the rental. It has clauses such as clause 9 in Figure 7–12, which states that the renter shall not have pets or a waterbed without prior written consent of the landlord or manager. The rental agreement should be signed and dated with a copy given to the resident. Waivers of residents' rights are prohibited and even if included in the agreement are invalid. Residential landlords must retain rental applications and eviction records for two years. Also, landlords must retain rental records until a final determination of any discrimination case has been made. Property managers, however, must keep records in compliance with their state Department of Real Estate regulations.

RENT CONTROL

Rent control dates back to World War II. In 1942, the Emergency Price Control Act froze rents. In New York City, many of the city's rental units remain under rent control while units added later are covered under rent stabilization. Currently, approximately 200 U.S. cities have residential rent control, representing 12 percent of the 35 million units in the nationwide rental market. In California, about half of the state's renters are covered under rent control, including the two major cities of Los Angeles and San Francisco. The social policy that fosters rent control strives to (1) preserve low- and middle-cost housing in the face of increasing new-construction costs as a result of the high cost of land, and (2) prevent displacement due to not being able to afford the local increased rental rate.

Rent control has traditionally been a local concern ignored by state and federal governments. The City of Santa Monica, in order to help the majority of its elderly residents, could not regulate the price of groceries, clothes, gasoline, and so on, but had the power to regulate rents and institute a rent-control ordinance. The federal government in 1981 spent $27 billion on low-cost housing, but only $11 billion in 1986. This decrease adds more pressure for rent control and passes the burden on to local government and the private sector (the landlord).

In areas of non–rent control, the landlord has benefited as many lenders and builders have curtailed building more apartments due to the threat of rent control, thus increasing existing rents. Many units that have been under rent control for years (such as many in New York City) have been abandoned, which reduces the existing rental stock.

Two major U.S. Supreme Court decisions (see Chapter 14) have upheld a city's power to regulate rents. Only state and/or federal intervention will repeal rent control and this will have to involve spending large sums of money to transfer the housing problem back to society as a whole rather than singling out the landlord.

Rent-Control Terms

Since each city may have its own rent-control ordinance, the property manager should obtain a copy and become thoroughly familiar with all codes.

Rental rate decontrol—When a tenant willingly moves, the owner may raise the rent to current market rates.

Annual increases—Amount of increase allowed each year.

Enforcement—Which agency handles enforcement?

Coverage—What types of units are covered; e.g., single-family houses may be exempt.

AGREEMENT TO RENT OR LEASE

Apt. _____

This Agreement is made and entered into between _____, hereinafter "Landlord" and (names of all adult residents and names and ages of children to reside on the premises):

Resident_____ Resident_____ (Age) _____

Resident_____ (Age) _____ Resident_____ (Age) _____

Resident_____ (Age) _____ Resident_____ (Age) _____

hereinafter "Resident". The word Residents as used herein shall each include the singular as well as the plural. Subject to the terms and conditions below, Landlord rents to Residents, and Residents rent from Landlord, for residential proposes only, the premises know as:

Apartment_____, located at_____California.

_____

Landlord and Residents mutually agree as follows:

1.   **TERM.** The term of the rental shall begin on _____, and shall continue as follows subject to the payment of rent for one month and the security deposit:

[ ]   For a period of _____ months and _____ days thereafter expiring on _____/_____ /9_____ (a Fixed-Term Lease). Renewal of the term shall be as described in Paragraph 24 of this Agreement.

[ ]   On a month-to-month basis, the residency terminable by Landlord or Residents by the giving of 30 day written notice to the other (A Month-To-Month Rental Agreement).

2.   **RENT.** Residents shall pay the monthly rent of $_____, in advance on or before the _____ DAY of each month without deduction or offset. Rent is payable in full at the Office only by personal check, cashier's check or money order. On signing this Agreement Residents shall pay one full months' rent in the form of a cashier's check or money order only. The Rent for the partial months period shall be prorated on the basis of a 30 day month and shall be paid on or before the next rental due date.

3.   **SECURITY DEPOSIT.** On signing this Agreement Residents shall pay to Landlord the sum of $_____ as a deposit to secure Residents performance of the agreements contained herein. No part of this deposit is to be considered as an advance payment of rent, including last months' rent, nor is it to be used or refunded prior to the leased premises being permanently and totally vacated by all Residents. After Residents have vacated the premises, Landlord shall furnish Residents with an itemized written statement of the basis for, and the amount of, any of the security deposit retained by Landlord. Landlord may withhold only that portion of Residents security deposit necessary (a) to remedy any default by Residents in the payment of rent or any other provision of this Agreement, (b) to repair damages to the premises to include repainting but exclusive of ordinary wear and tear, and/or, (c) to remove trash and clean the premises to meet Landlord's re-rental standards. The unused portion of this deposit shall be returned to Residents without interest, according to law.

4.   **LATE CHARGE/RETURNED CHECKS.** If Residents fail to pay the rent in full by the end of the **third day after it is due**, Residents shall pay a late charge of $_____ as additional rent. If Landlord elects to accept rent after the tenth day after it is due, payment in the form other than by personal check may be required. By this provision, Landlord does not waive the right to insist on payment of the rent in full on the day it is due. In the event Residents' checks are dishonored by the bank, Residents shall pay a returned check charge of $25.00 as additional rent. If the returned check causes the rent to be late, the late charge shall also be paid. After a check is dishonored, Landlord may require all future payments to be in a form other than a personal check.

5.   **OCCUPANCY.** Residents agree that the premises are to be used as a private residence for Residents listed hereinbefore, a total of _____ adults and _____ child/children and by no other persons and for no other reason. Guests may not stay more that 14 consecutive days in any 6 month period without prior written consent of Landlord.

6.   **POSSESSION OF PREMISES.** In the event Landlord is unable to deliver possession of the premises to Residents for any reason not within Landlord's control, including, but not limited to, failure of prior occupants to vacate as agreed or required by law, Landlord shall not be liable to Residents except for the return of all sums previously paid to Landlord in the event Residents choose to terminate this Lease.

7.   **ACCEPTANCE OF PREMISES.** Resident has inspected the premises, furnishings and equipment, and has found them to be satisfactory. All plumbing, heating and electrical systems are operative and deemed satisfactory.

8.   **UTILITIES.** Resident shall pay for all utilities services and charges, except _____.

9.   **PETS/WATER FILLED FURNITURE.** No animal, pet or water filled furniture shall be kept on or about the premises, without the prior written consent of the Landlord.

10.   **SECURITY.** Residents acknowledge that Landlord has made no representation that the property is a "secure" complex and that Residents are safe from theft, injury or damage. Gates, fences and locks are provided primarily for the protection of Landlord's property and is not a warranty of protection nor are they specifically provided for the protection of Residents or guest's person or property. Residents shall take appropriate measures to protect their own property and report to the Police any suspicious activities, persons or events occurring on or about the general premises.

11.   **QUIET ENJOYMENT/USE.** All Residents shall be entitled to quiet enjoyment of the premises. Residents shall not use the premises in such a way as to violate any law or ordinance, commit waste or nuisance, or annoy, disturb, inconvenience, or interfere with the quiet enjoyment of any other resident or nearby residents to include having loud or late parties or playing loud music. Residents shall ensure that their guests also comply with this provision. Violations constitute a breach of the Agreement and Landlord may take legal action to terminate the Agreement and remove Residents.

12.   **JOINT AND SEVERAL LIABILITY (CO-RESIDENTS).** If more than one Resident enters into this Agreement ("roommates"), the obligations are joint and several; each such Resident is individually, as well as jointly, liable for full performance of all agreed terms and payment of all sums required hereunder as long as any one of the Residents remain in possession of the premises. Any breach or abandonment by any one or more of the Residents shall not terminate the Agreement nor shall it relieve the remaining Residents from fulfilling the terms of this Agreement. Should one or more of the Residents terminate their residency apart and separately from other residents, no right to have another person substituted in their stead shall exist. Changes in residents during the rental term must be approved in advance by Landlord.

13.   **CARE AND MAINTENANCE.** Residents agree to keep the premises clean, in good order and repair, and free of trash and unsightly material and to immediately notify Landlord, in writing, of any defects or dangerous conditions in or about the premises, particularly any water penetration. Residents shall reimburse Landlord for the cost to repair damage by Residents through misuse or neglect including plumbing stoppages. Except as provided by law, no repairs, decorating or alterations shall be done by the resident without the Landlord's prior written consent.

Figure 7–12.   Rental Agreement

14. **RIGHT OF ENTRY.** Landlord or Landlord's agents shall have the right to enter the premises for purposes of performing inspections; to make necessary or agreed repairs, alterations or improvements; supplying agreed services; to exhibit the property to prospective residents; when the Resident has abandoned or surrendered the premises; and pursuant to court order. Except in cases of emergency, Landlord shall give Residents reasonable notice of intent to enter. Residents may be present, however, such entry shall not be conditioned upon such presence and Residents agree to indemnify and hold Landlord free and harmless for such entry.

15. **VEHICLES AND PARKING.** Landlord reserves the right to control the method of parking and to tow away, at Resident's expense, any vehicle causing an unsafe/hazardous condition or parked in spaces not authorized by Landlord. No automobile or any other motordriven vehicle or cycle may be brought onto the premises unless such vehicle is insured for public liability and property damage; is operable, currently registered, free of any leaking fluids, and in compliance with governmental noise limitations.

16. **LIABILITY/DAMAGE RESPONSIBILITY.** Residents agree to hold Landlord harmless from all claims of loss or damage to property, and of injury or death to persons caused by the intentional acts or negligence of the resident, his guest or invitees, or occurring on the premises rented for Residents exclusive use. **Resident expressly absolves Landlord from any and all liability for any loss or damage to Residents property or effects arising out of water leakage, or breaking pipes, or theft, or other causes beyond the reasonable control of Landlord.** This includes damage to Resident's or guest's vehicles while parked on the property. In the event the premises are damaged by fire or other casualty covered by insurance, Landlord shall have the option either to (1) repair such damage, this Agreement continuing in full force and effect, or (2) give notice to Residents terminating this Agreement. Landlord shall not be required to repair or replace any property brought onto the premises by Residents. Residents agree to accept financial responsibility for any damage to the premises from fire, water or casualty caused by Residents negligence. **Residents are encouraged to carry a standard renter's policy** or as an alternative, warrants that they will be financially responsible for losses not covered by Landlord's fire and extended coverage insurance policy. In no event shall Residents be entitled to any compensation or damage due to any extra expense, annoyance, or inconvenience for loss of use due to a casualty beyond the control of the Landlord.

17. **SUBLEASING/ASSIGNMENT.** Residents shall not sublet any part of the premises or assign this Agreement without the prior written consent of Landlord. Any such action without prior written consent is void.

18. **TERMINATION: CLEANING/REPAIRS.** Upon termination of the tenancy, Residents shall leave the premises in a clean and orderly condition free of trash and personal property. If this is not done, Resident expressly agrees that Landlord shall perform all cleaning services, including carpet cleaning/repair, which may be required in Landlord's discretion to restore the premises to Landlords standards for new occupancy. The costs incurred by Landlord for such services shall be deducted from Residents security deposit. If Landlord is required to perform any repair or renovation as a result of Residents decoration, modification or damage, regardless of the cause, the cost of such repair and/or renovation shall be deducted from Residents security deposit. In the event the deposit is not sufficient to pay all the lawful expenses and charges at the termination of this residency, Residents shall immediately, upon written notice, pay Landlord any additional sums necessary to pay all such charges in full.

19. **ATTORNEY FEES.** If any legal action or proceeding be brought by either party to enforce any part of this Agreement, the prevailing party shall recover, in addition to all other relief, reasonable attorney fees and costs, whether or not such action proceeds to judgment.

20. **RULES AND REGULATIONS.** Residents acknowledge receipt of, and have read a copy of the Apartment Rules and Regulations, which are hereby incorporated into this Agreement by this reference. Landlord may terminate this Agreement, as provided by law, if any of these Rules and Regulations are violated. Such Rules and Regulations may be amended from time to time upon giving notice to residents.

21. **SMOKE DETECTION DEVICE.** The premises are equipped with a smoke detection device(s), and: (a) the resident acknowledges the smoke detector(s) was tested and its operation explained by management in the presence of the resident at time of initial occupancy and the detector(s) in the unit was working properly at the time, (b) each resident shall test the smoke detector at least once a week to determine if the smoke detector(s) is (are) operating properly, and immediately inform the landlord, in writing, of any malfunction.

22. **TERMINATION.** At least 30 days written notice must be given to Landlord if Residents intend to vacate the premises whether the Agreement is on a month-to-month basis or for a fixed term. If Residents fail to give such notice when required, this Agreement shall continue in full force and effect. Until written notice is received in the Office, Residents shall be liable for rent under the terms of the Agreement. Once Residents establish a move out date in writing in the Office and the unit has been re-rented for a move-in based on the this date, Residents shall vacate as scheduled. Failure to do so may result in **DOUBLE** rent being charged for each day of continued occupancy.

23. **DEFAULT.** In the event of a default by Resident, Landlord may elect to (a) continue the lease in effect and enforce all his rights and remedies hereunder, including the right to recover the rent as it becomes due, or (b) at any time, terminate all of Resident's rights hereunder and recover from Resident all damages he may incur by reason of the breach of the lease, including the cost of recovering the premises, and including the worth at the time of such termination, or at the time of an award if suit be instituted to enforce this provision, of the amount by which the unpaid rent for the balance of the term exceeds the amount of such rental loss which the Resident proves could be reasonably avoided.

24. **RENEWAL/HOLDING OVER.** At the expiration of a fixed term lease, Residents may, **at the option of the Landlord**, continue residency on a month-to-month basis or by an extension of this lease for an additional fixed term providing such extension is executed by both parties in advance of the lease expiration date. In the absence of any communication between both parties, the residency shall continue on a month-to-month basis including any changes, i.e. rent adjustment, having been made by Landlord with proper written notice.

25. **ENTIRE AGREEMENT.** Each and every term, covenant, and agreement herein contained shall be deemed a condition hereof. No oral agreements have been entered into, and this Agreement shall not be modified unless such modification is reduced to writing. Waiver of any breach of any term or condition of this Agreement shall not constitute a waiver of subsequent breaches. The invalidity or partial invalidity of any provision of this Agreement shall not render the remainder of the Agreement invalid or unenforceable.

26. **GENERAL.** Time is of the essence of this Agreement and each provision herein contained. Words used in the singular shall include the plural where the context requires. The breach of any of the covenants or terms of this Agreement shall be deemed to be a material and total breach of this entire Agreement and shall give rise to all rights of termination. This Agreement shall be binding upon and shall inure to the benefit of the heirs, administrators, successors, and assigns of all the parties hereto, and all of the parties hereto shall be jointly and severally liable hereunder except there shall be no assignment or subletting by Resident.

IN SIGNING THIS AGREEMENT THE PARTIES HERETO INDICATE THAT THEY HAVE READ AND UNDERSTAND THIS ENTIRE AGREEMENT AND AGREE TO ALL THE TERMS, COVENANTS AND CONDITIONS STATED THEREIN. RESIDENTS ACKNOWLEDGE RECEIPT OF A COPY OF THIS AGREEMENT WITH ALL ADDENDUMS.

This Agreement is executed on _____   Resident_____

BY: _____   Resident_____

JD Property Management, Inc.
Agent for Landlord

Resident_____

Resident_____

Resident_____

EQUAL HOUSING
OPPORTUNITY

Figure 7–12. Continued

MANAGING SMALL PROPERTIES

Small properties are defined as single-family rentals of one to four units. There are over 10 million single-family rentals in the United States, or about 30 percent of the total number of rental units. Managing small properties is more time consuming and management intensive as there is no on-site manager and the central office must deal directly with tenants and vendors. This can take up a great deal of time and disrupt other property management operations in an office. In order to be successful, a separate division or operation should be established to centralize the single-family operations and hire an experienced property manager. Some areas to include are

Rental or leasing—Who will handle showing and leasing the houses? Will you charge separate rental fees?

Maintenance—Will outside vendors or in-house maintenance personnel be used?

Accounting—Who will collect the rent, or will rents be mailed to the main office? Centralized computer operation is a must.

Management fees—Will they be high enough to offset the additional personnel and costs?

Paying of bills—Often, the rent check does not cover the expenses and mortgage. How and when will the owner send you additional funds?

Statement to owner—should include rent roll, check register, and monthly profits, if any.

These are a few of the questions that need to be answered to successfully manage smaller properties. A book published by the Institute of Real Estate Management, *Managing Single-Family Homes* by Barbara Holland, CPM, is a good reference source.

SUMMARY

The largest area within the property management field is residential. Federal, state, and local laws that affect the property manager are varied and constantly changing. The property manager needs to consult with attorneys, CPAs, government officials, and organizations such as IREM or local apartment associations to keep abreast of new changes in the law. The Multifamily building falls into five classification areas: garden apartments (two- to three-story), mid-rise (four- to nine-story), high-rise (high-density), other (fourplexes), and government-assisted housing (HUD). The property manager, in order to create demand and desirability for an apartment community or building, should be aware of different marketing strategies. These include merchandising, signage and graphics, pricing, advertising, and effective sales presentations.

The property manager must balance vacancies with lower rents. If the complex has no vacancies, rents may be too low and should be increased. When determining base rents, property managers should complete a grid by comparing similar properties to the subject property. If the subject property is better than the comparable property, managers add to the rent of the comparable property to determine the rental value of the subject property. If the subject property is poorer than the comparable property, managers subtract from the rent of the comparable property to determine the rental value of the subject property. For example, if the subject property has a pool with a tenant value of $10.00 per month and the comparable property does not, you would add $10.00 to the comparable property rent to determine the rental value of the subject property.

When screening prospective tenants, property managers should be sure applicants complete credit applications. A consumer credit bureau report should be obtained and employment, references, and income level should be verified. The time and money spent qualifying tenants will reduce delinquencies and save the owner money as well as grief and aggravation in the long run. If a tenant leaves without paying the rent, skip-tracing sources are available to locate the tenant's new address. These include the Department of Motor Vehicles, the post office, voter registration, credit bureaus, Hanes-Polk XX Directories, and current or past employers.

Security-deposit laws vary among states but most states require that all deposits be refundable. Within a prescribed number of days after move-out, the tenant is entitled to an accounting and return of the balance of the deposit not used for unpaid rent or damage caused by the tenant. The property manager should remember that the tenant may be charged for normal wear and tear, which includes painting in most instances if a tenant has lived in the apartment over a year. A move-in/move-out form should be used, dated and signed by the tenant and manager. It is better to call the security deposit a security deposit, rather than breaking it down into key deposit, last month's rent, cleaning, and so on, as these deposits can be used only for that specific purpose. The more-generalized term *security deposit* can cover all of these items.

It would be a beneficial learning experience for the reader to answer the case study questions relating to Whiskey Manor Apartments at the end of this chapter and subsequent chapters to enhance the practical application of the material and to highlight the presented information and concepts in a "real world" perspective.

PERSONALITY PROFILE

Barbara Holland, CPM, is president and principal owner of H&L Realty & Management Company in Las Vegas, Nevada. She is the executive officer responsible for the development and growth of the property management, commercial brokerage, and leasing divisions. Barbara has been involved in real estate management since 1971.

Barbara has been very active both at the local and national IREM levels. She was the first Las Vegas ARM® chair in 1981, and the first Las Vegas IREM president in 1984. For IREM National, she has been the vice-division director of the communications division.

Along with an extensive teaching background that includes IREM's 101 and 301 courses, Barbara has written a number of articles for the *Journal of Property Management* on subjects ranging from energy conservation to employee motivation. Barbara is the first woman in the United States to be admitted to the *Journal of Property Management*'s Academy of Authors and has received IREM's Professional Achievements Award. Her academic credits include a master's degree in urban American history from the University of Connecticut.

REVIEW QUESTIONS

1. The largest area in property management is
   a. office building management.
   b. shopping center management.
   c. residential management.
   d. industrial management.

2. Classifications of multifamily buildings include
   a. garden.
   b. mid-rise.
   c. high-rise.
   d. only a and b
   e. a, b, and c

3. Marketing strategies include
   a. merchandising, signage, and advertising.
   b. DRE regulations.
   c. depreciation methods.
   d. budgeting.

4. In determining base rent, if the subject property, is poorer, you would
   a. add to comparable rent.
   b. subtract from comparable rent.
   c. add to subject rent.
   d. subtract from subject rent.

5. If a subject property has a garage worth $10.00 per month and a comparable does not, you would
   a. add $10.00 to comparable rent.
   b. subtract $10.00 from comparable rent.
   c. add $10.00 to subject rent.
   d. subtract $10.00 from subject rent.

6. The prudent property manager should
   a. get a credit application filled out and signed.
   b. check with the resident's parents.
   c. check with the resident's best friend.
   d. none of the above

7. The property manager can discriminate on the basis of
   a. religion.
   b. sex.
   c. color.
   d. ability to pay rent.

8. Security deposits are usually
   a. nonrefundable.
   b. refundable.
   c. last month's rent.
   d. first month's rent.

9. The move-in/move-out form is used to
   a. qualify renters.
   b. evict renters.
   c. return security deposits.
   d. discriminate against renters.

10. Which is more prudent for the property manager to request?
    a. a key deposit
    b. last month's rent
    c. a cleaning deposit
    d. a security deposit

11. Which ads produce the best results for advertising dollars?
    a. radio ads
    b. classified ads
    c. display ads
    d. TV ads

12. Apartment guides are
    a. leasing agents.
    b. discrimination testers.
    c. rental magazines.
    d. directional signs.

13. If an apartment complex has no vacancy, it probably means
    a. rents are too low.
    b. rents are too high.
    c. rents are maximum.

14. The purpose of an eviction proceeding is to
    a. create a vacancy.
    b. regain control of the unit.
    c. collect a large judgment.
    d. harass the tenant.

15. Standard forms for credit application should be
    a. five pages in length.
    b. two pages in length.
    c. reviewed by a real estate attorney.
    d. reviewed by an appraiser.

Refer to the case study scenario in Chapter Five, p. 89.

1. Would you have a model apartment?

2. What would you recommend to improve curb appeal?

3. Would you consider changing the name of the complex? Why or why not?

4. What would you choose for a new name?

5. Would you put up signage? Can you justify the cost?

6. Design a classified ad for apartment rental at Whiskey Manor using the new name.

7. What would you do about the present on-site manager?

8. What training programs would you implement for the present or new manager?

9. Would you raise rents, lower rents, or keep rents the same?

10. Determine the base rent of the 20-unit apartment complex which we will now call Civic Center Terrace, or another name you choose.

11. How would you change the present security deposit procedure?

12. Would you use a written rental agreement? Explain your reasoning.

ADDITIONAL READING AND REFERENCES

Basile, Frank, CPM, *Back to Basics with Basile*, Charisma Publications, Indianapolis, IN, 1982.

Blumberg, Richard, and James Grow, *The Rights of Tenants*, Avon Publishers, New York, NY, 1979.

California Apartment Association, *California Rental Housing Reference Book*, Sacramento, CA, 1985.

Glassman, Sidney, *New Guide to Residential Management*, National Multi-Housing Council, Washington, DC, 1984.

Gomer, Duane, CPM, *Creative Apartment Management*, Calabasas, CA, 1978.

Holco/Zimmerman Multifamily Investment Outlook (Quarterly), P.O. Box 3000, Denville, NJ 07834.

Holland, Barbara, CPM, *Managing Single Family Homes*, Institute of Real Estate Management, Chicago, IL, 1994.

I.D. Checking Guide, Driver License Guide Co., 1492 Oddstand Drive, Redwood City, CA 94063, 1995.

Institute of Real Estate Management, *Forms for Apartment Management*, Chicago, IL.

Institute of Real Estate Management, *Income/Expense Analysis—Apartments*, Chicago, IL, 1995.

Kelly, Edward N., CPM, *Practical Apartment House Management*, Institute of Real Estate Management, Chicago, IL, 1990.

Landlord-Tenant Relations Report (Monthly), CD Publications, 100 Summit Building, 8555 16th Street, Silver Spring, MD 20910.

McKenna-Harmon, Kathleen, CPM, and Lawrence, Harmon *Contemporary Apartment Marketing: Strategies & Applications*, Institute of Real Estate Management, Chicago, IL, 1993.

Moskovit, Myron, Ralph Warner, and Charles Sherman, *Tenants' Rights*, 4th Edition, Nolo Press, Berkeley, CA.

Professional Apartment Management (Monthly), Brownstone Publications, P.O. Box 4164 Grand Central Station, New York, NY 10163.

Chapter 8

Shopping Center Management

Key terms

CAM charges	Minibillboards	*Robbins v. Pruneyard*
Category killers	Neighborhood center	Strip center
Community center	Net lease	Tenant mix
Kiosk	Percentage lease	Tenant selection
Market share	Regional center	Trade area
Merchant association		

Food for thought

"When the going gets tough, the tough go shopping."

INTRODUCTION

This chapter will examine and analyze shopping center classifications and characteristics, types of leases, merchant associations, trade area, tenant mix, tenant selection, and common-area maintenance. As discussed in Chapter 1, shopping centers are a relatively new phenomenon and did not have a dominant presence until after World War II.

More than 42,000 shopping centers exist nationwide, which represents a 15-fold increase in the last three decades. California leads the way in malls with over 5,300; Florida has over 3,000; Texas over 2,800; and New York has approximately 1,550 to round out the top five states.

Shopping center retail sales are approximately $950 billion per year and account for 55 percent of all nonautomotive retail sales. Leasable space totaled 5 billion square feet which equates to over 18 square feet of retail space for every U.S. resident. Shopping centers employed over 10 million workers and generated 40 billion dollars in state sales tax revenue in 1995. The average center size was 120,000 and the average sales per square foot was approximately $170.

SHOPPING CENTER CLASSIFICATIONS
Strip Center

1. Small in size, consisting of several stores.

2. Usually laid out in a straight line, L, or U shape.

3. Trading area is usually the immediate neighborhood.

4. Convenience stores and 7–11 stores are typical anchor tenants.

5. The function of the strip center is to provide convenient and accessible one-stop shopping. The focus is strictly on location and community convenience.

Neighborhood Center

1. From 25,000 to 125,000 square feet in size.
2. Normally has one anchor (main) tenant such as a supermarket or discount store (Figure 8–1).
3. Trade area up to two miles.

Community Center

1. Size is 125,000 to 300,000 square feet.
2. Contains two or more anchors such as a home improvement store, junior department store, discount store, variety store, or supermarket.
3. Trade area is over three miles.

Regional Center

1. Size is up to 1,000,000 square feet.
2. Contains apparel, jewelry, and one or two department stores.
3. Trade area is over five miles.
4. Is often an enclosed mall.

Super-Regional Center

1. Size is over 1,000,000 square feet.
2. Is usually an enclosed mall.
3. Contains at least three department stores.
4. Contains specialty women's and men's apparel stores and specialty shops of all kinds.
5. Usually contains fast-food locations and one or more restaurants.
6. May contain community or cultural centers; i.e., library, music center, etc.
7. Trade area is 15 miles or more.

Figure 8–1. Neighborhood Center

Specialty Center

1. Usually small in size with a maximum of 100,000 square feet.

2. No anchor or large tenant.

3. Contains unique stores and boutiques.

4. May contain one or more restaurants.

5. Usually located near high-income areas or major tourist attraction centers.

Other Centers

Promotional, off-price, discount, factory outlet, and "power" centers which flourish through heavy advertising and low prices that produce high-volume dollar sales are a growing trend.

"Hypermart" is a different retailing concept from France; its first store opened in Dallas, Texas, in 1988. The retail store, which claims to be the largest in the country at 222,000 square feet, is all on one floor. Merchandise ranges from bananas to refrigerators to fine jewelry, a deli, a shoe repair shop, and 58 checkout stands. Sales clerks wear roller skates and the store philosophy is to undercut its competition on prices.

Future Trends

1. Anchorless strip centers.

2. Historic preservation themes—Ghiradelli Square in San Francisco.

3. Vertical shopping centers—Watertowner Center in Chicago, Nordstrom in San Francisco.

4. Underground centers—Toronto, Canada.

5. Power centers—category killers such as Toys 'Я' Us and Home Depot are tenants in over 300 power centers in the United States.

TYPES OF LEASES

In shopping centers, the net lease with annual increases is most prevalent. The percentage lease with a minimum base rent is the standard in larger centers and for national tenants. Both the merchant and the landlord want to maximize sales and work in closer harmony. See Chapter 6 for a review of these leases and their terms and clauses. Additional information can be obtained from *A Standard Manual of Accounting for Shopping Center Operations*, published by the Urban Land Institute, Washington, D.C. Depending on the size of the shopping center, the property manager may or may not do the leasing. Large regional centers usually have a separate leasing agent.

What constitutes gross sales for percentage-lease purposes? Some additional sources of percentage rent over sales alone include:

1. Services. A clothing store might charge extra for alterations or gift wrapping.

2. Equipment setup. A store might charge customers extra fees for setting up equipment (such as a washing machine installation in the customer's home).

3. Labor charges. An auto parts store might charge the customer extra for installing tires, batteries, etc.

4. Maintenance agreements. A retail appliance store might sell television maintenance contracts when televisions are purchased.

5. Service center charges. A retail store might do repair work in the customer's home.

Types of Percentage Leases

1. *Percentage-only.* The amount of rent is pegged to sales. There is no base or minimum rent. A percentage-only lease may be a good option for attracting socially conscious, quality tenants in depressed areas. The drawback is that no minimum rent is guaranteed if the business does poorly.

2. *Variable-scale.* There is no base rent. The percentage scale may increase or decrease according to various conditions. This lease is adaptable to the planning and rehab phases of "turnaround" projects for distressed or problem properties.

3. *Minimum percentage.* A minimum rent is established that, when added to all other base rents for the property, should cover all ownership expenses. A percentage of sales over a base amount serves as "overage" rent to provide the owner with net additions to annual cash flow and to serve as a hedge against inflation (see Figure 8–2).

```
                  SUMMARY OF PERCENTAGE RENT DUE


            For the Month of: _____



Gross Cash Sales                    $ _____

Gross Credit Sales                    _____

Other Gross Receipts                  _____

     Total Gross Receipts for month        $ _____

Less:  cash refunds/rebates         $ _____

        credit losses                 _____

        sales and use taxes           _____

     Adjusted Gross Receipts for month     $ _____

     Percentage Rent Rate                  x_____%

     Percentage Rent                       $ _____


     Less Minimum Rent Paid                $ _____


Percentage Rent Due:                       $ _____



I certify that the above information is true and correct to the best
of my knowledge and belief.



_____   _____   _____
By                            Title              Date
```

Figure 8–2. Percentage Reports

4. *Maximum percentage*. A minimum rent is negotiated. The percentage clause for overage rent may be straight or variable. However, a ceiling or maximum rent is also stipulated. Anchor tenants or franchises with bargaining leverage may pursue or insist on this type of lease. They may also wish to tie the maximum to an index.

Break Point

The break point is the point at which the percentage clause kicks in; the lessor gets a certain percentage of income from sales over the break point. The natural break point is determined by dividing the total base rent by the percentage. For example, if lease space is 1,000 square feet at $25 per square foot versus a 5 percent percentage clause, the natural break point would be $25,000 ÷ .05, or $500,000.

Merchants Association

Many leases require that the tenant belong to the merchants association. The purpose of the association is to help promote and advertise the merchants collectively and/or centerwide events in order to increase the center's traffic. The owner will usually contribute money and the property manager or staff will help run the association. The property manager must be careful, however, not to allow association meetings to turn into gripe sessions. The merchants association is controlled and managed by the store owners. Usually the property manager acts only in an advisory capacity. In larger centers, the association may be run by a marketing director whose background is in advertising and public relations. Marketing funds are replacing merchants associations in some regional centers because the marketing director administers the funds with complete control and responsibility, without the need for getting approval from store managers and owners who may not understand marketing.

MARKETING RETAIL SPACE

The marketing of a new center, especially a regional center, must start at project conception. Prospective anchor (key) tenants must be convinced that the proposed or existing site will offer sufficient retail sales potential. Unless commitments from anchor tenants are obtained prior to development, financing the project will be difficult.

Trade Area

The trade area is the area from which 70–80 percent of the typical retail sales will be attracted. A regional center usually needs a primary trade area of at least 150,000 population. Driving time must usually be less than 20 minutes, depending on the proximity to competing centers and customer loyalty to certain stores.

Topographical factors, including rivers, mountains, airports, and railroad tracks, may be a barrier to the trade area. A major center may also have a secondary trade area from which customers are attracted. This area may extend 30–50 miles and have a driving time of up to one hour. See Figure 8–3.

Market Research

Most property managers divide the trade area into census tracts in order to expedite information gathering (see map, Figure 8–3).

Populations and Income Data

Population multiplied by per-capita income equals total income for each census tract. Adding up the census tracts in the trade area gives total area income (see figures 8–4 and 8–5).

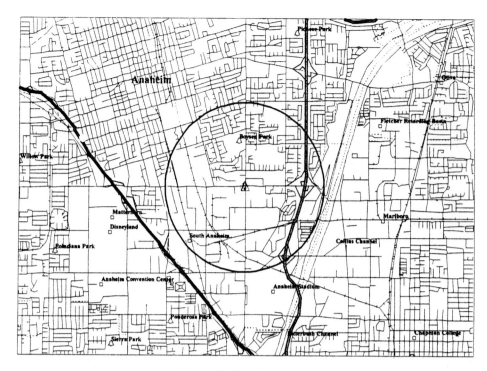

Figure 8–3. Trade Area

RETAIL SALES AND INCOME

Because a close correlation exists normally between personal income and the percentage of income spent in retail sales, total retail sales are derived by multiplying the trade-area income by the ratio of retail sales to personal income.

This demographic analysis can sometimes be misleading. Psychographic analysis may determine, for example, that the trade area is a well-established, conservative, "old money" community that spends less than normal ratios for retail merchandise. Also, proximity to a tourist attraction or vacation resort may contribute many additional shoppers not reflected in demographic studies of permanent residents.

Market Share

The market share should be based on estimates of both existing and projected competition. New centers usually do not create increased buying power but reallocate expenditures among existing businesses. A leakage or displaced sales from the trade area into other trade areas can occur.

Sales Potential of Department Stores

The sales potential of department stores is calculated by using retail trade area statistics and converting consumer dollar expenditures for department stores in census tracts of a trade area into a percentage of total retail sales. Multiplying this percentage by total potential retail sales in the area gives the total sales potential for all department stores in the trade area (Figure 8–6).

Tenant Mix

Shopping centers, even more so than office buildings, need to have a balanced, predetermined tenant makeup. The three things that matter most to owners and tenants in a shopping center are traffic, traffic, and more traffic. A good tenant mix helps attract and retain customers. The goal of a good tenant mix is having a variety of stores that work well together to enhance the performance of the entire center as well as the success of each individual store. The key is determining what types of tenants work well and have a symbiotic relationship.

BENCHMARK: POPULATION PROFILE
Anaheim, CA: Ball Rd & State College Blvd
1, 2 and 3 Mile Rings

Urban Decision Systems, Inc.

		1.00 Mile Ring	2.00 Mile Ring	3.00 Mile Ring
POPULATION	2000 Projection	17,755	88,899	224,073
	1995 Estimate	15,993	80,231	206,173
	1990 Census	14,482	71,535	187,713
	1980 Census	13,377	56,585	154,265
	% Change, 1990–1995	10.4%	12.2%	9.8%
	% Change, 1980–1990	8.3%	26.4%	21.7%
	In group quarters, 1995	1.0%	2.0%	2.9%
HOUSEHOLDS	2000 Projection	6,156	27,242	71,326
	1995 Estimate	5,480	24,467	65,329
	1990 Census	4,912	21,679	59,026
	1980 Census	4,854	20,748	56,754
	% Change, 1990–1995	11.6%	12.9%	10.7%
	% Change, 1980–1990	1.2%	4.5%	4.0%
FAMILIES	1995 Estimate	4,054	17,559	45,705
RACE 1995	White	74.4%	60.1%	65.2%
	Black	1.9%	2.5%	2.5%
	American Indian	0.3%	0.3%	0.4%
	Asian or Pacific Islander	12.8%	8.4%	10.0%
	Other	10.6%	28.7%	21.9%
HISPANIC ORIGIN 1995		28.8%	52.6%	45.8%
AGE 1995	0–5	7.3%	10.3%	9.9%
	6–13	10.9%	12.9%	12.5%
	14–17	5.5%	5.3%	5.4%
	18–20	4.0%	5.0%	4.8%
	21–24	7.5%	9.4%	8.7%
	25–34	18.2%	20.7%	20.5%
	35–44	15.2%	13.6%	13.9%
	45–54	12.9%	9.2%	9.1%
	55–64	9.2%	6.0%	6.5%
	65–74	6.6%	4.7%	5.1%
	75–84	2.3%	2.1%	2.6%
	85+	0.5%	0.8%	1.1%
	Median Age	33.1	28.3	29.2
	Male	32.0	27.5	28.1
	Female	34.3	29.3	30.5
HOUSEHOLD SIZE 1995	1 Person	18.1%	21.0%	22.4%
	2 Persons	34.6%	28.7%	29.4%
	3–4 Persons	33.8%	30.8%	30.8%
	5+ Persons	13.5%	19.5%	17.4%
TENURE 1995	Owner-Occupied Households	62.7%	44.2%	45.6%
	Renter-Occupied Households	37.3%	55.8%	54.4%

Source: 1980, 1990 Census, March 15, 1995 UDS Estimates

Urban Decision Systems Inc. / 4676 Admiralty Way Ste 624 / Marina del Rey, CA 90292 / (800) 633-9568

(XP5)

310083

Figure 8–4. Computerized Data

BENCHMARK: POPULATION PROFILE
Anaheim, CA: Ball Rd & State College Blvd
1, 2 and 3 Mile Rings

Urban Decision Systems, Inc.

		1.00 Mile Ring	2.00 Mile Ring	3.00 Mile Ring
AGGREGATE INCOME 1995	Total ($ Millions)	$329	$1,241	$3,226
	Per Capita	$20,557	$15,466	$15,649
HOUSEHOLDS 1995	Total	5,480	24,467	65,329
	Average Household Size	2.89	3.21	3.07
HOUSEHOLD INCOME 1995	Under $5,000	1.7%	2.5%	2.6%
	$5,000–$9,999	2.1%	4.5%	4.7%
	$10,000–$14,999	3.5%	6.6%	6.7%
	$15,000–$19,999	3.5%	4.9%	4.8%
	$20,000–$24,999	6.5%	6.8%	6.3%
	$25,000–$29,999	6.1%	7.9%	7.1%
	$30,000–$34,999	5.4%	6.4%	6.6%
	$35,000–$39,999	4.7%	5.5%	5.6%
	$40,000–$49,999	13.4%	12.4%	12.4%
	$50,000–$74,999	26.3%	21.5%	22.4%
	$75,000–$99,999	14.0%	11.0%	10.8%
	$100,000–$124,999	6.8%	5.3%	5.4%
	$125,000–$149,999	3.5%	2.4%	2.2%
	Over $150,000	2.6%	2.3%	2.2%
	Median Household Income	$52,836	$43,944	$44,439
	Average Household Income	$59,823	$49,813	$48,341
FAMILIES 1995	Total	4,054	17,559	45,705
	Average Family Size	3.24	3.62	3.52
FAMILY INCOME 1995	Under $5,000	1.1%	1.6%	1.6%
	$5,000–$9,999	0.9%	2.7%	2.4%
	$10,000–$14,999	1.9%	4.5%	4.5%
	$15,000–$19,999	2.7%	4.5%	4.2%
	$20,000–$24,999	5.0%	5.2%	4.7%
	$25,000–$29,999	5.7%	8.2%	7.2%
	$30,000–$34,999	4.2%	5.1%	5.3%
	$35,000–$39,999	4.4%	5.5%	5.5%
	$40,000–$49,999	12.9%	13.2%	13.1%
	$50,000–$74,999	28.3%	23.8%	25.6%
	$75,000–$99,999	16.7%	13.3%	13.4%
	$100,000–$124,999	8.5%	6.6%	6.9%
	$125,000–$149,999	4.5%	3.1%	2.8%
	Over $150,000	3.1%	2.8%	2.8%
	Median Family Income	$60,043	$49,649	$51,274
	Average Family Income	$66,984	$55,582	$54,852

Source: 1980, 1990 Census, March 15, 1995 UDS Estimates

(XP5)

Urban Decision Systems Inc. / 4676 Admiralty Way Ste 624 / Marina del Rey, CA 90292 / (800) 633-9568

310083

Figure 8–5. Computerized Data

RETAILER PRODUCTIVITY BREAKDOWN CHART

Type of Revenues	Annual Sales PSF Department Stores	Gross Margin	Annual Sales PSF Mass Merchandisers/ Variety Stores/ Specialty Shops	Gross Margin
Home Textiles	$116	40%	$120	34%
Toys	166	35	208	25
Housewares Non-Electric	150	30	142	16
Housewares Electric	195	22	242	16
Home Office/Stationery	114	41.4	148	37.8
Photo/Camera	227	18	545	16
Health/Beauty Aids	312	40	110	24
Sewing/Crafts	30.50	40	55	31
Sporting Goods	77	33.4	120	25.2
Home Furnishings	124	36.7	80	29.7
Consumer Electronics	235	19.6	247	15.0

Figure 8–6. Retailer Productivity

When determining the mix, the property manager starts with location, competition, and customer base. These factors determine the center's orientation and the property manager then pursues appropriate anchor and satellite stores that complement each other. For example, desirable satellite tenants for a neighborhood center with a supermarket as the anchor tenant might include a florist, stationery or gift store, barber or beauty shop, dry cleaner, pizza parlor, and so on. This would be called a "needs-based center." Research shows that clothes shopping is usually done on a separate shopping trip from needs. In a "fashion center," complementary stores would include shoe stores, men's and women's apparel stores, children's stores, and accessory stores.

In most instances, the anchor tenant (a supermarket, department store, etc.) establishes the profile of the center, with the satellite stores adapting to its lead. Research by Jodi Greenspan of the Knover Management Company showed that an athletic shoe store (usually found in a fashion-oriented center) located in a needs-based center anchored by a supermarket was not successful. A better choice would have been a photo shop or quick printer.

For a regional center with a major department store as the anchor, desirable complementary tenants would include women's and men's apparel stores, jewelry stores, specialty gift shops, and so forth. The rental rate per square foot is usually higher in a regional center than in a smaller center, so in addition to being complementary, the tenants must have either higher markups on their good or higher sales volumes in order to afford mall space. Regional centers tend to focus on fashion and apparel. Specialty businesses such as furniture stores may wish to cluster together to benefit from a wider draw. While two florists in a center would vie for business, certain retail uses benefit from proximity to one another such as jewelry stores.

Tenant Selection

Tenant selection will be discussed again in more depth in Chapter 9. If tenant selection is poor, the center loses money in lost rents and also suffers from a loss of goodwill and image. Empty or boarded-up stores that have gone bankrupt or out of business can stigmatize other merchants. Additional information can be obtained from *Dollars and Cents of Shopping Centers*, published by the Urban Land Institute, Washington, D.C., 1995.

LAYOUT OF SHOPPING CENTERS

When a center is designed, the physical layout should reflect the types of merchants and customers it hopes to attract (Figure 8–7). Shopping should be a fun, exciting, convenient event. The developer, owner, and property manager should try to evoke those feelings in the layout of the center.

Colors

Colors should be bright and cheerful. The use of banners, awnings, and flags that can be changed periodically to create a new and exciting atmosphere is desirable. Sodium vapor lamps are very bright and long lasting, while relatively inexpensive to operate. On the other hand, their eerie, yellow light can be unnerving and has become associated with high-crime areas. The new sodium vapor lights have improved color-correction and are now virtually indistinguishable from other parking lot lights, while retaining their cost and illumination benefits.

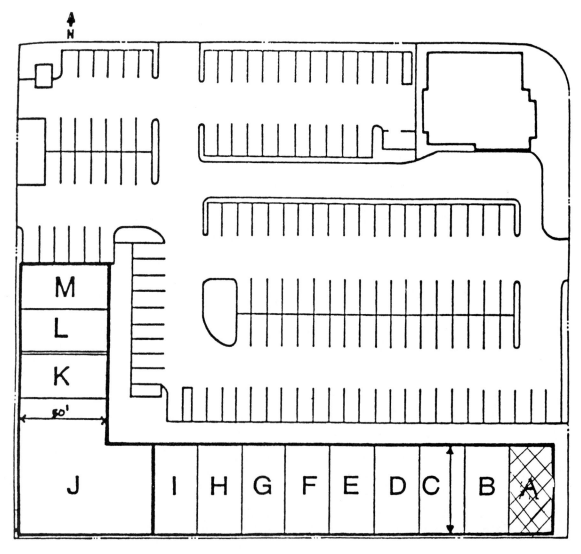

Figure 8–7. Layout of Center

Power Centers A recent trend is toward power centers in which each retailer is a dominant merchant in its merchandising area. These are called *category killers* and would include such names as Toys 'R Us, Home Depot, and Circuit City. Such centers may contain four or five large anchors and only a few small tenants. The term *power center* comes from the ability to attract customers from a much wider radius than similarly sized community shopping centers.

Space Planning Undesirable "bowling alley" centers exist when the developer tries to maximize floor space by making long, narrow retail spaces. Such designs eliminate the large window display space desired by tenants and usually create wasted space in the rear of the stores.

Hide-and-seek spaces located around corners or behind columns are also undesirable to the merchant, and confusing for the customer.

Enclosed malls are very desirable, and almost a necessity for the regional center today. Lighting, flooring, and decor should be coordinated to make the mall cheerful and bright.

Additional Profit Centers

1. *Kiosks* are free-standing shops (booths) located within a mall or center. They can be used to market custom signs, keys, costume jewelry, lettered T-shirts, and so on. Kiosks command a high rental rate per square foot (see Figure 8–8).

2. *Wall shops* are used in older centers that have long, blank walls. They are very shallow stores (ten feet deep) that liven up the center while at the same time producing income (see Figure 8–9).

3. *Seasonal holiday* tenants such as a Christmas gift-wrapping booth or a cheese and jam gift center operate in open mall space.

4. *Minibillboards* within the shopping center (see Figure 8–10).

Figure 8–8. Kiosk

Figure 8–9.   Wall Shop

Figure 8–10.   Mini Billboard

5. *Outparcels* such as fast-food outlets may also be built in the parking lot.

6. *Pushcarts* can add charm and are space-intensive, with the average size being only 4 feet by 6 feet.

7. *Car care malls* offer one-stop shopping for your car. Services include auto parts, tire sales, mufflers, brakes, transmission service, tune-ups, oil and lube, auto sound systems, and gasoline.

The property manager should check existing leases and receive permission if necessary prior to implementing any profit center strategy.

Layout Measurements

Space is usually measured from the center wall to the center wall, except freestanding spaces, which are measured to the outside of the outer wall. Some developers measure from the end of the eaves or overhang. The property manager should be familiar with the space sizes and how they were measured.

RENTAL RATES

Rental rates for retail commercial space vary depending on location. The location of retail enterprises depends on the need for traffic, either foot or vehicular. For example, it has been customary for banks to be located in the high-rent, prime space of the first floor. In today's society, with the advent of checks and credit cards, the majority of banking transactions are done by mail, courier, phone, or computer and no longer require physical pedestrian traffic to a bank. Thus, some banks are locating in less-desirable locations, such as the second floor of downtown office buildings, in order to reduce rental costs.

A recent survey shows that East 57th Street (New York City) has the highest ground-floor retail rents in the world, at $425 per square foot per year. In second place is Tokyo's Ginza at $400 per square foot. Third is Fifth Avenue (New York City) at $375 per square foot per year. An active leasing program may involve tasteful signage, "cold calling" existing desirable local merchants in other locations, soliciting broker assistance, contacting other property managers who may have good tenants and may be seeking opportunities to expand, and advertising in local and trade publications. Calling prospects from the Yellow Pages can also be appropriate. Attending ICSC (International Council of Shopping Centers) conventions, regional idea exchanges, and deal-making sessions are ideal ways to meet national and sometimes regional chains.

COMMON AREA MAINTENANCE

Common-area maintenance (CAM) charges are charges for maintaining, improving, and supplying common areas in a retail strip or mall. These costs include taxes, insurance, repairs, landscaping, utilities, and so forth, and are charged back to the tenant. The concept for CAM is that the manager and tenant need to act in a partnership in order for both to be successful. Each tenant relies on other tenants and a clean, cheerful center to generate consumer traffic and contribute to the overall success of the shared environment. CAM costs can range from $.10 per square foot to over $2.00 per square foot per month. The tenant must be aware of and budget for these costs, which are added to the base rent. From the owner's position, being able to pass on these CAM costs and any increases ensures profitability on the lease.

Calculation

A clause allowing additional rent must be included in the lease in order to charge tenants for common-area maintenance (CAM) costs.

Proration of costs is usually based on the prorated square footage of the space in relation to total rentable area. For example, if the merchant's space is 1,200 square feet and the total center is 100,000 square feet, his share would be 1.2 percent of the total amount of the CAM bills.

The billing cycle may be monthly, quarterly, or annual depending on lease terminology. This author prefers monthly billing based on an annual budget, with year-end adjustments. This improves the owner's cash flow while keeping the merchant's payments equal so he or she does not get hit with one large bill.

The most desirable and fastest method of calculation is through a computer program designed for the property manager. The hand format (Figure 8–11) is time consuming. The totals across the bottom must equal the totals

MONTH _____ YEAR_____

COMP #	RENT	SQ. FT.	KWH	ELECT	GAS	WATER	TRASH	CAM	TAX	INS	TOTAL CAM EXP.	% OF CAM for ADMIN.	MISC.	TOTAL
AMOUNT														
(1)														
(7)		2000												
(2)		925												
(3)		1500												
(4)		1050												
(5)		1200												
(6)		1200												
(7)		1200												
(9)		1200												
(10)		1380												
(11)		1110												
(12)		2400												
(13)		1200												
(14)		1200												
(15)		1200												
(16)		1200												
(17)		1200												
(18)		1580												
(19)		2960												
(8)		1200												
(20)		1000												
(21)		1027												
(22)		973												
(23)		3000												
(24)		3100												
		36005												

Comments:

Figure 8–11. CAM Hand Calculation

from top to bottom as a double check. The computer format (Figure 8–12) is much faster and easier.

Cost of Calculation

The cost of calculation and CAM supervision is usually charged back to the tenant, if permitted in the lease, at a percentage of total CAM charges. Supervisory charges such as this range from 5 percent to 15 percent. The property manager usually retains these charges for his or her efforts if the management agreement so permits.

BILLING SUMMARY FOR PROPERTY 60001   FROM 12/01/   TO 12/31/

STORE NAME NUMBER			RENT	SQ FT	KWH	ELECT	GAS	WATER	TRASH	CAM	TAX	INS	CAM TOTAL	CAM PCT	CAM CHARGE	SPECIAL ASSESS	TOTAL CHARGE
	BILLED AMOUNT:			40183		3777.60	110.82	101.46	368.06	2135.20	1023.83	255.00				945.50	
	RATIO:					.09401	.00354	.00282	.01119	.05930	.02844	.00708				.02626	
		(24)	3861.00	3100	0	0.00	0.00	8.74	0.00	183.83	88.16	21.95	302.68	30.26	214.09	81.41	4275.35
2037	10	(7)	0.00	2000	970	91.19	7.08	5.64	22.38	118.60	56.88	14.16	315.93	31.59	150.19	52.52	400.04
2093–95	10	(2)	555.00	925	840	78.97	3.27	2.61	10.35	54.85	26.31	6.55	182.91	18.29	73.14	24.29	780.49
2097	10	3)	1200.00	1500	1985	186.61	5.31	4.23	16.79	88.95	42.66	10.62	355.17	17.75	106.70	39.39	1612.31
2099	5	(4	700.00	1050	2720	255.71	3.72	2.96	11.75	62.27	29.86	7.43	373.70	37.37	99.64	27.57	1138.64
2101	10	(5)	699.61	1200	1635	153.71	4.25	3.38	13.43	71.16	34.13	8.50	288.56	28.85	100.01	31.51	1048.53
2103	10	(6)	900.00	1200	1830	172.04	4.25	3.38	13.43	71.16	34.13	8.50	306.89	30.68	101.84	31.51	1269.08
2105	10	(7)	1105.95	1200	1465	137.72	4.25	3.38	13.43	71.16	34.13	8.50	272.57	27.25	98.41	31.51	1437.28
2107	10	(9)	750.60	1200	1790	168.28	4.25	3.38	13.43	71.16	34.13	8.50	303.13	30.31	101.47	31.51	1115.55
2109	10	(10)	925.00	1380	1070	100.59	4.89	3.89	15.44	81.83	39.25	9.77	255.66	25.56	107.39	36.24	1242.46
2111	10	(11)	666.00	1110	1785	167.81	3.93	3.13	12.42	65.82	31.57	7.86	292.54	29.25	95.07	29.15	1016.94
2113	10	(12)	1422.14	2400	0	0.00	8.50	6.77	26.86	142.32	0.00	16.99	201.44	10.07	152.39	63.02	1696.67
2115–17	5	(13)	698.00	1200	4695	441.38	4.25	3.38	13.43	71.16	34.13	8.50	576.23	28.81	99.97	31.51	1334.55
2119	5	(14)	780.00	1200	2425	227.97	4.25	3.38	13.43	71.16	34.13	8.50	362.82	36.28	107.44	31.51	1210.61
2121	10	(15)	540.00	1200	1950	183.32	4.25	3.38	13.43	71.16	34.13	8.50	318.17	31.81	102.97	31.51	921.49
2123	10	(16)	540.00	1200	2510	235.97	4.25	3.38	13.43	71.16	34.13	8.50	370.82	37.08	108.24	31.51	979.41
2125	10	(17	591.82	1200	0	0.00	4.25	3.38	13.43	71.16	34.13	8.50	134.85	6.74	77.90	31.51	764.92
2127	5	(18)	700.00	1580	0	0.00	0.00	4.46	17.68	93.69	0.00	0.00	115.83	11.58	105.27	41.49	868.90
2129	10	(19)	1861.80	2960	2955	277.80	10.48	8.35	33.12	175.53	84.18	20.96	610.42	61.04	236.57	77.73	2610.99
2131–5	10	(8)	500.00	1200	1020	95.89	4.25	3.38	13.43	71.16	34.13	8.50	230.74	23.07	94.23	31.51	785.32
2137	10	(20)	575.30	1000	1395	131.14	3.54	2.82	11.19	59.30	28.44	7.08	243.51	24.35	83.65	26.26	869.42
2139	10	(21)	610.28	1027	920	86.49	3.64	2.90	11.49	60.90	29.21	7.27	201.90	20.19	81.09	26.97	859.34
2141	10	(22)	685.00	973	905	85.08	3.44	2.74	10.89	57.70	27.67	6.89	194.41	19.44	77.14	25.55	924.40
2143	10	(23)	0.00	3000	0	0.00	10.62	8.46	33.57	177.90	0.00	0.00	230.55	11.52	189.42	78.78	320.85
2145	5																
			20867.50	36005	34865	3277.67	110.92	101.50	368.23	2135.09	825.49	222.53	7041.43	629.23	2764.32	945.47	29483.63

SQ FT FOR GAS RATIO =   31325
SQ FT FOR WATER RATIO = 36005
SQ FT FOR TRASH RATIO = 32905

OTHER CAM EXPENSES...... 1635.26
+ ELECTRICAL DIFFERENCE... 499.94
= TOTAL CAM BILLED AMOUNT 2135.20

TAX DIFFERENCE........ 198.34
+ INSURANCE DIFFERENCE.. 32.47
= ABSORBED BY OWNER..... 230.81

Figure 8–12. CAM Computer Calculation

Additional CAM Items

1. *Security.* Security should include adequate lighting in both the center and parking lots. Security guards are usually employed in larger centers to protect both customers and merchants.

2. *Insurance.* Insurance policies should have a high liability amount to protect against injury in common areas. Each merchant should have insurance for his or her own store's contents and interior liability. The property manager should require Certificates of Additionally Insured on both the owner's and tenants' policies.

   The property manager must periodically review the entire center and eliminate or minimize every "risk" exposure. Frequently, insurance company representatives are willing to inspect and share their observations and insight. Risk avoidance or management is an important part of every property manager's job.

3. *Real estate taxes.* The lease should specify who pays the increased taxes if a property is sold, as the reassessment may increase astronomically the amount included in the CAM expenses and also the building taxes if allocated back to the tenant.

LEGAL CONSIDERATIONS

A U.S. Supreme Court decision in *Robbins v. Pruneyard* said that shopping centers—even if privately owned—are quasi-public and must allow solicitors such as religious groups and cults as well as Girl Scout cookie sales. The property manager can, however, set reasonable rules, regulations, and insurance requirements to be observed by these groups.

In *Kendall v. Ernest Pestana*, a 1985 California Supreme Court decision, the court said a commercial lessor cannot withhold their consent to an assignment of a lease unless there is a commercially reasonable objection to the assignee or to his or her proposed use. A lease document can include a clause prohibiting certain types of assignments as well as call for increased rents at the time of the assignment if freely negotiated at the time of signing.

Commercial Rent Control

Many states such as California have a statewide ban on local commercial rent-control laws. This ban does not apply to residential.

Bankruptcy Law Amendments

The Bankruptcy Reform Act of 1994 made changes in the handling of unexpired nonresidential leases. The debtors-in-possession or trustees must assume or reject a lease within 60 days from filing the case. The court may grant more time if the request is made within the 60-day period. On rejection, either by choice or when the 60-day period expires, the lessee must immediately surrender the property to the lessor. If the lease is assumed, a subsequent breach will elevate the lessor's claim to the cost of administration of the estate. This receives the highest payment priority, rather than becoming an unsecured claim. Pending decision on whether to assume the lease, all obligations and payment of rent and CAM charges must be made in accordance with the lease.

When assuming or assigning an unexpired lease, the revised Bankruptcy Amendment states that the lessee's financial and operating statement must be at least equal to the present tenant's and that all provisions such as percentage rent, radius, and use clauses are applicable to the new tenant. Any lease that expires before or during the bankruptcy period is not part of the estate.

SUMMARY

After World War II, with the advent of the automobile and the creation of suburbia, a major shift in retailing occurred. Stores moved out of downtown areas to shopping centers in suburban areas to be closer to their customers. The different classifications of shopping centers include strip, neighborhood, community, regional, super-regional, and specialty. Leases in shopping centers are usually percentage or net leases. Merchants associations were formed to help promote and advertise the merchants in the center collectively and to increase customer traffic. The trade area of the center varies according to its classification. A strip center, for example, is for convenience shopping and draws from the immediate neighborhood. At the other end of the spectrum, the super-regional center trade area may extend 30 to 50 miles in radius.

Market research uses demographics to obtain data on income, age, home ownership, and so on, as a close correlation exists between personal income and percentage of income spent in retail sales. Market share compares the number of people who shop at competing centers. The sales potential of department stores is calculated by using consumer retail trade area statistics to convert dollar expenditures for department stores of census tracts in a trade area to a percentage of total retail sales. Tenant mix is very important in a shopping center, it offers the center a wide selection of goods and brings in customers who will shop at more than one store on their trip (cross-shop). When leasing, property managers should select tenants that complement each other in a symbiotic relationship.

The physical layout of the center should reflect the types of merchants and customers the developer/owner hopes to attract. Shopping should be a fun, exciting, convenient event. Colors should be bright and cheerful. Long, narrow stores and hide-and-seek spaces should be avoided. Additional profit centers include kiosks, wall shops, and holiday tenants. Rental rates vary from area to area and where in the center the store is located. The trend is toward high-margin retailers, for example Gucci's replacing traditional ground-floor tenants such as banks in prime downtown locations in major cities. The *Robbins v. Pruneyard* U.S. Supreme Court decision classified shopping centers as quasi-public places that must allow groups to solicit. The manager can establish rules, regulations, and insurance requirements, however. Common-area maintenance (CAM) costs such as taxes, insurance, maintenance, utilities, and so forth, are billed back to the merchant on a pro rata share depending on what percentage of the total space each merchant in the center rents.

Shopping center management is distinctly different from residential management, requiring unique skills and specialized knowledge. Unlike residential property management, in which most agreements are month-to-month, shopping center leases may be long term, costing the owner "mega-bucks" for a bad decision. Shopping centers are a new phenomenon that has changed the shopping habits of America. The customers have moved from downtown areas to outlying suburbs. The property manager has to be informed not only about his or her center's trade area, but about trends in retailing so he or she can correctly select the best tenant mix to make a success of the center. The center owner and merchant truly constitute a partnership. A successful merchant will contribute to a successful center and vice versa.

PERSONALITY PROFILE

The management of a regional shopping center takes a dynamic, detail-oriented person in order to be successful. Don Smith fits this profile with an MBA degree from Stanford and the achievement of both the CPM (certified property manager) designation from the Institute of Real Estate Management (IREM) and the CSM (certified shopping center manager) designation from the International

Council of Shopping Centers (ICSC). Additionally, Don was also a colonel in the army reserve.

Don deals with large institutional owners such as pension plans, insurance companies, and REITs. He deals with vendors, leasing brokers, and asset managers and he does budget and forecast planning. As president of a property management company (DWA Smith Co.), he is a third-party fee manager and has to help solicit and attract new clients to his firm. He does this through word of mouth, referrals, and advertising in trade publications.

REVIEW QUESTIONS

1. Which of the following is usually the smallest-size shopping center?
   a. community center
   b. strip center
   c. super-regional center
   d. regional center

2. Which of the following is usually the largest-size shopping center?
   a. community center
   b. strip center
   c. super-regional center
   d. regional center

3. Specialty centers usually have how many anchor tenants?
   a. one
   b. two or more
   c. none
   d. five or more

4. A lease in which the merchant pays a portion of gross sales as rent is
   a. percentage.
   b. gross.
   c. net.
   d. industrial.

5. Merchants associations are made up of
   a. tenants.
   b. attorneys.
   c. CPMs.
   d. CSMs.

6. Regional center trade areas usually have a population of at least
   a. 50,000.
   b. 100,000.
   c. 150,000.
   d. 500,000.

7. A likely anchor tenant for a neighborhood shopping center would be
   a. a large department store.
   b. a supermarket.
   c. an office building.
   d. a florist shop.

8. Additional profit areas for a shopping center include
   a. kiosks.
   b. wall shops.
   c. seasonal tenants.
   d. all of the above
   e. only b and c

9. Items in common-area maintenance include
   a. real estate taxes.
   b. base rent.
   c. percentage rent.
   d. CPI.

10. The U.S. Supreme Court decision establishing that shopping centers are quasi-public is
    a. *Robbins v. Pruneyard*.
    b. *Costa Mesa v. DRE*.
    c. *DeCarlo v. McLelland*.
    d. *Kendall v. Ernest Pestana*.

11. The number of shopping centers in the United States is approximately
    a. 30,000.
    b. 42,000.
    c. 50,000.
    d. 100,000.

12. The average sales per square foot in retail is approximately
    a. $110.
    b. $150.
    c. $170.
    d. $250.

13. Which classification of shopping center would most commonly have an L-shaped design?
   a. strip
   b. neighborhood
   c. community
   d. regional

14. What would be a typical anchor tenant for a power center?
   a. grocery store
   b. restaurant
   c. jewelry store
   d. Home Depot

15. Which type of store has the highest gross margin?
   a. consumer electronics
   b. housewares
   c. stationery
   d. camera

ADDITIONAL READING AND REFERENCES

Andrew Report (Monthly), P.O. Box 80209, Indianapolis, IN 46208.

Crittenden Retail Space News (Biweekly), Crittenden Business Publications, P.O. Box 1150, Novato, CA 94948.

Directory of Major Malls, P.O. Box 1708, 7 So. Myrtle Ave., Spring Valley, NY 1992.

Institute of Real Estate Management, *Managing the Shopping Center*, Chicago, IL, 1983.

International Council of Shopping Centers, *The Competitive Edge*, New York, NY, 1988.

International Council of Shopping Centers, *Food Courts*, New York, NY, 1985.

International Council of Shopping Centers, *Leasing Opportunities*, New York, NY, 1986.

International Council of Shopping Centers, *The Legal Edge*, New York, NY, 1986.

International Council of Shopping Centers, *The Operating Edge*, New York, NY, 1987.

Retail Leasing Reporter (Twice Monthly), P.O. Box 248, Kendall Park, NJ 08824.

Shopping Center Directory (West) (Annual), National Research Bureau, 310 S. Michigan Ave., Ste. 1150, Chicago, IL 60664.

Shopping Centers Today (Monthly), International Council of Shopping Centers, 665 Fifth Ave., New York, NY 10022.

Chapter 9

The Office Building

Key terms

Break-even analysis
CBD
Grade A
Grade B
Grade C
Gross area

Gross rentable area
Location
Major tenant
Money-created
   demand

Net rentable area
Perks
Space-created demand
Space planner
Status tenant

Food for thought

"Use not only all the brains you have—but all you can borrow."

INTRODUCTION

An office building can be defined as a property that provides facilities (space) to a tenant engaged in services (legal, accounting) rather than a location where goods are sold (shopping center) or manufactured (industrial building). As we discussed in Chapter 2, the U.S. economy has been moving away from manufacturing due to competition from countries such as Japan and Korea where production costs are lower. These countries can export their products to the United States more cheaply than our domestic manufacturers can produce them. This trend—unless tariffs are imposed—will continue into the next century.

SUPPLY AND DEMAND

Developers build office space dependent on two types of demand:

1. *Space-created demand.* Typically, developers build only when the vacancy rate drops below 7 percent or when they anticipate a declining vacancy.

2. *Money-created demand.* Developers build because lenders (banks, savings and loans) have money to lend. The availability of money for their projects encourages developers to proceed with development. This results in high vacancy rates as it ignores basic principles of supply and demand. The reason for this imbalance is that real estate has become a favorite investment for pension funds, banks, insurance companies, and syndicators. With the long holding ability of such institutional investors, oversupply vacancies are not as negative a factor to lenders as they would be to other "cash-poor" customers. Bankers lend because they obtain large loan transaction fees (points) and they feel real estate investors are more favorable borrowers than other customers such as Third World countries and farmers. Syndicators and insurance companies like the favorable tax shelter benefits. However, lenders and investors were only fooling themselves, as chronic overbuilding reduced rents and values of both new and used

(older) office buildings in the 1980s. In the 90s development has slowed and investors are concentrating on cash flow rather than appreciation or tax shelter.

Size Sizes range from small, one-story buildings to the enormous Sears Tower, 110 stories and 1,454 feet in height in Chicago (one of the world's tallest buildings). As we discussed in Chapter 1, new technological advances in elevators, design, and energy management allowed for the construction of skyscrapers. Initially, skyscrapers were all constructed in central business districts (CBDs), but they have now moved into the suburbs as well.

The size of the office market throughout U.S. cities varies. New York City leads with almost 300 million square feet, followed by Chicago, Washington, D.C., and Los Angeles.

Desirability Why are some office buildings at full occupancy with high rental rates while others are half empty at bargain-basement rents? The answer is "desirability". Office desirability is divided into four categories or grades (see Figure 9–1). The grades are achieved by ranking 12 criteria.

1. *Location.* Based more on prestige than geographic area (see Figure 9–2).

2. *Neighborhood.* Based on appearance and upkeep of other buildings in the surrounding area.

GRADE	LOCATION	RENTAL RATE	TENANTS
A	*Best*	*Highest*	*Most Prestigious*
B	Second best	Slightly less than A	Good, solid
C	Older area	Below A & B	Lower income
D	Near CBD	Lowest	Not usually maintained

Figure 9–1. Location Desirability

Figure 9–2. Location Benefits

3. *Transportation*. Are freeways and rapid transit systems convenient?

4. *Prestige of building*. Does the reputation of the tenants enhance the building and vice versa?

5. *Appearance*. Does the building have an attractive facade and entrance (so-called "curb appeal") which enhances an older building?

6. *Lobby*. Is it clean, neat, and cheerful; is the directory neat and organized?

7. *Elevators*. Are they conveniently located; are they clean; are they high-speed?

8. *Corridors*. Are the colors and design coordinated; are they cheerfully decorated and well lighted?

9. *Office interiors*. Do offices have window views, good column spacing, sufficient ceiling height?

10. *Management*. Are common areas and restrooms clean?

11. *Tenant mix*. What is the reputation of the tenants (i.e., attorneys, CPAs, etc.)? Are their services compatible?

12. *Tenant services*. Are the janitorial and security services of high quality? Does the building have built-in telecommunications?

OFFICE BUILDING STATISTICS

The Institute of Real Estate Management (IREM) publishes an annual report entitled *Income and Expense Analysis: Office Buildings*. This publication compares building types, age groups, rental ranges, and building sizes. Using IREM criteria, the property manager can compare a building to a sample of over 11,000 buildings, divided by national, regional, and metropolitan areas. These figures, used as benchmarks, make analysis and comparison of the property manager's operation and performance more meaningful (Figure 9–3).

MEASURING THE BUILDING

The two most common methods of measuring a building are those developed by BOMI and IREM. In this chapter we will use the IREM method.

Gross Area of Entire Building

This is the total sum of the areas of each floor, including lobbies and corridors, within the outside faces of the exterior walls.

Gross Rentable Area

The gross rentable area includes all areas within the outside walls, less pipe shafts, vertical ducts, elevator shafts, balconies, and stairs.

Net Rentable Area

The net rentable area is computed by deducting the following from gross rentable area: public corridors, washrooms, janitorial and electrical closets, air-conditioning rooms, and other rooms or areas not available to the tenant and the tenant's employees.

The property manager should be sure that figures are accurate and truthful to avoid confusion and lawsuits. In describing the space, the lease document should contain language such as "Suite 300, which is approximately 3,000 square feet." As a rule of thumb, the higher the loss or "load factor" (unusable space), the lower the rent, because the tenant receives less usable space. For example, if the net rentable area is 80,000 square feet, but only 70,000 square feet are usable due to corridors, the load factor is:

$$\frac{10,000}{80,000} = 12.5\%$$

Downtown Office Buildings—Metropolitan Dallas, Texas

Chart of Accounts	$/Gross Area of Entire Bldg.				$/Gross Rentable Office Area				$/Net Rentable Office Area			
	Blgs (10,000)	Med.	Range Low	$ High	Blgs (10,000)	Med.	Range Low	$ High	Blgs (10,000)	Med.	Range Low	$ High
Income												
Offices	14 1397	12.44	9.86	13.53	9 803	13.28	10.17	15.06	13 961	14.20	11.70	20.14
Retail	5 795	.10	.07	.12	3 462	.11	.06	.11	4 492	.13	.08	.13
Parking	10 1267	.68	.29	.83	7 698	.68	.26	.92	9 856	.77	.37	.98
Pass-Throughs	14 1397	1.27	.26	1.93	9 803	1.38	.28	2.15	13 961	1.43	.32	2.24
Retail % Income	5 715	.03	.02	.03	4 547	.03	.02	.03	4 440	.04	.03	.04
Misc. Income	11 1373	.11	.07	.24	8 798	.13	.10	.19	10 942	.13	.08	.25
Vacancy/Delin. Rents	14 1397	3.64	.53	4.63	9 803	3.64	3.22	5.10	13 961	3.89	.64	5.97
Total Collections	14 1397	11.95	9.05	15.45	9 803	11.79	8.36	12.82	13 961	13.65	11.93	18.66
Expenses												
Electricity	1 23	1.43	1.43	1.43	1 22	1.48	1.48	1.48	1 19	1.70	1.70	1.70
Water	15 1527	.04	.03	.04	10 913	.04	.03	.09	13 961	.05	.04	.07
Sewer	5 361	.03	.02	.03	3 304	.03	.01	.03	3 33	.03	.01	.03
HVAC Fuel												
Gas												
Fuel Oil	1 164	.00	.00	.00					1 131	.00	.00	.00
Electricity												
Steam												
Other												
Combination Electric	14 1504	1.18	.97	1.47	9 891	1.27	1.15	1.57	12 942	1.65	1.38	1.66
Total Energy Plant												
Subtotal Utilities	15 1527	1.22	1.02	1.53	10 913	1.53	1.21	1.62	13 961	1.72	1.41	1.82
Janitorial												
Payroll/Contract	15 1527	.46	.35	.47	10 913	.47	.38	.53	13 961	.50	.45	.60
Cleaning Supplies	10 1463	.03	.02	.03	7 868	.03	.02	.04	8 908	.04	.03	.04
Miscellaneous	1 192	.00	.00	.00	1 129	.00	.00	.00	1 125	.00	.00	.00
Maintenance & Repair												
Payroll	14 1521	.21	.18	.27	9 908	.25	.20	.28	12 956	.26	.22	.33
Supplies	13 1348	.03	.01	.11	9 908	.03	.01	.04	11 815	.04	.01	.12
Htg/Ven. & A.C. Repairs	15 1527	.08	.05	.12	10 913	.09	.06	.12	13 961	.09	.06	.14
Electric Repairs	14 1516	.05	.03	.06	10 913	.06	.03	.07	12 953	.07	.04	.08

(Continued)

Figure 9–3. Office Income and Expense
Published annually, © Institute of Real Estate Management, 430 N. Michigan, Chicago, IL 60611.

Chart of Accounts	$/Gross Area of Entire Bldg. Blgs	Sq. Ft. (10,000)	Med.	$ Range Low	$ Range High	$/Gross Rentable Office Area Blgs	Sq. Ft. (10,000)	Med.	$ Range Low	$ Range High	$/Net Rentable Office Area Blgs	Sq. Ft. (10,000)	Med.	$ Range Low	$ Range High
Plumbing Repairs	12	1392	.02	.01	.03	9	807	.02	.01	.03	10	853	.02	.01	.03
Elev Repr/Maintenance	15	1527	.19	.08	.20	10	913	.22	.08	.24	13	961	.23	.09	.25
Exterior Repairs	8	941	.04	.03	.05	7	702	.05	.01	.05	7	582	.05	.05	.05
Roof Repairs	7	501	.01	.00	.02	6	319	.01	.00	.02	7	415	.01	.00	.02
Parking Lot Repairs	7	610	.03	.01	.04	5	301	.04	.02	.08	6	362	.03	.01	.10
Decorating—Tenant	2	23	.08	.01	.08	2	23	.08	.01	.08	2	20	.09	.02	.09
Decorating—Public	6	806	.05	.03	.06	5	586	.05	.04	.09	5	485	.06	.04	.10
Misc. Repairs	12	1486	.11	.04	.13	9	891	.11	.04	.14	10	928	.13	.04	.16
Subtot Jan/Maint/Rpr	15	1527	1.18	.98	1.35	10	913	1.29	1.18	1.39	13	961	1.46	1.35	1.69
Administrative															
Payroll—Administ.	12	1503	.20	.14	.21	9	908	.21	.19	.28	10	942	.24	.16	.27
Advertising	8	653	.06	.00	.07	7	448	.07	.00	.10	8	522	.07	.00	.10
Management Fee	15	1527	.26	.23	.35	10	913	.27	.24	.33	13	961	.35	.28	.43
Other Administrative	13	1509	.16	.10	.19	10	913	.17	.12	.21	11	947	.20	.10	.21
Other Payroll Costs															
Payroll Taxes	8	951	.05	.05	.06	7	706	.06	.05	.08	6	502	.06	.05	.06
Employee Benefits	8	957	.13	.12	.13	7	762	.13	.09	.14	6	531	.14	.11	.15
Subtotal Admin/Payrl	15	1527	.74	.50	.80	10	913	.91	.80	1.05	13	961	.88	.61	1.01
Insurance	14	1397	.10	.07	.14	9	803	.08	.08	.16	13	961	.10	.08	.13
Services															
Landscape	13	1509	.04	.03	.06	10	913	.06	.03	.06	11	947	.06	.03	.07
Trash Removal	13	1509	.02	.02	.03	10	913	.02	.02	.04	11	947	.02	.02	.04
Security—Payroll	8	1135	.24	.17	.25	5	574	.26	.25	.28	7	754	.26	.01	.27
Security—Contracted	12	1319	.10	.07	.27	9	742	.08	.05	.10	11	947	.09	.06	.12
Window Washing	13	1352	.02	.01	.02	10	913	.02	.02	.03	11	823	.03	.02	.03
Snow Removal	2	215	.00	.00	.00	2	202	.00	.00	.00	2	169	.00	.00	.00
Miscellaneous	11	1328	.08	.03	.14	9	896	.05	.04	.15	9	802	.05	.04	.10
Subtotal Insur/Srvcs	15	1527	.53	.36	.60	10	913	.60	.50	.61	13	961	.57	.54	.71
Net Operating Costs	15	1527	3.70	3.44	4.02	10	913	4.10	3.97	4.68	13	961	4.72	4.31	4.78
Real Estate Taxes	15	1527	1.11	.75	1.25	10	913	1.33	.82	1.37	13	961	1.32	.93	1.61
Other Tax/Fee/Permit	8	846	.00	.00	.02	7	617	.00	.00	.02	6	418	.00	.00	.03
Total Operating Costs	15	1527	4.73	4.26	5.35	10	913	5.45	4.92	6.32	13	961	5.95	5.54	6.55

OCCUPANCY LEVEL	75%	E/I RATIO (NOC/TAC)	.31
VACANCY LEVEL	25%	CLEANG SERVICES (% YES)	100%

TENANTS ALTERATNS 3-YEAR (11) $8.00 5-YEAR (13) $15.00

Footnote: Square footage figures (sq. ft.) are reported in multiples of ten thousand. See guidelines section for explanation of reports and interpretation of data. Copyright 1995, IREM.

Figure 9–3. Continued

Measuring the Building

> Gross area of entire building
>
> – shafts, ducts, balconies, and stairs
>
> = rentable area (tenant pays rent on)
>
> – public corridors, restrooms, mechanical rooms
>
> = usable area (tenant occupies)

In the United States and Canada, three additional methods exist for measuring rentable area in office buildings. All three measure total square footage.

1. *BOMA International (Building Owners and Managers Association International)*—from the inside of the outside wall (or in new buildings, from the glass line) to the outside of the inside wall (or hall wall), and center to center on the division walls. Columns are included.

2. *General Services Administration*—same as the previous method except that all columns, division walls, service closets, and so on, are excluded from the calculation of net usable space. In negotiating leases with the federal government, this method must be used. After October 1993, the General Services Administration required federal government leases to be in metric and not square footage.

3. *So-called New York method*—space is measured right across the floor from glass line to glass line, subtracting only elevator shafts and stairwells. In the case of multiple occupancy on one floor, the common space, usable and nonusable, is apportioned among the tenants according to the size of their respective areas.

Usable Area

Usable area refers to any area in a given floor that could be used by the tenant. This area includes a point from the perimeter glass line to demising walls; it also includes column areas within such a space.

Although these are the most commonly used methods, other methods may be encountered; for example, drip-line method in which the rentable area includes that portion outside the building that is within the area whose perimeter is defined by a line formed by the water dripping off the roof or canopy.

SETTING THE RENT SCHEDULE

When setting the rent schedule, the property manager must take into account the twelve criteria for ranking the building, additional amenities, general economic conditions, and the owner's break-even point.

Market Survey

The property manager should conduct a market survey of the competition. A form similar to the one used for a residential market survey can be used, and at least three comparable properties should be analyzed. The rental rate measure most commonly used is "cost per square foot." On the West Coast, this is usually quoted on a monthly basis, but in other parts of the country it is annualized. For example, if the rent is $4,000 per month on 2,500 square feet of space, on the West Coast, the quoted rate would be $1.60 per square foot per month. The rate in the East would be twelve months times $1.60 or an annualized rate of $19.20 per square foot. The cost is really the same; the only difference is in the semantics.

Break-Even Analysis

A break-even analysis determines the minimum rent needed to pay all of the building's expenses and costs, as well as the owner's expected return. The formula to calculate the break-even rent is as follows:

$$\text{B/E rent} = \frac{\text{expenses} + \text{mortgage} + \text{return}}{\text{Rentable area of building in square feet}}$$

For example:

Rentable space = 50,000 s.f.

Expenses = $291,258

Owner's equity = $1,000,000

Owner's rate of return = 10% = $100,000

Mortgage payment = $568,742

Mortgage = $4,500,000

Therefore:

$$\text{B/E rent} = \frac{\$291,258 + \$568,742 + \$100,00}{50,000 \text{ s.f.}} = \frac{\$960,000}{50,000 \text{ s.f.}} = \$19.20/\text{s.f.}$$

Thus, the minimum rent we can charge is $19.20 per square foot per year, or $1.60 per square foot per month, to cover all of the building's expenses, costs, and the owner's return.

TENANT SELECTION

The selection of commercial tenants is different from and much more important than the selection of residential tenants due to the length of times leases may run and the large rental sums therefore involved. A mistake can be very expensive.

Major Tenants

Major tenants can be checked by using Dun & Bradstreet (D&B) reports and ratings, contacting tenants' bank account managers, and checking with tenants' vendors and landlords at other locations. Also, copies of tenant financial statements can be obtained and analyzed. See Figure 9–4 for a D&B rating report.

Small Tenants

Small tenants such as "Ma and Pa" companies usually are not rated and may not have other locations. With smaller tenants, look more to the individuals than the business. Run credit reports (TRWs) on their personal credit histories. Also contact their banks and vendors. Additionally, ask for business plans (verbal or written) to ascertain their goals and objectives. To ensure rent payment, the property manager should in some cases ask for a "personal guarantee," much as a bank does, if the entity is a corporation. The property manager should obtain written permission from the prospective tenant before checking credit to avoid violating privacy laws.

In summary, a conscientious effort by the property manager in tenant selection will save considerable time, expense, and aggravation in the future.

ATTRACTING TENANTS

In order to screen and obtain tenants, property managers need to make them aware of the property. The cost, (rental rate) is not always the deciding factor. Creativity and hard work are important in finding prospective tenants. For example, because image is important, a small office building with interior courtyards may be named "The Courtyards." A project that has

D&B Rating System

The D&B Rating System is a widely used tool that uses a two-part code to represent a firm's estimated financial strength and composite credit appraisal. A Rating may be based on a book financial statement or on an estimated financial statement submitted by the company.

	Estimated Financial Strength			Composite Credit Appraisal			
				High	Good	Fair	Limited
Estimated financial strength, based on an actual book financial statement.	$50,000,000	and over	**5A**	1	2	3	4
	$10,000,000	to $49,999,999	**4A**	1	2	3	4
For example, if a company has a Rating of "3A3," this means its financial strength is between $1,000,000 and $9,999,999 and its composite credit appraisal is "fair."	$1,000,000	to $9,999,999	**3A**	1	2	3	4
	$750,000	to $999,999	**2A**	1	2	3	4
	$500,000	to $749,999	**1A**	1	2	3	4
Copyright 1991.	$300,000	to $499,999	**BA**	1	2	3	4
Dun & Bradstreet, Inc.	$200,000	to $299,999	**BB**	1	2	3	4
All Rights Reserved.	$125,000	to $199,999	**CB**	1	2	3	4
Reprinted With Permission.	$75,000	to $124,999	**CC**	1	2	3	4
	$50,000	to $74,999	**DC**	1	2	3	4
Estimated financial strength, based on either an actual book financial statement or an estimated financial statement.	$35,000	to $49,999	**DD**	1	2	3	4
	$20,000	to $34,999	**EE**	1	2	3	4
	$10,000	to $19,999	**FF**	1	2	3	4
	$5,000	to $9,999	**GG**	1	2	3	4
		up to $4,999	**HH**	1	2	3	4
Estimated financial strength, based on an estimated financial statement (when an actual book financial statement is not available to us).	$125,000	and over	**1R**		2	3	4
	$50,000	to $124,999	**2R**		2	3	4

Symbols in the Rating column — what do they mean?

-- (Absence of a Rating)

A Business Information Report is available on this business, and other information products may be available as well. However, a D&B Rating has not been assigned. A "--" symbol should not be interpreted as indicating that credit should be denied. It simply means that the information available to Dun & Bradstreet does not permit us to classify the company within our Rating key and that further inquiry should be made before reaching a credit decision.

In many cases, a "--" symbol is used because a current financial statement on the business is not available to us. Some other reasons for using a "--" symbol include:

☐ Unavailability of the source and amount of starting capital — in the case of a new business
☐ A deficit net worth ☐ Bankruptcy proceedings ☐ A critical financial condition

ER (Employee Range)

Certain lines of business, primarily banks, insurance companies and other service-type businesses, do not lend themselves to classification under the D&B Rating System. Instead, we assign these types of businesses an Employee Range symbol based on the number of people employed. No other significance should be attached to this symbol.

For example, a Rating of "ER7" means there are between 5 and 9 employees in the company.

"ERN" should not be interpreted negatively. It simply means we don't have information indicating how many people are employed at this firm.

Key to Employee Range	
1000 or more employees	ER 1
500 to 999	ER 2
100 to 499	ER 3
50 to 99	ER 4
20 to 49	ER 5
10 to 19	ER 6
5 to 9	ER 7
1 to 4	ER 8
Not available	ER N

Questions? Please call your D&B Customer Service Center at 1-800-234-DUNS (1-800-234-3867). Our Customer Service Representatives will be happy to help you interpret the D&B Rating System and other symbols.

Figure 9–4. D&B Rating

Figure 9–5. Marketing Strategies

a pond or overlooks water may be named "The Lakes." Such a name gives the building an identity.

The most productive forms of advertising are shown in Figure 9–5.

Newspaper Advertisements Place advertisements in newspapers and magazines that businesspeople will read. *The Wall Street Journal*, as an example, has separate editions for different parts of the country. It also has a real estate mart in Friday's edition.

Direct Mail Direct mail can be an effective tool if you target your markets properly. Word processors can be used to send individual, personalized letters to prospects, such as doctors, attorneys, accountants, and so on.

Publicity Arrange for grand openings and open houses for prospective tenants and other leasing agents. Write articles for newspapers about unique building features or tenants; for example, a prestigious tenant such as IBM.

Signage Signage is very important, especially for a new building. The sign should include the name of the building and the address and phone number of the leasing contact.

Brochures Brochures should create excitement about the building and its location, amenities, and features. A brochure should have pictures and a map of how to get to the building.

Miscellaneous Media Radio and television are expensive and not as effective as the printed media. They target a mass market rather than an individual market. Advertising medical building space in a medical association magazine can be very effective, too.

Perks Perks are items such as free rent, extra tenant improvements (TIs), and amenities such as free parking and exercise rooms. Most popular as perks for existing tenants are lunches and Christmas parties (Figure 9–6). One of the newer perks is the addition of a "concierge" in an office building to help busy executives.

Tenant Happy Factor*	Action	Frequency	(Unit Cost) Annual Cost	Cost/Sq. Ft.	Annual % Return on Investment
☺☺☺☺☺	Lunches/Meals	[monthly] 12	($50) $600	$.09	16,922%
☺☺☺	Flowers/Plants	[quarterly] 3	($40) $120	$.02	85,011%
☺☺☺☺	Christmas Party	[annual] 1	$500	$.07	20,326%
☺	Holiday Cards	[bi-annual] 2	($2) $4	$.0005	2,553,219%
☺☺	Cookies/Candy	[quarterly] 3	($10) $30	$.004	340,343%
	TOTAL		$1254	$.18	8,045%

* Tenant Happy Factor — Amount of good will generated by the different tenant relations activities, with five smiles the high and one smile the low.

Figure 9–6. Existing Tenant Perks

LEASING CONSIDERATIONS

On-site versus Off-site

The question of whether there should be an on-site leasing agent is often asked. The answer: it depends on the size of the building and its vacancy level. For a new 100,000 square-foot office building, an on-site leasing agent is desirable. If the building is 96 percent occupied after one year, however, an on-site agent may no longer be needed.

Property Management versus Leasing Agents

Should the property manager and leasing agent be the same person from the same firm or should they be from different companies? The answer again depends on size, location, other duties of the property manager, time, and so forth. The leasing agent's job is usually complete when the tenant signs the lease; the property manager will live with the lease for its entire term. As a result, the property manager may be more diligent in looking at the long-term benefits of the lease.

Small versus Large Leasing Firms

Is it best to hire a small, local leasing firm or a large, national company? We recommend compromise. A large firm, due to its national exposure, may be retained to solicit and lease major anchor tenants for large rental spaces (over 5,000 square feet). A small, local firm is usually more effective in renting smaller stores and offices attractive to "Ma and Pa" type tenants. Attention should be paid not only to the reputation of the leasing company, but also to that of the individual leasing agent. The agent will be the "man or woman on the spot" and it will be primarily his or her efforts that get results.

LEASING TECHNIQUES

Some leasing techniques have been covered under tenant selection, but additional techniques need to be discussed. An empty building does not make for good rapport with the owner. The importance of leasing cannot be overemphasized.

Cold-Calling

Cold-calling by the property manager on the telephone and through personal visits is important. Again, the market should be targeted to achieve the best results. Cold-calling is difficult for the property manager due to the high rate of rejection, but it can often be a very effective tool for reaching certain potential tenants. A script should be developed to assist and enhance cold-calling success.

Space Planner A space planner should be available to help potential tenants design an office to meet their needs. Space planning can be done in a computerized format, helping the tenant lower costs by better utilization of space. Well-planned but smaller space at higher rental rates can benefit both the owner and tenant. In the past, each employee averaged 250 square feet of work space, but due to telecommunicating (computer and fax) it is estimated in a study by Link Resources Corporation that over eight million employees use phone technology to work from home. The latest guestimate is down to an average of 180 square feet per employee.

Existing Tenants Retention is the best tool for maintaining high occupancy rates. Find out existing tenant concerns and problems well before the lease expires.

High-Status Tenants High-status tenants can attract other tenants to your building. A rent concession to draw family practitioners and pediatricians can be beneficial for leasing to specialists who hope to obtain referrals from these general practitioners.

Comparison of Buildings The property manager should, from time to time, compare his or her buildings to those of competitors. This information can be useful for planning, refinancing, prospecting, or selling.

> *Objective data*—ownership, total square footage, name of management company, name of leasing agent, quoted rental range, names of tenants, tenant mix, vacancies, floor plans, financing, and type of construction. Sources of this data would be the assessor's office, realty trade associations, chambers of commerce, and government agencies.

> *Subjective data*—actual rents and lease terms, renewal data and options, concessions or incentives being given, condition of building, effectiveness of management, and any anticipated management or ownership changes. Sources for this information include tenants, the management company, brokers, on-site personnel, contractors, vendors, and other owners and managers.

MAINTENANCE When high vacancy rates occur in the office rental market, keeping existing tenants happy so they will renew their leases is imperative. BOMI, in addition to the RPA designation, has a systems maintenance administrator (SMA) designation for those who operate and maintain today's complex commercial building systems. Candidates must complete eight courses ranging from heating and air-conditioning to electrical systems, building design, energy management, control systems, and supervision.

After World War II, central air-conditioning was installed in most new buildings, but temperature is still the major source of complaints. It is difficult to satisfy everyone when it comes to temperature. Some buildings are airtight and have few or no drafts. Space locations vary within the building, construction materials differ, and climates differ—so common sense must be used to establish ideal temperatures or temperature zones for each building.

Standard Temperature Guidelines

	Temperature	Humidity
Summer	73–79 degrees	20–60%
Winter	68–74 degrees	30–70%
Ideal	75 degrees	50%
Air velocity	15 feet per minute	

Source: Skylines (December 1987)

SMART (INTELLIGENT) BUILDINGS

A buzzword being used today in office building management and development is "smart" or "intelligent" buildings. Intelligent building features include the amount of automation, communication, and information-processing technologies present in the building. The higher the intelligence, the more desirable the building will be to most tenants.

Five Classifications of Smart Buildings

Level Zero—has no intelligent amenities and does not qualify.

Level One—provides infrastructural core, including computerized energy management, HVAC, elevators, and security and life-safety systems.

Level Two—provides Level One capabilities, plus shared conference space, photocopying, and word-processing centers.

Level Three—provides Level Two capabilities, plus telecommunications services utilizing building cabling system.

Level Four—provides Level Three capabilities, plus sophisticated office automation and information-processing services. These buildings are sometimes called "Einstein" buildings.

Commercial Building Organizations

The Intelligent Building Institute (IBI) is an international trade association established in 1986 to serve the needs of all sectors involved in advanced technologies used in commercial, institutional, and industrial buildings.

IBI Headquarters
2101 "L" St., N.W., Ste. 300
Washington, DC 20037

The International Facilities Management Association (IFMA) offers a certified facilities manager (CFM) designation. This designation involved education, work, experience, and an examination.

IFMA
1 E. Greenway Plaza, 11th Floor
Houston, TX 77046

SICK BUILDINGS

A recent *Wall Street Journal* report stated that more office workers are filing lawsuits, claiming they were made ill by indoor air pollution from such things as insect sprays, industrial cleaners, cigarette smoke, and fumes from new carpets, drapes, and copiers. Most of the suits involve airtight, energy-efficient buildings. Plaintiffs usually don't prevail; however, there have been several out-of-court settlements. The most frequent targets of such suits are landlords, architects, contractors, building product manufacturers, and real estate managers.

Scientists have identified more than 1,500 bacterial and chemical indoor air pollutants from such sources as carpets and copy machines. The buildup of bacteria in the indoor air of the county courthouse in Barton, Florida, led to the evacuation of the building in 1992. This ten-story building, which cost $30 million to build, had to be rehabbed with new air-conditioning and ventilation systems at an additional expense of $37 million.

Buildings are not designed to vent out contaminants and depend on the air-conditioning systems to cleanse and recirculate air and introduce fresh air. The industry standard for the amount of outdoor air that should be mixed with indoor air is 20 cubic feet per minute.

SUMMARY

The office building provides space for tenants to engage in services such as legal, accounting, and so on. Since our economy is moving away from production and toward service, office buildings have experienced overdevelopment so that many areas have an abundance of space and a high vacancy rate. The two main reasons for new developments are space-created and money-created demand. During periods of high vacancy, the availability of money causes developers to create office buildings built on speculation without being preleased to tenants.

Four grades of office buildings exist, with Grade A being the best and having the highest rents. Grade D buildings are the poorest and are not usually well maintained. They are in less desirable areas and have the lowest rental rates. Statistics for office buildings can be obtained from the Institute of Real Estate Management's annual report entitled *Income and Expense Analysis: Office Buildings* as well as from BOMI.

The measurement of gross and net rentable area varies, so the property manager should double-check measurements before quoting to tenants. When establishing the rent schedule, a market survey should be made of competing buildings. On the West Coast, rental rates are quoted per square foot per month rather than per square foot per year. A break-even analysis is made to determine the minimum rent needed to pay all operating and debt-service expenses. When screening tenants for financial ability to pay rent, the major (larger) tenant rating can be found in Dun & Bradstreet (D&B). Smaller "Ma and Pa" type tenants should be checked out personally much like a residential tenant, as described in Chapter 7. Bank references, financial statements, and income tax returns may be checked.

When marketing space in an office building, the property manager or leasing agent may use newspaper ads, direct mail, publicity, signage, brochures, media, and perks. Some leasing considerations include hiring an on-site versus an off-site leasing agent, a property manager versus a leasing agent, or small versus large leasing firms. Leasing techniques include cold-calling, offering space planning, retaining existing tenants, and attracting prestige tenants.

Property managers of office buildings can help reduce vacancy by ensuring proper temperature settings so tenants are comfortable and satisfied. Newer "smart buildings" have built-in features for automation, communications, and information processing. Sick buildings are becoming a problem for owners and managers and will be a more serious problem in the future.

Office buildings are a growth area in property management as our society moves from an emphasis on industrial goods manufacturing to a service orientation.

Rick Burnett, who works for a major Los Angeles bank, originally started his career as a radio announcer. He entered the real estate industry by pursuing a career as a real estate agent and then ran a small brokerage company. He then entered the property management area by working for several firms including a real estate development subsidiary of a major corporation, a real estate syndicator, and an international real estate owner. During this time, Rick decided that education was critical to his success. He pursued and attained the CPM designation from the Institute of Real Estate Management (IREM), the real property administrator (RPA) designation from the Building Owners and Managers Association (BOMA), and the certified shopping center manager (CSM) designation from the International Council of Shopping Centers (ICSC). He then pursued and attained his B.S. degree, attending college at night while working for his current firm.

In his position as vice president of real estate operations, he has responsibility for site identification and lease negotiations in certain states west of the Mississippi, while also administering a portfolio of corporate-owned and -leased premises. He stays involved with industry changes while actively participating in the real estate organizations he belongs to. He was acknowledged for his work in the greater Los Angeles chapter of IREM by being named "CPM® of the Year" for 1994. He is also an instructor for IREM's Course 200.

REVIEW QUESTIONS

1. The most desirable office building category is
   a. Grade A.
   b. Grade B.
   c. Grade C.
   d. Grade D.
   e. none of the above

2. Criteria for ranking office buildings include
   a. debt service.
   b. appearance.
   c. tenant mix.
   d. both a and b
   e. both b and c

3. A compatible tenant mix would include
   a. CPAs and attorneys.
   b. CPAs and a massage parlor.
   c. CPAs and a second-hand store.
   d. all of the above
   e. none of the above

4. Net rentable space includes
   a. A/C rooms.
   b. washrooms.
   c. public corridors.
   d. all of the above
   e. none of the above

5. Usable area usually means
   a. the gross area of the building.
   b. the area the tenant occupies.
   c. the area for which the tenant pays rent.
   d. the gross area plus the parking lot.

6. Large commercial tenant screening is usually checked by using
   a. a CPA.
   b. the DRE.
   c. D&B.
   d. TRW.

7. Methods of attracting office tenants include
   a. an apartment guide.
   b. signage.
   c. brochures.
   d. both a and b
   e. both b and c

8. On-site leasing agents for commercial buildings are usually
   a. required at all times.
   b. never needed.
   c. needed for large buildings with high vacancy rates.
   d. required by law.

9. Office leasing techniques include
   a. percentage rents.
   b. model offices.
   c. space planning.
   d. both a and b
   e. both b and c

10. The best source for new office tenants is
    a. radio ads.
    b. existing tenants.
    c. television ads.
    d. an apartment guide.

11. Which office building has the higher rental rates?
    a. Grade A
    b. Grade B
    c. Grade C
    d. Grade D

12. The square foot office requirements per employee are
    a. increasing.
    b. decreasing.
    c. remaining the same.

13. The break-even point is
    a. the mortgage payment divided by the square footage.
    b. the mortgage payment and real estate taxes divided by the square footage.
    c. building expenses, the mortgage payment and the owner's return divided by the square footage.
    d. the management fee and mortgage payment divided by the square footage.

14. Office leases are usually
    a. short term.
    b. long term.
    c. month-to-month.

15. An "Einstein" building would be
    a. Level One.
    b. Level Two.
    c. Level Three.
    d. Level Four.

ADDITIONAL READING AND REFERENCES

Alexander, Alan, and Richard Muhlebach, *Managing and Leasing Commercial Properties*, John Wiley & Sons, Colorado Springs, CO, 1990.

Beard, Bodick, and Cher Zucker, *Forms for Office Building Management and Operations Manual Guidance*, Institute of Real Estate Management, Chicago, IL, 1985.

BOMA, *The Changing Office Workplace*, Washington, DC, 1990.

BOMA, *Experience Exchange Report*, Washington, DC, 1983.

BOMA, *Leasing Concepts: A Guide to Leasing Office Space*, Washington, DC, 1983.

Buildings (Monthly), Stamats Communications, Inc., 427 Sixth Street, S.E., Cedar Rapids, IA 52406.

Commercial Investment Journal (Quarterly), National Association of Realtors, 430 N. Michigan Avenue, Chicago, IL 60611.

Income and Expense Analysis: Office Buildings, Institute of Real Estate Management, Chicago, IL, 1996.

Institute of Real Estate Management, *Managing the Office Building*, Chicago, IL, 1981.

Skylines (Monthly), BOMI, 1250 Eye Street, N.W., Suite 200, Washington, DC 20005.

Smith, Charles, *A Guide to Commercial Management*, BOMA, Washington, DC, 1983.

Urban Land Institute, *Office Development Handbook*, Washington, DC.

Chapter 10

Condominium Management

Key terms

Association	CC&Rs	Per diem fee
Board of directors	Committee	PUD
Bylaws	Condominium	Rules and regulations
CAI	Cooperative	Townhouse

Food for thought

> "Let everyone sweep in front of his own door, and the whole world will be clean."

COMMUNITY ASSOCIATIONS

The nature of community association types of ownership and operations, whether residential or commercial, is an area of much confusion. In this chapter we will examine these issues with a concentration on residential condominiums, co-ops, and planned unit developments (PUDs). We will place special emphasis on these types of ownership as well as the special problems inherent in their management.

DEFINITION OF TERMS

Condominium   A condominium is a property in which there is separate fee ownership of individual units (by grant deed) and an assigned interest in common with all other owners in the "common elements" (e.g., lawns, parking lots, pool, etc.). The owner of the "condo" unit owns an "interest in space" within the walls of the unit. Any maintenance problems with internal fixtures, such as a broken garbage disposal, are the owner's responsibility.

The owner has a separate mortgage and tax bill, but pays a monthly association fee to cover common-area expenses. Common-area expenses may include, but are not limited to, landscape maintenance, pool repairs and maintenance, common-area utilities, management, exterior building maintenance, and so on. Insurance of the building for common-area liability is usually included in the association fee, while interior liability and contents insurance is carried separately by the owner.

Cooperative (Co-Op)   A cooperative is a stock corporation that owns the building(s) and land. The buyer is issued a share of stock and a long-term proprietary lease for the unit. For example, in a 100-unit building there would be 100 shares; therefore, each owner would have 1/100th interest.

In some cases, separate tax bills and mortgages are issued. This form of ownership has not been as desirable as that of a condo due to difficulties in financing, since the purchaser is not issued a grant deed.

Planned Unit Development (PUD)   In a planned unit development, the person owns the living unit plus the land underneath, with an undivided interest in the common areas. Typically, no units are above or below another in a PUD.

Timeshare   The owner typically buys an interest in time in a building. A fee title may or may not be involved. For example, the buyer would have the right to occupy a unit for a week each year. Timeshare ownership is associated primarily with resort property.

Townhouse   Townhouses are a type of architecture (usually two-story), not a form of ownership.

SIZE OF THE CONDO MARKET

Due to increased land costs, PUDs and condos are an attractive way for a developer to obtain the highest and best use of the land. Forecasters have predicted that by the year 2000, approximately 35 million residents will be living in 14 million units in over 225,000 community associations in the United States. The average size of a community association is 95 units.

The state of California alone has over 25,000 associations, with a median size of approximately 43 units per association, accounting for over two million units in the state.

According to a research study sponsored by the California Department of Real Estate, entitled *Common Interest Homeowner's Association Management Study* (Sacramento, CA, 1987), 44 percent of associations are self-managed (usually the smaller complexes), 16 percent have on-site management, and 40 percent have off-site management.

GOVERNMENT OF CONDOS

A condominium development is usually formed into a nonprofit corporation governed by a board of directors using articles of incorporation; covenants, conditions, and restrictions (CC&Rs); bylaws; and rules and regulations.

The homeowners association is created by the previously mentioned documents and is responsible for the operation of the community. The community's board of directors establishes and enforces rules and regulations, fees, collection procedures, budgets, and an overall management policy for the community.

The homeowners elect members to the board of directors in much the same manner as a city elects its city council. The number can vary depending on the articles of incorporation, but five to seven is most typical. The property manager is selected by and reports to the board of directors.

The board usually elects its own officers, which typically include a president, vice president, secretary, and treasurer.

Government of the Board

The rights and duties of the board of directors and homeowners are set forth in the following documents:

1. *Articles of incorporation*—establish the corporation.

2. *Bylaws*—provide procedures for the operation of the corporation; for example, election procedures.

3. *CC&Rs*—covenants, conditions, and restrictions; provide land-use and deed restrictions.

4. *Grant deeds*—a mechanisms that convey ownership interest.

5. *Rules and regulations*—everyday rules to guide the conduct of owners and/or their tenants; i.e., pool hours, parking, pets, etc.

Election of Officers

The association bylaws normally set forth the notice period for an election meeting and mandate that the date, time, place, and general nature of the business to be discussed be included in the notice. Most state laws mandate notices not less than 10 days nor more than 90 days before the date of a meeting at which members are permitted to take action such as elections. A written notice must be sent by first class mail. Nomination procedures should include

1. A reasonable means of nominating persons.

2. Reasonable opportunities for nominees to communicate to members.

3. Reasonable opportunities for all nominees to solicit votes.

4. A reasonable opportunity for all members to choose among the nominees.

The bylaws usually provide for a nominating committee to select candidates and also for the acceptance of written nominations and nominations from the floor. If a proxy is used, it should not be confused with a mail-in ballot, which is not permitted by law. The proxy giver vests the proxy holder with the power to vote at the meeting in a predetermined manner. The election ballots should not be issued until the meeting date. All members who register at the meeting should be given a ballot for themselves and proxies. Most bylaws allow for cumulative voting. For example, if a member owns one unit and five directors are to be elected, the member has one vote for each director, or a total of five votes. The member may then accumulate those votes, casting them all for any one director or some for one and some for another. The bylaws also set forth the way a quorum is determined. For example, a set of bylaws might state that 50 percent of the homeowners must cast ballots. If a quorum is not attained, 25 percent would constitute a quorum in a second election.

FISCAL REPORTING

The property manager is usually responsible for supplying the board of directors with the financial statements and an annual budget, in which the income, expenses, and reserves for the following year are projected (see Figure 10–1). Financial reports to the homeowners must also be sent, usually on a yearly basis (see Figure 10–2). Actual income and expenses are compared with the projected budget; the differences are called variances. A negative variance in income would be bad, and a variance in expenses over budget would be undesirable. If dealing with several large condo associations, computerization is essential to streamline bookkeeping and reduce costs for the property manager. Individual median annual expenses for condominiums can be found in Figure 10–3.

An association must, in some states, prepare a financial statement and distribute it to its members no less than 45 and no more than 60 days prior to the beginning of the association's fiscal year. The budget should include

1. An estimate of revenue and expenses on an accrual basis.

2. An identification of total cash reserves set aside.

3. An identification of estimated remaining life and method of funding to defray future repairs.

4. A general statement addressing the procedure for establishing and calculating reserves.

5. A statement describing association lien rights or other remedies of default.

	BUDGET/MO	BUDGET/UNIT 256	BUDGET/YR
400 Monthly Dues	35,990	N/A	431,880
401 Interest	450	1.76	5,400
405 Delinquency Fees	100	0.39	1,200
410 Other Income	200	0.78	2,400
415 Laundry	1,300	5.08	15,600
TOTAL INCOME		38,040 148.59	456,480
500 Landscape-Basic	2,000	7.81	24,000
501 Sprinkler Repairs	150	0.59	1,800
505 Landscape-Extra	100	0.39	1,200
510 Pool-Basic	330	1.29	3,960
515 Pool-Extra	300	1.17	3,600
516 Pest Control-Basic	225	0.88	2,700
517 Pest Control-Termites	75	0.29	900
520 Common Area Repairs	775	3.03	9,300
523 Salaries-Cash	1,500	5.86	18,000
525 Street Sweeping	275	1.07	3,300
526 Plumbing Repairs	1,200	4.69	14,400
527 Sewer Service	100	0.39	1,200
530 Common Area Supplies	400	1.56	4,800
545 Roof Maintenance	75	0.29	900
546 Security Expense	2,200	8.59	26,400
547 Security Gate Repair	150	0.59	1,800
TOTAL MAINTENANCE		9,855 38.50	118,260
550 * Gas	4,860	18.98	58,320
550 Gas (Common)	1,215	4.75	
555 Electric	1,850	7.23	22,200
560 * Water	1,480	5.78	17,760
560 Water (Common)	370	1.45	
565 Trash	1,900	7.42	22,800
570 Telephone	50	0.20	600
TOTAL UTILITIES		11,725 45.80	140,700
600 Management Fee	1,400	5.47	16,800
610 Accounting	175	0.68	2,100
620 Taxes & Permits	50	0.20	600
630 Printing & Postage	375	1.46	4,500
640 Bad Debts		0.00	0
645 Legal & Collection	600	2.34	7,200
646 * Insurance (Property)	4,141	16.18	49,692
646 Insurance (Liability)	1,784		
TOTAL ADMINISTRATIVE		8,525 33.30	102,300
RESERVES			
705 Air Conditioners	15	0.06	180
706 * Water Heaters	325	1.27	3,900
707 Decking	975	3.81	11,700
710 * Painting	1,415	5.53	16,980
715 * Roofing	1,625	6.35	19,500
720 Driveways	325	1.27	3,900

** PAGE 1 **

Figure 10–1.   Condo Budget

(Continued)

724 Carpet	30	0.12	360
725 Recreation Facil. (Pool)	780	3.05	9,360
726 Furnishings	50	0.20	600
728 Playground Equipment	65	0.25	780
730 Fences	325	1.27	3,900
731 Iron Fences	25	0.10	300
732 Security Gates	45	0.18	540
745 Other (Contingency)	585	2.29	7,020
761 Irrigation System	65	0.25	780
765 Tree Trimming	540	2.11	6,480
775 Lighting	745	2.91	8,940
TOTAL RESERVE ALLOCATION	7,935	31.00	95,220
TOTAL COSTS	38,040	148.59	456,480
NET INCOME	0	0.00	0

ASSESSMENT BREAKDOWN

Total Prorated Expenses	13,846 (Designated with an " * ")
Flat Expense	24,194
less Other Income	2,050
Total Equal Share	22,144
TOTAL	35,990

UNITS	RATIO	PRORATED AMOUNT	FLAT RATE AMOUNT	LAST YEAR ASSESSMENT	NEW ASSESSMENT
12	0.00290	40.15	86.50	107.79	126.65
32	0.00356	49.29	86.50	114.46	135.79
44	0.00357	49.43	86.50	114.74	135.93
44	0.00382	52.89	86.50	117.34	139.39
32	0.00385	53.31	86.50	117.66	139.81
80	0.00427	59.12	86.50	122.06	145.62
6	0.00509	70.48	86.50	130.78	156.98
6	0.00513	71.03	86.50	131.24	157.53

256

Figure 10-1. Continued

6. A review of the quarterly reconciliations of reserves, operating accounts, and bank statements.

7. A statement comparing actual reserve account revenue against budget reserves.

8. The names of the two board members (at least) whose signatures are required to withdraw reserve funds.

An accountant or CPA is usually hired to assist the property manager in financial reporting.

	CURRENT MONTH ACTUAL	CURRENT MONTH BUDGET	CURRENT MONTH VARIANCE*	YEAR-TO-DATE ACTUAL	YEAR-TO-DATE BUDGET	YEAR-TO-DATE VARIANCE*	ANNUAL BUDGET	ANNUAL VARIANCE*
INCOME								
OPERATING INCOME								
4110 ASSESSMENT INCOME	4,341.18	3,851.50	489.68	7,905.08	7,703.00	202.08	46,218.00	(38,312.92)
4122 INTEREST INCOME	193.94	226.50	(32.56)	406.47	453.00	(46.53)	2,718.00	(2,311.53)
TOTAL OPERATING INCOME	4,535.12	4,078.00	457.12	8,311.55	8,156.00	155.55	48,936.00	(40,624.45)
TOTAL INCOME	4,535.12	4,078.00	457.12	8,311.55	8,156.00	155.55	48,936.00	(40,624.45)
OPERATING EXPENSES								
G & A EXPENSE								
6205 GROUNDS UPKEEP		50.00	50.00		100.00	100.00	600.00	600.00
6212 PAINTING		41.67	41.67		83.34	83.34	500.04	500.04
6213 PLUMBING		25.00	25.00		50.00	50.00	300.00	300.00
6217 HEATING/COOLING	187.26	135.00	(52.26)	187.26	270.00	82.74	1,620.00	1,432.74
6220 ROOFING		83.33	83.33		166.66	166.66	999.96	999.96
6221 TAXES		50.00	50.00		100.00	100.00	600.00	600.00
6222 MISCELLANEOUS REPAIRS	136.41	83.33	(53.08)	1,242.64	166.66	(1,075.98)	999.96	(242.68)
6224 WATER		108.33	108.33	220.37	216.66	(3.71)	1,299.96	1,079.59
6225 GAS	25.94	25.00	(0.94)	48.23	50.00	1.77	300.00	251.77
6226 ELECTRIC	386.66	433.33	46.67	718.24	866.66	148.42	5,199.96	4,481.72
6230 LANDSCAPE MAINTENANCE	503.00	375.00	(128.00)	2,060.00	750.00	(1,310.00)	4,500.00	2,440.00
6233 RUBBISH COLLECTION		91.67	91.67	78.40	183.34	104.94	1,100.04	1,021.64
6246 TELEPHONE		16.67	16.67		33.34	33.34	200.04	200.04
6249 SECURITY SERVICE	150.00	65.00	(85.00)	225.00	130.00	(95.00)	780.00	555.00
6250 ACCOUNTING		108.33	108.33		216.66	216.66	1,299.96	1,299.96
6255 SIDEWALK CLEANING		100.00	100.00		200.00	200.00	1,200.00	1,200.00
6272 MANAGEMENT FEE	500.00	500.00		1,000.00	1,000.00		6,000.00	5,000.00
6273 MISCELLANEOUS	260.00	83.33	(176.67)	251.77	166.66	(85.11)	999.96	748.19
6290 INSURANCE		250.00	250.00		500.00	500.00	3,000.00	3,000.00
6296 JANITORIAL SUPPLIES		12.50	12.50		25.00	25.00	150.00	150.00
6305 JANITORIAL	450.00	333.33	(116.67)	1,350.00	666.66	(683.34)	3,999.96	2,649.96
6325 ELEVATOR MAINT	197.07	191.67	(4.60)	374.14	383.34	9.20	2,300.04	1,925.90
6345 ANSWERING SERVICE	53.51	75.00	21.49	138.46	150.00	11.54	900.00	761.54
6350 FIRE EXTINGUISHERS		8.33	8.33		16.66	16.66	99.96	99.96
6375 CARPET REPAIRS		41.67	41.67		83.34	83.34	500.04	500.04
6905 WINDOW WASHING		41.67	41.67		83.34	83.34	500.04	500.04
TOTAL G & A EXPENSE	2,839.35	3,329.16	489.31	7,894.51	6,658.32	(1,236.19)	39,949.92	32,055.41
RESERVE ALLOCATIONS								
6256 CONTINGENCY RESERVE	70.83	76.00	5.17	141.66	152.00	10.34	912.00	770.34
6274 PAINTING RESERVE	172.00	100.00	(72.00)	344.00	200.00	(144.00)	1,200.00	856.00
6275 ROOF RESERVE	285.00	100.00	(185.00)	570.00	200.00	(370.00)	1,200.00	630.00
6383 PARKING AREA & ROAD RES	86.25	86.00	(0.25)	172.50	172.00	(0.50)	1,032.00	859.50
6384 BUILDING MAINTENANCE RE	154.00	100.00	(54.00)	308.00	200.00	(108.00)	1,200.00	892.00
6680 ELEVATOR RESERVE	45.00	45.00		90.00	90.00		540.00	450.00
TOTAL RESERVE ALLOCATIONS	813.08	507.00	(306.08)	1,626.16	1,014.00	(612.16)	6,084.00	4,457.84
TOTAL OPERATING EXPENSES	3,652.93	3,836.16	183.23	9,520.67	7,672.32	(1,848.35)	46,033.92	36,513.25
NET PROFIT OR LOSS	882.19	241.84	640.35	(1,209.12)	483.68	(1,692.80)	2,902.08	(4,111.20)

Figure 10–2. Condo Profit and Loss Statement

Assessment Increases

In addition to any limitations placed on the board by the governing documents, state-mandated maximum increase in dues, such as 20 percent may exist in some states. The property manager should be familiar with the laws of his or her state in order to assist the board.

Collection

The property manager is usually responsible for collecting dues, banking, and sending late notices. The bank account is normally in the name of the associ-

Median Annual Expenses—Condominiums Low Rise

Expenses	Projects	Units	Med	Low	High
				Dollars per Unit	
				--------$--------	
Administrative Exp.			Med	Low	High
Office Salaries	1	115	16.60	16.60	16.60
Office Expense	57	6,760	19.88	13.65	28.58
Management Fee	58	6,875	139.96	130.00	157.38
Legal Fees	55	6,587	14.15	6.68	37.00
Audit Fees	32	4,177	9.73	7.50	14.93
Professional Fees	14	1,401	10.37	2.81	14.35
Other	51	5,867	12.12	3.11	20.59
Subtotal Administ.	58	6,875	211.33	175.13	274.29
Operating Expenses					
Elevator	3	315	38.46	21.50	38.46
Heating Fuel	3	305	75.27	12.83	75.27
Electricity	58	6,875	86.99	64.90	147.12
Water/Sewer	57	6,855	364.05	269.42	450.02
Natural Gas	30	3,856	117.70	96.82	181.93
Exterminating	52	6,104	16.47	7.66	24.01
Rubbish Removal	57	6,855	56.48	44.83	72.09
Window Washing					
Miscellaneous	39	4,496	109.88	97.43	122.59
Subtotal Operating	58	6,875	689.78	559.69	808.34
Repair and Maint.					
Security	39	5,056	55.90	25.98	138.35
Snow Removal					
Ground Maintenance	56	6,497	191.18	139.28	243.07
Custodial	44	5,418	72.51	20.25	131.73
General Maintenance	57	6,839	102.24	61.54	200.24
Heat/AC/Vent	23	2,619	26.97	10.39	53.90
Paint—Int Ca Only	27	2,926	18.92	6.04	22.50
Paint—Exterior	26	2,867	99.09	46.42	142.16
Recreational	56	6,819	36.67	25.58	56.86
Garage & Parking	43	5,318	23.36	6.44	45.77
Subtotal Rep/Maint.	58	6,875	577.19	418.27	817.91
Fixed Expenses					
Real Estate Tax	1	27	440.56	440.56	440.56
Other Tax	41	4,848	13.50	3.13	32.63
Insurance	54	6,500	161.15	97.82	226.91
Subtotal Fixed Exp.	57	6,760	177.85	109.04	242.34
Total All Expenses	58	6,875	1584.77	1328.25	2140.46
Ground Rent	2	144	1576.94	6.48	1576.94
Replacement Reserve	45	5,245	408.50	191.60	623.25
Amenities					
Pool	55	6,735	32.91	24.81	47.53
Rec Building	12	2,058	2.81	.41	3.47
Outdoor Rec Facility	4	948	.67	.08	.67
Other	22	2,750	6.95	2.86	9.93

Published annually by the Institute of Real Estate Management, 430 N. Michigan, Chicago, IL 60611.

Figure 10–3. Median Annual Expenses—Condos
© Institute of Real Estate Management,
430 N. Michigan, Chicago, IL 60611.

ation. Reserves are usually put into interest-bearing savings accounts. Each member of the board of directors is given an accounting of the cash balances in the different accounts, usually on a monthly basis.

In some states, associations are subject to the "one action rule" which requires the holder of the lien to first foreclose the lien and prohibit filing personal action against the delinquent owner until the lien rights were exhausted. Other states allow the association to sue for personal money judgments. If the owner has little equity in a unit, this might be an advisable course of action.

Late Charges

When homeowners do not pay dues in a timely manner, state law may allow for a late charge such as $10 or 10 percent whichever is greater, after 15 days. Property managers should consult an attorney to verify state law.

Paying the Bills

The property manager usually solicits bids for work to be done and gains approval from the board of directors for large amounts (typically $500 and over, except for routine monthly bills such as utilities). The bills are coded according to a chart of accounts, and amounts are checked for accuracy and further certified against the purchase order. The checks are then drawn up by the property manager and given to the designated board member(s) to sign. It is customary to have the books of the association audited at least annually and to have the tax return prepared by an accountant. See Figure 10–3, the Institute of Real Estate Management's median annual expense sample chart for Houston, Texas. *Income and Expense Analysis: Condominiums*, published annually, is available through the Institute.

Insurance

The property manager is usually responsible for obtaining bids and making recommendations on insurance coverage to the board of directors. A prudent property manager will enlist the assistance of a competent insurance broker to ensure proper coverage and also comply with coverage requirements set forth in the bylaws and CC&Rs. We will cover insurance in more depth in Chapter 13, but the following coverages are usually recommended:

1. Fire insurance

2. General liability

3. Workers' compensation on employees

4. Fidelity bond to protect from embezzlement

5. Directors' and officers' liability (D&O coverage) to protect the board of directors if they become personally liable due to an "act, error, or omission in their performance."

Liability of the Association

A condominium owner's unit was burglarized. The owner requested the association to install better lighting, but the board of directors refused. The owner then installed her own lighting, but the association removed it as a violation of the CC&Rs. The owner, after removal of the lights, was sexually assaulted and subsequently sued the association for failure to prevent (with better lighting) the crime that caused her injury.

The state court in California ruled that when an association is aware of hazards or potential injury and fails to take reasonable steps to prevent them, the association, like a landlord, is liable. This liability ruling is probably applicable in most other states.

ROLE OF THE PROPERTY MANAGER

Even though a community association is a nonprofit entity, it is big business. A 300-unit complex with association fees of $100 per month would have an annual income of $360,000. The elected members of the board of directors usually hold nonpaying positions, and the operation of management is complex, time consuming, and requires expertise and training. This is where the property management team comes into play, with its computerized systems and procedures to professionally run the business. In many instances, condos are purchased as an investment and the owners live off site, renting the units to tenants. The ratio of tenants to owners has surpassed 50 percent in some complexes, leading to problems between on-site owners and tenants.

Resident Relations

Resident relations are more difficult in community association management since each "tenant" is also usually an owner. In a 300-unit complex, the property manager may feel there are 300 bosses rather than just the board of directors. The property manager should be familiar with the CC&Rs, bylaws, and rules and regulations, as well as the management agreement, so that decisions made are within the scope and guidelines of the property manager's authority. Newsletters prepared by the association and published on a regular basis are a good way to transmit official notices and rule changes, as well as to promote a feeling of togetherness and camaraderie.

The leading sources of problems, according to a Department of Real Estate study (Common Interest Homeowners Association Management Study, 1987, Sacramento, CA), were "parking violations, followed by late payments, pet violations, rules for common areas, unauthorized changes in dwellings, and noise and disorderly conduct."

Maintenance and Security

The property manager is responsible for supervising maintenance of the common areas (e.g., landscaping, parking lot repairs, exterior painting, etc.) to preserve and enhance the value of the complex. The budget and priorities of maintenance must be decided by the board of directors, but the property manager is responsible for implementation. The property manager should avoid showing favoritism among the homeowners.

Proper outside lighting and security precautions also must be considered to protect the homeowners and prevent undue liability exposure to the association.

Association Meetings

Many associations hold regular monthly meetings of the board of directors which are open to homeowners. The property manager usually prepares the agendas and provides income and expense reports, delinquency reports, bank balances, and so on. The property manager also usually sets up and coordinates elections of the members of the board of directors.

Committees

Most associations have several committees such as finance, social, architectural, rules, ground, nominating, and so forth, which report back to the board of directors with their recommendations. The property manager will oftentimes coordinate and help facilitate these efforts (see Figure 10–4).

Employees

Someone must hire, fire, supervise, and train employees for office work, housekeeping, maintenance, and so on. They must be paid at least minimum wage and have deductions such as income tax and Social Security withheld from their pay. In many instances this is the responsibility of the property manager.

Rentals

Theoretically, rentals do not exist in a condo complex since the owners are residents. In actuality, however, almost half of some complexes are rented. Rules, regulations, and procedures governing such rentals must be established. In

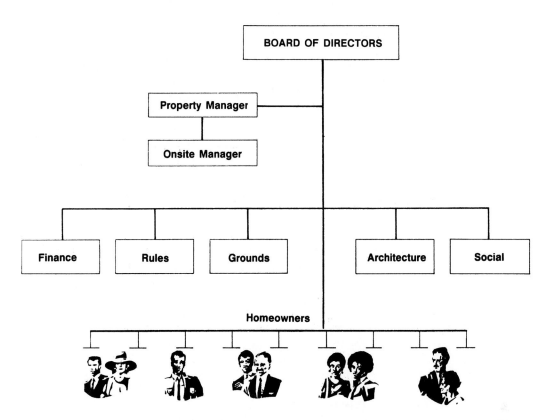

Figure 10–4. Organizational Chart

some instances, for an additional fee, the property manager will handle rentals to ensure the quality of the tenants. The association can suggest credit and qualifying criteria so long as such criteria are not discriminatory.

Restriction of Children

The Federal Amendments Act of 1988 (Fair Housing) prohibits rules and regulations restricting children unless the rules are reasonable and other facilities are available. Some associations may qualify as "senior complexes" and would be exempt from these regulations.

The Management Contract

The property manager should have a signed management agreement, although this is not required by law if the term is less than one year. The agreement should spell out the term in years, fees, and duties of management. Duties should be detailed as specifically as possible. A hold-harmless clause covering both parties is essential. Additionally, a spending limit should be established for the property manager. Extra charges to the association should be stated, such as copying, postage, transfer fees, and so forth. Additional meetings the property manager is required to attend, other than regular monthly meetings, are often charged to the association at an hourly rate or a flat charge per meeting. By explicitly stating the authority and responsibilities of the property manager, the management agreement (Figure 10–5) should eliminate future misunderstandings.

MANAGEMENT FEE STRUCTURE

Traditionally, the fee structure has been low and is usually based on a cost per door (unit); for example, $10 per unit times 100 units equals $1,000 per month. Management companies thus need to handle several thousand units (a high volume) in order to make a profit.

The management company should disclose all interests it may have in vendors, such as landscaping, plumbing, and so on, in writing. Nondisclosure would be considered "secret profit." The management company may in some cases act strictly as a bookkeeping operation or a paid consultant, with the association being self-managed. This is especially true for associations under 100 units.

CHOOSING THE MANAGEMENT COMPANY

Maintaining clients is difficult for condo management companies, as boards of directors frequently change and new directors want to make their own selections. Choosing the property manager is also a difficult task for the association, as this facet of the management industry is still relatively new. The background, reputation, and references of the property manager should be checked. Does the firm employ CPMs or PCAMs? Does the firm belong to the Community Association Institute (CAI)? What accounts does it presently manage? How do the firm's present clients rate the firm? Does the management firm have a real estate license? Does the firms specialize in condo management?

Additional Information

Additional information may be obtained through the following organizations:

Institute of Real Estate Management (IREM)
430 N. Michigan Avenue
Chicago, IL 60611
(312) 661-1930

Community Associations Institute (CAI)
1630 Duke Street, 3rd floor
Alexandria, VA 22314
(703) 548-8600

EDUCATION Reports

The Community Associations Institution (CAI) published a series of monographs called GAP (Guide for Association Practitioners) Reports. Professionals and homeowner experts throughout the country are authors of these comprehensive and detailed guidebooks. The GAP Reports provide needed information for persons involved in the community association industry, including association managers, property managers, lenders, homeowners, association board members, and so on. Some selected topics of the available GAP Reports include:

GAP #1—Association Management

GAP #2—Architectural Control

GAP #3—Transition from Developer's Control

GAP #4—Insurance

GAP #5—Association Collections; Legal Remedies

GAP #6—Property Tax and HOAs

GAP #7—Drafting Association Rules

GAP #8—Choosing a Management Company

GAP #9—Bid Specification & Contract Negotiations

GAP #10—Assessment Collection; Creating a System

JD PROPERTY
MANAGEMENT
INCORPORATED

3520 Cadillac Avenue / Suite B
Costa Mesa, California / 92626
714 751-2787 / Fax 714 751-0126

THIS AGREEMENT, made and entered into this _____ day of _____, 19 ,
by and between the Board of Directors (hereafter called "The Board") of the   ,
and JD PROPERTY MANAGEMENT, INC. (hereafter called "The Agent").

1.0   THE BOARD employs The AGENT exclusively to manage the condominium for a period of
_____ years, beginning to time, unless on or before (30) thirty days prior to the expiration of any such
renewal period, either party shall notify the other in writing that it elects to terminate this agreement, in which case this
agreement shall be terminated at the end of that period.

2.0   THE AGENT shall perform the following services in the name of and on behalf of the BOARD, and the
BOARD hereby gives the AGENT the authority and powers required to perform these services:

2.1   The AGENT shall collect all monthly dues, due to the BOARD for operation of the Condominium. Any late
fees collected shall remain in possession of the AGENT as its fee.

2.2   The AGENT shall maintain records showing all its receipts and expenditures relating to the Condominium and
shall promptly submit to the BOARD a cash receipts and disbursements statement for the preceding month and a
statement indicating the balance or deficit in the AGENT'S account for the Condominium.

2.3   Subject to the direction and at the expense of the BOARD, the AGENT shall cause the common elements of the
Condominium to be maintained according to appropriate standards of maintenance consistent with the character of the
Condominium, including:

_____

_____

_____

_____

2.4   Subject to the direction of the BOARD, the AGENT shall negotiate and execute on behalf of the BOARD
contracts for water, electricity, gas, telephone, and such other services for the common elements of the Condominium as
may be necessary or advisable. The AGENT also shall purchase on behalf of the BOARD such equipment, tools,
appliances, materials, and supplies as are necessary for the proper operation and maintenance of the condominium. All
such purchases and contracts shall be in the name and at the terms of this agreement or pursuant to other authority
granted by the BOARD.

2.5   The AGENT shall pay from the funds of the BOARD all taxes, building and elevator inspection fees, water
rates and other governmental charges, and all other charges or obligations incurred by the BOARD with respect to the
maintenance or operation of the Condominium or incurred by the AGENT on behalf of the BOARD pursuant to the
terms of this agreement or pursuant to other authority granted by the BOARD.

Figure 10–5.   Condo Management Agreement

(Continued)

2.6   The AGENT shall maintain appropriate records of all insurance coverage carried by the BOARD. The AGENT shall cooperate with the BOARD in investigating and reporting all accidents or claims for damage relating to the ownership, operation, and maintenance of the common elements of the Condominium including any damage or destruction to them.

3.0   In discharging its responsibilities under paragraph 2 of this agreement, the AGENT shall not make any expenditures nor incur any nonrecurring contractual obligation exceeding $_____ without the prior consent of the BOARD, provided that no such consent shall be required to repay any advances made by the AGENT under the terms of paragraph 5. Notwithstanding these limitations, the AGENT may, on behalf of the BOARD without prior consent, expend any amount or incur a contractual obligation in any amount required to deal with emergency conditions which may involve a danger of life or property or may threaten the safety of the Condominium or the OWNERS and occupants or may threaten the suspension of any necessary service to the Condominium.

4.0   All monies collected by the AGENT on behalf of the BOARD shall be deposited in a custodial account in a state or national bank where deposits are insured by the Federal Deposit Insurance Corporation separate and apart from AGENT'S own funds.

4.1   All expenses of operation and management may be paid from the BOARD'S funds held by the AGENT, and the AGENT is authorized to pay any amounts owed to the AGENT by the BOARD from such account at any time without prior notice to the BOARD. The AGENT shall have no obligation to advance funds to the BOARD for any purpose whatsoever.

4.2   All AGENT'S employees who handle or are responsible for the safekeeping of any monies of the BOARD shall be covered by a fidelity bond protecting the BOARD, such bond to be in an amount and with a company determined by the AGENT.

5.0   The BOARD shall pay the AGENT a management fee equal to $ 425.00 per month. The management fee shall be paid monthly in advance. Any clerical services performed for the BOARD, such as preparation and circulation of notices and newsletters and general correspondence of the BOARD, shall be at the expense of the BOARD. This includes all xeroxing, postage, and stationery expense.

6.0   One of the AGENT'S employee's shall be designated Site Manager for the Condominium. The Site Manager or other representative of the AGENT shall attend ALL regular meetings (not to exceed six meetings per year, additional meetings will be billed singularly at a rate of $75.00 per hour to the BOARD). The Site Manager shall be custodian of the official record of the BOARD and the condominium association but shall not be required to record the minutes of meetings.

7.0   The BOARD shall designate a single individual who shall be authorized to deal with the AGENT on any matter relating to the management of the Condominium. The AGENT is directed not to accept directions or instructions with regard to the management of the Condominium from anyone else. In the absence of any other designation by the BOARD, the President of the BOARD shall have this authority.

7.1   The AGENT is authorized to charge $300.00 for any transfer of ownership, through the respective escrow, for providing all the necessary documents and information.

8.0   The AGENT shall have no authority to make any structural changes in the Condominium or to make any other major alterations or additions in or to any building or equipment therein, except such emergency repairs as may be required because of danger to life or property or which are immediately necessary for the preservation and safety of the Condominium or safety of the OWNERS and occupants or are required to avoid the suspension of any necessary service to the Condominium.

Figure 10–5.   Continued

8.2   The AGENT has no responsibility for the compliance of the Condominium or any of its equipment with the requirements of any ordinances, laws, rules, or regulations (including those relating to the disposal of solid, liquid, and gaseous wastes) of the City, County, State, or Federal Government, or any public authority or official thereof having jurisdiction over it, except any complaints, warnings, notices, or summonses received by it relating to such matters. The OWNERS represent that to the best of their knowledge the condominium complies with all such requirements, and authorize the AGENT to disclose the ownership of the Condominium to any such officials, and agree to indemnify and hold harmless the AGENT, its representatives, servants, and employees, of and from all loss, cost expense, and liability whatsoever which may be imposed on them or any of them by reason of any present or future violation or alleged violation of such laws, ordinances, rules, or regulations.

9.0   The BOARD shall:

9.1   Indemnify, defend, and save the AGENT harmless from all suits in connection with the Condominium and from liability for damage to property and injuries to or death of any employee or other person whomsoever, and carry at its own expense public liability, boiler, elevator liability (if elevators are part of the equipment of the Condominium), and workers compensation insurance naming the BOARD and the AGENT and adequate to protect their interests and in form, substance, and amounts reasonably satisfactory to the AGENT, and furnish to the AGENT certificates evidencing the existence of such insurance and furnish such certificates within (30) thirty days from the date of this agreement, the Agent may, but shall not be obligated to, place said insurance and charge the cost thereof to the account of the BOARD. The AGENT shall also be named as additionally insured on all Board insurance policies.

9.2   Pay all expenses incurred by the AGENT including, without limitation, attorneys' fees for counsel to represent the AGENT or the BOARD in any proceeding or suit involving an alleged violation by the AGENT or the BOARD, or both, of any governmental body pertaining to environmental protection, fair housing, or fair employment including, without limitation, race, creed, color, religion, or national origin in the sale, rental, or other disposition of housing or any services rendered in connection therewith or in connection with employment practices (unless, in either, the AGENT is finally adjudicated to have personally and not in a representative capacity violated such constitutional provision, statue, ordinance, law, or regulation), but nothing herein contained shall require the AGENT to employ counsel to represent the BOARD in any such proceeding or suit.

9.3   Indemnify, defend, and save the AGENT harmless from all claims, investigations, and suits with respect to any alleged or actual violation of state or federal labor laws. The BOARD'S obligation under this paragraph 9.3 shall include the payment of all settlements, judgments, damages, liquidated damages, penalties, forfeitures, back pay awards, court costs, litigation expense, and attorneys' fees.

10.0   This agreement shall be binding upon and inure to the benefit of the successors and assigns of the AGENT and heirs, administrators,, successors, and assigns of the BOARD. Notwithstanding the preceding sentence the AGENT shall not assign its interest under this agreement except in connection with the sale of all or substantially all the assets of its business; in the event of such a sale, AGENT shall be released from all liability hereunder upon the express assumption of such liability by its assignee.

11.0   Schedule Of Fees

11.1   The following items will be billed singularly in addition to the base monthly fee:

11.2   Postage, Printing and Xerox Copies $ 1.50 per unit

11.4   Long Distance Telephone Calls - Net plus 25%

11.5   Collection of delinquent dues - no charge, but late charge to belong to J.D. Property Management for collection fees.

11.6   Management service such as bids, contract supervision, maintenance, etc.

Figure 10–5. Continued

12.0   Schedule Of Rates

12.1   Certified Property Manager $100.00 per hour

12.2   Property Manager $ 75.00 per hour

12.3   Extra Accounting $ 50.00 per hour

The parties have affixed or caused to be affixed their respective signature this_____day of_____19____

BOARD   AGENT

_____   _____

_____   Firm_____

_____   By_____

POWER OF ATTORNEY

KNOWN ALL MEN BY THESE PRESENT, THAT _____

_____

LOCATED AT_____

has made, constituted and appointed, and, by these present does hereby make, constitute and appoint J.D. Property Management, Inc. a resident of the United States, whose address 3520 Cadillac Ave., Suite B Costa Mesa, CA 92626 is true and lawful attorney to collect assessments, deposit funds and execute checks for the homeowners association.

Dated at_____this_____day of_____19___.

Signature of the Board Members:

President_____

Vice-President_____

Secretary/Treasurer_____

Figure 10–5.   Continued

Programs   The following programs are available through the Community Associations Institute:

1. *PCAM (Professional Community Association Manager)* is a designation for managers of condominiums, cooperatives, or homeowners associations who are interested in career growth. This *program* honors association managers who demonstrate an advanced degree of skill and knowledge.

2. *The Operations and Management Program* offers intensive coursework on the complexities of association operation and management. This program is for board members, developers, and managers who want to have a solid understanding of responsibility, liability, and authority.

3. *The Professional Management Development Program* is a comprehensive educational program with over 100 hours of instruction. Courses included in the program are the legal basis of community associations, communications and meetings, operations, asset protection, and management practices.

MARKETING CONDOS

The property manager may have an opportunity to sell individual condo units. The sale of individual condos is similar to that of single-family homes. In many states, the agent must have an agency form completed and signed (Figure 10–6). Agency forms are required on sales of four or fewer residential units and in some states on all properties. Even though commercial properties are exempt, it may be prudent to use these forms on all transactions to reduce the liability risk.

Unique marketing conditions in the sale of a condo include:

1. Posting For Sale signs in compliance with the CC&Rs.

2. Holding open houses and showing the condo in security-gated complexes where access is limited.

3. In the sale of a new condo, a document (approved by the Department of Real Estate) must be given to the buyer stating the proposed dues and budget.

4. Copies of the bylaws, CC&Rs, current budget, and reserve study must be given to buyers prior to close.

5. A statement from the management company as to dues and any assessments owed and change of ownership paperwork. A charge of $50 to $100 is usually made by the management company for supplying this information.

CONDO MANAGEMENT PROBLEMS

Office and industrial buildings may also be condo associations. The individual units are either owner/user-occupied or the unit owner may lease out the unit. A major difference between such associations and residential associations is that, if rented, the lessee usually pays a triple net lease. Also, usually no statutory limit exists on the increase percentage for commercial association dues.

Denise Arant, a former condo association board president, described nine problem types of condo owners.

1. *Veteran*—knows everything and wants to go back to the old ways.

2. *Cheapskate*—wants to hoard association funds and not maintain the complex.

3. *Time burner*—places no value on time and wants to drag out meetings and get 100 bids on every project.

REAL ESTATE AGENCY CONFIRMATION FORM

SUBJECT PROPERTY:

Street Address _____ City _____ State _____ Zip _____

The following agency relationship(s) is/are hereby disclosed and confirmed for this transaction:

LISTING AGENT:

is the agent of (check one):

☐ the Landlord exclusively; or
☐ both the Tenant and Landlord

SELLING AGENT:

(if not the same as Listing Agent)

is the agent of (check one):

☐ the Tenant exclusively; or
☐ the Landlord exclusively; or
☐ both the Tenant and Landlord

I/WE ACKNOWLEDGE RECEIPT OF A COPY OF THIS CONFIRMATION.

Seller/Landlord _____ Date _____ Buyer/Tenant _____ Date _____

Seller/Landlord _____ Date _____ Buyer/Tenant _____ Date _____

Listing Agent _____ By _____ Date _____
(Please Print) (Signature)

Selling Agent _____ By _____ Date _____
(Please Print) (Signature)

Figure 10–6. Agency Confirmation Form

4. *Dictator*—wants rules for everything; for example, no bicycles, no lit cigarettes on grounds, etc.

5. *Slob*—wants special permission to store washing machines and old furniture on balcony.

6. *Blamer*—accuses other residents of worse infractions.

7. *Party animal*—plays loud music at 4 A.M. and is offended when people complain.

8. *Variance freak*—wants to add extra room, windows, doors, etc.

9. *Bushwacker*—confronts board members with "earth-shattering" issues such as burnt-out light bulbs, dog poop on lawn, etc.

BUDGETING

A budget is a financial plan to accomplish the goals and maintain the standards of the association. The board of directors estimates future income and expenses, usually with the assistance of the property managers (see Figure 10–7). Different types of budgets exist, such as an annual operating budget. In order to keep the association on course, actual expenditures are compared to the budget on a regular basis. This is called variance analysis and it will be either favorable or unfavorable. The property manager then adds up the variances to see how the total compares (also see Company Budget in Chapter 13).

Examples of Variances

- Our budgeted dues are $10,000 per month and collections were $10,200. This is a favorable variance of $200 or 2 percent.

- Repairs were budgeted at $5,000 and only $4,500 was spent. This is a favorable variance of $500 or 10 percent of our expenses.

- If landscaping was budgeted at $500 and the association spent $600, this is an unfavorable variance of $100 or 20 percent.

Variance Analysis

Dues collections	+ $200
Repairs	+ $500
Landscaping	– $100
	+ $600 Total favorable variance

Accounting Methods

Two main accounting methods exist for reporting income and expenses.

1. *Cash basis*—Revenues (dues) are declared in the month collected and expenses are declared in the month paid. This is the easiest method but can lead to some distortions on the monthly statement. For example, if the insurance premium is paid once a year, the expenses in the month paid (January) would be artificially higher. If delinquent dues are collected, it would increase the income level for that month.

2. *Accrual basis*—Revenues (dues) are declared in the accounting period for which they are earned and not the month paid. For example, if laundry income was paid quarterly, it would be prorated to a monthly basis. The insurance premium bill would be divided by 12 months and spread over the year rather than having the entire bill appear in January.

Summary by Metropolitan Area
Expenses Reported as Median Dollars per Unit

High Rise	No. of Units	Admin. Exp.	Oper. Exp.	Repair & Mnt.	Fixed Exp.	Total Exp.	Replac. Resrv.
Atlanta, GA	247	221.70	774.93	561.88	129.35	1667.67	305.26
Baltimore, MD	898	447.45	986.70	2147.80	211.47	3912.88	243.78
Boston, MA	3,661	491.63	1277.50	1422.26	185.94	3396.48	423.47
Chicago, IL	6,253	402.47	943.91	1525.09	125.97	2640.02	671.78
Cincinnati, OH	321	397.27	1297.22	3863.80	236.11	6151.14	480.00
Cleveland, OH	1,201	236.58	1072.30	1348.66	101.73	3234.89	268.86
Denver, CO	444	626.06	1331.52	1056.23	176.16	3138.01	772.35
Honolulu, HI	7,662	536.36	1108.92	558.09	295.74	2462.28	470.03
Lexington, KY	195	261.33	696.90	933.56	225.12	2410.15	220.18
Los Angeles, CA	1,037	396.62	837.52	751.26	316.08	2300.17	290.34
Memphis, TN	309	272.73	824.00	851.03	223.10	2073.86	226.45
Myrtle Beach, SC	3,415	268.43	944.54	954.28	498.69	2626.68	258.75
New Jersey Southern	464	783.46	1392.83	1412.65	721.14	3458.28	480.76
New Orleans, LA	250	643.39	1132.28	1692.64	417.86	3675.20	337.04
New York City, NY	1,085	573.01	1614.99	2034.22	511.56	4210.03	
Orlando, FL	587	215.75	558.67	411.92	86.83	1257.54	303.38
Philadelphia, PA	1,283	557.10	1199.18	1898.36	256.05	3695.71	720.49
Pittsburgh, PA	744	455.02	1274.96	1779.75	312.18	4066.00	425.55
Washington, DC	1,192	498.26	933.10	772.44	151.76	2408.09	368.47
Worcester, MA	242	435.39	620.47	899.11	207.01	2528.89	248.00
Low Rise							
Albuquerque, NM	524	326.41	575.80	247.00	182.66	1331.87	164.84
Anchorage, AK	232	232.94	620.42	618.55	265.18	1712.72	341.79
Atlanta, GA	123	247.75	571.15	594.88	138.06	1419.23	250.00
Austin, TX	623	209.87	543.00	483.78	111.89	1460.36	142.86
Baltimore, MD	1,509	163.65	117.59	501.43	84.26	875.64	214.29
Boston, MA	1,533	230.67	893.98	595.00	168.02	1989.03	133.33
Charlotte, NC	766	149.46	127.27	567.83	285.97	1162.54	143.50
Chicago, IL	463	187.86	676.60	568.71	200.40	1520.65	285.71
Cincinnati, OH	238	134.07	212.75	421.95	82.25	997.88	239.17
Columbus, OH	401	188.85	275.90	606.53	56.19	1052.10	290.25
Dallas, TX	2,501	207.86	443.32	527.15	151.98	1308.83	143.36
Denver, CO	1,122	319.17	385.77	477.34	114.25	1270.86	232.71
Detroit, MI	711	263.40	533.61	1458.84	142.00	2387.57	124.21
El Paso, TX	428	266.74	495.88	750.76	180.69	1693.61	70.00
Fayetteville, NC	256	143.58	481.25	550.98	194.40	1114.74	284.44
Fresno, CA	680	219.29	389.05	520.95	97.31	1217.29	398.69
Ft. Worth, TX	1,251	336.44	461.80	342.98	163.55	1446.72	146.34
Gainesville, FL	454	197.11	328.85	389.06	50.53	909.44	231.49
Hagerstown, MD	1,179	261.81	501.50	520.42	97.11	1340.50	204.24
Honolulu, HI	982	518.62	680.25	334.40	258.59	1954.66	427.90
Houston, TX	6,875	211.33	689.78	577.19	177.85	1584.77	408.50
Las Vegas, NV	260	130.78	341.53	629.08	99.34	1162.56	296.88
Little Rock, AR	200	131.21	265.75	374.58	144.52	925.63	
Los Angeles, CA	4,378	265.31	658.15	574.68	266.83	1806.60	360.00

Figure 10–7. Expenses by Unit
© Institute of Real Estate Management,
430 N. Michigan, Chicago, IL 60611.

Low Rise	No. of Units	Admin. Exp.	Oper. Exp.	Repair & Mnt.	Fixed Exp.	Total Exp.	Replac. Resrv.
Milwaukee, WI	1,111	158.26	307.21	570.73	100.42	1175.92	142.40
Minneapolis–Saint Paul, MN	218	172.50	572.50	411.75	157.75	1298.21	315.00
Myrtle Beach, SC	1,004	216.08	699.50	607.28	449.53	1556.15	256.51
New Jersey Northern	2,456	259.55	286.86	709.92	119.70	1255.24	229.94
New Jersey Southern	371	263.18	629.93	643.75	146.29	1836.49	260.61
Orange County, CA	1,348	191.25	393.61	428.74	177.07	1268.19	305.91
Orlando, FL	5,195	167.00	318.24	451.00	77.82	1054.64	208.22
Pensacola, FL	375	134.33	160.05	402.94	85.24	790.24	282.08
Philadelphia, PA	568	278.96	545.29	948.37	268.45	1805.65	45.57
Phoenix, AZ	573	190.55	553.61	578.81	84.51	1467.59	255.17
Pittsburgh, PA	478	385.33	1244.41	1402.92	141.04	3519.23	307.69
San Antonio, TX	358	194.98	429.60	679.50	125.00	1500.15	150.00
San Bernardino, CA	404	189.75	278.40	635.05	188.44	1395.70	339.73
San Diego, CA	826	334.06	698.06	556.12	223.38	1934.29	256.26
San Francisco, CA	710	301.26	635.62	857.83	244.57	1923.58	654.60
San Jose, CA	1,703	245.98	516.36	565.64	228.06	1494.92	478.05
St. Louis, MO	282	149.71	294.14	282.60	111.99	1041.20	235.13
Tampa–St. Peter., FL	281	169.74	582.36	506.93	81.37	1533.77	102.86
Tucson, AZ	390	95.67	388.86	360.45	94.50	900.47	110.03
Washington, DC	1,418	327.40	953.92	740.24	119.03	2263.15	699.47
Wichita, KS	189	206.94	299.40	760.77	169.50	1426.28	427.71
Townhouse							
Atlanta, GA	721	185.54	431.20	476.40	118.74	1404.97	202.11
Baltimore, MD	888	147.01	89.39	309.98	87.88	575.60	156.84
Boston, MA	1,278	282.95	217.86	904.87	198.32	1798.64	342.95
Cincinnati, OH	1,350	174.82	434.56	848.58	109.92	1585.93	360.00
Cleveland, OH	297	187.38	143.94	579.36	74.19	852.88	382.87
Columbus, OH	2,314	154.21	287.83	489.23	72.95	919.22	170.45
Dallas, TX	424	151.12	174.03	310.37	15.43	993.37	
Denver, CO	294	166.25	451.67	354.74	119.00	1082.54	366.04
Detroit, MI	2,411	224.96	381.60	752.14	132.00	1439.10	282.93
Fayetteville, NC	316	129.00	186.05	476.90	126.74	795.38	121.24
Harrisburg, PA	171	99.62	22.07	919.95	135.78	1199.86	300.62
Honolulu, HI	1,239	446.15	795.39	815.95	392.40	2469.69	351.88
Houston, TX	1,518	163.32	548.32	490.92	20.22	1466.50	284.13
Las Vegas, NV	399	124.00	318.74	277.67	102.71	915.79	188.68
Lexington, KY	191	170.13	112.87	548.78	49.08	992.73	378.19
Little Rock, AR	451	201.03	288.67	715.06	177.79	1395.31	130.66
Los Angeles, CA	10,771	205.39	416.92	447.84	194.86	1341.06	410.12
Louisville, KY	439	144.69	305.81	365.94	111.25	857.48	208.33
Madison, WI	366	188.53	127.88	292.86	95.38	805.09	
Memphis, TN	115	178.43	267.83	678.77	203.29	1201.45	466.66
Milwaukee, WI	336	183.13	295.06	904.25	129.17	1450.44	125.00
Minneapolis–Saint Paul, MN	369	215.70	147.68	719.36	132.08	1183.10	314.54
Myrtle Beach, SC	375	166.11	103.92	321.04	14.35	605.42	77.78
Nashville, TN	1,125	134.01	401.69	620.84	116.00	1177.71	318.46
New Jersey Northern	2,489	302.11	255.00	870.44	167.41	1768.14	326.27

Figure 10–7. Continued

(Continued)

Townhouse	No. of Units	Admin. Exp.	Oper. Exp.	Repair & Mnt.	Fixed Exp.	Total Exp.	Replac. Resrv.
Omaha, NE	419	121.35	165.40	1125.79	174.69	1709.65	
Orange County, CA	1,927	174.29	349.80	481.84	159.10	1222.50	406.34
Orlando, FL	2,866	89.87	123.43	314.00	18.71	716.27	120.00
Oxnard–Ventura, CA	901	181.56	278.98	551.52	229.31	1399.50	508.00
Pensacola, FL	169	123.96	142.17	371.33	25.48	648.64	52.79
Phoenix, AZ	1,666	135.90	432.49	371.90	39.87	996.50	220.69
Portland, OR	229	201.18	456.73	474.41	69.95	1112.86	173.84
San Diego, CA	777	215.03	537.79	626.47	168.72	1434.17	325.69
Tampa–St. Peter, FL	450	221.04	596.48	749.71	93.18	1549.54	610.96
Toronto, ON	638	347.07	412.87	568.82	74.57	1362.16	260.05
Tucson, AZ	192	96.94	392.04	276.23	94.25	958.18	139.80
Wichita, KS	194	225.04	141.67	548.22	99.00	980.33	383.40

Published annually by the Institute of Real Estate Management, 430 N. Michigan Ave., Chicago, IL 60611.

Figure 10–7. Continued

Reserve Studies

The board of directors needs to anticipate and plan for future capital replacements such as roofs, paving, painting, fencing, and so on. In order to accomplish this, replacement reserves should be set aside over a number of years during the useful life of the component. The board of directors should have a reserve study prepared by the management company or an outside consultant to establish life spans, remaining useful life, and costs of replacement. Some states require certain reserve levels and mandate that studies be done periodically. Usually the time period is 10–20 years. The study determines the amount of money from association dues to be set aside each month for replacement reserves. Included in the calculation of funds should be the inflation rate, the interest rate of funds held, and taxes on earned interest. Many associations assume that the inflation and interest rates cancel each other out to simplify the calculation (see Figure 10–8).

Example of Reserve Assessment

A new roof will be needed in five years at a cost of $100,000 and there are 100 condo units.

100,000 cost ÷ 5 years = 20,000 per year reserve

20,000 ÷ 12 months = $1,667 per month (rounded off)

1,667 ÷ 100 units = $16.67 per unit per month is roof reserve set aside

SUMMARY

Condominiums are defined as separate fee ownership of an individual unit and an assigned interest in the common areas with other owners. In a cooperative, on the other hand, a stock corporation owns the building and the land, and the buyer is issued a share of stock and a long-term proprietary lease

Base assessment	$ 140.00 2/28/96	$ 168.00 96/97	$ 201.60 97/98	$ 241.92 98/99	$ 290.30 99/00	$ 348.36 00/01	$ 418.04 01/02	$ 501.65 02/03	$ 601.97 03/04	$ 722.37 04/05	$ 866.84 05/06
Beginning reserve cash	$15,000.00	$11,693.76	$ 4,408.34	$ 7,776.42	$23,427.71	$ 6,792.42	$ 710.04	$ 763.55	$37,958.02	$28,671.64	$20,987.83
Monthly assessment—20% increase	—	8,736.00	10,483.20	12,579.84	15,095.81	18,114.97	21,737.96	28,085.56	—	—	—
Special assessment—Board assessed	—	4,132.80	4,959.35	5,951.23	7,141.48	6,569.77	10,283.73	12,340.47	—	—	—
Special assessment—member assessed	—	20,500.00	—	—	—	—	84,050.00	—	—	—	—
	—	33,368.80	15,442.56	18,531.07	22,237.29	26,684.74	116,071.89	38,428.03	—	—	—
Anticipated reserve expenditures:	1	2	3	4	5	6	7	8	9	10	11
Composition rolled roof	—	—	—	—	—	—	36,982.76	—	—	—	—
Wood shake roof	—	—	—	—	—	—	45,085.15	—	—	—	—
Painting—wood trim	—	5,866.46	—	—	—	—	—	—	—	—	—
Painting—woodwork exterior	—	8,426.49	—	—	—	—	—	—	—	—	—
Painting—wrought iron	2,584.14	—	—	—	—	—	—	—	—	—	—
Painting—stucco	—	7,861.27	—	—	—	—	—	—	—	—	—
Painting—interior	—	—	—	—	—	3,754.56	—	—	—	—	—
Driveway—slurry seal	—	—	4,188.49	—	—	—	—	—	—	—	—
Driveway—repairs	—	—	1,084.93	—	—	—	—	—	—	—	—
Driveway—overlay	—	—	—	—	—	—	23,849.77	—	—	—	—
Fencing—wrought iron	—	—	—	—	—	22,702.62	—	—	—	—	—
Fencing—wood fence	—	—	—	—	20,764.43	—	—	—	—	—	—
Fencing—trash gates	—	—	—	—	—	—	885.06	—	—	—	—
Fencing—block walls	—	—	—	—	—	—	—	—	—	1,878.86	—
Fencing—slumpstone	—	—	—	—	—	—	—	—	—	4,635.58	—
Lighting—exterior	—	—	—	—	—	—	—	—	2,454.53	—	—
Lighting—interior	—	—	—	—	—	—	—	—	834.86	—	—
Pool—replaster	—	—	—	—	5,186.80	—	—	—	—	—	—
Pool—heater	—	—	1,767.52	—	—	—	—	—	—	—	—
Pool—filter	—	—	—	—	1,176.21	—	—	—	—	—	—
Spa—replaster	—	—	1,617.55	—	—	—	—	—	—	—	—
Spa—heater	—	—	1,285.47	—	—	—	—	—	—	—	—
Spa—filter	722.10	—	—	—	—	—	—	1,231.57	—	—	—
Pool—deck caulking	—	—	—	—	738.76	—	—	—	—	—	—
Pool—expansion joint caulking	—	—	—	—	1,956.53	—	—	—	—	—	—
Sauna—wood replacement	—	—	—	—	—	—	5,636.14	—	—	—	—
Clubhouse—ceramic shower	—	—	—	—	—	1,178.85	—	—	—	—	—
Clubhouse—doors	—	—	—	—	—	—	—	—	1,805.35	—	—
Clubhouse—plumbing fixtures	—	—	—	—	—	—	—	—	—	1,169.37	—
Clubhouse—vinyl tile	—	—	—	—	—	5,131.09	—	—	—	—	—
Clubhouse—water heater	—	—	—	—	654.09	—	—	—	—	—	—
Entry system—enterphone	—	—	—	1,846.02	—	—	—	—	—	—	—
Entry system—card readers	—	—	—	799.94	—	—	—	—	—	—	—
Entry system—gate operators	—	—	—	—	6,827.78	—	—	—	—	—	—
Directory board—replacement	—	—	—	235.82	—	—	—	—	—	—	—
Directory board—replacement	—	—	—	—	—	—	—	—	—	—	963.72
Landscape—controller	—	18,500.00	—	—	—	—	—	—	—	—	—
Termite control—fumigation	—	—	2,128.52	—	—	—	—	—	—	—	—
Mailboxes—replacement	—	—	—	—	—	—	1,450.50	—	—	—	—
Miscellaneous—fire extinguishers	—	—	—	—	1,567.98	—	—	—	—	—	—
Miscellaneous—wood railings	—	—	—	—	—	—	—	—	4,191.64	—	—
Miscellaneous—hallway carpets	—	—	—	—	—	—	2,128.80	—	—	—	—
Total anticipated expenditures	3,306.24	40,654.22	12,072.48	2,881.78	38,872.58	32,767.12	116,018.18	1,231.57	9,286.38	7,683.81	963.72
Projected ending cash balance	$11,893.76	$ 4,408.34	$ 7,778.42	$23,427.71	$ 6,792.42	$ 710.04	$ 763.55	$37,958.02	$28,671.64	$20,987.83	$20,024.11

Figure 10–8. Reserve Study

203

on a unit. A townhouse is often confused with a condominium, but in actuality is a type of architecture (usually two stories). Condominium associations are governed by boards of directors based on articles of incorporation, CC&Rs, bylaws, and rules and regulations. The board of directors is elected by the homeowners, usually at annual elections, and the most common number of board members is five. The board usually meets once a month.

The property manager is responsible for preparing the fiscal reports and budgets for the board of directors. Collection of dues, payments of bills, and vendor selection are also usually assigned duties of the property manager. Other duties include resident relations, maintenance and security, and supervision of employees. The most frequent problems in condominium associations involve parking violations, late payments, pet violations, common-area rule violations, and unauthorized changes in the dwellings. The association usually has several committees, which may include finance, social, rules, architectural, and nominating.

Fees for condominium management have traditionally been low and unprofitable for many management firms. Prices are usually quoted per door or per unit; for example, $6 per unit for a 200-unit complex equals a $1,200 management fee. Reasons for the low fees include high and frequent turnover of boards of directors and the fact that, in many states, a real estate license is not required to manage condominiums, which eliminates the need for trust accounts and other consumer protection procedures required by the Department of Real Estate in other forms of management. This lack of control has led to missing and unaccounted-for funds in some associations. The Institute of Real Estate Management (IREM) and the Community Associations Institute (CAI) have designations, educational programs, and books available to help better educate the property manager in condominium management.

Condominium management is a large and specialized market which is very competitive since no license and little money are required to become established. It is, however, a service-intensive industry requiring that the property manager have not only excellent financial reporting skills, but also a thorough knowledge of maintenance and public relations.

PERSONALITY PROFILE

The management of condos is a unique management specialty that requires special training and specific courses. In a 200-unit condo association, you potentially have 200 bosses although in reality the manager deals with and takes direction from the board of directors. The board is constantly changing so the property manager is constantly re-educating and training new board members. Marge Blaine, CPM and Stanford University graduate, is a successful property manager who has specialized in condo management. She is an instructor for the Institute of Real Estate Management (IREM) condo seminar, a professional community association manager (PCAM), and a member of the CAI national faculty for over 10 years. Marge is also a member of the California Community Association (CCAM) and a member of their faculty.

Marge relayed a couple of interesting personal experiences she had at condo board meetings. One time, while she and the board quickly left a board meeting and went into an "executive session" elsewhere, whether or not it was legal, a disgruntled owner came into the meeting room menacingly bearing a shotgun. Another time, Marge shared, during an annual meeting, a drunk homeowner who was angry with the developer threw a large, mud-clotted weed at his representative with a snarl, "there's your wonderful landscaping." Clearly these examples confirm how unique condo management can be and the benefit of special training.

1. In a condominium, the owner gets
   a. a life estate.
   b. a grant deed.
   c. stock ownership.
   d. a rental agreement.

2. In a cooperative, the owner gets
   a. a life estate.
   b. a grant deed.
   c. stock ownership.
   d. a rental agreement.

3. In a PUD, the person owns
   a. the living unit plus the land underneath.
   b. nothing, but has a common interest.
   c. his or her unit only.
   d. the land only.

4. Timeshare complexes are usually found in
   a. rural areas.
   b. urban areas.
   c. resort areas.
   d. depressed areas.

5. The board of directors is
   a. elected by the homeowners.
   b. appointed by the Department of Real Estate (DRE).
   c. elected by the city.
   d. elected by the county.

6. Condominiums are usually
   a. profit corporations.
   b. nonprofit corporations.
   c. limited partnerships.
   d. general partnerships.

7. Accounting and cash balance statements are usually given to the board of directors
   a. on an annual basis.
   b. when requested.
   c. only when required by law.
   d. on a monthly basis.

8. Insurance provided by the homeowners association covers
   a. the inside of individual units.
   b. pools only.
   c. all common areas.
   d. liability inside the units.

9. The property manager usually reports directly to
   a. each individual homeowner.
   b. the board of directors.
   c. The Department of Real Estate.
   d. The city council.

10. If the association pays a fee of $9 per door per month, what would be the monthly management fee for 200 units?
    a. $900
    b. $1,800
    c. $18,000
    d. $2,000

11. Approximately how many condo associations are forecasted in the United States by the year 2000?
    a. 80,000
    b. 120,000
    c. 150,000
    d. 200,000

12. What document governs the procedures to run the condo corporation?
    a. articles of incorporation
    b. bylaws
    c. CC&Rs
    d. rules and regulations

13. What document governs deed restrictions?
    a. articles of incorporation
    b. bylaws
    c. CC&Rs
    d. rules and regulations

14. What document governs the pool house?
   a. articles of incorporation
   b. bylaws
   c. CC&Rs
   d. rules and regulations

15. The authority and responsibility of the property manager is contained in the
   a. bylaws.
   b. CC&Rs.
   c. management agreement.
   d. charter.

ADDITIONAL READING AND REFERENCES

Condominium Management Agreement, Institute of Real Estate Management, Chicago, IL.

Giese, Lester J., and Robert W. Kuehn, *Model Business Policies for Community Associations*, Condominium Management Maintenance Corporation, Clinton, NJ.

Holeman, Jack, *Condominium Management*, Prentice-Hall, Englewood Cliffs, NJ, 1980.

Hyatt, Wayne, and Phillip Downer, *Condominium and Homeowners Association Litigation*, John Wiley & Sons, Somerset, NJ, 1987.

Income/Expense Analysis: Condominiums and Cooperatives, Institute of Real Estate Management, Chicago, IL, 1996.

McKenzie, Evan, *Privatopia: An Objective Look at Community Association Living*, Yale University Press, New Haven, CT, 1993.

The Owner's and Manager's Guide to Condominium Management, Institute of Real Estate Management, Chicago, IL, 1984.

Reserve Study Guidelines for Homeowners Association Budgets, California Department of Real Estate, Sacramento, CA., 1990.

Wade, J., *Condominiums: The Professional's Complete Manual and Guide*, Prentice-Hall, Englewood Cliffs, NJ, 1983.

Chapter 11

Other Types of Management

Key terms

EIR   Multitenant   Retirement community
"Keenager"   Parking requirements   Sale/leaseback
Key money   R&D building   SSSA
Medical building   Rating   Subdivision laws
Mobile home park

Food for thought

"If you don't have the time to do things right—When will you have the time to do them over?"

INTRODUCTION

Professional property management encompasses a wide and diversified classification of properties. In this chapter we will discuss management as it relates to some of these, such as industrial, research and development, mobile home parks, mini-storage facilities, medical buildings, retirement communities, and motel and resort rentals.

Each of these specialized areas embodies unique characteristics and customs, many of which can be learned only through years of experience. For example, a successful property manager may be adept at managing shopping centers and yet have little experience in the management of mini-storage facilities.

INDUSTRIAL BUILDING CHARACTERISTICS

In previous chapters we discussed the trend of the U.S. economy away from manufacturing and toward more service-oriented industries. Even though industrial property includes all land and facilities used for heavy and light manufacturing, today's emphasis is related to the storage and distribution of goods. Throughout history, most industrial buildings have been owned and managed by the occupant manufacturer who endeavored to locate close to the source of raw materials. (A good example of this is the steel industry in the Pennsylvania/Ohio area.)

As the trend away from the production of goods and toward that of services became more apparent, the size of industrial buildings changed. Newer facilities became single-story as opposed to multistoried. Locations were found closer to freeways and employee sources rather than to raw materials. Modern building layouts became more streamlined, and automated handling of goods by forklift and pallet became common practice. Many of the new buildings were conveniently located in industrial parks rather than on single-entity sites.

Types of Buildings

1. *Single-tenant*. These buildings have increased in size and are usually leased on a long-term basis, with 5–10 percent of the space devoted to office functions.

2. *Multi-tenant*. These are usually older multistory buildings located in urban areas, such as in the garment industry area. A smaller portion of the space is devoted to office activities.

3. *Industrial parks*. These are often located in the suburbs and include several tenants. They are frequently small (Ma and Pa) incubator startup users with short leases and usually experience a high business failure rate. The office space most often encompasses 10 percent of the total area.

Parking Requirements

Unlike office buildings where employees come and go at peak periods (7:30–9:30 A.M. and 3:30–5:30 P.M.), traffic flow for industrial buildings can be diversified utilizing two or three shifts. Using several shifts requires less machinery, space, and capital outlay per employee. This is especially true as manufacturers become more automated. Spacing work shifts means less traffic congestion and more lenient parking requirements than are necessary for office buildings and shopping centers.

Typical Parking Requirements

Building Type	No. of Spaces per 1,000 s.f.
Industrial	3
Office	4
Medical building	6
Restaurant	10
Financial (banks)	5
Retail store	4
Furniture store	2

Location

Industrial buildings are usually located near sources of transportation. In the past, water and rail were the major transportation methods, but today, modern highways and airports are emerging as the key elements.

Industry Categories

There are six basic categories of industry.

1. *Market-oriented*—finished products are sold directly to consumers; for example, food, beverages, electronics, and printing. Locations tend to be close to population centers to reduce transportation costs and perishability for some food products.

2. *Raw materials and resource-oriented*—companies that fall into this category need to be close to sources of raw materials to reduce transportation costs; for instance, aluminum, steel, and grain elevators.

3. *Transportation-oriented*—companies in which freight, storage, and inventory costs are a major influence. Examples would be oil refineries (near a seaport) or high-tech computer parts producers (near an airport).

4. *Labor intensity-oriented*—where labor rates and productivity are dominant factors. This can range from furniture assembly requiring cheap, unskilled labor to high-tech computer assembly requiring highly skilled technicians.

5. *Energy-oriented*—companies that use large amounts of fuel such as electricity and coal tend to be located near their sources to reduce costs. Due to environmental concerns and constraints, energy and raw-material-oriented companies have been leaving California for other states with fewer restrictions.

6. *Nondescript-oriented*—these are companies that do not fall into the other five categories. Transportation, labor costs, or raw materials are not dominant and these companies can locate in most areas. Such companies are sometimes lured by tax incentives to certain communities.

In the United States, most industries must be "clean" and not cause pollution or environmental problems. This prevents new, large manufacturing operations such as steel mills or auto plants from establishing in many areas. A detailed analysis of locational industry is covered starting on page 41 of the book, *Industrial Real Estate*, published by the Society of Industrial Realtors (4th Edition), Washington, D.C., 1984.

Management

Once industrial space is leased, it is one of the easiest types to manage and, as a result, management fees are usually lower than for other types of property. Most expenses are paid directly by the tenant or billed back as common-area maintenance (CAM) charges to the tenant. Also, leases are generally long term.

Types of Leases

1. *Gross lease.* A lease in which the tenant pays one flat rental amount. This type of lease is typical of older buildings in urban areas. These leases may have annual cost-of-living adjustments or increased cost "pass-throughs." The term is usually for several years with possible options due to the high expense of moving machinery. (See Figure 11–1, Standard Industrial Gross Lease.)

2. *Net lease or triple net lease.* This is the most common type of lease. The tenant pays a base rent as well as a separate amount based on taxes, insurance, and maintenance. These leases almost always include cost-of-living increases. Like gross leases, they are usually given for long periods of time (see Figure 11–1).

3. *Sale/leaseback.* This is a new concept that allows the manufacturer to sell a building to an investor, thus freeing up the manufacturer's capital for use in the business. It benefits both parties as it gives the investor a tax shelter (depreciation), and a guaranteed income stream (lease) while the manufacturer has additional funds for operations.

RESEARCH AND DEVELOPMENT (R&D) BUILDING CHARACTERISTICS

R&D buildings are an offshoot of industrial buildings and are considered a rapidly growing area in both development and property management.

1. *Location.* These buildings are often located near major highways, educational centers (universities), and in suburban areas.

2. *Employment.* They usually employ highly skilled and educated individuals.

3. *Building layout.* They are usually two stories in height, with 50 percent or more of the area devoted to office space and/or laboratories.

STANDARD INDUSTRIAL/COMMERCIAL MULTI-TENANT LEASE—GROSS
AMERICAN INDUSTRIAL REAL ESTATE ASSOCIATION

1. **Basic Provisions ("Basic Provisions").**

    1.1   **Parties:** This Lease (**"Lease"**), dated for reference purposes only, _____, 19 _____, is made by and between_____(**"Lessor"**) and _____(**"Lessee"**), (collectively the **"Parties,"** or individually a **"Party"**).

    1.2(a)   **Premises:** That certain portion of the Building, including all improvements therein or to be provided by Lessor under the terms of this Lease, commonly known by the street address of _____, located in the City of _____, County of _____, State of _____, with zip code _____, as outlined on Exhibit ____ attached hereto (**"Premises"**). The **"Building"** is that certain building containing the Premises and generally described as (describe briefly the nature of the Building):_____
_____.

In addition to Lessee's rights to use and occupy the Premises as hereinafter specified, Lessee shall have non-exclusive rights to the Common Areas (as defined in Paragraph 2.7 below) as hereinafter specified, but shall not have any rights to the roof, exterior walls or utility raceways of the Building or to any other buildings in the Industrial Center. The Premises, the Building, the Common Areas, the land upon which they are located, along with all other buildings and improvements thereon, are herein collectively referred to as the **"Industrial Center."** (Also see Paragraph 2.)

    1.2(b)   **Parking:** _____ unreserved vehicle parking spaces (**"Unreserved Parking Spaces"**); and _____ reserved vehicle parking spaces (**"Reserved Parking Spaces"**). (Also see Paragraph 2.6.)

    1.3   **Term:** _____ years and _____ months (**"Original Term"**) commencing_____ (**"Commencement Date"**) and ending _____ (**"Expiration Date"**). (Also see Paragraph 3.)

    1.4   **Early Possession:** _____(**"Early Possession Date"**). (Also see Paragraphs 3.2 and 3.3.)

    1.5   **Base Rent:** $_____ per month (**"Base Rent"**), payable on the_____ day of each month commencing _____ (Also see Paragraph 4.)

[   ]   If this box is checked, this Lease provides for the Base Rent to be adjusted per Addendum _____, attached hereto.

    1.6(a)   **Base Rent Paid Upon Execution:** $_____ as Base Rent for the period _____.

    1.6(b)   **Lessee's Share of Common Area Operating Expenses:** _____ percent (%) (**"Lessee's Share"**) as determined by [ ] prorata square footage of the Premises as compared to the total square footage of the Building or [   ] other criteria as described in Addendum _____.

    1.7   **Security Deposit:** $_____ (**"Security Deposit"**). (Also see Paragraph 5.)

    1.8   **Permitted Use:** _____
_____ (**"Permitted Use"**) (Also see Paragraph 6.)

    1.9   **Insuring Party.** Lessor is the **"Insuring Party."** (Also see Paragraph 8.)

    1.10(a) **Real Estate Brokers.** The following real estate broker(s) (collectively, the **"Brokers"**) and brokerage relationships exist in this transaction and are consented to by the Parties (check applicable boxes):

[ ] _____ represents Lessor exclusively (**"Lessor's Broker"**);

[ ] _____ represents Lessee exclusively (**"Lessee's Broker"**); or

[ ] _____ represents both Lessor and Lessee (**"Dual Agency"**). (Also see Paragraph 15.)

    1.10(b) **Payment to Brokers.** Upon the execution of this Lease by both Parties, Lessor shall pay to said Broker(s) jointly, or in such separate shares as they may mutually designate in writing, a fee as set forth in a separate written agreement between Lessor and said Broker(s) (or in the event there is no separate written agreement between Lessor and said Broker(s), the sum of $_____) for brokerage services rendered by said Broker(s) in connection with this transaction.

    1.11   **Guarantor.** The obligations of the Lessee under this Lease are to be guaranteed by_____
_____
(**"Guarantor"**). (Also see Paragraph 37.)

    1.12   **Addenda and Exhibits.** Attached hereto is an Addendum or Addenda consisting of Paragraphs _____ through _____, and Exhibits _____ through _____, all of which constitute a part of this Lease.

2. **Premises, Parking and Common Areas.**

    2.1   **Letting.** Lessor hereby leases to Lessee, and Lessee hereby leases from Lessor, the Premises, for the term, at the rental, and upon all of the terms, covenants and conditions set forth in this Lease. Unless otherwise provided herein, any statement of square footage set forth in this Lease, or that may have been used in calculating rental and/or Common Area Operating Expenses, is an approximation which Lessor and Lessee agree is reasonable and the rental and Lessee's Share (as defined in Paragraph 1.6(b)) based thereon is not subject to revision whether or not the actual square footage is more or less.

    2.2   **Condition.** Lessor shall deliver the Premises to Lessee clean and free of debris on the Commencement Date and warrants to Lessee that the existing plumbing, electrical systems, fire sprinkler system, lighting, air conditioning and heating systems and loading doors, if any, in the Premises, other than those constructed by Lessee, shall be in good operating condition on the Commencement Date. If a non-compliance with said warranty exists as of the Commencement Date, Lessor shall, except as otherwise provided in this Lease, promptly after receipt of written notice from Lessee setting forth with specificity the nature and extent of such non-compliance, rectify same at Lessor's expense. If Lessee does not give Lessor written notice of a non-compliance with this warranty within thirty (30) days after the Commencement Date, correction of that non-compliance shall be the obligation of Lessee at Lessee's sole cost and expense.

    2.3   **Compliance with Covenants, Restrictions and Building Code.** Lessor warrants that any improvements (other than those constructed by Lessee or at Lessee's direction) on or in the Premises which have been constructed or installed by Lessor or with Lessor's consent or at Lessor's direction shall comply with all applicable covenants or restrictions of record and applicable building codes, regulations and ordinances in effect on the Commencement Date. Lessor further warrants to Lessee that Lessor has no knowledge of any claim having been made by any governmental agency that a violation or violations of applicable building codes, regulations, or ordinances exist with regard to the Premises as of the Commencement Date. Said warranties shall not apply to any Alterations or Utility Installations (defined in Paragraph 7.3(a)) made or to be made by Lessee. If the Premises do not comply with said warranties, Lessor shall, except as otherwise provided in this Lease, promptly after receipt of written notice from Lessee given within six (6) months following the Commencement Date and setting forth with specificity the nature and extent of such non-compliance, take such action, at Lessor's expense, as may be reasonable or appropriate to rectify the non-compliance. Lessor makes no warranty that the Permitted Use in Paragraph 1.8 is permitted for the Premises under Applicable Laws (as defined in Paragraph 2.4).

    2.4   **Acceptance of Premises.** Lessee hereby acknowledges: (a) that it has been advised by the Broker(s) to satisfy itself with respect to the condition of the Premises (including but not limited to the electrical and fire sprinkler systems, security, environmental aspects, seismic and earthquake requirements, and compliance with the Americans with Disabilities Act and applicable zoning, municipal, county, state and federal laws, ordinances and regulations and any covenants or restrictions of record (collectively, **"Applicable Laws"**) and the present and future suitability of the Premises for Lessee's intended use; (b) that Lessee has made such investigation as it deems necessary with reference to such matters, is satisfied with reference thereto, and assumes all responsibility therefore as the same relate to Lessee's occupancy of the Premises and/or the terms of this Lease; and (c) that neither Lessor, nor any of Lessor's agents, has made any oral or written representations or warranties with respect to said matters other than as set forth in this Lease.

    2.5   **Lessee as Prior Owner/Occupant.** The warranties made by Lessor in this Paragraph 2 shall be of no force or effect if immediately prior to the date set forth in Paragraph 1.1 Lessee was the owner or occupant of the Premises. In such event, Lessee shall, at Lessee's sole cost and expense, correct any non-compliance of the Premises with said warranties.

Initials: _____

_____

Figure 11–1.   Standard Industrial Lease

2.6   **Vehicle Parking.** Lessee shall be entitled to use the number of Unreserved Parking Spaces and Reserved Parking Spaces specified in Paragraph 1.2(b) on those portions of the Common Areas designated from time to time by Lessor for parking. Lessee shall not use more parking spaces than said number. Said parking spaces shall be used for parking by vehicles no larger than full-size passenger automobiles or pick-up trucks, herein called "**Permitted Size Vehicles.**" Vehicles other than Permitted Size Vehicles shall be parked and loaded or unloaded as directed by Lessor in the Rules and Regulations (as defined in Paragraph 40) issued by Lessor. (Also see Paragraph 2.9.)

(a) Lessee shall not permit or allow any vehicles that belong to or are controlled by Lessee or Lessee's employees, suppliers, shippers, customers, contractors or invitees to be loaded, unloaded, or parked in areas other than those designated by Lessor for such activities.

(b) If Lessee permits or allows any of the prohibited activities described in this Paragraph 2.6, then Lessor shall have the right, without notice, in addition to such other rights and remedies that it may have, to remove or tow away the vehicle involved and charge the cost to Lessee, which cost shall be immediately payable upon demand by Lessor.

(c) Lessor shall at the Commencement Date of this Lease, provide the parking facilities required by Applicable Law.

2.7   **Common Areas—Definition.** The term "**Common Areas**" is defined as all areas and facilities outside the Premises and within the exterior boundary line of the Industrial Center and interior utility raceways within the Premises that are provided and designated by the Lessor from time to time for the general non-exclusive use of Lessor, Lessee and other lessees of the Industrial Center and their respective employees, suppliers, shippers, customers, contractors and invitees, including parking areas, loading and unloading areas, trash areas, roadways, sidewalks, walkways, parkways, driveways and landscaped areas.

2.8   **Common Areas—Lessee's Rights.** Lessor hereby grants to Lessee, for the benefit of Lessee and its employees, suppliers, shippers, contractors, customers and invitees, during the term of this Lease, the non-exclusive right to use, in common with others entitled to such use, the Common Areas as they exist from time to time, subject to any rights, powers, and privileges reserved by Lessor under the terms hereof or under the terms of any rules and regulations or restrictions governing the use of the Industrial Center. Under no circumstances shall the right herein granted to use the Common Areas be deemed to include the right to store any property, temporarily or permanently, in the Common Areas. Any such storage shall be permitted only by the prior written consent of Lessor or Lessor's designated agent, which consent may be revoked at any time. In the event that any unauthorized storage shall occur then Lessor shall have the right, without notice, in addition to such other rights and remedies that it may have, to remove the property and charge the cost to Lessee, which cost shall be immediately payable upon demand by Lessor.

2.9   **Common Areas—Rules and Regulations.** Lessor or such other person(s) as Lessor may appoint shall have the exclusive control and management of the Common Areas and shall have the right, from time to time, to establish, modify, amend and enforce reasonable Rules and Regulations with respect thereto in accordance with Paragraph 40. Lessee agrees to abide by and conform to all such Rules and Regulations, and to cause its employees, suppliers, shippers, customers, contractors and invitees to so abide and conform. Lessor shall not be responsible to Lessee for the non-compliance with said rules and regulations by other lessees of the Industrial Center.

2.10   **Common Areas—Changes.** Lessor shall have the right, in Lessor's sole discretion, from time to time:

(a) To make changes to the Common Areas, including, without limitation, changes in the location, size, shape and number of driveways, entrances, parking spaces, parking areas, loading and unloading areas, ingress, egress, direction of traffic, landscaped areas, walkways and utility raceways;

(b) To close temporarily any of the Common Areas for maintenance purposes so long as reasonable access to the Premises remains available;

(c) To designate other land outside the boundaries of the Industrial Center to be a part of the Common Areas;

(d) To add additional buildings and improvements to the Common Areas;

(e) To use the Common Areas while engaged in making additional improvements, repairs or alterations to the Industrial Center, or any portion thereof; and

(f) To do and perform such other acts and make such other changes in, to or with respect to the Common Areas and Industrial Center as Lessor may, in the exercise of sound business judgment, deem to be appropriate.

3. Term.

3.1   **Term.** The Commencement Date, Expiration Date and Original Term of this Lease are as specified in Paragraph 1.3.

3.2   **Early Possession.** If an Early Possession Date is specified in Paragraph 1.4 and if Lessee totally or partially occupies the Premises after the Early Possession Date but prior to the Commencement Date, the obligation to pay Base Rent shall be abated for the period of such early occupancy. All other terms of this Lease, however, (including but not limited to the obligations to pay Lessee's Share of Common Area Operating Expenses and to carry the insurance required by Paragraph 8) shall be in effect during such period. Any such early possession shall not affect nor advance the Expiration Date of the Original Term.

3.3   **Delay in Possession.** If for any reason Lessor cannot deliver possession of the Premises to Lessee by the Early Possession Date, if one is specified in Paragraph 1.4, or if no Early Possession Date is specified, by the Commencement Date, Lessor shall not be subject to any liability therefor, nor shall such failure affect the validity of this Lease, or the obligations of Lessee hereunder, or extend the term hereof, but in such case, Lessee shall not, except as otherwise provided herein, be obligated to pay rent or perform any other obligation of Lessee under the terms of this Lease until Lessor delivers possession of the Premises to Lessee. If possession of the Premises is not delivered to Lessee within sixty (60) days after the Commencement Date, Lessee may, at its option, by notice in writing to Lessor within ten (10) days after the end of said sixty (60) day period, cancel this Lease, in which event the parties shall be discharged from all obligations hereunder; provided further, however, that if such written notice of Lessee is not received by Lessor within said ten (10) day period, Lessee's right to cancel this Lease hereunder shall terminate and be of no further force or effect. Except as may be otherwise provided, and regardless of when the Original Term actually commences, if possession is not tendered to Lessee when required by this Lease and Lessee does not terminate this Lease, as aforesaid, the period free of the obligation to pay Base Rent, if any, that Lessee would otherwise have enjoyed shall run from the date of delivery of possession and continue for a period equal to the period during which the Lessee would have otherwise enjoyed under the terms hereof, but minus any days of delay caused by the acts, changes or omissions of Lessee.

4. Rent.

4.1   **Base Rent.** Lessee shall pay Base Rent and other rent or charges, as the same may be adjusted from time to time, to Lessor in lawful money of the United States, without offset or deduction, on or before the day on which it is due under the terms of this Lease. Base Rent and all other rent and charges for any period during the term hereof which is for less than one full month shall be prorated based upon the actual number of days of the month involved. Payment of Base Rent and other charges shall be made to Lessor at its address stated herein or to such other persons or at such other addresses as Lessor may from time to time designate in writing to Lessee.

4.2   **Common Area Operating Expenses.** Lessee shall pay to Lessor during the term hereof, in addition to the Base Rent, Lessee's Share (as specified in Paragraph 1.6(b)) of all Common Area Operating Expenses, as hereinafter defined, during each calendar year of the term of this Lease, in accordance with the following provisions:

(a) "Common Area Operating Expenses" are defined, for purposes of this Lease, as all costs incurred by Lessor relating to the ownership and operation of the Industrial Center, including, but not limited to, the following:

(i)   The operation, repair and maintenance, in neat, clean, good order and condition, of the following:

(aa) The Common Areas, including parking areas, loading and unloading areas, trash areas, roadways, sidewalks, walkways, parkways, driveways, landscaped areas, striping, bumpers, irrigation systems, Common Area lighting facilities, fences and gates, elevators and roof.

(bb) Exterior signs and any tenant directories.

(cc) Fire detection and sprinkler systems.

(ii)   The cost of water, gas, electricity and telephone to service the Common Areas.

(iii)   Trash disposal, property management and security services and the costs of any environmental inspections.

(iv)   Reserves set aside for maintenance and repair of Common Areas.

(v)   Any increase above the Base Real Property Taxes (as defined in Paragraph 10.2(b)) for the Building and the Common Areas.

(vi)   Any "Insurance Cost Increase" (as defined in Paragraph 8.1).

(vii)   The cost of insurance carried by Lessor with respect to the Common Areas.

(viii)   Any deductible portion of an insured loss concerning the Building or the Common Areas.

(ix)   Any other services to be provided by Lessor that are stated elsewhere in this Lease to be a Common Area Operating Expense.

(b) Any Common Area Operating Expenses and Real Property Taxes that are specifically attributable to the Building or to any other building in the Industrial Center or to the operation, repair and maintenance thereof, shall be allocated entirely to the Building or to such other building. However, any Common Area Operating Expenses and Real Property Taxes that are not specifically attributable to the Building or to any other building or to the operation, repair and maintenance thereof, shall be equitably allocated by Lessor to all buildings in the Industrial Center.

(c) The inclusion of the improvements, facilities and services set forth in Subparagraph 4.2(a) shall not be deemed to impose an obligation upon Lessor to either have said improvements or facilities or to provide those services unless the Industrial Center already has the same, Lessor already provides the services, or Lessor has agreed elsewhere in this Lease to provide the same or some of them.

(d) Lessee's Share of Common Area Operating Expenses shall be payable by Lessee within ten (10) days after a reasonably detailed statement of actual expenses is presented to Lessee by Lessor. At Lessor's option, however, an amount may be estimated by Lessor from time to time of Lessee's Share of annual Common Area Operating Expenses and the same shall be payable monthly or quarterly, as Lessor shall designate, during each 12-month period of the Lease term, on the same day as the Base Rent is due hereunder. Lessor shall deliver to Lessee within sixty (60) days after the expiration of each calendar year a reasonably detailed statement showing Lessee's Share of the actual Common Area Operating Expenses incurred during the preceding year. If Lessee's payments under this Paragraph 4.2(d) during said preceding year exceed Lessee's Share as indicated on said statement, Lessor shall be credited the amount of such over-

Initials: _____

_____

—2—

Figure 11–1.   Continued

(Continued)

payment against Lessee's Share of Common Area Operating Expenses next becoming due. If Lessee's payments under this Paragraph 4.2(d) during said preceding year were less than Lessee's Share as indicated on said statement, Lessee shall pay to Lessor the amount of the deficiency within ten (10) days after delivery by Lessor to Lessee of said statement.

5. Security Deposit. Lessee shall deposit with Lessor upon Lessee's execution hereof the Security Deposit set forth in Paragraph 1.7 as security for Lessee's faithful performance of Lessee's obligations under this Lease. If Lessee fails to pay Base Rent or other rent or charges due hereunder, or otherwise Defaults under this Lease (as defined in Paragraph 13.1), Lessor may use, apply or retain all or any portion of said Security Deposit for the payment of any amount due Lessor or to reimburse or compensate Lessor for any liability, cost, expense, loss or damage (including attorneys' fees) which Lessor may suffer or incur by reason thereof. If Lessor uses or applies all or any portion of said Security Deposit, Lessee shall within ten (10) days after written request therefore deposit monies with Lessor sufficient to restore said Security Deposit to the full amount required by this Lease. Any time the Base Rent increases during the term of this Lease, Lessee shall, upon written request from Lessor, deposit additional monies with Lessor as an addition to the Security Deposit so that the total amount of the Security Deposit shall at all times bear the same proportion to the then current Base Rent as the initial Security Deposit bears to the initial Base Rent set forth in Paragraph 1.5. Lessor shall not be required to keep all or any part of the Security Deposit separate from its general accounts. Lessor shall, at the expiration or earlier termination of the term hereof and after Lessee has vacated the Premises, return to Lessee (or, at Lessor's option, to the last assignee, if any, of Lessee's interest herein), that portion of the Security Deposit not used or applied by Lessor. Unless otherwise expressly agreed in writing by Lessor, no part of the Security Deposit shall be considered to be held in trust, to bear interest or other increment for its use, or to be prepayment for any monies to be paid by Lessee under this Lease.

6. Use.

6.1 **Permitted Use.**

(a) Lessee shall use and occupy the Premises only for the Permitted Use set forth in Paragraph 1.8, or any other legal use which is reasonably comparable thereto, and for no other purpose. Lessee shall not use or permit the use of the Premises in a manner that is unlawful, creates waste or a nuisance, or that disturbs owners and/or occupants of, or causes damage to the Premises or neighboring premises or properties.

(b) Lessor hereby agrees to not unreasonably withhold or delay its consent to any written request by Lessee, Lessee's assignees or subtenants, and by prospective assignees and subtenants of Lessee, its assignees and subtenants, for a modification of said Permitted Use, so long as the same will not impair the structural integrity of the improvements on the Premises or in the Building or the mechanical or electrical systems therein, does not conflict with uses by other lessees, is not significantly more burdensome to the Premises or the Building and the improvements thereon, and is otherwise permissible pursuant to this Paragraph 6. If Lessor elects to withhold such consent, Lessor shall within five (5) business days after such request give a written notification of same, which notice shall include an explanation of Lessor's reasonable objections to the change in use.

6.2 **Hazardous Substances.**

(a) **Reportable Uses Require Consent.** The term **"Hazardous Substance"** as used in this Lease shall mean any product, substance, chemical, material or waste whose presence, nature, quantity and/or intensity of existence, use, manufacture, disposal, transportation, spill, release or effect, either by itself or in combination with other materials expected to be on the Premises, is either: (i) potentially injurious to the public health, safety or welfare, the environment, or the Premises; (ii) regulated or monitored by any governmental authority; or (iii) a basis for potential liability of Lessor to any governmental agency or third party under any applicable statute or common law theory. Hazardous Substance shall include, but not be limited to, hydrocarbons, petroleum, gasoline, crude oil or any products or by-products thereof. Lessee shall not engage in any activity in or about the Premises which constitutes a Reportable Use (as hereinafter defined) of Hazardous Substances without the express prior written consent of Lessor and compliance in a timely manner (at Lessee's sole cost and expense) with all Applicable Requirements (as defined in Paragraph 6.3). **"Reportable Use"** shall mean (i) the installation or use of any above or below ground storage tank, (ii) the generation, possession, storage, use, transportation, or disposal of a Hazardous Substance that requires a permit from, or with respect to which a report, notice, registration or business plan is required to be filed with, any governmental authority, and (iii) the presence in, on or about the Premises of a Hazardous Substance with respect to which any Applicable Laws require that a notice be given to persons entering or occupying the Premises or neighboring properties. Notwithstanding the foregoing, Lessee may, without Lessor's prior consent, but upon notice to Lessor and in compliance with all Applicable Requirements, use any ordinary and customary materials reasonably required to be used by Lessee in the normal course of the Permitted Use, so long as such use is not a Reportable Use and does not expose the Premises or neighboring properties to any meaningful risk of contamination or damage or expose Lessor to any liability therefor. In addition, Lessor may (but without any obligation to do so) condition its consent to any Reportable Use of any Hazardous Substance by Lessee upon Lessee's giving Lessor such additional assurances as Lessor, in its reasonable discretion, deems necessary to protect itself, the public, the Premises and the environment against damage, contamination or injury and/or liability therefor, including but not limited to the installation (and, at Lessor's option, removal on or before Lease expiration or earlier termination) of reasonably necessary protective modifications to the Premises (such as concrete encasements) and/or the deposit of an additional Security Deposit under Paragraph 5 hereof.

(b) **Duty to Inform Lessor.** If Lessee knows, or has reasonable cause to believe, that a Hazardous Substance has come to be located in, on, under or about the Premises or the Building, other than as previously consented to by Lessor, Lessee shall immediately give Lessor written notice thereof, together with a copy of any statement, report, notice, registration, application, permit, business plan, license, claim, action, or proceeding given to, or received from, any governmental authority or private party concerning the presence, spill, release, discharge of, or exposure to, such Hazardous Substance including but not limited to all such documents as may be involved in any Reportable Use involving the Premises. Lessee shall not cause or permit any Hazardous Substance to be spilled or released in, on, under or about the Premises (including, without limitation, through the plumbing or sanitary sewer system).

(c) **Indemnification.** Lessee shall indemnify, protect, defend and hold Lessor, its agents, employees, lenders and ground lessor, if any, and the Premises, harmless from and against any and all damages, liabilities, judgments, costs, claims, liens, expenses, penalties, loss of permits and attorneys' and consultants' fees arising out of or involving any Hazardous Substance brought onto the Premises by or for Lessee or by anyone under Lessee's control. Lessee's obligations under this Paragraph 6.2(c) shall include, but not be limited to, the effects of any contamination or injury to person, property or the environment created or suffered by Lessee, and the cost of investigation (including consultants' and attorneys' fees and testing), removal, remediation, restoration and/or abatement thereof, or of any contamination therein involved, and shall survive the expiration or earlier termination of this Lease. No termination, cancellation or release agreement entered into by Lessor and Lessee shall release Lessee from its obligations under this Lease with respect to Hazardous Substances, unless specifically so agreed by Lessor in writing at the time of such agreement.

6.3 **Lessee's Compliance with Requirements.** Lessee shall, at Lessee's sole cost and expense, fully, diligently and in a timely manner, comply with all **"Applicable Requirements,"** which term is used in this Lease to mean all laws, rules, regulations, ordinances, directives, covenants, easements and restrictions of record, permits, the requirements of any applicable fire insurance underwriter or rating bureau, and the recommendations of Lessor's engineers and/or consultants, relating in any manner to the Premises (including but not limited to matters pertaining to (i) industrial hygiene, (ii) environmental conditions on, in, under or about the Premises, including soil and groundwater conditions, and (iii) the use, generation, manufacture, production, installation, maintenance, removal, transportation, storage, spill, or release of any Hazardous Substance), now in effect or which may hereafter come into effect. Lessee shall, within five (5) days after receipt of Lessor's written request, provide Lessor with copies of all documents and information, including but not limited to permits, registrations, manifests, applications, reports and certificates, evidencing Lessee's compliance with any Applicable Requirements specified by Lessor, and shall immediately upon receipt, notify Lessor in writing (with copies of any documents involved) of any threatened or actual claim, notice, citation, warning, complaint or report pertaining to or involving failure by Lessee or the Premises to comply with any Applicable Requirements.

6.4 **Inspection; Compliance with Law.** Lessor, Lessor's agents, employees, contractors and designated representatives, and the holders of any mortgages, deeds of trust or ground leases on the Premises (**"Lenders"**) shall have the right to enter the Premises at any time in the case of an emergency, and otherwise at reasonable times, for the purpose of inspecting the condition of the Premises and for verifying compliance by Lessee with this Lease and all Applicable Requirements (as defined in Paragraph 6.3), and Lessor shall be entitled to employ experts and/or consultants in connection therewith to advise Lessor with respect to Lessee's activities, including but not limited to Lessee's installation, operation, use, monitoring, maintenance, or removal of any Hazardous Substance on or from the Premises. The costs and expenses of any such inspections shall be paid by the party requesting same, unless a Default or Breach of this Lease by Lessee or a violation of Applicable Requirements or a contamination, caused or materially contributed to by Lessee, is found to exist or to be imminent, or unless the inspection is requested or ordered by a governmental authority as the result of any such existing or imminent violation or contamination. In such case, Lessee shall upon request reimburse Lessor or Lessor's Lender, as the case may be, for the costs and expenses of such inspections.

7. Maintenance, Repairs, Utility Installations, Trade Fixtures and Alterations.

7.1 **Lessee's Obligations.**

(a) Subject to the provisions of Paragraphs 2.2 (Condition), 2.3 (Compliance with Covenants, Restrictions and Building Code), 7.2 (Lessor's Obligations), 9 (Damage or Destruction), and 14 (Condemnation), Lessee shall, at Lessee's sole cost and expense and at all times, keep the Premises and every part thereof in good order, condition and repair (whether or not such portion of the Premises requiring repair, or the means of repairing the same, are reasonably or readily accessible to Lessee, and whether or not the need for such repairs occurs as a result of Lessee's use, any prior use, the elements or the age of such portion of the Premises), including, without limiting the generality of the foregoing, all equipment or facilities specifically serving the Premises, such as plumbing, heating, air conditioning, ventilating, electrical, lighting facilities, boilers, fired or unfired pressure vessels, fire hose connections if within the Premises, fixtures, interior walls, interior surfaces of exterior walls, ceilings, floors, windows, doors, plate glass, and skylights, but excluding any items which are the responsibility of Lessor pursuant to Paragraph 7.2 below. Lessee, in keeping the Premises in good order, condition and repair, shall exercise and perform good maintenance practices. Lessee's obligations shall include restorations, replacements or renewals when necessary to keep the Premises and all improvements thereon or a part thereof in good order, condition and state of repair.

(b) Lessee shall, at Lessee's sole cost and expense, procure and maintain a contract, with copies to Lessor, in customary form and substance for and with a contractor specializing and experienced in the inspection, maintenance and service of the heating, air conditioning and ventilation system for the Premises. However, Lessor reserves the right, upon notice to Lessee, to procure and maintain the contract for the heating, air conditioning and ventilating systems, and if Lessor so elects, Lessee shall reimburse Lessor, upon demand, for the cost thereof.

(c) If Lessee fails to perform Lessee's obligations under this Paragraph 7.1, Lessor may enter upon the Premises after ten (10) days' prior written notice to Lessee (except in the case of an emergency, in which case no notice shall be required), perform such obligations on Lessee's behalf, and put the Premises in good order, condition and repair, in accordance with Paragraph 13.2 below.

7.2 **Lessor's Obligations.** Subject to the provisions of Paragraphs 2.2 (Condition), 2.3 (Compliance with Covenants, Restrictions and Building Code), 4.2 (Common Area Operating Expenses), 6 (Use), 7.1 (Lessee's Obligations), 9 (Damage or Destruction) and 14 (Condemnation), Lessor, subject to reimbursement pursuant to Paragraph 4.2, shall keep in good order, condition and repair the foundations, exterior walls, structural condition of interior bearing walls, exterior roof, fire sprinkler and/or standpipe and hose (if located in the Common Areas) or other automatic fire extinguishing system including fire alarm and/or smoke detection

Initials: ____________

____

MULTI-TENANT—GROSS

—3—

Figure 11–1. Continued

systems and equipment, fire hydrants, parking lots, walkways, parkways, driveways, landscaping, fences, signs and utility systems serving the Common Areas and all parts thereof, as well as providing the services for which there is a Common Area Operating Expense pursuant to Paragraph 4.2. Lessor shall not be obligated to paint the exterior or interior surfaces of exterior walls nor shall Lessor be obligated to maintain, repair or replace windows, doors or plate glass of the Premises. Lessee expressly waives the benefit of any statute now or hereafter in effect which would otherwise afford Lessee the right to make repairs at Lessor's expense or to terminate this Lease because of Lessor's failure to keep the Building, Industrial Center or Common Areas in good order, condition and repair.

7.3 **Utility Installations, Trade Fixtures, Alterations.**

(a) **Definitions; Consent Required.** The term **"Utility Installations"** is used in this Lease to refer to all air lines, power panels, electrical distribution, security, fire protection systems, communications systems, lighting fixtures, heating, ventilating and air conditioning equipment, plumbing, and fencing in, on or about the Premises. The term **"Trade Fixtures"** shall mean Lessee's machinery and equipment which can be removed without doing material damage to the Premises. The term **"Alterations"** shall mean any modification of the improvements on the Premises which are provided by Lessor under the terms of this Lease, other than Utility Installations or Trade Fixtures. **"Lessee-Owned Alterations and/or Utility Installations"** are defined as Alterations and/or Utility Installations made by Lessee that are not yet owned by Lessor pursuant to Paragraph 7.4(a). Lessee shall not make nor cause to be made any Alterations or Utility Installations in, on, under or about the Premises without Lessor's prior written consent. Lessee may, however, make non-structural Utility Installations to the interior of the Premises (excluding the roof) without Lessor's consent but upon notice to Lessor, so long as they are not visible from the outside of the Premises, do not involve puncturing, relocating or removing the roof or any existing walls, or changing or interfering with the fire sprinkler or fire detection systems and the cumulative cost thereof during the term of this Lease as extended does not exceed $2,500.00.

(b) **Consent.** Any Alterations or Utility Installations that Lessee shall desire to make and which require the consent of the Lessor shall be presented to Lessor in written form with detailed plans. All consents given by Lessor, whether by virtue of Paragraph 7.3(a) or by subsequent specific consent, shall be deemed conditioned upon: (i) Lessee's acquiring all applicable permits required by governmental authorities; (ii) the furnishing of copies of such permits together with a copy of the plans and specifications for the Alteration or Utility Installation to Lessor prior to commencement of the work thereon; and (iii) the compliance by Lessee with all conditions of said permits in a prompt and expeditious manner. Any Alterations or Utility Installations by Lessee during the term of this Lease shall be done in a good and workmanlike manner, with good and sufficient materials, and be in compliance with all Applicable Requirements. Lessee shall promptly upon completion thereof furnish Lessor with as-built plans and specifications therefor. Lessor may, (but without obligation to do so) condition its consent to any requested Alteration or Utility Installation that costs $2,500.00 or more upon Lessee's providing Lessor with a lien and completion bond in an amount equal to one and one-half times the estimated cost of such Alteration or Utility Installation.

(c) **Lien Protection.** Lessee shall pay when due all claims for labor or materials furnished or alleged to have been furnished to or for Lessee at or for use on the Premises, which claims are or may be secured by any mechanic's or materialmen's lien against the Premises or any interest therein. Lessee shall give Lessor not less than ten (10) days' notice prior to the commencement of any work in, on, or about the Premises, and Lessor shall have the right to post notices of non-responsibility in or on the Premises as provided by law. If Lessee shall, in good faith, contest the validity of any such lien, claim or demand, then Lessee shall, at its sole expense, defend and protect itself, Lessor and the Premises against the same and shall pay and satisfy any such adverse judgment that may be rendered thereon before the enforcement thereof against the Lessor or the Premises. If Lessor shall require, Lessee shall furnish to Lessor a surety bond satisfactory to Lessor in an amount equal to one and one-half times the amount of such contested lien claim or demand, indemnifying Lessor against liability for the same, as required by law for the holding of the Premises free from the effect of such lien or claim. In addition, Lessor may require Lessee to pay Lessor's attorneys' fees and costs in participating in such action if Lessor shall decide it is to its best interest to do so.

7.4 **Ownership, Removal, Surrender, and Restoration.**

(a) **Ownership.** Subject to Lessor's right to require their removal and to cause Lessee to become the owner thereof as hereinafter provided in this Paragraph 7.4, all Alterations and Utility Installations made to the Premises by Lessee shall be the property of and owned by Lessee, but considered a part of the Premises. Lessor may, at any time and at its option, elect in writing to Lessee to be the owner of all or any specified part of the Lessee-Owned Alterations and Utility Installations. Unless otherwise instructed per Subparagraph 7.4(b) hereof, all Lessee-Owned Alterations and Utility Installations shall, at the expiration or earlier termination of this Lease, become the property of Lessor and remain upon the Premises and be surrendered with the Premises by Lessee.

(b) **Removal.** Unless otherwise agreed in writing, Lessor may require that any or all Lessee-Owned Alterations or Utility Installations be removed by the expiration or earlier termination of this Lease, notwithstanding that their installation may have been consented to by Lessor. Lessor may require the removal at any time of all or any part of any Alterations or Utility Installations made without the required consent of Lessor.

(c) **Surrender/Restoration.** Lessee shall surrender the Premises by the end of the last day of the Lease term or any earlier termination date, clean and free of debris and in good operating order, condition and state of repair, ordinary wear and tear excepted. Ordinary wear and tear shall not include any damage or deterioration that would have been prevented by good maintenance practice or by Lessee performing all of its obligations under this Lease. Except as otherwise agreed or specified herein, the Premises, as surrendered, shall include the Alterations and Utility Installations. The obligation of Lessee shall include the repair of any damage occasioned by the installation, maintenance or removal of Lessee's Trade Fixtures, furnishings, equipment, and Lessee-Owned Alterations and Utility Installations, as well as the removal of any storage tank installed by or for Lessee, and the removal, replacement, or remediation of any soil, material or ground water contaminated by Lessee, all as may then be required by Applicable Requirements and/or good practice. Lessee's Trade Fixtures shall remain the property of Lessee and shall be removed by Lessee subject to its obligation to repair and restore the Premises per this Lease.

8. Insurance; Indemnity.

8.1 **Payment of Premium Increases.**

(a) As used herein, the term **"Insurance Cost Increase"** is defined as any increase in the actual cost of the insurance applicable to the Building and required to be carried by Lessor pursuant to Paragraphs 8.2(b), 8.3(a) and 8.3(b), (**"Required Insurance"**), over and above the Base Premium, as hereinafter defined, calculated on an annual basis. "Insurance Cost Increase" shall include, but not be limited to, requirements of the holder of a mortgage or deed of trust covering the Premises, increased valuation of the Premises, and/or a general premium rate increase. The term "Insurance Cost Increase" shall not, however, include any premium increases resulting from the nature of the occupancy of any other lessee of the Building. If the parties insert a dollar amount in Paragraph 1.9, such amount shall be considered the **"Base Premium."** If a dollar amount has not been inserted in Paragraph 1.9 and if the Building has been previously occupied during the twelve (12) month period immediately preceding the Commencement Date, the "Base Premium" shall be the annual premium applicable to such twelve (12) month period. If the Building was not fully occupied during such twelve (12) month period, the "Base Premium" shall be the lowest annual premium reasonably obtainable for the Required Insurance as of the Commencement Date, assuming the most nominal use possible of the Building. In no event, however, shall Lessee be responsible for any portion of the premium cost attributable to liability insurance coverage in excess of $1,000,000 procured under Paragraph 8.2(b).

(b) Lessee shall pay any Insurance Cost Increase to Lessor pursuant to Paragraph 4.2. Premiums for policy periods commencing prior to, or extending beyond, the term of this Lease shall be prorated to coincide with the corresponding Commencement Date or Expiration Date.

8.2 **Liability Insurance.**

(a) **Carried by Lessee.** Lessee shall obtain and keep in force during the term of this Lease a Commercial General Liability policy of insurance protecting Lessee, Lessor and any Lender(s) whose names have been provided to Lessee in writing (as additional insureds) against claims for bodily injury, personal injury and property damage based upon, involving or arising out of the ownership, use, occupancy or maintenance of the Premises and all areas appurtenant thereto. Such insurance shall be on an occurrence basis providing single limit coverage in an amount not less than $1,000,000 per occurrence with an "Additional Insured-Managers or Lessors of Premises" endorsement and contain the "Amendment of the Pollution Exclusion" endorsement for damage caused by heat, smoke or fumes from a hostile fire. The policy shall not contain any intra-insured exclusions as between insured persons or organizations, but shall include coverage for liability assumed under this Lease as an **"Insured contract"** for the performance of Lessee's indemnity obligations under this Lease. The limits of said insurance required by this Lease or as carried by Lessee shall not, however, limit the liability of Lessee nor relieve Lessee of any obligation hereunder. All insurance to be carried by Lessee shall be primary to and not contributory with any similar insurance carried by Lessor, whose insurance shall be considered excess insurance only.

(b) **Carried by Lessor.** Lessor shall also maintain liability insurance described in Paragraph 8.2(a) above, in addition to and not in lieu of, the insurance required to be maintained by Lessee. Lessee shall not be named as an additional insured therein.

8.3 **Property Insurance-Building, Improvements and Rental Value.**

(a) **Building and Improvements.** Lessor shall obtain and keep in force during the term of this Lease a policy or policies in the name of Lessor, with loss payable to Lessor and to any Lender(s), insuring against loss or damage to the Premises. Such insurance shall be for full replacement cost, as the same shall exist from time to time, or the amount required by any Lender(s), but in no event more than the commercially reasonable and available insurable value thereof if, by reason of the unique nature or age of the improvements involved, such latter amount is less than full replacement cost. Lessee-Owned Alterations and Utility Installations, Trade Fixtures and Lessee's personal property shall be insured by Lessee pursuant to Paragraph 8.4. If the coverage is available and commercially appropriate, Lessor's policy or policies shall insure against all risks of direct physical loss or damage (except the perils of flood and/or earthquake unless required by a Lender or included in the Base Premium), including coverage for any additional costs resulting from debris removal and reasonable amounts of coverage for the enforcement of any ordinance or law regulating the reconstruction or replacement of any undamaged sections of the Building required to be demolished or removed by reason of the enforcement of any building, zoning, safety or land use laws as the result of a covered loss, but not including plate glass insurance. Said policy or policies shall also contain an agreed valuation provision in lieu of any co-insurance clause, waiver of subrogation, and inflation guard protection causing an increase in the annual property insurance coverage amount by a factor of not less than the adjusted U.S. Department of Labor Consumer Price Index for All Urban Consumers for the city nearest to where the Premises are located.

(b) **Rental Value.** Lessor shall also obtain and keep in force during the term of this Lease a policy or policies in the name of Lessor, with loss payable to Lessor and any Lender(s), insuring the loss of the full rental and other charges payable by all lessees of the Building to Lessor for one year (including all Real Property Taxes, insurance costs, all Common Area Operating Expenses and any scheduled rental increases). Said insurance may provide that in the event the Lease is terminated by reason of an insured loss, the period of indemnity for such coverage shall be extended beyond the date of the completion of repairs or replacement of the Premises, to provide for one full year's loss of rental revenues from the date of any such loss. Said insurance shall contain an agreed valuation provision in lieu of any co-insurance clause, and the amount of coverage shall be adjusted annually to reflect the projected rental income, Real Property Taxes, insurance premium costs and other expenses, if any, otherwise payable, for the next 12-month period. Common Area Operating Expenses shall include any deductible amount in the event of such loss.

(c) **Adjacent Premises.** Lessee shall pay for any increase in the premiums for the property insurance of the Building and for the Common Areas or other buildings in the Industrial Center if said increase is caused by Lessee's acts, omissions, use or occupancy of the Premises.

Initials: ____________

____

MULTI-TENANT–GROSS

—4—

Figure 11–1. Continued

(Continued)

(d) **Lessee's Improvements.** Since Lessor is the Insuring Party, Lessor shall not be required to insure Lessee-Owned Alterations and Utility Installations unless the item in question has become the property of Lessor under the terms of this Lease.

8.4 **Lessee's Property Insurance.** Subject to the requirements of Paragraph 8.5, Lessee at its cost shall either by separate policy or, at Lessor's option, by endorsement to a policy already carried, maintain insurance coverage on all of Lessee's personal property, Trade Fixtures and Lessee-Owned Alterations and Utility Installations in, on, or about the Premises similar in coverage to that carried by Lessor as the Insuring Party under Paragraph 8.3(a). Such insurance shall be full replacement cost coverage with a deductible not to exceed $1,000 per occurrence. The proceeds from any such insurance shall be used by Lessee for the replacement of personal property and the restoration of Trade Fixtures and Lessee-Owned Alterations and Utility Installations. Upon request from Lessor, Lessee shall provide Lessor with written evidence that such insurance is in force.

8.5 **Insurance Policies.** Insurance required hereunder shall be in companies duly licensed to transact business in the state where the Premises are located, and maintaining during the policy term a "General Policyholders Rating" of at least B+, V, or such other rating as may be required by a Lender, as set forth in the most current issue of "Best's Insurance Guide." Lessee shall not do or permit to be done anything which shall invalidate the insurance policies referred to in this Paragraph 8. Lessee shall cause to be delivered to Lessor, within seven (7) days after the earlier of the Early Possession Date or the Commencement Date, certified copies of, or certificates evidencing the existence and amounts of, the insurance required under Paragraph 8.2(a) and 8.4. No such policy shall be cancelable or subject to modification except after thirty (30) days' prior written notice to Lessor. Lessee shall at least thirty (30) days prior to the expiration of such policies, furnish Lessor with evidence of renewals or "insurance binders" evidencing renewal thereof, or Lessor may order such insurance and charge the cost thereof to Lessee, which amount shall be payable by Lessee to Lessor upon demand.

8.6 **Waiver of Subrogation.** Without affecting any other rights or remedies, Lessee and Lessor each hereby release and relieve the other, and waive their entire right to recover damages (whether in contract or in tort) against the other, for loss or damage to their property arising out of or incident to the perils required to be insured against under Paragraph 8. The effect of such releases and waivers of the right to recover damages shall not be limited by the amount of insurance carried or required, or by any deductibles applicable thereto. Lessor and Lessee agree to have their respective insurance companies issuing property damage insurance waive any right to subrogation that such companies may have against Lessor or Lessee, as the case may be, so long as the insurance is not invalidated thereby.

8.7 **Indemnity.** Except for Lessor's negligence and/or breach of express warranties, Lessee shall indemnify, protect, defend and hold harmless the Premises, Lessor and its agents, Lessor's master or ground lessor, partners and Lenders, from and against any and all claims, loss of rents and/or damages, costs, liens, judgments, penalties, loss of permits, attorneys' and consultants' fees, expenses and/or liabilities arising out of, involving, or in connection with, the occupancy of the Premises by Lessee, the conduct of Lessee's business, any act, omission or neglect of Lessee, its agents, contractors, employees or invitees, and out of any Default or Breach by Lessee in the performance in a timely manner of any obligation on Lessee's part to be performed under this Lease. The foregoing shall include, but not be limited to, the defense or pursuit of any claim or any action or proceeding involved therein, and whether or not (in the case of claims made against Lessor) litigated and/or reduced to judgment. In case any action or proceeding be brought against Lessor by reason of any of the foregoing matters, Lessee upon notice from Lessor shall defend the same at Lessee's expense by counsel reasonably satisfactory to Lessor and Lessor shall cooperate with Lessee in such defense. Lessor need not have first paid any such claim in order to be so indemnified.

8.8 **Exemption of Lessor from Liability.** Lessor shall not be liable for injury or damage to the person or goods, wares, merchandise or other property of Lessee, Lessee's employees, contractors, invitees, customers, or any other person in or about the Premises, whether such damage or injury is caused by or results from fire, steam, electricity, gas, water or rain, or from the breakage, leakage, obstruction or other defects of pipes, fire sprinklers, wires, appliances, plumbing, air conditioning or lighting fixtures, or from any other cause, whether said injury or damage results from conditions arising upon the Premises or upon other portions of the Building of which the Premises are a part, from other sources or places, and regardless of whether the cause of such damage or injury or the means of repairing the same is accessible or not. Lessor shall not be liable for any damages arising from any act or neglect of any other lessee of Lessor nor from the failure by Lessor to enforce the provisions of any other lease in the Industrial Center. Notwithstanding Lessor's negligence or breach of this Lease, Lessor shall under no circumstances be liable for injury to Lessee's business or for any loss of income or profit therefrom.

9. Damage or Destruction.

9.1 **Definitions.**

(a) **"Premises Partial Damage"** shall mean damage or destruction to the Premises, other than Lessee-Owned Alterations and Utility Installations, the repair cost of which damage or destruction is less than fifty percent (50%) of the then Replacement Cost (as defined in Paragraph 9.1(d)) of the Premises (excluding Lessee-Owned Alterations and Utility Installations and Trade Fixtures) immediately prior to such damage or destruction.

(b) **"Premises Total Destruction"** shall mean damage or destruction to the Premises, other than Lessee-Owned Alterations and Utility Installations, the repair cost of which damage or destruction is fifty percent (50%) or more of the then Replacement Cost of the Premises (excluding Lessee-Owned Alterations and Utility Installations and Trade Fixtures) immediately prior to such damage or destruction. In addition, damage or destruction to the Building, other than Lessee-Owned Alterations and Utility Installations and Trade Fixtures of any lessees of the Building, the cost of which damage or destruction is fifty percent (50%) or more of the then Replacement Cost (excluding Lessee-Owned Alterations and Utility Installations and Trade Fixtures of any lessees of the Building) of the Building shall, at the option of Lessor, be deemed to be Premises Total Destruction.

(c) **"Insured Loss"** shall mean damage or destruction to the Premises, other than Lessee-Owned Alterations and Utility Installations and Trade Fixtures, which was caused by an event required to be covered by the insurance described in Paragraph 8.3(a) irrespective of any deductible amounts or coverage limits involved.

(d) **"Replacement Cost"** shall mean the cost to repair or rebuild the improvements owned by Lessor at the time of the occurrence to their condition existing immediately prior thereto, including demolition, debris removal and upgrading required by the operation of applicable building codes, ordinances or laws, and without deduction for depreciation.

(e) **"Hazardous Substance Condition"** shall mean the occurrence or discovery of a condition involving the presence of, or a contamination by, a Hazardous Substance as defined in Paragraph 6.2(a), in, on, or under the Premises.

9.2 **Premises Partial Damage—Insured Loss.** If Premises Partial Damage that is an Insured Loss occurs, then Lessor shall, at Lessor's expense, repair such damage (but not Lessee's Trade Fixtures or Lessee-Owned Alterations and Utility Installations) as soon as reasonably possible and this Lease shall continue in full force and effect. In the event, however, that there is a shortage of insurance proceeds and such shortage is due to the fact that, by reason of the unique nature of the improvements in the Premises, full replacement cost insurance coverage was not commercially reasonable and available, Lessor shall have no obligation to pay for the shortage in insurance proceeds or to fully restore the unique aspects of the Premises unless Lessee provides Lessor with the funds to cover same, or adequate assurance thereof, within ten (10) days following receipt of written notice of such shortage and request therefor. If Lessor receives said funds or adequate assurance thereof within said ten (10) day period, Lessor shall complete them as soon as reasonably possible and this Lease shall remain in full force and effect. If Lessor does not receive such funds or assurance within said period, Lessor may nevertheless elect by written notice to Lessee within ten (10) days thereafter to make such restoration and repair as is commercially reasonable with Lessor paying any shortage in proceeds, in which case this Lease shall remain in full force and effect. If Lessor does not receive such funds or assurance within such ten (10) day period, and if Lessor does not so elect to restore and repair, then this Lease shall terminate sixty (60) days following the occurrence of the damage or destruction. Unless otherwise agreed, Lessee shall in no event have any right to reimbursement from Lessor for any funds contributed by Lessee to repair any such damage or destruction. Premises Partial Damage due to flood or earthquake shall be subject to Paragraph 9.3 rather than Paragraph 9.2, notwithstanding that there may be some insurance coverage, but the net proceeds of any such insurance shall be made available for the repairs if made by either Party.

9.3 **Partial Damage—Uninsured Loss.** If Premises Partial Damage that is not an Insured Loss occurs, unless caused by a negligent or willful act of Lessee (in which event Lessee shall make the repairs at Lessee's expense and this Lease shall continue in full force and effect), Lessor may at Lessor's option, either (i) repair such damage as soon as reasonably possible at Lessor's expense, in which event this Lease shall continue in full force and effect, or (ii) give written notice to Lessee within thirty (30) days after receipt by Lessor of knowledge of the occurrence of such damage of Lessor's desire to terminate this Lease as of the date sixty (60) days following the date of such notice. In the event Lessor elects to give such notice of Lessor's intention to terminate this Lease, Lessee shall have the right within ten (10) days after the receipt of such notice to give written notice to Lessor of Lessee's commitment to pay for the repair of such damage totally at Lessee's expense and without reimbursement from Lessor. Lessee shall provide Lessor with the required funds or satisfactory assurance thereof within thirty (30) days following such commitment from Lessee. In such event this Lease shall continue in full force and effect, and Lessor shall proceed to make such repairs as soon as reasonably possible after the required funds are available. If Lessee does not give such notice and provide the funds or assurance thereof within the times specified above, this Lease shall terminate as of the date specified in Lessor's notice of termination.

9.4 **Total Destruction.** Notwithstanding any other provision hereof, if Premises Total Destruction occurs (including any destruction required by any authorized public authority), this Lease shall terminate sixty (60) days following the date of such Premises Total Destruction, whether or not the damage or destruction is an Insured Loss or was caused by a negligent or willful act of Lessee. In the event, however, that the damage or destruction was caused by Lessee, Lessor shall have the right to recover Lessor's damages from Lessee except as released and waived in Paragraph 9.7.

9.5 **Damage Near End of Term.** If at any time during the last six (6) months of the term of this Lease there is damage for which the cost to repair exceeds one month's Base Rent, whether or not an Insured Loss, Lessor may, at Lessor's option, terminate this Lease effective sixty (60) days following the date of occurrence of such damage by giving written notice to Lessee of Lessor's election to do so within thirty (30) days after the date of occurrence of such damage. Provided, however, if Lessee at that time has an exercisable option to extend this Lease or to purchase the Premises, then Lessee may preserve this Lease by (a) exercising such option, and (b) providing Lessor with any shortage in insurance proceeds (or adequate assurance thereof) needed to make the repairs on or before the earlier of (i) the date which is ten (10) days after Lessee's receipt of Lessor's written notice purporting to terminate this Lease, or (ii) the day prior to the date upon which such option expires. If Lessee duly exercises such option during such period and provides Lessor with funds (or adequate assurance thereof) to cover any shortage in insurance proceeds, Lessor shall, at Lessor's expense repair such damage as soon as reasonably possible and this Lease shall continue in full force and effect. If Lessee fails to exercise such option and provide such funds or assurance during such period, then this Lease shall terminate as of the date set forth in the first sentence of this Paragraph 9.5.

9.6 **Abatement of Rent; Lessee's Remedies.**

(a) In the event of (i) Premises Partial Damage or (ii) Hazardous Substance Condition for which Lessee is not legally responsible, the Base Rent, Common Area Operating Expenses and other charges, if any, payable by Lessee hereunder for the period during which such damage or condition, its repair, remediation or restoration continues, shall be abated in proportion to the degree to which Lessee's use of the Premises is impaired, but not in excess of proceeds from insurance required to be carried under Paragraph 8.3(b). Except for abatement of Base Rent, Common Area Operating Expenses and other charges, if any, as aforesaid, all other obligations of Lessee hereunder shall be performed by Lessee, and Lessee shall have no claim against Lessor for any damage suffered by reason of any such damage, destruction, repair, remediation or restoration.

Initials: ____________

____

MULTI-TENANT—GROSS

—5—

Figure 11–1. Continued

(b) If Lessor shall be obligated to repair or restore the Premises under the provisions of this Paragraph 9 and shall not commence, in a substantial and meaningful way, the repair or restoration of the Premises within ninety (90) days after such obligation shall accrue, Lessee may, at any time prior to the commencement of such repair or restoration, give written notice to Lessor and to any Lenders of which Lessee has actual notice of Lessee's election to terminate this Lease on a date not less than sixty (60) days following the giving of such notice. If Lessee gives such notice to Lessor and such Lenders and such repair or restoration is not commenced within thirty (30) days after receipt of such notice, this Lease shall terminate as of the date specified in said notice. If Lessor or a Lender commences the repair or restoration of the Premises within thirty (30) days after the receipt of such notice, this Lease shall continue in full force and effect. **"Commence"** as used in this Paragraph 9.6 shall mean either the unconditional authorization of the preparation of the required plans, or the beginning of the actual work on the Premises, whichever occurs first.

9.7   **Hazardous Substance Conditions.** If a Hazardous Substance Condition occurs, unless Lessee is legally responsible therefor (in which case Lessee shall make the investigation and remediation thereof required by Applicable Requirements and this Lease shall continue in full force and effect, but subject to Lessor's rights under Paragraph 6.2(c) and Paragraph 13), Lessor may at Lessor's option either (i) investigate and remediate such Hazardous Substance Condition, if required, as soon as reasonably possible at Lessor's expense, in which event this Lease shall continue in full force and effect, or (ii) if the estimated cost to investigate and remediate such condition exceeds twelve (12) times the then monthly Base Rent or $100,000 whichever is greater, give written notice to Lessee within thirty (30) days after receipt by Lessor of knowledge of the occurrence of such Hazardous Substance Condition of Lessor's desire to terminate this Lease as of the date sixty (60) days following the date of such notice. In the event Lessor elects to give such notice of Lessor's intention to terminate this Lease, Lessee shall have the right within ten (10) days after the receipt of such notice to give written notice to Lessor of Lessee's commitment to pay for the excess costs of (a) investigation and remediation of such Hazardous Substance Condition to the extent required by Applicable Requirements, over (b) an amount equal to twelve (12) times the then monthly Base Rent or $100,000, whichever is greater. Lessee shall provide Lessor with the funds required of Lessee or satisfactory assurance thereof within thirty (30) days following said commitment by Lessee. In such event this Lease shall continue in full force and effect, and Lessor shall proceed to make such investigation and remediation as soon as reasonably possible after the required funds are available. If Lessee does not give such notice and provide the required funds or assurance thereof within the time period specified above, this Lease shall terminate as of the date specified in Lessor's notice of termination.

9.8   **Termination—Advance Payments.** Upon termination of this Lease pursuant to this Paragraph 9, Lessor shall return to Lessee any advance payment made by Lessee to Lessor and so much of Lessee's Security Deposit as has not been, or is not then required to be, used by Lessor under the terms of this Lease.

9.9   **Waiver of Statutes.** Lessor and Lessee agree that the terms of this Lease shall govern the effect of any damage to or destruction of the Premises and the Building with respect to the termination of this Lease and hereby waive the provisions of any present or future statute to the extent it is inconsistent herewith.

10. Real Property Taxes.

10.1   **Payment of Taxes.** Lessor shall pay the Real Property Taxes, as defined in Paragraph 10.2(a), applicable to the Industrial Center, and except as otherwise provided in Paragraph 10.3, any increases in such amounts over the Base Real Property Taxes shall be included in the calculation of Common Area Operating Expenses in accordance with the provisions of Paragraph 4.2.

10.2   **Real Property Tax Definitions.**

(a) As used herein, the term **"Real Property Taxes"** shall include any form of real estate tax or assessment, general, special, ordinary or extraordinary, and any license fee, commercial rental tax, improvement bond or bonds, levy or tax (other than inheritance, personal income or estate taxes) imposed upon the Industrial Center by any authority having the direct or indirect power to tax, including any city, state or federal government, or any school, agricultural, sanitary, fire, street, drainage, or other improvement district thereof, levied against any legal or equitable interest of Lessor in the Industrial Center or any portion thereof, Lessor's right to rent or other income therefrom, and/or Lessor's business of leasing the Premises. The term **"Real Property Taxes"** shall also include any tax, fee, levy, assessment or charge, or any increase therein, imposed by reason of events occurring, or changes in Applicable Law taking effect, during the term of this Lease, including but not limited to a change in the ownership of the Industrial Center or in the improvements thereon, the execution of this Lease, or any modification, amendment or transfer thereof, and whether or not contemplated by the Parties.

(b) As used herein, the term **"Base Real Property Taxes"** shall be the amount of Real Property Taxes, which are assessed against the Premises, Building or Common Areas in the calendar year during which the Lease is executed. In calculating Real Property Taxes for any calendar year, the Real Property Taxes for any real estate tax year shall be included in the calculation of Real Property Taxes for such calendar year based upon the number of days which such calendar year and tax year have in common.

10.3   **Additional Improvements.** Common Area Operating Expenses shall not include Real Property Taxes specified in the tax assessor's records and work sheets as being caused by additional improvements placed upon the Industrial Center by other lessees or by Lessor for the exclusive enjoyment of such other lessees. Notwithstanding Paragraph 10.1 hereof, Lessee shall, however, pay to Lessor at the time Common Area Operating Expenses are payable under Paragraph 4.2, the entirety of any increase in Real Property Taxes if assessed solely by reason of Alterations, Trade Fixtures or Utility Installations placed upon the Premises by Lessee or at Lessee's request.

10.4   **Joint Assessment.** If the Building is not separately assessed, Real Property Taxes allocated to the Building shall be an equitable proportion of the Real Property Taxes for all of the land and improvements included within the tax parcel assessed, such proportion to be determined by Lessor from the respective valuations assigned in the assessor's work sheets or such other information as may be reasonably available. Lessor's reasonable determination thereof, in good faith, shall be conclusive.

10.5   **Lessee's Property Taxes.** Lessee shall pay prior to delinquency all taxes assessed against and levied upon Lessee-Owned Alterations and Utility Installations, Trade Fixtures, furnishings, equipment and all personal property of Lessee contained in the Premises or stored within the Industrial Center. When possible, Lessee shall cause its Lessee-Owned Alterations and Utility Installations, Trade Fixtures, furnishings, equipment and all other personal property to be assessed and billed separately from the real property of Lessor. If any of Lessee's said property shall be assessed with Lessor's real property, Lessee shall pay Lessor the taxes attributable to Lessee's property within ten (10) days after receipt of a written statement setting forth the taxes applicable to Lessee's property.

11. Utilities. Lessee shall pay directly for all utilities and services supplied to the Premises, including but not limited to electricity, telephone, security, gas and cleaning of the Premises, together with any taxes thereon. If any such utilities or services are not separately metered to the Premises or separately billed to the Premises, Lessee shall pay to Lessor a reasonable proportion to be determined by Lessor of all such charges jointly metered or billed with other premises in the Building, in the manner and within the time periods set forth in Paragraph 4.2(d).

12. Assignment and Subletting.

12.1   **Lessor's Consent Required.**

(a) Lessee shall not voluntarily or by operation of law assign, transfer, mortgage or otherwise transfer or encumber (collectively, "assign") or sublet all or any part of Lessee's interest in this Lease or in the Premises without Lessor's prior written consent given under and subject to the terms of Paragraph 36.

(b) A change in the control of Lessee shall constitute an assignment requiring Lessor's consent. The transfer, on a cumulative basis, of twenty-five percent (25%) or more of the voting control of Lessee shall constitute a change in control for this purpose.

(c) The involvement of Lessee or its assets in any transaction, or series of transactions (by way of merger, sale, acquisition, financing, refinancing, transfer, leveraged buy-out or otherwise), whether or not a formal assignment or hypothecation of this Lease or Lessee's assets occurs, which results or will result in a reduction of the Net Worth of Lessee, as hereinafter defined, by an amount equal to or greater than twenty-five percent (25%) of such Net Worth of Lessee as it was represented to Lessor at the time of full execution and delivery of this Lease or at the time of the most recent assignment to which Lessor has consented, or as it exists immediately prior to said transaction or transactions constituting such reduction, at whichever time said Net Worth of Lessee was or is greater, shall be considered an assignment of this Lease by Lessee to which Lessor may reasonably withhold its consent. **"Net Worth of Lessee"** for purposes of this Lease shall be the net worth of Lessee (excluding any Guarantors) established under generally accepted accounting principles consistently applied.

(d) An assignment or subletting of Lessee's interest in this Lease without Lessor's specific prior written consent shall, at Lessor's option, be a Default curable after notice per Paragraph 13.1, or a non-curable Breach without the necessity of any notice and grace period. If Lessor elects to treat such unconsented to assignment or subletting as a non-curable Breach, Lessor shall have the right to either: (i) terminate this Lease, or (ii) upon thirty (30) days' written notice **("Lessor's Notice")**, increase the monthly Base Rent for the Premises to the greater of the then fair market rental value of the Premises, as reasonably determined by Lessor, or one hundred ten percent (110%) of the Base Rent then in effect. Pending determination of the new fair market rental value, if disputed by Lessee, Lessee shall pay the amount set forth in Lessor's Notice, with any overpayment credited against the next installment(s) of Base Rent coming due, and any underpayment for the period retroactively to the effective date of the adjustment being due and payable immediately upon the determination thereof. Further, in the event of such Breach and rental adjustment, (i) the purchase price of any option to purchase the Premises held by Lessee shall be subject to similar adjustment to the then fair market value as reasonably determined by Lessor (without the Lease being considered an encumbrance or any deduction for depreciation or obsolescence, and considering the Premises at its highest and best use and in good condition) or one hundred ten percent (110%) of the price previously in effect, (ii) any index-oriented rental or price adjustment formulas contained in this Lease shall be adjusted to require that the base index be determined with reference to the index applicable to the time of such adjustment, and (iii) any fixed rental adjustments scheduled during the remainder of the Lease term shall be increased in the same ratio as the new rental bears to the Base Rent in effect immediately prior to the adjustment specified in Lessor's Notice.

(e) Lessee's remedy for any breach of this Paragraph 12.1 by Lessor shall be limited to compensatory damages and/or injunctive relief.

12.2   **Terms and Conditions Applicable to Assignment and Subletting.**

(a) Regardless of Lessor's consent, any assignment or subletting shall not (i) be effective without the express written assumption by such assignee or sublessee of the obligations of Lessee under this Lease, (ii) release Lessee of any obligations hereunder, nor (iii) alter the primary liability of Lessee for the payment of Base Rent and other sums due Lessor hereunder or for the performance of any other obligations to be performed by Lessee under this Lease.

(b) Lessor may accept any rent or performance of Lessee's obligations from any person other than Lessee pending approval or disapproval of an assignment. Neither a delay in the approval or disapproval of such assignment nor the acceptance of any rent for performance shall constitute a waiver or estoppel of Lessor's right to exercise its remedies for the Default or Breach by Lessee of any of the terms, covenants or conditions of this Lease.

(c) The consent of Lessor to any assignment or subletting shall not constitute a consent to any subsequent assignment or subletting by Lessee or to any subsequent or successive assignment or subletting by the assignee or sublessee. However, Lessor may consent to subsequent sublettings and assignments of the sublease or any amendments or modifications thereto without notifying Lessee or anyone else liable under this Lease or the sublease and without obtaining their consent, and such action shall not relieve such persons from liability under this Lease or the sublease.

Initials: _____

_____

MULTI-TENANT—GROSS
© American Industrial Real Estate Association 1993   —6—

Figure 11–1.   Continued

(Continued)

(d) In the event of any Default or Breach of Lessee's obligation under this Lease, Lessor may proceed directly against Lessee, any Guarantors or anyone else responsible for the performance of the Lessee's obligations under this Lease, including any sublessee, without first exhausting Lessor's remedies against any other person or entity responsible therefor to Lessor, or any security held by Lessor.

(e) Each request for consent to an assignment or subletting shall be in writing, accompanied by information relevant to Lessor's determination as to the financial and operational responsibility and appropriateness of the proposed assignee or sublessee, including but not limited to the intended use and/or required modification of the Premises, if any, together with a non-refundable deposit of $1,000 or ten percent (10%) of the monthly Base Rent applicable to the portion of the Premises which is the subject of the proposed assignment or sublease, whichever is greater, as reasonable consideration for Lessor's considering and processing the request for consent. Lessee agrees to provide Lessor with such other or additional information and/or documentation as may be reasonably requested by Lessor.

(f) Any assignee of, or sublessee under, this Lease shall, by reason of accepting such assignment or entering into such sublease, be deemed, for the benefit of Lessor, to have assumed and agreed to conform and comply with each and every term, covenant, condition and obligation herein to be observed or performed by Lessee during the term of said assignment or sublease, other than such obligations as are contrary to or inconsistent with provisions of an assignment or sublease to which Lessor has specifically consented in writing.

(g) The occurrence of a transaction described in Paragraph 12.2(c) shall give Lessor the right (but not the obligation) to require that the Security Deposit be increased by an amount equal to six (6) times the then monthly Base Rent, and Lessor may make the actual receipt by Lessor of the Security Deposit increase a condition to Lessor's consent to such transaction.

(h) Lessor, as a condition to giving its consent to any assignment or subletting, may require that the amount and adjustment schedule of the rent payable under this Lease be adjusted to what is then the market value and/or adjustment schedule for property similar to the Premises as then constituted, as determined by Lessor.

12.3 **Additional Terms and Conditions Applicable to Subletting.** The following terms and conditions shall apply to any subletting by Lessee of all or any part of the Premises and shall be deemed included in all subleases under this Lease whether or not expressly incorporated therein:

(a) Lessee hereby assigns and transfers to Lessor all of Lessee's interest in all rentals and income arising from any sublease of all or a portion of the Premises heretofore or hereafter made by Lessee, and Lessor may collect such rent and income and apply same toward Lessee's obligations under this Lease; provided, however, that until a Breach (as defined in Paragraph 13.1) shall occur in the performance of Lessee's obligations under this Lease, Lessee may, except as otherwise provided in this Lease, receive, collect and enjoy the rents accruing under such sublease. Lessor shall not, by reason of the foregoing provision or any other assignment of such sublease to Lessor, nor by reason of the collection of the rents from a sublessee, be deemed liable to the sublessee for any failure of Lessee to perform and comply with any of Lessee's obligations to such sublessee under such Sublease. Lessee hereby irrevocably authorizes and directs any such sublessee, upon receipt of a written notice from Lessor stating that a Breach exists in the performance of Lessee's obligations under this Lease, to pay to Lessor the rents and other charges due and to become due under the sublease. Sublessee shall rely upon any such statement and request from Lessor and shall pay such rents and other charges to Lessor without any obligation or right to inquire as to whether such Breach exists and notwithstanding any notice from or claim from Lessee to the contrary. Lessee shall have no right or claim against such sublessee, or, until the Breach has been cured, against Lessor, for any such rents and other charges so paid by said sublessee to Lessor.

(b) In the event of a Breach by Lessee in the performance of its obligations under this Lease, Lessor, at its option and without any obligation to do so, may require any sublessee to attorn to Lessor, in which event Lessor shall undertake the obligations of the sublessor under such sublease from the time of the exercise of said option to the expiration of such sublease; provided, however, Lessor shall not be liable for any prepaid rents or security deposit paid by such sublessee to such sublessor or for any other prior defaults or breaches of such sublessor under such sublease.

(c) Any matter or thing requiring the consent of the sublessor under a sublease shall also require the consent of Lessor herein.

(d) No sublessee under a sublease approved by Lessor shall further assign or sublet all or any part of the Premises without Lessor's prior written consent.

(e) Lessor shall deliver a copy of any notice of Default or Breach by Lessee to the sublessee, who shall have the right to cure the Default of Lessee within the grace period, if any, specified in such notice. The sublessee shall have a right of reimbursement and offset from and against Lessee for any such Defaults cured by the sublessee.

13. Default; Breach; Remedies.

13.1 **Default; Breach.** Lessor and Lessee agree that if an attorney is consulted by Lessor in connection with a Lessee Default or Breach (as hereinafter defined), $350.00 is a reasonable minimum sum per such occurrence for legal services and costs in the preparation and service of a notice of Default, and that Lessor may include the cost of such services and costs in said notice as rent due and payable to cure said default. A **"Default"** by Lessee is defined as a failure by Lessee to observe, comply with or perform any of the terms, covenants, conditions or rules applicable to Lessee under this Lease. A **"Breach"** by Lessee is defined as the occurrence of any one or more of the following Defaults, and, where a grace period for cure after notice is specified herein, the failure by Lessee to cure such Default prior to the expiration of the applicable grace period, and shall entitle Lessor to pursue the remedies set forth in Paragraphs 13.2 and/or 13.3:

(a) The vacating of the Premises without the intention to reoccupy same, or the abandonment of the Premises.

(b) Except as expressly otherwise provided in this Lease, the failure by Lessee to make any payment of Base Rent, Lessee's Share of Common Area Operating Expenses, or any other monetary payment required to be made by Lessee hereunder as and when due, the failure by Lessee to provide Lessor with reasonable evidence of insurance or surety bond required under this Lease, or the failure of Lessee to fulfill any obligation under this Lease which endangers or threatens life or property, where such failure continues for a period of three (3) days following written notice thereof by or on behalf of Lessor to Lessee.

(c) Except as expressly otherwise provided in this Lease, the failure by Lessee to provide Lessor with reasonable written evidence (in duly executed original form, if applicable) of (i) compliance with Applicable Requirements per Paragraph 6.3, (ii) the inspection, maintenance and service contracts required under Paragraph 7.1(b), (iii) the rescission of an unauthorized assignment or subletting per Paragraph 12.1, (iv) a Tenancy Statement per Paragraphs 16 or 37, (v) the subordination or non-subordination of this Lease per Paragraph 30, (vi) the guaranty of the performance of Lessee's obligations under this Lease if required under Paragraphs 1.11 and 37, (vii) the execution of any document requested under Paragraph 42 (easements), or (viii) any other documentation or information which Lessor may reasonably require of Lessee under the terms of this lease, where any such failure continues for a period of ten (10) days following written notice by or on behalf of Lessor to Lessee.

(d) A Default by Lessee as to the terms, covenants, conditions or provisions of this Lease, or of the rules adopted under Paragraph 40 hereof that are to be observed, complied with or performed by Lessee, other than those described in Subparagraphs 13.1(a), (b) or (c), above, where such Default continues for a period of thirty (30) days after written notice thereof by or on behalf of Lessor to Lessee; provided, however, that if the nature of Lessee's Default is such that more than thirty (30) days are reasonably required for its cure, then it shall not be deemed to be a Breach of this Lease by Lessee if Lessee commences such cure within said thirty (30) day period and thereafter diligently prosecutes such cure to completion.

(e) The occurrence of any of the following events: (i) the making by Lessee of any general arrangement or assignment for the benefit of creditors; (ii) Lessee's becoming a "debtor" as defined in 11 U.S. Code Section 101 or any successor statute thereto (unless, in the case of a petition filed against Lessee, the same is dismissed within sixty (60) days); (iii) the appointment of a trustee or receiver to take possession of substantially all of Lessee's assets located at the Premises or of Lessee's interest in this Lease, where possession is not restored to Lessee within thirty (30) days; or (iv) the attachment, execution or other judicial seizure of substantially all of Lessee's assets located at the Premises or of Lessee's interest in this Lease, where such seizure is not discharged within thirty (30) days; provided, however, in the event that any provision of this Subparagraph 13.1(e) is contrary to any applicable law, such provision shall be of no force or effect, and shall not affect the validity of the remaining provisions.

(f) The discovery by Lessor that any financial statement of Lessee or of any Guarantor, given to Lessor by Lessee or any Guarantor, was materially false.

(g) If the performance of Lessee's obligations under this Lease is guaranteed: (i) the death of a Guarantor, (ii) the termination of a Guarantor's liability with respect to this Lease other than in accordance with the terms of such guaranty, (iii) a Guarantor's becoming insolvent or the subject of a bankruptcy filing, (iv) a Guarantor's refusal to honor the guaranty, or (v) a Guarantor's breach of its guaranty obligation on an anticipatory breach basis, and Lessee's failure, within sixty (60) days following written notice by or on behalf of Lessor to Lessee of any such event, to provide Lessor with written alternative assurances of security, which, when coupled with the then existing resources of Lessee, equals or exceeds the combined financial resources of Lessee and the Guarantors that existed at the time of execution of this Lease.

13.2 **Remedies.** If Lessee fails to perform any affirmative duty or obligation of Lessee under this Lease, within ten (10) days after written notice to Lessee (or in case of an emergency, without notice), Lessor may at its option (but without obligation to do so), perform such duty or obligation on Lessee's behalf, including but not limited to the obtaining of reasonably required bonds, insurance policies, or governmental licenses, permits or approvals. The costs and expenses of any such performance by Lessor shall be due and payable by Lessee to Lessor upon invoice therefor. If any check given to Lessor by Lessee shall not be honored by the bank upon which it is drawn, Lessor, at its own option, may require all future payments to be made under this Lease by Lessee to be made only by cashier's check. In the event of a Breach of this Lease by Lessee (as defined in Paragraph 13.1), with or without further notice or demand, and without limiting Lessor in the exercise of any right or remedy which Lessor may have by reason of such Breach, Lessor may:

(a) Terminate Lessee's right to possession of the Premises by any lawful means, in which case this Lease and the term hereof shall terminate and Lessee shall immediately surrender possession of the Premises to Lessor. In such event Lessor shall be entitled to recover from Lessee: (i) the worth at the time of the award of the unpaid rent which had been earned at the time of termination; (ii) the worth at the time of award of the amount by which the unpaid rent which would have been earned after termination until the time of award exceeds the amount of such rental loss that the Lessee proves could have been reasonably avoided; (iii) the worth at the time of award of the amount by which the unpaid rent for the balance of the term after the time of award exceeds the amount of such rental loss that the Lessee proves could be reasonably avoided; and (iv) any other amount necessary to compensate Lessor for all the detriment proximately caused by the Lessee's failure to perform its obligations under this Lease or which in the ordinary course of things would be likely to result therefrom, including but not limited to the cost of recovering possession of the Premises, expenses of reletting, including necessary renovation and alteration of the Premises, reasonable attorneys' fees, and that portion of any leasing commission paid by Lessor in connection with this Lease applicable to the unexpired term of this Lease. The worth at the time of award of the amount referred to in provision (iii) of the immediately preceding sentence shall be computed by discounting such amount at the discount rate of the Federal Reserve Bank of San Francisco or the Federal Reserve Bank District in which the Premises are located at the time of award plus one percent (1%). Efforts by Lessor to mitigate damages caused by Lessee's Default or Breach of this Lease shall not waive Lessor's right to recover damages under this Paragraph 13.2. If termination of this Lease is obtained through the provisional remedy of unlawful detainer, Lessor shall have the right to recover in such pro-

Initials: ___________

____

MULTI-TENANT—GROSS

—7—

Figure 11–1. Continued

ceeding the unpaid rent and damages as are recoverable therein, or Lessor may reserve the right to recover all or any part thereof in a separate suit for such rent and/or damages. If a notice and grace period required under Subparagraph 13.1(b), (c) or (d) was not previously given, a notice to pay rent or quit, or to perform or quit, as the case may be, given to Lessee under any statute authorizing the forfeiture of leases for unlawful detainer shall also constitute the applicable notice for grace period purposes required by Subparagraph 13.1(b),(c) or (d). In such case, the applicable grace period under the unlawful detainer statue shall run concurrently after the one such statutory notice, and the failure of Lessee to cure the Default within the greater of the two (2) such grace periods shall constitute both an unlawful detainer and a Breach of this Lease entitling Lessor to the remedies provided for in this Lease and/or by said statute.

(b) Continue the Lease and Lessee's right to possession in effect (in California under California Civil Code Section 1951.4) after Lessee's Breach and recover the rent as it becomes due, provided Lessee has the right to sublet or assign, subject only to reasonable limitations. Lessor and Lessee agree that the limitations on assignment and subletting in this Lease are reasonable. Acts of maintenance or preservation, efforts to relet the Premises, or the appointment of a receiver to protect the Lessor's interest under this Lease, shall not constitute a termination of the Lessee's right to possession.

(c) Pursue any other remedy now or hereafter available to Lessor under the laws or judicial decisions of the state wherein the Premises are located.

(d) The expiration or termination of this Lease and/or the termination of Lessee's right to possession shall not relieve Lessee from liability under any indemnity provisions of this Lease as to matters occurring or accruing during the term hereof or by reason of Lessee's occupancy of the Premises.

13.3 **Inducement Recapture In Event of Breach.** Any agreement by Lessor for free or abated rent or other charges applicable to the Premises, or for the giving or paying by Lessor to or for Lessee of any cash or other bonus, inducement or consideration for Lessee's entering into this Lease, all of which concessions are hereinafter referred to as **"Inducement Provisions"** shall be deemed conditioned upon Lessee's full and faithful performance of all of the terms, covenants and conditions of this Lease to be performed or observed by Lessee during the term hereof as the same may be extended. Upon the occurrence of a Breach (as defined in Paragraph 13.1) of this Lease by Lessee, any such Inducement Provision shall automatically be deemed deleted from this Lease and of no further force or effect, and any rent, other charge, bonus, inducement or consideration theretofore abated, given or paid by Lessor under such an Inducement Provision shall be immediately due and payable by Lessee to Lessor, and recoverable by Lessor, as additional rent due under this Lease, notwithstanding any subsequent cure of said Breach by Lessee. The acceptance by Lessor of rent or the cure of the Breach which initiated the operation of this Paragraph 13.3 shall not be deemed a waiver by Lessor of the provisions of this Paragraph 13.3 unless specifically so stated in writing by Lessor at the time of such acceptance.

13.4 **Late Charges.** Lessee hereby acknowledges that late payment by Lessee to Lessor of rent and other sums due hereunder will cause Lessor to incur costs not contemplated by this Lease, the exact amount of which will be extremely difficult to ascertain. Such costs include, but are not limited to, processing and accounting charges, and late charges which may be imposed upon Lessor by the terms of any ground lease, mortgage or deed of trust covering the Premises. Accordingly, if any installment of rent or other sum due from Lessee shall not be received by Lessor or Lessor's designee within ten (10) days after such amount shall be due, then, without any requirement for notice to Lessee, Lessee shall pay to Lessor a late charge equal to six percent (6%) of such overdue amount. The parties hereby agree that such late charge represents a fair and reasonable estimate of the costs Lessor will incur by reason of late payment by Lessee. Acceptance of such late charge by Lessor shall in no event constitute a waiver of Lessee's Default or Breach with respect to such overdue amount, nor prevent Lessor from exercising any of the other rights and remedies granted hereunder. In the event that a late charge is payable hereunder, whether or not collected, for three (3) consecutive installments of Base Rent, then notwithstanding Paragraph 4.1 or any other provision of this Lease to the contrary, Base Rent shall, at Lessor's option, become due and payable quarterly in advance.

13.5 **Breach by Lessor.** Lessor shall not be deemed in breach of this Lease unless Lessor fails within a reasonable time to perform an obligation required to be performed by Lessor. For purposes of this Paragraph 13.5, a reasonable time shall in no event be less than thirty (30) days after receipt by Lessor, and by any Lender(s) whose name and address shall have been furnished to Lessee in writing for such purpose, of written notice specifying wherein such obligation of Lessor has not been performed; provided, however, that if the nature of Lessor's obligation is such that more than thirty (30) days after such notice are reasonably required for its performance, then Lessor shall not be in breach of this Lease if performance is commenced within such thirty (30) day period and thereafter diligently pursued to completion.

14. Condemnation. If the Premises or any portion thereof are taken under the power of eminent domain or sold under the threat of the exercise of said power (all of which are herein called "condemnation"), this Lease shall terminate as to the part so taken as of the date the condemning authority takes title or possession, whichever first occurs. If more than ten percent (10%) of the floor area of the Premises, or more than twenty-five percent (25%) of the portion of the Common Areas designated for Lessee's parking, is taken by condemnation, Lessee may, at Lessee's option, to be exercised in writing within ten (10) days after Lessor shall have given Lessee written notice of such taking (or in the absence of such notice, within ten (10) days after the condemning authority shall have taken possession) terminate this Lease as of the date the condemning authority takes such possession. If Lessee does not terminate this Lease in accordance with the foregoing, this Lease shall remain in full force and effect as to the portion of the Premises remaining, except that the Base Rent shall be reduced in the same proportion as the rentable floor area of the Premises taken bears to the total rentable floor area of the Premises. No reduction of Base Rent shall occur if the condemnation does not apply to any portion of the Premises. Any award for the taking of all or any part of the Premises under the power of eminent domain or any payment made under threat of the exercise of such power shall be the property of Lessor, whether such award shall be made as compensation for diminution of value of the leasehold or for the taking of the fee, or as severance damages; provided, however, that Lessee shall be entitled to any compensation, separately awarded to Lessee for Lessee's relocation expenses and/or loss of Lessee's Trade Fixtures. In the event that this Lease is not terminated by reason of such condemnation, Lessor shall to the extent of its net severance damages received, over and above Lessee's Share of the legal and other expenses incurred by Lessor in the condemnation matter, repair any damage to the Premises caused by such condemnation authority. Lessee shall be responsible for the payment of any amount in excess of such net severance damages required to complete such repair.

15. Brokers' Fees.

15.1 **Procuring Cause.** The Broker(s) named in Paragraph 1.10 is/are the procuring cause of this Lease.

15.2 **Additional Terms.** Unless Lessor and Broker(s) have otherwise agreed in writing, Lessor agrees that: (a) if Lessee exercises any Option (as defined in Paragraph 39.1) granted under this Lease or any Option subsequently granted, or (b) if Lessee acquires any rights to the Premises or other premises in which Lessor has an interest, or (c) if Lessee remains in possession of the Premises with the consent of Lessor after the expiration of the term of this Lease after having failed to exercise an Option, or (d) if said Brokers are the procuring cause of any other lease or sale entered into between the Parties pertaining to the Premises and/or any adjacent property in which Lessor has an interest, or (e) if Base Rent is increased, whether by agreement or operation of an escalation clause herein, then as to any of said transactions, Lessor shall pay said Broker(s) a fee in accordance with the schedule of said Broker(s) in effect at the time of the execution of this Lease.

15.3 **Assumption of Obligations.** Any buyer or transferee of Lessor's interest in this Lease, whether such transfer is by agreement or by operation of law, shall be deemed to have assumed Lessor's obligation under this Paragraph 15. Each Broker shall be an intended third party beneficiary of the provisions of Paragraph 1.10 and of this Paragraph 15 to the extent of its interest in any commission arising from this Lease and may enforce that right directly against Lessor and its successors.

15.4 **Representations and Warranties.** Lessee and Lessor each represent and warrant to the other that it has had no dealings with any person, firm, broker or finder other than as named in Paragraph 1.10(a) in connection with the negotiation of this Lease and/or the consummation of the transaction contemplated hereby, and that no broker or other person, firm or entity other than said named Broker(s) is entitled to any commission or finder's fee in connection with said transaction. Lessee and Lessor do each hereby agree to indemnify, protect, defend and hold the other harmless from and against liability for compensation or charges which may be claimed by any such unnamed broker, finder or other similar party by reason of any dealings or actions of the indemnifying Party, including any costs, expenses, and/or attorneys' fees reasonably incurred with respect thereto.

16. Tenancy and Financial Statements.

16.1 **Tenancy Statement.** Each Party (as **"Responding Party"**) shall within ten (10) days after written notice from the other Party (the **"Requesting Party"**) execute, acknowledge and deliver to the Requesting Party a statement in writing in a form similar to the then most current **"Tenancy Statement"** form published by the American Industrial Real Estate Association, plus such additional information, confirmation and/or statements as may be reasonably requested by the Requesting Party.

16.2 **Financial Statement.** If Lessor desires to finance, refinance, or sell the Premises or the Building, or any part thereof, Lessee and all Guarantors shall deliver to any potential lender or purchaser designated by Lessor such financial statements of Lessee and such Guarantors as may be reasonably required by such lender or purchaser, including but not limited to Lessee's financial statements for the past three (3) years. All such financial statements shall be received by Lessor and such lender or purchaser in confidence and shall be used only for the purposes herein set forth.

17. Lessor's Liability. The term **"Lessor"** as used herein shall mean the owner or owners at the time in question of the fee title to the Premises. In the event of a transfer of Lessor's title or interest in the Premises or in this Lease, Lessor shall deliver to the transferee or assignee (in cash or by credit) any unused Security Deposit held by Lessor at the time of such transfer or assignment. Except as provided in Paragraph 15.3, upon such transfer or assignment and delivery of the Security Deposit, as aforesaid, the prior Lessor shall be relieved of all liability with respect to the obligations and/or covenants under this Lease thereafter to be performed by the Lessor. Subject to the foregoing, the obligations and/or covenants in this Lease to be performed by the Lessor shall be binding only upon the Lessor as hereinabove defined.

18. Severability. The invalidity of any provision of this Lease, as determined by a court of competent jurisdiction, shall in no way affect the validity of any other provision hereof.

19. Interest on Past-Due Obligations. Any monetary payment due Lessor hereunder, other than late charges, not received by Lessor within ten (10) days following the date on which it was due, shall bear interest from the date due at the prime rate charged by the largest state chartered bank in the state in which the Premises are located plus four percent (4%) per annum, but not exceeding the maximum rate allowed by law, in addition to the potential late charge provided for in Paragraph 13.4.

20. Time of Essence. Time is of the essence with respect to the performance of all obligations to be performed or observed by the Parties under this Lease.

21. Rent Defined. All monetary obligations of Lessee to Lessor under the terms of this Lease are deemed to be rent.

22. No Prior or other Agreements; Broker Disclaimer. This Lease contains all agreements between the Parties with respect to any matter mentioned herein, and no other prior or contemporaneous agreement or understanding shall be effective. Lessor and Lessee each represents and warrants to the Brokers that it has made, and is relying solely upon, its own investigation as to the nature, quality, character and financial responsibility of the other Party to this Lease and as to the nature, quality and character of the Premises. Brokers have no responsibility with respect thereto or with respect to any default or breach hereof by either Party. Each Broker shall be an intended third party beneficiary of the provisions of this Paragraph 22.

Initials: ____________

____

MULTI-TENANT–GROSS

—8—

Figure 11–1. Continued

(Continued)

23. Notices.

23.1   **Notice Requirements**. All notices required or permitted by this Lease shall be in writing and may be delivered in person (by hand or by messenger or courier service) or may be sent by regular, certified or registered mail or U.S. Postal Service Express Mail, with postage prepaid, or by facsimile transmission during normal business hours, and shall be deemed sufficiently given if served in a manner specified in this Paragraph 23. The addresses noted adjacent to a Party's signature on this Lease shall be that Party's address for delivery or mailing of notice purposes. Either Party may by written notice to the other specify a different address for notice purposes, except that upon Lessee's taking possession of the Premises, the Premises shall constitute Lessee's address for the purpose of mailing or delivering notices to Lessee. A copy of all notices required or permitted to be given to Lessor hereunder shall be concurrently transmitted to such party or parties at such addresses as Lessor may from time to time hereafter designate by written notice to Lessee.

23.2   **Date of Notice**. Any notice sent by registered or certified mail, return receipt requested, shall be deemed given on the date of delivery shown on the receipt card, or if no delivery date is shown, the postmark thereon. If sent by regular mail, the notice shall be deemed given forty-eight (48) hours after the same is addressed as required herein and mailed with postage prepaid. Notices delivered by United States Express Mail or overnight courier that guarantees next day delivery shall be deemed given twenty-four (24) hours after delivery of the same to the United States Postal Service or courier. If any notice is transmitted by facsimile transmission or similar means, the same shall be deemed served or delivered upon telephone or facsimile confirmation of receipt of the transmission thereof, provided a copy is also delivered via delivery or mail. If notice is received on a Saturday or a Sunday or a legal holiday, it shall be deemed received on the next business day.

24. Waivers. No waiver by Lessor of the Default or Breach of any term, covenant or condition hereof by Lessee, shall be deemed a waiver of any other term, covenant or condition hereof, or of any subsequent Default or Breach by Lessee of the same or any other term, covenant or condition hereof. Lessor's consent to, or approval of, any such act shall not be deemed to render unnecessary the obtaining of Lessor's consent to, or approval of, any subsequent or similar act by Lessee, or be construed as the basis of an estoppel to enforce the provision or provisions of this Lease requiring such consent. Regardless of Lessor's knowledge of a Default or Breach at the time of accepting rent, the acceptance of rent by Lessor shall not be a waiver of any Default or Breach by Lessee of any provision hereof. Any payment given Lessor by Lessee may be accepted by Lessor on account of moneys or damages due Lessor, notwithstanding any qualifying statements or conditions made by Lessee in connection therewith, which such statements and/or conditions shall be of no force or effect whatsoever unless specifically agreed to in writing by Lessor at or before the time of deposit of such payment.

25. Recording. Either Lessor or Lessee shall, upon request of the other, execute, acknowledge and deliver to the other a short form memorandum of this Lease for recording purposes. The Party requesting recordation shall be responsible for payment of any fees or taxes applicable thereto.

26. No Right To Holdover. Lessee has no right to retain possession of the Premises or any part thereof beyond the expiration or earlier termination of this Lease. In the event that Lessee holds over in violation of this Paragraph 26 then the Base Rent payable from and after the time of the expiration or earlier termination of this Lease shall be increased to two hundred percent (200%) of the Base Rent applicable during the month immediately preceding such expiration or earlier termination. Nothing contained herein shall be construed as a consent by Lessor to any holding over by Lessee.

27. Cumulative Remedies. No remedy or election hereunder shall be deemed exclusive but shall, wherever possible, be cumulative with all other remedies at law or in equity.

28. Covenants and Conditions. All provisions of this Lease to be observed or performed by Lessee are both covenants and conditions.

29. Binding Effect; Choice of Law. This Lease shall be binding upon the Parties, their personal representatives, successors and assigns and be governed by the laws of the State in which the Premises are located. Any litigation between the Parties hereto concerning this Lease shall be initiated in the county in which the Premises are located.

30. Subordination; Attornment; Non-Disturbance.

30.1   **Subordination.** This Lease and any Option granted hereby shall be subject and subordinate to any ground lease, mortgage, deed of trust, or other hypothecation or security device (collectively, **"Security Device"**), now or hereafter placed by Lessor upon the real property of which the Premises are a part, to any and all advances made on the security thereof, and to all renewals, modifications, consolidations, replacements and extensions thereof. Lessee agrees that the Lenders holding any such Security Device shall have no duty, liability or obligation to perform any of the obligations of Lessor under this Lease, but that in the event of Lessor's default with respect to any such obligation, Lessee will give any Lender whose name and address have been furnished Lessee in writing for such purpose notice of Lessor's default pursuant to Paragraph 13.5. If any Lender shall elect to have this Lease and/or any Option granted hereby superior to the lien of its Security Device and shall give written notice thereof to Lessee, this Lease and such Options shall be deemed prior to such Security Device, notwithstanding the relative dates of the documentation or recordation thereof.

30.2   **Attornment.** Subject to the non-disturbance provisions of Paragraph 30.3, Lessee agrees to attorn to a Lender or any other party who acquires ownership of the Premises by reason of a foreclosure of a Security Device, and that in the event of such foreclosure, such new owner shall not: (i) be liable for any act or omission of any prior lessor or with respect to events occurring prior to acquisition of ownership, (ii) be subject to any offsets or defenses which Lessee might have against any prior lessor, or (iii) be bound by prepayment of more than one month's rent.

30.3   **Non-Disturbance.** With respect to Security Devices entered into by Lessor after the execution of this lease, Lessee's subordination of this Lease shall be subject to receiving assurance (a "non-disturbance agreement") from the Lender that Lessee's possession and this Lease, including any options to extend the term hereof, will not be disturbed so long as Lessee is not in Breach hereof and attorns to the record owner of the Premises.

30.4   **Self-Executing.** The agreements contained in this Paragraph 30 shall be effective without the execution of any further documents; provided, however, that upon written request from Lessor or a Lender in connection with a sale, financing or refinancing of Premises, Lessee and Lessor shall execute such further writings as may be reasonably required to separately document any such subordination or non-subordination, attornment and/or non-disturbance agreement as is provided for herein.

31. Attorneys' Fees. If any Party or Broker brings an action or proceeding to enforce the terms hereof or declare rights hereunder, the Prevailing Party (as hereafter defined) in any such proceeding, action, or appeal thereon, shall be entitled to reasonable attorneys' fees. Such fees may be awarded in the same suit or recovered in a separate suit, whether or not such action or proceeding is pursued to decision or judgment. The term **"Prevailing Party"** shall include, without limitation, a Party or Broker who substantially obtains or defeats the relief sought, as the case may be, whether by compromise, settlement, judgment, or the abandonment by the other Party or Broker of its claim or defense. The attorneys' fee award shall not be computed in accordance with any court fee schedule, but shall be such as to fully reimburse all attorneys' fees reasonably incurred. Lessor shall be entitled to attorneys' fees, costs and expenses incurred in preparation and service of notices of Default and consultations in connection therewith, whether or not a legal action is subsequently commenced in connection with such Default or resulting Breach. Broker(s) shall be intended third party beneficiaries of this Paragraph 31.

32. Lessor's Access; Showing Premises; Repairs. Lessor and Lessor's agents shall have the right to enter the Premises at any time, in the case of an emergency, and otherwise at reasonable times for the purpose of showing the same to prospective purchasers, lenders, or lessees, and making such alterations, repairs, improvements or additions to the Premises or to the Building, as Lessor may reasonably deem necessary. Lessor may at any time place on or about the Premises or Building any ordinary "For Sale" signs and Lessor may at any time during the last one hundred eighty (180) days of the term hereof place on or about the Premises any ordinary "For Lease" signs. All such activities of Lessor shall be without abatement of rent or liability to Lessee.

33. Auctions. Lessee shall not conduct, nor permit to be conducted, either voluntarily or involuntarily, any auction upon the Premises without first having obtained Lessor's prior written consent. Notwithstanding anything to the contrary in this Lease, Lessor shall not be obligated to exercise any standard of reasonableness in determining whether to grant such consent.

34. Signs. Lessee shall not place any sign upon the exterior of the Premises or the Building, except that Lessee may, with Lessor's prior written consent, install (but not on the roof) such signs as are reasonably required to advertise Lessee's own business so long as such signs are in a location designated by Lessor and comply with Applicable Requirements and the signage criteria established for the Industrial Center by Lessor. The installation of any sign on the Premises by or for Lessee shall be subject to the provisions of Paragraph 7 (Maintenance, Repairs, Utility Installations, Trade Fixtures and Alterations). Unless otherwise expressly agreed herein, Lessor reserves all rights to the use of the roof of the Building, and the right to install advertising signs on the Building, including the roof, which do not unreasonably interfere with the conduct of Lessee's business; Lessor shall be entitled to all revenues from such advertising signs.

35. Termination; Merger. Unless specifically stated otherwise in writing by Lessor, the voluntary or other surrender of this Lease by Lessee, the mutual termination or cancellation hereof, or a termination hereof by Lessor for Breach by Lessee, shall automatically terminate any sublease or lesser estate in the Premises; provided, however, Lessor shall, in the event of any such surrender, termination or cancellation, have the option to continue any one or all of any existing subtenancies. Lessor's failure within ten (10) days following any such event to make a written election to the contrary by written notice to the holder of any such lesser interest, shall constitute Lessor's election to have such event constitute the termination of such interest.

36. Consents.

(a) Except for Paragraph 33 hereof (Auctions) or as otherwise provided herein, wherever in this Lease the consent of a Party is required to an act by or for the other Party, such consent shall not be unreasonably withheld or delayed. Lessor's actual reasonable costs and expenses (including but not limited to architects', attorneys', engineers' and other consultants' fees) incurred in the consideration of, or response to, a request by Lessee for any Lessor consent pertaining to this Lease or the Premises, including but not limited to consents to an assignment a subletting or the presence or use of a Hazardous Substance, shall be paid by Lessee to Lessor upon receipt of an invoice and supporting documentation therefor. In addition to the deposit described in Paragraph 12.2(e), Lessor may, as a condition to considering any such request by Lessee, require that Lessee deposit with Lessor an amount of money (in addition to the Security Deposit held under Paragraph 5) reasonably calculated by Lessor to represent the cost Lessor will incur in considering and responding to Lessee's request. Any unused portion of said deposit shall be refunded to Lessee without interest. Lessor's consent to any act, assignment of this Lease or subletting of the Premises by Lessee shall not constitute an acknowledgment that no Default or Breach by Lessee of this Lease exists, nor shall such consent be deemed a waiver of any then existing Default or Breach, except as may be otherwise specifically stated in writing by Lessor at the time of such consent.

(b) All conditions to Lessor's consent authorized by this Lease are acknowledged by Lessee as being reasonable. The failure to specify herein any particular condition to Lessor's consent shall not preclude the impositions by Lessor at the time of consent of such further or other conditions as are then reasonable with reference to the particular matter for which consent is being given.

37. Guarantor.

37.1   **Form of Guaranty**. If there are to be any Guarantors of this Lease per Paragraph 1.11, the form of the guaranty to be executed by each such Guarantor shall be in the form most recently published by the American Industrial Real Estate Association, and each such Guarantor shall have the same obligations as Lessee under this lease, including but not limited to the obligation to provide the Tenancy Statement and information required in Paragraph 16.

Initials: _____

_____

MULTI-TENANT—GROSS
© American Industrial Real Estate Association 1993   —9—

Figure 11–1.   Continued

37.2 **Additional Obligations of Guarantor.** It shall constitute a Default of the Lessee under this Lease if any such Guarantor fails or refuses, upon reasonable request by Lessor to give: (a) evidence of the due execution of the guaranty called for by this Lease, including the authority of the Guarantor (and of the party signing on Guarantor's behalf) to obligate such Guarantor on said guaranty, and resolution of its board of directors authorizing the making of such guaranty, together with a certificate of incumbency showing the signatures of the persons authorized to sign on its behalf, (b) current financial statements of Guarantor as may from time to time be requested by Lessor, (c) a Tenancy Statement, or (d) written confirmation that the guaranty is still in effect.

38. Quiet Possession. Upon payment by Lessee of the rent for the Premises and the performance of all of the covenants, conditions and provisions on Lessee's part to be observed and performed under this Lease, Lessee shall have quiet possession of the Premises for the entire term hereof subject to all of the provisions of this Lease.

39. Options.

39.1 **Definition.** As used in this Lease, the word **"Option"** has the following meaning: (a) the right to extend the term of this Lease or to renew this Lease or to extend or renew any lease that Lessee has on other property of Lessor; (b) the right of first refusal to lease the Premises or the right of first offer to lease the Premises or the right of first refusal to lease other property of Lessor or the right of first offer to lease other property of Lessor; (c) the right to purchase the Premises, or the right of first refusal to purchase the Premises, or the right of first offer to purchase the Premises, or the right to purchase other property of Lessor, or the right of first refusal to purchase other property of Lessor, or the right of first offer to purchase other property of Lessor.

39.2 **Options Personal to Original Lessee.** Each Option granted to Lessee in this Lease is personal to the original Lessee named in Paragraph 1.1 hereof, and cannot be voluntarily or involuntarily assigned or exercised by any person or entity other than said original Lessee while the original Lessee is in full and actual possession of the Premises and without the intention of thereafter assigning or subletting. The Options, if any, herein granted to Lessee are not assignable, either as a part of an assignment of this Lease or separately or apart therefrom, and no Option may be separated from this Lease in any manner, by reservation or otherwise.

39.3 **Multiple Options.** In the event that Lessee has any multiple Options to extend or renew this Lease, a later option cannot be exercised unless the prior Options to extend or renew this Lease have been validly exercised.

39.4 **Effect of Default on Options.**

(a) Lessee shall have no right to exercise an Option, notwithstanding any provision in the grant of Option to the contrary: (i) during the period commencing with the giving of any notice of Default under Paragraph 13.1 and continuing until the noticed Default is cured, or (ii) during the period of time any monetary obligation due Lessor from Lessee is unpaid (without regard to whether notice thereof is given Lessee), or (iii) during the time Lessee is in Breach of this Lease, or (iv) in the event that Lessor has given to Lessee three (3) or more notices of separate Defaults under Paragraph 13.1 during the twelve (12) month period immediately preceding the exercise of the Option, whether or not the Defaults are cured.

(b) The period of time within which an Option may be exercised shall not be extended or enlarged by reason of Lessee's inability to exercise an Option because of the provisions of Paragraph 39.4(a)

(c) All rights of Lessee under the provisions of an Option shall terminate and be of no further force or effect, notwithstanding Lessee's due and timely exercise of the Option, if, after such exercise and during the term of this Lease, (i) Lessee fails to pay to Lessor a monetary obligation of Lessee for a period of thirty (30) days after such obligation becomes due (without any necessity of Lessor to give notice thereof to Lessee), or (ii) Lessor gives to Lessee three (3) or more notices of separate Defaults under Paragraph 13.1 during any twelve (12) month period, whether or not the Defaults are cured, or (iii) if Lessee commits a Breach of this Lease.

40. Rules and Regulations. Lessee agrees that it will abide by, and keep and observe all reasonable rules and regulations ("Rules and Regulations") which Lessor may make from time to time for the management, safety, care, and cleanliness of the grounds, the parking and unloading of vehicles and the preservation of good order, as well as for the convenience of other occupants or tenants of the Building and the Industrial Center and their invitees.

41. Security Measures. Lessee hereby acknowledges that the rental payable to Lessor hereunder does not include the cost of guard service or other security measures, and that Lessor shall have no obligation whatsoever to provide same. Lessee assumes all responsibility for the protection of the Premises, Lessee, its agents and invitees and their property from the acts of third parties.

42. Reservations. Lessor reserves the right, from time to time, to grant, without the consent or joinder of Lessee, such easements, rights of way, utility raceways, and dedications that Lessor deems necessary, and to cause the recordation of parcel maps and restrictions, so long as such easements, rights of way, utility raceways, dedications, maps and restrictions do not reasonably interfere with the use of the Premises by Lessee. Lessee agrees to sign any documents reasonably requested by Lessor to effectuate any such easement rights, dedication, map or restrictions.

43. Performance Under Protest. If at any time a dispute shall arise as to any amount or sum of money to be paid by one Party to the other under the provisions hereof, the Party against whom the obligation to pay the money is asserted shall have the right to make payment "under protest" and such payment shall not be regarded as a voluntary payment and there shall survive the right on the part of said Party to institute suit for recovery of such sum. If it shall be adjudged that there was no legal obligation on the part of said Party to pay such sum or any part thereof, said Party shall be entitled to recover such sum or so much thereof as it was not legally required to pay under the provisions of this Lease.

44. Authority. If either Party hereto is a corporation, trust, or general or limited partnership, each individual executing this Lease on behalf of such entity represents and warrants that he or she is duly authorized to execute and deliver this Lease on its behalf. If Lessee is a corporation, trust or partnership, Lessee shall, within thirty (30) days after request by Lessor, deliver to Lessor evidence satisfactory to Lessor of such authority.

45. Conflict. Any conflict between the printed provisions of this Lease and the typewritten or handwritten provisions shall be controlled by the typewritten or handwritten provisions.

46. Offer. Preparation of this Lease by either Lessor or Lessee or Lessor's agent or Lessee's agent and submission of same to Lessee or Lessor shall not be deemed an offer to lease. This Lease is not intended to be binding until executed and delivered by all Parties hereto.

47. Amendments. This Lease may be modified only in writing, signed by the parties in interest at the time of the modification. The Parties shall amend this Lease from time to time to reflect any adjustments that are made to the Base Rent or other rent payable under this Lease. As long as they do not materially change Lessee's obligations hereunder, Lessee agrees to make such reasonable non-monetary modifications to this Lease as may be reasonably required by an institutional insurance company or pension plan Lender in connection with the obtaining of normal financing or refinancing of the property of which the Premises are a part.

48. Multiple Parties. Except as otherwise expressly provided herein, if more than one person or entity is named herein as either Lessor or Lessee, the obligations of such multiple parties shall be the joint and several responsibility of all persons or entities named herein as such Lessor or Lessee.

Initials: _____

_____

(Continued)

Figure 11–1. Continued

Research and Development (R&D) Building Characteristics   **219**

LESSOR AND LESSEE HAVE CAREFULLY READ AND REVIEWED THIS LEASE AND EACH TERM AND PROVISION CONTAINED HEREIN, AND BY THE EXECUTION OF THIS LEASE SHOW THEIR INFORMED AND VOLUNTARY CONSENT THERETO. THE PARTIES HEREBY AGREE THAT, AT THE TIME THIS LEASE IS EXECUTED, THE TERMS OF THIS LEASE ARE COMMERCIALLY REASONABLE AND EFFECTUATE THE INTENT AND PURPOSE OF LESSOR AND LESSEE WITH RESPECT TO THE PREMISES.

IF THIS LEASE HAS BEEN FILLED IN, IT HAS BEEN PREPARED FOR YOUR ATTORNEY'S REVIEW AND APPROVAL. FURTHER, EXPERTS SHOULD BE CONSULTED TO EVALUATE THE CONDITION OF THE PROPERTY FOR THE POSSIBLE PRESENCE OF ASBESTOS, UNDERGROUND STORAGE TANKS OR HAZARDOUS SUBSTANCES. NO REPRESENTATION OR RECOMMENDATION IS MADE BY THE AMERICAN INDUSTRIAL REAL ESTATE ASSOCIATION OR BY THE REAL ESTATE BROKERS OR THEIR CONTRACTORS, AGENTS OR EMPLOYEES AS TO THE LEGAL SUFFICIENCY, LEGAL EFFECT, OR TAX CONSEQUENCES OF THIS LEASE OR THE TRANSACTION TO WHICH IT RELATES; THE PARTIES SHALL RELY SOLELY UPON THE ADVICE OF THEIR OWN COUNSEL AS TO THE LEGAL AND TAX CONSEQUENCES OF THIS LEASE. IF THE SUBJECT PROPERTY IS IN A STATE OTHER THAN CALIFORNIA, AN ATTORNEY FROM THE STATE WHERE THE PROPERTY IS LOCATED SHOULD BE CONSULTED.

The parties hereto have executed this Lease at the place and on the dates specified above their respective signatures.

Executed at: _____   Executed at: _____

on: _____   on: _____

By **LESSOR**:   By **LESSEE**:

_____   _____

_____   _____

By: _____   By: _____

Name Printed: _____   Name Printed: _____

Title: _____   Title: _____

By: _____   By: _____

Name Printed: _____   Name Printed: _____

Title: _____   Title: _____

Address: _____   Address: _____

_____   _____

Telephone: (   ) _____   Telephone: (   ) _____

Facsimile: (   ) _____   Facsimile: (   ) _____

BROKER: **BROKER:**

Executed at: _____   Executed at: _____

on: _____   on: _____

By: _____   By: _____

Name Printed: _____   Name Printed: _____

Title: _____   Title _____

Address: _____   Address: _____

_____   _____

Telephone: (   ) _____   Telephone: (   ) _____

Facsimile: (   ) _____   Facsimile: (   ) _____

NOTE: These forms are often modified to meet changing requirements of law and needs of the industry. Always write or call to make sure you are utilizing the most current form: AMERICAN INDUSTRIAL REAL ESTATE ASSOCIATION, 345 So. Figueroa St., M-1, Los Angeles, CA 90071. (213) 687-8777.

Initials: _____

_____

MULTI-TENANT—GROSS
© American Industrial Real Estate Association 1993   —11—

Figure 11–1. Continued

4. *Rental rates.* The rents are considerably higher than for industrial buildings, but lower than for office buildings.

5. *Trends.* The trend is for conversion of existing industrial buildings into research and development space.

Government Approvals   In some states, before construction of a building, the environmental impact must be considered. Some environmental quality laws declare that "the long-term protection of the environment, consistent with the provision of a decent home and suitable living environment, shall be the guiding criterion in public decisions."

An assessment of a proposed project or activity must be made to determine whether it will have significant environmental effects on our man-made or natural environment. When no significant environmental impact will result, an environmental impact report (EIR) is not needed. Instead, a "negative declaration" is submitted and signed by the city or county planning department on the proposed project. Some significant environmental effects would be:

1. the displacing of existing homeowners or tenants (e.g., tearing down old homes inhabited by blue-collar workers and building luxury condominiums);

2. the altering or disrupting of a scenic, recreational, or historical site (e.g., an Indian burial ground);

3. the altering or disrupting of air or water quality (e.g., causing air pollution by building a steel mill);

4. the changing of land use or the causing of traffic congestion (e.g., converting farmland into a housing subdivision);

5. the threatening or endangering of rare birds or plants (e.g., development on a bird sanctuary).

In order to comply with environmental quality laws, the developer may be required to undertake mitigation measures such as dedicating park land, building roads, or having an archaeologist on site during grading.

MOBILE HOME PARK MANAGEMENT

A mobile home park is defined by the California Department of Real Estate as "any area or tract of land where one or more mobile homes are rented or leased." A mobile home is actually a hybrid between a dwelling and a vehicle, and as larger and more attractive units are being built they have become more permanent and frequently are only moved once.

In some states, new mobile homes are taxed as real and not personal property. Park jurisdiction may fall under a state agency such as Housing and Community Development.

1. *Evictions.* Evictions from mobile home parks are more difficult and take longer than for residential income properties in some states. For example, in California a 60-day rather than a 30-day notice to vacate may be required from the manager. Eviction for cause must be proved by the manager: (1) nonpayment of space rent; (2) willful and malicious violation of park rules and covenants.

2. *Notices.* Rent increases may require a 60- to 90-day notice. Park rule changes may require six months' notice unless all residents agree. These involve pets, noise, speed limits, etc.

3. *Billing.* In addition to paying rent, the expenses of water, gas, and electricity are frequently metered and rebilled for payment by the tenants.

4. *Tenant unions.* Many parks have tenant unions and the park manager must deal with them and their demands.

5. *Tenant mix.* Senior citizens, many of whom are on fixed incomes, make up the majority of tenants. Mobile home parks or apartment buildings can qualify for a senior citizen exemption to the Amendments Acts of 1988 on

discrimination against children in one of two ways. First is housing, intended solely for persons 62 years and older. Second is where 80 percent of the units have at least one resident over the age of 55. Careful screening of new tenants by the property manager, similar to that in residential management (Chapter 7), is essential to avoid claims discrimination.

6. *Ratings*. Parks are rated according to location, layout, amenities, etc., with a five-star rating being the highest.

7. *Trends*. Prime-location mobile home parks, such as those near the ocean, are being sold so that the land will become a more profitable venture. Many mobile home parks near the ocean are being converted to condominium developments.

8. *Management opportunities*. This is a specialized area of management and one that should not be entered into casually. It requires expertise in its unique laws and regulations.

Federal Law

The Manufactured Home Construction and Safety Act (1976) established federal construction standards for design and installation of fire resistant and energy saving materials to meet minimum ratings. This law also regulates installation and standards for plumbing, air-conditioning, heating, and electrical for mobile homes.

State Law

Many states require inspection of mobile homes and mobile home parks at least once every five years. If violations are found, citations are issued to either the homeowner or park owner, depending on who is the responsible party.

Associations

Many states have their own association of mobile home park owners. Following is one such organization:

Western Mobile Home Association (WMA)
1007 7th Street, 3rd Floor
Sacramento, CA 95814

MINI-STORAGE FACILITIES MANAGEMENT

A recent phenomenon that began in the Southwest, but which has now spread nationwide, is the practice of using mini-storage or self-storage units. These facilities provide separate self-storage units of various sizes for individuals and businesses on a rental basis within one secure complex.

Layout

The typical layout consists of long, narrow buildings facing each other across large driveways (Figure 11–2). Units vary in size from 5' by 5' to 20' by 20' or larger. The average unit size is 115 square feet, with an average number of units per facility of approximately 544. The typical facility contains an average readable square footage of 56,073 according to a report by the Self Storage Association (*Profile of Self Storage Facilities Characteristics*, Cincinnati, Ohio, 1995). The report further states that the average office size is 486 square feet and that the national occupancy vote was 89 percent. More than half of all storage facilities use computerized record keeping. The Self Storage Association offers seminars and monthly publications to property managers and owners.

A good reference source for rental agreements and specific state laws is the *Self-Service Storage Rental Agreement: Handbook for Owners and Managers*, published by the Self-Service Storage Association.

According to a 1996 survey by the *Mini-Storage Messenger*, the four largest self-storage companies are U-Haul International, Public Storage, Storage USA, and Shurgard Storage Centers.

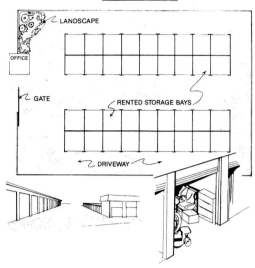

Figure 11-2. Mini-storage Layout

On-site Management

The management team usually includes a resident on-site manager. Duties of the on-site manager include collecting rents, preparing reports, screening applicants, renting units, and taking care of maintenance.

Property Management

The property manager's responsibilities include marketing, providing 24-hour security, obtaining insurance, managing finances, collecting rent, supervising the on-site manager, and being responsible for evictions. Computer gate access can control visitors and nonpaying tenants whose codes no longer work when rent is delinquent.

Other Important Information

The customer base varies according to locality. The normal mix is 70 percent residential and 30 percent commercial. In areas near expensive office buildings, businesses utilize the majority of storage space.

Security and safety are important, so mini-storage facilities often utilize closed-circuit cameras, gates, fences, and a method of screening visitors and customers for the successful operation of the complex.

MEDICAL BUILDING MANAGEMENT

Some investors consider office and medical building management identical. However, some major distinctions exist between the two. For this reason, it takes a professional property manager to properly manage medical buildings.

Location

The best location for a medical building is in close proximity to (within blocks of) a hospital. This helps doctors keep in close communication with their patients. They are also able to capitalize on being near such services as radiology and laboratories of various kinds. Having quick access to equipment not in the doctor's office generates additional income for the practice.

Maintenance

This is of particular concern to the property manager. Lobbies and hallways must be kept clean. Frequently, an emergency source of power (generator) is needed to automatically kick in during power outages. Window washers should be scheduled on weekends to provide patient privacy during exams.

Trash, such as contaminated needles, bandages, and so forth, must often be segregated into separate containers for special disposal.

Tenant Mix This is of utmost importance in a medical building. The most desirable arrangement is to have several general practitioners and pediatricians so they can refer patients to specialists such as orthopedists, plastic surgeons, in the same building.

Rental Rates Rental rates are usually higher in a medical building than in an ordinary office building. A pharmacy off the main lobby, for example, will command premium rent, including bonus or key money, which is an amount paid at the beginning of the lease for the privilege of renting in a desirable location.

RETIREMENT COMMUNITY MANAGEMENT

By the year 2000, over 13 percent of the U.S. population will be over the age of 62, and by 2030 the figure will be over 21 percent. This is due to higher life expectancy rates and the maturing of baby boomers. The names given to this older age group include senior citizens, Gray Panthers, elderly, retirees, and others. This author prefers a more positive and youthful-sounding name—"keenagers." The housing for these people falls into three major categories.

1. *Independent living*—retirement residence communities.
2. *Semi-independent living*—meals provided.
3. *Supported living*—nursing homes.

We will concentrate on retirement communities in which subdivisions, towns, and villages have been built expressly for the keenager. They are usually located near urban centers and cater to the middle and upper classes. These communities include amenities such as pools, recreation halls, handicraft centers, and other facilities to give residents a self-contained and secure place to live (protected by security gates). The communities contain anywhere from 500 to 20,000 units and frequently require full-time management personnel to operate.

The management staff for these operations includes clerical personnel, gardeners, maintenance people, an on-site manager, security personnel, and so on. The book, *Housing for the Elderly* by Rosetta Parker (IREM, 1984) lists the property manager's duties. These include functioning as a community worker and organizer as well as the property supervisor who enforces policy, directs staff work, monitors costs, and so on. As is very apparent, empathy and patience, along with expertise, knowledge, and experience in the area, are required of the property manager in order to be successful in the area of retirement community management.

RESORT RENTAL MANAGEMENT

Resort rentals are usually located near beaches, mountains, or other resort areas. The term of the rental is usually short (days or weeks). The manager needs a housekeeping or maintenance crew to ensure that cleanup is done quickly and properly.

Reservations and referral systems are a must. The management fee is very high, often exceeding 25 percent of the gross rental.

An offshoot area of resort management is that of timeshare complexes. These complexes have on-site managers, but many times need sophisticated control systems to streamline operations. For example, a 100-unit complex sold for occupancy one week in the year would handle 5,200 requests in order to match available dates. Most timeshares are run by an elected board of directors much like condominiums (Chapter 10).

HOSPITALITY (HOTEL) MANAGEMENT

In the language of today's hotel industry, a hotel is any facility that accommodates transient guests. From the downtown high-rise $750-a-room Hyatt Regency to the 11-room country bed and breakfast, all are included in the generic name—hotel.

While a hotel in the generic sense is any transient lodging facility, the terminology does get more specific. A "full-service hotel" has multistories; food, beverage, and other services; a lobby entrance; interior corridors; and remote parking. The word *motel* has disappeared from use, with a variety of more descriptive terms replacing it. *Motor inn* (exterior corridor, parking at the door) and *motor hotel* (interior corridor, parking at the building) are two of these.

Hotels are also distinguished by the price of the room, with full-service and luxury hotels having the highest prices, mid-market properties (usually motor hotels and motor inns) having mid-range prices, and economy having the lowest prices. The fastest-growing segment of the hotel market is, and has been for the last five years, the economy segment.

While many hotels have no brand name (these are called "independents"), many more belong to franchise groups or membership organizations. The primary benefits of affiliations are national and international reservations systems and group marketing and advertising programs.

The biggest of the franchising organizations are Holiday Inns, including Hampton Inns, and Choice International, which includes Quality Inns and Quality Suites, Clarion Hotels, Comfort Inns, Comfort Suites, Sleep Inns, Econolodge, Rodeway Inns, and Friendship Inns. In both cases, the parent organization may own some of the facilities, but most are owned and operated by the franchisees.

By far the largest of the affiliation groups is Best Western International, with over 2,000 worldwide affiliates and an aggressive program for growth.

Each state has at least one trade association for hotel owners and managers. California has two, the California Lodging Industry Association (formerly the California Motel Association) and the California Hotel & Motel Association. CLIA is primarily a lobbying organization that also seeks to provide such membership services as group-discounted insurance rates.

CH&MA also emphasizes lobbying, but as an affiliate of the American Hotel & Motel Association it has a broader perspective. At the national level the organization provides educational programs and the only professional designation available for hotel managers, certified hotel administrator (CHA).

FEDERALLY SUBSIDIZED HOUSING PROGRAMS

History and Background

Federal government involvement in housing was almost nonexistent until 1918 when, after World War I, Congress created the U.S. Housing Corporation. During the Depression years, the Federal Housing Authority (FHA) was created along with other programs to help provide more and better housing in the United States. During World War II, we saw the Soldiers and Sailors Relief Act, which provided mortgage relief for servicemen. In 1942, the Emergency Price Control Act authorized federal rent control. The Housing Act of 1949 established the federal government's commitment to housing by establishing the goal of "a decent home and a suitable living environment to every American family." This act created grants for urban renewal. The Housing Act of 1959 created new programs for elderly rental projects. The Department of Housing and Urban Development (HUD) was established in 1965. It was also the beginning of a rent supplement program to assist lower-income tenants so rent would not exceed 25 percent of income. The Housing and Urban Renewal Recovery Act of 1983 reduced some of the rent supplements and created a voucher system.

Section 8 Program

Under this program, a low-income tenant pays rent equal to 30 percent of net income. The government pays the difference between that amount and the fair market rent. Both payments go directly to the landlord. HUD does rental surveys to establish guidelines for fair market value depending on the size of the unit, utilities, and so forth. The landlord must accept this level and cannot request the tenant to pay any additional monies above the stated rent in the contract.

An inspection is also made to see if the unit meets HUD habitability standards. This program is voluntary and the landlord/manager does not have to participate. The program is based unit by unit and not on the entire building. For example, in a 20-unit building you may have any number of units rented to Section 8 tenants, but you need not rent them all in this manner. The lease term is usually for one year and is renegotiated annually.

Tenants, in order to qualify for eligibility, must make no more than 80 percent of the area median income with adjustments for household size. In some states, many area median incomes exceed $40,000 per year, which means tenants earning up to $32,000 could qualify.

Public Housing Authority

A public housing project is built by a joint venture of local and federal governments using tax-exempt bonds. The bond debt service is paid by the federal governments, and after the bonds are paid off, federal subsidies are paid. The tenant pays no more than 30 percent of income for rent. In some cases, however, the tenant's income could make the rent negligible. A minimum rent of 5 percent of the tenant's gross income or a portion of welfare payments stipulated for housing, whichever is greater, must be paid. Tenant selection and rent increases are based on complex guidelines that make management very difficult and cumbersome.

Elderly Housing

In the United States in 1995, more than 12.7 percent of the population was over the age of 65, according to the *World Almanac* (Mahwah, N.J., 1995). According to the National Council of Senior Citizens, approximately one-third of our elderly are living below the poverty level. The Housing Act of 1959, Section 202 Program, provides direct loans at below-market rates for up to 40 years for elderly housing. The Section 202 Program is also linked to Section 8, so that a tenant does not have to pay more than 30 percent of income for rent. Nonprofit corporations, limited-dividend partnerships, consumer cooperatives, and public agencies can be Section 202 sponsors.

Another elderly program is Section 231, a mortgage insurance program in which one-half of the units must be rented to the elderly or handicapped. Under Section 231, HUD will insure loans for the construction and rehabilitation of nursing homes.

Following is a list of multifamily HUD programs:

Section 207—loans for middle-income family housing projects.

Section 221(d)(3)—provided below-market-rate loans and direct subsidies.

Replaced by Section 236, the Mortgage Interest Reduction Program.

Section 223(f)—allows owners to realize equity buildup by refinancing or selling a project in older, declining urban areas.

Section 213—refers to cooperative programs.

Section 234—refers to condominium programs.

The management of subsidized housing is very detailed and exacting. A property manager should not accept such projects without proper training and/or backup support. Projects are usually large with huge density and high maintenance costs. Property management is very intensive with high turnover, rent loss, and collection problems. Tenant unions and more vocal residents often create management headaches. The Institute of Real Estate Management offers HUD-approved programs to train managers. Computer programs exist to help compile the many reports, forms, and statistics necessary for compliance. One such program for an IBM PC is called Micro-HUD.

HUD MANAGEMENT

Congress passed the Housing Act in 1935. The act recognized the need for housing for low-income families and created programs to meet that need. Congress has amended the act many times over the years to accommodate housing needs. Amendments to the act have created various programs for subsidizing mortgage interest rates while other programs subsidized the families themselves. Until the early 1980s, all of the various programs for family subsidies had their own sets of entrance requirements and paperwork. In the early 1980s, many of the programs for family subsidies were phased out and converted to current programs, and the paperwork became uniform and streamlined.

Although HUD is not currently issuing subsidy contracts except for senior citizen housing, it has a huge inventory of properties to oversee. A large majority of properties are privately owned, federally subsidized, and managed by fee managers. Owners and management agents must be approved by HUD on a case-by-case basis.

When approved, the agent must manage the property within HUD guidelines—using the government charts of accounts, submitting monthly income and expense reports when required, and setting up an annual certified audit. Of course, HUD has the right to inspect both the property and the agent's records to ensure they are being properly maintained.

The key to success in dealing with HUD is to make sure the owner knows and will follow the guidelines as described in the regulatory agreement. This document, written in plain English, describes the things the owner can and cannot do. Most HUD-related problems occur when the owner disregards the guidelines.

Agents should be willing to adapt to some minor changes in their accounting, leases/rental forms, and management agreements. Agents should also recognize the fact that HUD has a real interest (either by way of mortgage insurance or other subsidy) in the property and its goals are the same as those of the manager, to manage the property to its best potential.

Dealing with tenants in subsidized properties is not vastly different from dealing with tenants in conventional properties. However, there are some differences in the management processes. The screening of the residents is much the same as for conventional management except that many more personal financial questions must be asked and documented. In many cases, the house rules are easier to enforce because of the possibility of eviction for noncompliance. Tenants are possibly more motivated to comply knowing that they are not likely to find other suitable housing at such low rates. Eviction proceedings require much more documentation than unsubsidized, but evictions are not impossible. One vast difference between subsidized housing and conventional housing is that there is virtually no need for marketing once a subsidized project is built as there is always a waiting list of people who want to move in.

As stated at the beginning of this chapter, each type of property has its own area of specialization, and HUD management is no different. In order to demonstrate the paperwork involved, some HUD forms appear in Figures 11–3 to 11–5.

Owner's Certification of Compliance with HUD's Tenant Eligibility and Rent Procedures

U.S. Department of Housing and Urban Development

Office of Housing
Federal Housing Commissioner

Important: Read the Instructions in Appendix I of Handbook 4350.3 before completing this form.

OMB No. 2502-0204

Part I - GENERAL INFORMATION

1. Date this Form will be Effective. MM DD YY
2. Date Tenant Moved into this Project. MM DD YY
3. Project Name:

6. Action Processed: (See Instructions)
a. Always Enter One Code:
1= Move-Ins
2= Converted from:
3= Initial Certification
4= Annual Recertification
5= Interim Recertification

b. See Instructions:
1= Correction to prior 50059
2= Unit Transfer
3= Gross Rent Change
4= Rent Rebate

7. Type of Subsidy:
a. Subsidy Tenant will receive (Enter One Code):
1= Section 8
2= Rent Supplement
3= RAP
4= Section 236
5= BMIR
6= HUD-owned

b. Is this the type of subsidy the Family is NOW receiving? ☐ Yes ☐ No

4. FHA/Eh/Hon-Insured Project No.:
5. Section 8 Project Contract Number:

8. Complete this Item ONLY for Tenants who were already converted from Rent Supp. or RAP.
8a. Date Code (See Instructions)
8b. Was the Head or Spouse age 62 or older at time of conversion? ☐ Yes ☐ No
8c. Has the Family received Section 8 continuously since being converted? ☐ Yes ☐ No

9a. Race of Head of Household (Enter One Code):
1= White
2= Black
3= American Indian or Alaskan Native
4= Asian or Pacific Islander

9b. Ethnicity of Head of Household (Enter One Code):
1= Hispanic
2= Non-Hispanic

Use the Instructions to complete Items 10, 11, and 12.

10. Previous Housing Code (For Move-Ins ONLY)
11. Displace-ment Code (For Move-Ins or Initial Certifications ONLY)
12. Preference Code (For Move-Ins or Initial Certifications ONLY)

Part II - HOUSEHOLD COMPOSITION

13. Mbr. No.	14a. Last Name of Family Member	14b. First 8 Letters of First Name	14c. M.I.	15. Relationship to Head of Household	16. Sex	17. Date of Birth MM DD YY	18. Age	19. Spec Status Code
Head				Head of Household				
2								
3								
4								
5								
6								
7								
8								
9								

13. Mbr. No.	20. Social Security Number or Alien Registration Number	21. Elig. Code	22. Place of Birth	23. Family Member Occupation	
Head					24a. Number of Family Members
2					
3					24b. Number of Foster Children and Live-In Attendants
4					
5					
6					25. Number of Dependents
7					
8					
9					

Part III - NET FAMILY ASSETS AND INCOME (Read instructions before completing this Chart.)

26a. Type of Assets	26b. C or I	26c. Cash Value of Assets	26d. Actual Yearly Income from Assets
TOTALS			

IF the Total in Column 26c exceeds $5,000, complete Item 27, Otherwise, enter "N.A." in Item 27 AND GO TO Item 28.

27. IMPUTED INCOME FROM ASSETS: Enter the HUD-approved Passbook Rate here (%) and multiply the Total in Item 26c by that rate. $

28. INCOME (USE ANNUAL AMOUNTS) (Read instructions before completing this Chart.)

28. Mbr. No.	28a. Care Code	28b. Employment or Business	28c. Social Security, Pensions, etc.	28d. Public Assistance	28e. Other Income

28f. Total income from each source.

29. Income from all sources except Assets (Add all amounts on Line 28f above.) $

30. Income from Assets (Enter the Greater of Item 27 or Total in Item 26d.) $

31. ANNUAL INCOME (Item 29 plus Item 30.) $

32. INCOME LIMITS:
a. Lower... $
b. Very Low. $

33. Eligibility Universe (See Instructions)
☐ Pre-1981 ☐ Post 1981

34. Tenant's Current Income Status (See Instructions):
☐ Lower ☐ Very Low.

35a. Did Tenant begin receiving Section 8 assistance on or after July 1, 1984? ☐ Yes ☐ No

35b. If "Yes", enter one of the exception codes listed in the Instructions.

Part IV - ALLOWANCES AND ADJUSTED INCOME

36. Allowance for Dependents (Item 25 x $480) $
37. Child Care Allowance $
38. 3% of Annual Income (.03 x Item 31) $
39a. Total Handicapped Assistance Expenses $
39b. Allowance for Handicap Assistance (See Inst.) $
40a. Total Medical Expenses (Elderly Households ONLY) $
40b. Allowance for Medical Expenses (See Instructions) $
41. Elderly Household Allowance (See Instructions) $
42. Total Allowances (Add Lines 36, 37, 39b, 40b and 41) $
43. ADJUSTED INCOME (Line 31 minus Line 42.) $

Part V - PROJECT RENT INFORMATION (Use amounts that will be in effect on date shown in Item 1.)

44. CONTRACT RENT $
45. UTILITY ALLOWANCE $
46. GROSS RENT (Line 44 plus Line 45.) $

Part VI - FAMILY RENT & SUBSIDY INFORMATION (See Instructions)

47. WELFARE RENT $
48. HCDA percentage (leave blank if BMIR) ☐ 29% ☐ 30%
49. HUD-50059 Worksheet used (See Instructions):
50. TOTAL TENANT PAYMENT (TTP) $
51. TENANT RENT $
52. UTILITY REIMBURSEMENT $
53. ASSISTANCE PAYMENT (Line 46 minus Line 50) $
54. Percentage of Adjusted Income Charged %
55. Did the 1983 HURRA Rent Limitations affect the Tenant's Rent? ☐ Yes ☐ No

Part VII - UNIT ASSIGNMENT AND RECERTIFICATION INFORMATION

56. Date Next Annual Recertification Effective MM DD YY
57. Number of Bedrooms
58. Building Identification Code
59. Unit Number (See Inst.)

Part VIII - CERTIFICATIONS - SIGN ONLY AFTER READING THE STATEMENT THAT APPLIES TO YOU ON THE COVER FLAP.

	Date
Head of Household	
Spouse/Co-Head	
Owner/Agent	

PREVIOUS EDITIONS OBSOLETE

HUD-50059 (10-84)
HB 4350.3

Figure 11-3. Owner's Certification

Form FmHA 1944-8
(Rev. 5-86)

USDA – FARMERS HOME ADMINISTRATION

TENANT CERTIFICATION

FORM APPROVED
OMB NO. 0575-0033

WARNING: Section 1001 of Title 18, United States Code provides, "Whoever, in any matter within the jurisdiction of any department or agency of the United States knowingly and willfully falsifies, conceals or covers up by any trick, scheme, or device a material fact, or makes any false, fictitious or fraudulent statements or representations, or makes or uses any false writing or document knowing the same to contain any false, fictitious or fraudulent statement or entry, shall be fined not more than $10,000 or imprisoned not more than five years, or both."

ALL MONETARY FIGURES SHOULD BE ROUNDED TO THE NEAREST DOLLAR

STATEMENT REQUIRED BY THE PRIVACY ACT:
The Farmers Home Adminstration (FmHA) is authorized by Title V of the Housing Act of 1949, as amended (42 U.S.C. 1471 et. seq.), to solicit the information requested on this form. Disclosure of the information requested is voluntary. However, failure to disclose certain items of information may result in a delay in the processing of your eligibility or rejection, except that it is unlawful for FmHA to deny eligibility because of the refusal to disclose the Social Security Account Number.

The principal purposes for collecting the requested information are to determine eligibility for occupancy in the FmHA financed rental project and to determine the amount of tenant contribution for rent. The information collected on this form may be released to appropriate Federal, State, and Local Agencies when relevant to civil, criminal or regulatory proceedings.

PART I – TENANT HOUSEHOLD INFORMATION

1. Household Member Name *(Last, First and Middle Initial)*	2. Sex	3. Date of Birth M M D D Y Y	4. Minor, Disabled or Handicapped	5. Elderly, Disabled or Handicapped	6. Race/National Origin of Tenant

(Complete this only when household member *is not* the Tenant or a Co-Tenant)

(Complete this only when household member *is a* Tenant or Co-Tenant)

(Check below when coded above)

1 - White, Non Hispanic
2 - Black, Non Hispanic
3 - Asian, Pacific Isld.
4 - American Indian Alaskan Native
5 - Hispanic

1.a. Number of Foster Children *(if any)*

Total *(Line 4)*

Elderly Status

Enter Race/National Origin Code

PART II – UNIT IDENTIFICATION

7. Unit Number

8. Unit Type

PART III – ASSET INCOME

9. Net Family Assets (NOTE: If Line 9 does not exceed $5,000, enter zero on Line 10.) $

10. Imputed Income from Assets *(Bank Passbook Savings Rate (·) x Line 9.)* $

11. Income from Assets $

PART IV – INCOME CALCULATIONS

12. Income

a. Wages, Salaries, etc. $

b. Soc. Sec., Pensions, etc. $

c. Public Assistance $

d. Income Contributed by Assets *(Greater of Line 10 or Line 11)* $

e. Other $

f. Annual Income

13. Adjustments to Income

a. $480 x total of Line 4 $

b. $400 if elderly status $

c. Medical *(if elderly handicapped or disabled)* $

d. Child Care $

e. Total Adjustments

14. Adjusted Annual Income *(Line 12.f. minus 13.e.)* $

PART V – INCOME LEVELS

15. Number of Household Members

16. Current Eligibility Income Level *(Enter Code)*

17. Date of Initial Project Entry M M D D Y Y

18. Eligibility Income Level at Initial Project Entry *(Enter Code)*

PART VI – CERTIFICATION BY TENANT

I/we certify that the information in PARTS I through VI is true and correct to the best of my/our knowledge and belief. Inquiries may be made to verify this information.

a. Date: M M D D Y Y

b. Soc. Sec. No.

c. Tenant Signature

d. Date: M M D D Y Y

e. Soc. Sec. No.

f. Co-Tenant Signature

This form is used to certify tenant income, establish tenant eligibility, and assure compliance with Federal Regulations. The information is required as a condition to obtain a benefit. This statement is provided pursuant to P.L. 96-511.

Figure 11–4. Tenant Certification

(Continued)

PART VII – PRELIMINARY CALCULATIONS

19. Adjusted Monthly Income *(Line 14 ÷ 12)*   a. $ [ ]   × .30   = b. $ [ ]

20. Monthly Income *(Line 12.f. ÷ 12)*   a. $ [ ]   × .10   = b. $ [ ]

21. Designated Monthly Welfare Shelter Payment $ [ ]

22. Highest of Line 19.b., Line 20.b., or Line 21. $ [ ]

23. Gross Basic Rent
   a. Basic Rent $ [ ]
   b. Utility Allowance $ [ ]
   c. *(Line 23.a. + Line 23.b.)* $ [ ]

24. Gross Market Rent
   a. Market Rent $ [ ]
   b. Utility Allowance $ [ ]
   c. *(Line 24.a. + Line 24.b.)* $ [ ]

PART VIII – PRELIMINARY GROSS TENANT CONTRIBUTION (PGTC)

Decision: *(check one)*

☐ A. If tenant *Receives rental assistance (RA)* enter line 22 on line 25 below.

☐ B. If tenant *does not receive RA* and this project receives Plan II Interest Credit, enter the greater of line 22 or line 23.c. (but not to exceed line 24.c.) on line 25 below.

☐ C. If tenant *does not receive RA* and this project is a Plan I, Full Profit or Labor Housing project complete lines C.1. thru C.3. and enter C.3. on line 25.

   C.1. Enter line 24.c $ [ ]   25. PGTC
   C.2. Add Plan I Surcharge *(if any)* $ [ ]
   C.3. Total *(enter on line 25)* $ [ ] $ [ ]

PART IX – DOES PGTC BECOME FINAL GROSS TENANT CONTRIBUTION?

Decision: *(check one)* If you check Decision A, B, C, D, or E, Enter Line 25 on Line 26 Below

☐ A. Tenant initially occupied the project on or after October 1, 1986.

☐ B. You checked Decision B in PART VIII *and entered Line 23.c. on Line 25.*

☐ C. You checked Decision C in PART VIII.

☐ D. Change in PGTC is *entirely* due to a change in household size, rental rate, or utility allowance *(recertifications only)*.

☐ E. The most recently completed PART XIV, "Tenant Certification Worksheet" indicated this tenant is no longer subject to the Tenant Contribution Increase Limits.

☐ F. None of the above apply. IF YOU CHECK THIS BOX, YOU MUST COMPLETE PART XIV, "Tenant Certification Worksheet", enter the answer from Line G-1 of Part XIV on line 26 of Part X.

PART X – DETERMINING NET TENANT CONTRIBUTION (NTC)

26. Gross Tenant Contribution *(See PART IX)* $ [ ]
27. Utility Allowance *(Line 23.b. or Line 24.b.)* $ [ ]
28. Preliminary NTC *(Line 26 minus Line 27)* $ [ ]

   Decision: *(check one)*

☐ A. If you checked Decision A in PART VIII (PGTC) enter Line 28 on Line 29 below and compare Line 23.c. and Line 28. If Line 23.c. is smaller, return to PART VIII (PGTC) and check Decision B since this tenant will not receive RA.

☐ B. If you checked Decision B in PART VIII (PGTC), enter the greater of Line 23.a. or Line 28 (but not to exceed Line 24.a.) on Line 29 below.

☐ C. If you checked Decision C in PART VIII (PGTC) enter Line 28 on Line 29 below.

29. Final NTC *(amount Tenant pays Borrower for rent)*
   (If Line 29 is negative, Borrower pays difference to Tenant for utilities) $ [ ]

PART XI – PROJECT IDENTIFICATION

30. Project Case Number [ ]   31. Project Number [ ]

PART XII – CERTIFICATION BY BORROWER

I certify that the information on this form has been verified as required by federal law and the tenant household ☐ is eligible to live in the unit, or ☐ has been granted ineligible occupancy by FmHA.

a. Effective Date   M M D D Y Y | b. Signature of Borrower or Borrowers Representative | c. Date Signed   M M D D Y Y

PART XIII – CERTIFICATION BY FmHA

Based on information provided by the Borrower, the calculations for this form are correct.

a. Date   M M D D Y Y | b. Signature of FmHA Representative

Form FmHA 1944-8 *(Rev. 5-86)*

–2–

Figure 11–4.   Continued

PART XIV – TENANT CERTIFICATION WORKSHEET

NOTE: Use only if directed by PART IX. When this worksheet is used, it is subject to the certification statements signed and dated by the borrower (PART XII) and FmHA (PART XIII).

ENTER THE FOLLOWING

From This Form FmHA 1944-8:

From the Most Recently Approved Tenant Certification:

	from Form FmHA 1944-8	from Form FmHA 444-8

A-1 _____ PGTC (Line 25)

B-1 _____ Gross Tenant Contribution (Line 25) (Line 9.d. plus Line 10.d.)

A-2 _____ Annual Income (Line 12.f.)

B-2 _____ Annual Income (Line 12.f.) (Line 4.a.)

A-3 _____ Adjustments (Line 13.e.)

B-3 _____ Adjustments (Line 13.e.) (Line 4.b. plus Line 4.c.)

A-4 _____ Affect of Imputed Income from Assets
[If household has net family assets greater than $5000 and imputed income from Assets (Line 10) is greater than actual income from Assets (Line 11) then enter the difference (Line 10 minus Line 11)]

Test # 1

C-1 _____ PGTC (A-1)

C-2 _____ Portion of PGTC Automatically Allowable (B-1 times 1.10)

C-3 _____ Portion of PGTC Which may be Allowable (C-1 minus C-2)

Decision Test # 1

(check one) ☐ If C-3 is zero or less, enter C-1 on G-1 and omit Test # 2 Test # 3 and Test # 4

☐ If C-3 is greater than zero, go to Test # 2

Test # 2

D-1 _____ Change in Annual Income (A-2 minus B-2)

D-2 _____ Affect of Imputed Income from Assets (A-4)

D-3 _____ Net Change in Annual Income (D-1 minus D-2)

Decision Test # 2

(check one) ☐ If D-3 is zero or less, enter C-2 on G-1 and omit Test # 3 and Test # 4

☐ If D-3 is greater than zero, go to Test # 3

Test # 3

E-1 _____ Net Change in Annual Income (D-3)

E-2 _____ Change in Adjustments (A-3 minus B-3)

E-3 _____ Total Net Change (E-1 plus E-2)

Decision Test # 3

(check one) ☐ If E-3 is zero or less, enter C-2 on G-1 and omit Test # 4

☐ If E-3 is greater than zero, go to Test # 4

Test # 4

F-1 _____ Portion of Total Net Change Attributable to Annual Income (E-1 divided by E-3)

F-2 _____ Portion of C-3 Allowable (C-3 times F-1)

F-3 _____ Total PGTC Allowable (C-2 plus F-2)

Decision Test # 4

(check one) ☐ If F-3 is less than A-1, enter F-3 on G-1

☐ If F-3 is equal to or greater than A-1, enter A-1 on G-1.
(NOTE: When this box is checked, this tenant household is no longer subject to the tenant contribution increase limits.)

Gross Tenant Contribution

G-1 _____ (Enter on Line 26 of Part X)

–3– Form FmHA 1944-8 (Rev. 5-86)

Figure 11–4. Continued

The Easy Worksheet for Computing Total Tenant Payment/Tenant Rent (All Programs)

U.S. Department of Housing and Urban Development
Office of Housing
Federal Housing Commissioner

OMB No. 2502-0204 (exp. 3/31/87)

IMPORTANT: Read Appendix 2 of Handbook 4350.3 before you complete this Form. The Appendix tells you which version of the Worksheet you must use.

Name or Tenant	Name of Project	Unit Number

PART A. COMPUTE THE TOTAL TENANT PAYMENT/TENANT RENT. Complete only one Section. Select the Section that applies to the type of subsidy the Tenant will be receiving.

Sec. 8/RAP Tenants	Rent Supplement Tenants
A-1. _____ Monthly Income (Item 31 ÷ 12).	A-1. ///// Monthly Income.
A-2. _____ Monthly Adjusted Income (Item 43 ÷ 12).	A-2. _____ Monthly Adjusted Income (Item 43 ÷ 12).
A-3. _____ HCDA Percentage (Item 48).	A-3. _____ HCDA Percentage (Item 48).
A-4. _____ Monthly Adjusted Income × HCDA Percentage (A2 × A3).	A-4. _____ Gross Rent (Item 46).
A-5. _____ 10% of Monthly Income (A1 × .10).	A-5. _____ 30% of Gross Rent (A4 × .30).
A-6. _____ Welfare Rent *(Applies only to welfare recipients in as-paid States or Counties).*	A-6. _____ Monthly Adjusted Income × HCDA Percentage. (A2 × A3).
A-7. _____ **TOTAL TENANT PAYMENT (TTP)** (Enter the **largest** of A4, A5 or A6).	A-7. _____ **TOTAL TENANT PAYMENT (TTP)** (Enter the **larger** of A5 or A6).
	NOTE: If this is a *move-in* or an *initial* certification, Tenant is eligible ONLY if Total Tenant Payment (TTP) is less than 90 percent of Gross Rent - i.e., A7 is less than (.90 × A4).
Go to Part B	**Go to Part B**

Section 236 Tenants
Complete only one column under this Part. Select the utility arrangement that applies to this Tenant.

No Utility Allowance	With Utility Allowance
A-1. ///// Monthly Income.	A-1. ///// Monthly Income.
A-2. _____ Monthly Adjusted Income (Item 43 ÷ 12).	A-2. _____ Monthly Adjusted Income (Item 43 ÷ 12).
A-3. _____ HCDA Percentage (Item 48).	A-3. _____ HCDA Percentage (Item 48).
A-4. _____ Monthly Adjusted Income × HDCA Percentage (A2 × A3).	A-4. _____ Monthly Adjusted Income × HDCA Percentage (A2 × A3).
A-5. _____ *Basic Rent (Item 44).	A-5. _____ *Utility Allowance (Item 45).
A-6. _____ *Market Rent (From Rent Schedule).	A-6. _____ A4 minus A5.
A-7. _____ **TENANT RENT** (Enter the **larger** of A4 or A5 but never more than A6).	A-7. _____ *Basic Rent (Item 44).
	A-8. _____ Higher of A6 or A7.
	A-9. _____ Minimum Rent (25% of A2).
	A-10. _____ *Market Rent (From Rent Schedule).
	A-11. _____ **TENANT RENT** (Enter the **larger** of A8 or A9 but never more than A10).
Go to Part B	**Go to Part B**

*NOTE: *Use the Rents and Utility Allowance that will be in effect on the date this Tenant Rent will become effective.*

PART B. TRANSFER THIS WORKSHEET DATA TO THE HUD-50059

	HUD-50059 Item No:
• Enter the Answer from Part A in:	
—for Section 236 Tenants	51
—for All Other Tenants	50
• Enter HCDA Percentage from A3 in	54
• Check "No" in	55

Prepared By (Name and Date)	Supervisory Review By (Initials and Date)

HUD-50059 e (10-84)
HB 4350.3

Figure 11-5. Assistance Payments

SUMMARY

Each specialized area of professional property management has its own unique features and peculiarities, many of which are derived from local customs. The property manager should have expertise and experience in a specialized area before undertaking management.

Industrial buildings are usually classified as single-tenant, multitenant, or industrial parks. Industrial tenants are classified into six basic categories.

1. Market-oriented

2. Raw material and resource-oriented

3. Transportation-oriented

4. Labor intensity-oriented

5. Energy-oriented

6. Nondescript-oriented

Research and development (R&D) buildings are an outgrowth of industrial building and are considered a hybrid of office and industrial.

The government approval process for new development usually involves an environmental impact report (EIR) that must consider tenant displacement; historical sites; traffic, air, and water quality; endangered species; and so on.

Mobile home park management involves different rules and regulations from apartment management. For example, the notice period to raise rents is longer than for apartments.

Mini-storage is a growing and unique type of management that requires specific expertise and knowledge. The Self-Service Storage Association (SSSA), a trade association, is a source of forms, information, and seminars.

Management of medical buildings is unique in that it has special tenant mix requirements. Maintenance is frequently more intense and specialized, such as disposal of contaminated waste including needles and bandages.

Retirement communities are broken into three basic categories: independent, semi-independent, and supported living.

Hotels are categorized by price of rooms, with full service hotels having the highest room rates. The benefits of national franchise affiliations are reservation systems and advertising programs.

Federally subsidized housing programs such as Section 8, in which the government pays the difference between 20–30 percent of the tenant's income and fair market rent, require special knowledge of HUD rules and regulations. Government forms need to be accurately filled out in order to comply and be paid. The use of special computer programs is very desirable in this area.

In this chapter we covered specialized and unique areas of property management. As pointed out, the property management field is wide and varied and no one book can contain all the answers. Common sense and a willingness to seek out and accept challenges are necessary for successful property management.

PERSONALITY PROFILE

The management of specialized properties such as mobile home parks, mini-storage, or hospitality properties requires additional training and experience. Judith Ricker of Santa Barbara, California, heads up a company that in addition to managing residential and commercial properties, manages a large portfolio of hotel properties. These properties require additional computer software and have a large payroll, due to all of the clerks, maids, and so forth, employed at each hotel.

Judy encountered a problem when the city had a water shortage and did not allow laundry facilities at a newly built motel. Judy's solution was to purchase a local coin-op laundromat. The motel operated it as a laundromat for outside customers during the day and washed the hotel linens at night, obtaining almost 24-hour use of the machines and facilities.

Judy has her B.A. degree and teaches at the local community college. She also has earned her certified property manager (CPM) designation and the certified hotel administrator (CHA) designation.

REVIEW QUESTIONS

1. Industrial buildings usually have stiffer parking regulations than
   a. office buildings.
   b. retail buildings.
   c. medical buildings.
   d. none of the above

2. Industrial buildings are usually located
   a. near major transportation.
   b. only in rural areas.
   c. only in urban areas.
   d. only in Sunbelt areas.

3. Management fees for industrial management are usually
   a. higher than for residential.
   b. higher than for commercial.
   c. among the lowest.
   d. among the highest.

4. Which of the following is not a typical industrial lease?
   a. gross
   b. net
   c. percentage

5. R&D buildings are usually
   a. skyscrapers.
   b. one to two stories.
   c. a minimum of 10 stories.
   d. a minimum of 20 stories.

6. Mobile home parks usually require
   a. a month-to-month lease.
   b. a short-term lease.
   c. no lease.
   d. a long-term lease.

7. The highest rating for a mobile home park is
   a. two stars.
   b. three stars.
   c. five stars.
   d. ten stars.

8. Mini-storage parks are usually located
   a. on prime land.
   b. on cheaper land.
   c. only in rural areas.
   d. near hospitals.

9. The best location for a medical building is near
   a. a hospital.
   b. a shopping center.
   c. an office building.
   d. a river.

10. The most desirable tenants for a medical building are
    a. real estate brokers.
    b. general practitioners.
    c. veterinarians.
    d. insurance companies.

11. Industrial leases are usually
    a. long term.
    b. percentage rents.
    c. month-to-month.
    d. both a and b
    e. both b and c

12. Which type of business usually has the highest parking requirements?
    a. furniture stores
    b. retail stores
    c. doctors' offices
    d. restaurants

13. Environmental reports consider
    a. affirmative action.
    b. discrimination.
    c. endangered species.
    d. parking ratios.

14. The standard industrial lease is usually over _____ pages in length.
    a. one
    b. two
    c. three
    d. four or more

15. Key money is
    a. a bonus to be kept by the management agent.
    b. a bonus to be kept by the leasing agent.
    c. a bonus to go to the landlord for desirable location.
    d. a bonus paid to a locksmith.

ADDITIONAL READING AND REFERENCES

American Hotel & Motel Association, 1201 New York Avenue, N.W., Washington, DC 20005.

California Department of Real Estate, *Common Interest Homeowner's Association Management Study*, Sacramento, CA, 1987.

California Department of Real Estate, *A Guide to Mobile-Home Park Purchases by Residents*, Sacramento, CA, 1986.

Inside Self-Storage (Monthly), 4141 N. Scottsdale Rd., #316, Scottsdale, AZ 85251.

The Mini-Storage Messenger (Monthly), 2531 W. Dunlap Avenue, Suite 201, Phoenix, AZ 85021.

Mobilehome Parks Report (Monthly), 3807 Pasadena Avenue, Suite 100, Sacramento, CA 95821.

Pappas, Stephen G., *Managing Mobile Home Parks*, Institute of Real Estate Management, Chicago, IL, 1991.

Parker, Rosetta A., CPM, *Housing for the Elderly*, Institute of Real Estate Management, Chicago, IL, 1984.

Society of Industrial Realtors, *A Guide to Industrial Site Selection*, Washington, DC, 1984.

Society of Industrial Realtors, *Industrial Real Estate*, Washington, DC, 1984.

Society of Industrial Realtors, *Industrial Real Estate Market Survey*, Washington, DC, 1984.

Society of Industrial Realtors, *S.I.R. Reports* (Bimonthly newsletter), Washington, DC.

Urban Land Institute, *Hotel/Motel Development*, Washington, DC.

Urban Land Institute, *PUDs in Practice*, Washington, DC, 1985.

Urban Land Institute, *Shared Parking*, Washington, DC, 1983.

Urban Land Institute, *Timesharing II*, Washington, DC, 1982.

Western Mobilehome Association Reporter (WMA) (Monthly), 1007–7th Street, 3rd Floor, Sacramento, CA 95814.

Chapter 12

Maintenance

Key terms

Asbestos	Flow restrictor	Routine maintenance
Btu	Photoelectric timer	Security complex
Circuit breaker	Preventive	Service maintenance
Controllable cost	maintenance	Thermostat
Electrolysis	Recirculation pump	Toxic waste

Food for thought

"I'd hate to fly seven miles above the ground in something repaired by the low bidder."

THE ROLE OF THE PROPERTY MANAGER IN MAINTENANCE

Maintenance is one of the most important and visible roles of property management. If you ask a tenant if a building is well managed, he or she will reply either, "Yes, they fix things right away" or "No, they always procrastinate and never fix things correctly." The tenant views management and maintenance as the same entity (see Figure 12–1). Since retaining existing tenants is the best method for keeping vacancy low and turnover at a minimum, a good maintenance program is imperative. The property manager, in a quest to increase NOI, must not only increase rents but also develop programs and guidelines to reduce costs. Maintenance is a controllable cost, unlike the mortgage payment over which the property manager has no control. Budgeting should be set in place with a priority plan to handle problems so the property manager controls rather than reacts to maintenance problems.

The property manager need not be an expert in maintenance, but should learn the terminology and be willing to get dirty when dealing with maintenance personnel and contractors.

THE FOUR TYPES OF MAINTENANCE
Service Maintenance

Service maintenance includes maintenance items requested by the tenant or manager. It also includes emergency issues such as stopped-up toilets, leaking faucets, lack of hot water, broken windows, lack of heat, and so on. Property managers should prioritize requests by marking one of the following numbers on the work order:

1. Emergency

2. Repair within 24 hours

3. When time permits

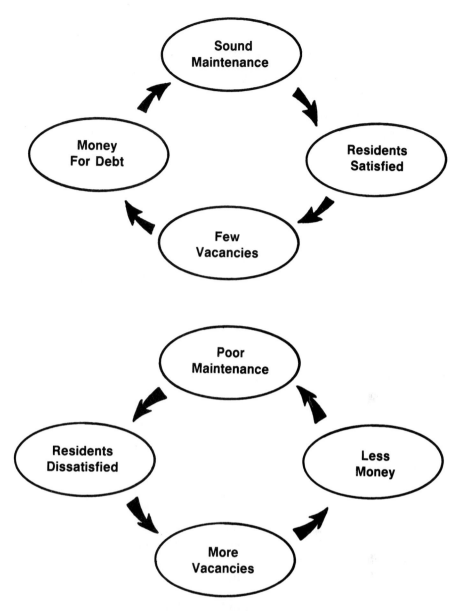

Figure 12–1. Maintenance Circle

Routine Maintenance

Routine maintenance includes general maintenance to the common areas, landscaping, equipment, and janitorial duties. These items are not tenant requested, but are necessary to give the building good "curb appeal"—desirability. In office buildings, the lobby, halls, and restrooms should be maintained on a regular schedule; don't wait for a tenant to complain. Record of work should begin with a written work order (see Figure 12–2).

Preventive Maintenance

This is a system of performing repair tasks on a regularly scheduled basis to prevent minor problems from leading to major breakdowns or problems. Examples include replacing air-conditioning filters; lubricating, oiling, and adjusting equipment; exterminating; exterior painting; and so forth. Often, outside contractors are used for these tasks.

JD MAINTENANCE AND CONSTRUCTION

P.O. BOX 1438
COSTA MESA, CA 92666
(714) 751-2787

WORK ORDER   # 2216

DATE: _____

PHONES

NAME: _____

(H) _____

(B) _____

(MGR.) _____

WORK REQUESTED				

MATERIALS		
QTY.	DESCRIPTION	UNIT COST

WORKMAN	DATE	IN	OUT	HOURS

Figure 12–2. Work Order

Extraordinary Maintenance

This task involves major rehabilitation, replacement, or refurbishment of units, buildings, or grounds (see Figure 12–3). Examples include a new facade, roof replacement, replumbing, conversion from master meter to individual meters, and so on. The property manager will frequently charge a supervision fee to handle these items.

LICENSED VERSUS UNLICENSED CONTRACTORS

The basic difference between licensed and unlicensed contractors is that licensed contractors have to pass a state exam and meet experience criteria set forth by the contractor's state license board (or other state agency). They must also have a bond and are subject to having their licenses revoked or suspended. An unlicensed contractor doing work (including labor and material) costing $300 or more is committing a misdemeanor in some states.

MAINTENANCE AREAS

Plumbing

Plumbing is one of the most frequent problem areas. The plumbing system can be divided into three parts: fresh water supply, drainage system, and gas piping.

Following is a list of areas of interest to the property manager and the on-site manager:

1. Shutoff valve locations in the complex.

2. Electrolysis is corrosion due to connecting dissimilar metal pipes, such as an iron pipe and a copper connector pipe. Steel (gas) pipe laid in close proximity to copper (water) pipe may cause a chemical reaction (electrolysis) to occur between the two dissimilar metals. This results in a pitting action that leads to pinhole leaks in the steel pipe.

3. Insulation of hot water pipes will result in energy savings. A 40°F temperature loss between the hot water heater and a remote outlet can occur without proper insulation.

4. Recirculating pumps also reduce energy costs by constantly keeping hot water in the lines. Pump timers can reduce energy costs during low tenant usage (nighttime).

---

10 RULES OF SERVICE

1. Do not enter without permission
2. Have a witness, when possible
3. Knock before entering
4. Keep mouth *shut*
5. Authorized work only
6. No false promises
7. Keep mouth *shut*
8. Do not browse
9. Do not touch
10. Be courteous and considerate

Source: E. Robert Miller, CPM

Figure 12–3. Rules of Service

5. Hot water heaters should be properly serviced to remove heavy mineral deposits which can cause them to burst. The temperature should not exceed 120°F, although higher temperatures may be required in special-use buildings (e.g., medical) or for dishwashers (140°F).

6. Repairs—try to replace broken parts with identical parts from the same manufacturer.

7. Parts—faucets and garbage disposals should be purchased in quantity in order to obtain lower prices. Using one brand can make replacement or repair easier and less time consuming.

8. Proper tools—seat-dressing wrench, socket wrench, wax seals (toilet), and pipe wrenches should always be readily available.

9. Always try to standardize the type of repair and replacement parts used.

10. Maintain a working relationship with a qualified plumbing and electrical company to be on call 24 hours a day to handle plumbing and heating emergencies.

Heating System

Like plumbing, lack of heat is a habitability problem (see Chapter 14 for further discussion) and needs immediate attention.

1. The most comfortable temperature range for the human body in summer is 72–79°F, and 68–74°F in winter.

2. Airflow motion by fans, windows, or vents increases the evaporation rate of heat from the body. This is desirable during the summer months.

3. Drapes (lined) covering windows will prevent heat loss in the winter.

4. Older people usually prefer higher temperatures.

5. A "heat pump" is a system in which the refrigeration system is used to remove heat and discharge it to the outdoors in the summer. In colder weather this process is reversed.

6. Heat exchange is a method of transferring heat from one liquid to another without mixing the liquids; the process is used for hot water systems.

7. The British thermal unit (Btu) is the unit of heat required to raise the temperature of one pound of water from 62°F to 63°F.

8. Performance ratio is calculated by converting fuel usage into Btu. These Btu are divided by conditioned square footage of the building—which is then divided by the total heating and cooling days. The lower the performance ratio, the less energy the building consumes per square foot per degree per day. Information on heating- and cooling-degree days can be obtained from the local weather bureau.

9. High-pressure gas piping should always be installed by a licensed plumber.

Electrical System

1. Wiring systems include the following descriptions and cautions:
   a) 120/240-volt, single-phase, 3-wire system is used for smaller buildings and residential buildings.
   b) 120/208-volt, 3-phase, 4-wire system is usually used in office, apartment, and commercial buildings.
   c) 480/277-volt, 3-phase, 4-wire system is used mainly for large industrial buildings.

2. Electrical repairs should be performed by a licensed electrician for safety and insurance reasons.

3. The property manager should maintain electrical blueprints so the electrician can more readily trace problems.

4. Circuit-breakers versus fuses—both perform the same function, which is to cut off electricity when the system is overloaded. Appliances should be turned off before replacing fuses or resetting circuit breakers to avoid power surges when the current is restored.

5. Watt (power)—a measurement of electricity. Appliances, lights, motors, air-conditioning, and so on, should not exceed the capacity of the service panel.

6. Always turn off the power at the circuit breaker before doing any electrical work.

7. In some medical buildings and large office buildings, self-starting diesel generators are installed which automatically activate when the power goes out.

Carpeting

1. Carpeting with patterns and in darker colors hides dirt and wears well. Hi-lo or plush covering is better and more aesthetically pleasing than shag.

2. Padding increases the comfort, quiet, and insulation of residential carpet, but sometimes is not used in commercial areas as it increases wear (increased movement causes more wear on the fibers).

3. Frequent vacuuming will prolong carpet life. A heavy-duty, upright vacuum cleaner is the best.

4. Spot and stain removal should be done immediately.
   a) Use a wet cloth to soak up damp spills and transfer the stain from the carpet to the cloth.
   b) Remedies for dissolving stains:
      (1) Water-soluble removers for sugars and starches
      (2) Dry-cleaning fluids for butter, oils, and fats
      (3) Detergent solutions:
         (a) Juices—diluted ammonia solution
         (b) Bleach and urine—diluted vinegar solution

5. Carpet grade should be FHA-approved to give longer wear—five to eight years in many instances.

Pest Control

1. Regularly scheduled monthly service contracts should be established with a licensed pest control vendor (Figure 12–4).

2. Cockroaches are best handled by regular spraying or by putting boric acid under sinks and areas they frequent. Caution must be used to keep acid away from areas accessible to children.

3. Clean premises and good housekeeping are the best deterrent to pest problems.

4. Spraying one unit may cause roaches to flee to neighboring units, so it is desirable also to spray surrounding units.

Roofing

1. Most properly maintained roofs will last 20–25 years.

2. Schedule inspections by a roofing contractor at least once a year, with repair work performed in the dry season for best prices.

3. Don't walk unnecessarily on the roof.

Figure 12–4. Pest Control

4. When doing repairs, such as major patching, be sure that rotted boards are replaced before putting down new felt and patching. Always have large areas repaired using the same materials and specifications as the original roof.

Summary

We have covered only the highlights of a few major maintenance areas. An in-depth analysis appears in Mel Shear's *Handbook of Building Maintenance Management* (Reston Publishing, Reston, VA, 1983).

SECURITY AND SAFETY

The property manager is responsible for more than the repair of plumbing and roofs for tenants. To most tenants, security represents the peaceful enjoyment of the unit and a secure complex. It is really a service the tenant has a legal right to expect from the management company or owner. Therefore, the property manager should develop programs and take preventive measures to promote tenant security. However, the manager should never promise more security than he or she can actually provide.

1. *Hardware*—locks, deadbolts, doors, adequate lighting, fences, gates, and so forth. If security gates are installed, they should be working at all times to limit liability. A complex should not be advertised as a "security complex." Even the President of the United States, with all his Secret Service personnel, cannot be guaranteed security. By implying that your building is "secure," you expose yourself to additional liability.

2. *Guards*—to patrol the complex; can be either employees or an outside service.

3. *Tenant participation*—many cities have either the Community Organized Police (COP), Neighborhood Watch, or Safety Management Alliance of Residents and Tenants (SMART) Partners programs in place, in which tenants watch each other's units.

4. *Police*—renting to police as tenants at a slightly reduced rate is a good way to ward off problems.

5. *Site improvements*—install lighting in dark areas, high fences, closed-circuit television monitors.

6. *Smoke detectors*—the Orange County fire department estimates that an 87 percent reduction in deaths and serious injury and a 40 percent reduction in property loss would be achieved through implementation of a comprehensive smoke detection alarm system and maintenance program. Many states place the burden of responsibility for testing the smoke detector on a regular basis on the owner/manager. In some states, it is incumbent upon the owner to notify tenants, provide test forms, and maintain records of compliance for a minimum of three years (see figures 12–5 and 12–6).

7. *Telephone jack*—In some states, the landlord is responsible for installing at least one jack and maintaining the inside telephone wiring in good working order.

ENERGY MANAGEMENT

The largest single expense in office buildings is master-metered utilities, which may represent over 32 percent of operating costs. The cost of master-metered utilities in apartment buildings is over 25 percent of operating costs. The property manager must therefore institute an energy management program as a means of reducing expenses and increasing net operating income. The cap rate method of valuation will increase property value if expenses go down and NOI increases. The comfort level of the tenant must, however, also be considered as no one likes to take cold showers or wear a coat to bed at night.

Steps in an Energy Management Program

1. Gather background information—past utility bills, prior energy programs.
2. Analyze information—fuel usage per unit or per square foot.

SMOKE ALARM

INSTALLATION RECORD

PROPERTY: ______________________

INSTALLATION CODE

A= New alarm and battery installed

B= New battery for existing detector

Record date and installation code letter in box farthest left

UNIT #									

J. D. Property Mgt Form

Figure 12–5. Smoke Detector Log

Page ________

SMOKE DETECTOR AGREEMENT

THIS AGREEMENT is entered into this _____ day of ______________, 199___,

by and between ____, "Owner" (Landlord),

and ____, "Resident" (Tenant).

IN CONSIDERATION OF THEIR MUTUAL PROMISES, OWNER AND RESIDENT AGREE AS FOLLOWS:

1. Resident is renting from Owner the premises located at:

   ____, CA

2. This agreement is an Addendum and part of the Rental Agreement and/or Lease between Owner and Resident.

3. The premises is equipped with a smoke detection device(s).

4. The resident acknowledges the smoke detector(s) was tested and its operation explained by management in the presence of the Resident at time of initial occupancy and the detector(s) in the unit was working properly at that time.

5. Each resident shall perform the manufacturer's recommended test to determine if the smoke detector(s) is (are) operating properly at least once a week.

6. Initial in box ONLY if BATTERY OPERATED: ☐

   By initialing as provided, each Resident understands that said smoke detector(s) and alarm is a battery operated unit and it shall be each Resident's responsibility to:

   a. ensure that the battery is in operating condition at all times;
   b. replace the battery as needed (unless otherwise provided by law); and
   c. if, after replacing the battery, the smoke detector(s) do *not* work, inform the Owner or authorized agent immediately in writing.

7. Resident(s) must inform the owner or authorized agent immediately in writing of any defect, malfunction or failure of any detector(s).

________________________ ________________________

Owner/Agent Resident

____

Resident

UNAUTHORIZED REPRODUCTION SHALL RENDER THIS FORM NULL AND VOID

CAA APPROVED FORM
CALIFORNIA APARTMENT ASSOCIATION

Figure 12–6. Smoke Detector Agreement

3. Develop alternative measures—hot water heater efficiency, replacement needs, payback period.

4. Implement selected measures—purchase equipment and put it into use.

5. Follow up and maintain control—review fuel bills and operating costs periodically.

Specific Measures to Reduce Energy Consumption

1. Caulk outside cracks, joints, holes, vents, pipes, windows, air-conditioners, doors, and so on, to prevent drafts that can increase heating and cooling costs by as much as 30 percent.

2. Install photoelectric timers for inside and outside lighting (Figure 12–7).

3. Adjust thermostat settings in the common areas to 60–65°F in winter and 78–80°F in summer.

4. Cover room air-conditioners in winter to reduce heat loss.

5. Install hot water recirculating pumps and set hot water at 110°F (when appropriate).

6. Install tamperproof boxes over thermostats.

7. Submeter or separate-meter master-metered buildings if possible. Studies show this reduces energy consumption by 20 percent. Reminder: Tenants conserve energy when they pay directly.

8. Install flow restrictors on shower heads as this uses 50–75 percent less water.

9. Repair any plumbing leaks or drips, especially of hot water.

10. Replace incandescent bulbs with low-energy fluorescent bulbs which last ten times longer and use only a third as much energy.

11. Use two dummy bulbs in four-bulb light fixtures, which reduces energy by almost 50 percent.

12. Charge tenants in office and commercial buildings for using air-conditioning after 6:00 P.M. and on Sundays if these are not considered normal operating hours. The lease provision to this effect should be in writing.

Solar Energy

In the past, the property manager recommended purchasing solar energy to receive large rebates. These rebates, however, are usually no longer available, but the owner may still get a 20–40 percent return on investment depending on the dollar amount of gas bills, rent structure, and income tax status. A well-designed solar system can reduce gas bills by 50 percent. In California, the Public Utilities Commission (PUC) allows the gas company to allocate a discounted baseline rate. This allocation does not consider the number of people, bedrooms, bathrooms, or size of units. Once the building exceeds the baseline allowance, the rate increases.

Large units or those with heated swimming pools have the greatest need to reduce gas expenses. If the building is under rent control, the owner may be able to pass the cost of the solar installation on to the tenants in the form of higher rents and reduce expenses at the same time, which will increase resale value. Solar installations may receive both federal and state tax credits.

Water Conservation

Toilets   Approximately 70 percent of the water flushed down a traditional toilet is not required for effective sewage. The residential toilet consumes

Item	Condition	Remarks
Roof		
Surface		
Vents		
Flashings		
Gutters		
Other		
Lighting		
Fixtures		
Timers		
Bulbs		
Other		
Surface Walls		
Structure		
Cleanliness		
Paint		
Trim		
Other		
Grounds		
Landscaping		
Cleanliness		
Trash enclosures		
Other		
Signage		
Building sign		
Manager's office		
Vacancy		
Other		
Mailboxes		
Doors		
Locks		
Other		
Decking		
Stairs		
Railing		
Deck		
Other		
Laundry Room		
Cleanliness		
Machines		
Other		
Hallway		
Cleanliness		
Paint		
Carpet		
Other		
Entryways		
Cleanliness		
Paint		
Locks		
Other		

Property_____ Date_____

Address_____ Inspector_____

Figure 12–7. Exterior Inspection Report Form

Property_____ Date_____

Address_____ Inspector_____

Unit No._____ No. of occupants: Adults_____ Children_____ Other_____

Room	Condition	Remarks
Bedroom(s)		
Carpet		
Windows		
Drapes		
Walls & ceiling		
Doors & locks		
Electrical		
Closets		
Paint		
Other		
Kitchen		
Floor		
Walls & ceiling		
Electrical		
Refrigerator		
Stove		
Sink		
Garbage disposal		
Doors & locks		
Paint		
Other		
Living Room		
Carpet		
Walls & ceiling		
Windows		
Drapes		
Electrical		
Doors & locks		
Paint		
Other		
Bathroom(s)		
Floor		
Walls & ceiling		
Windows		
Shower		
Toilet		
Sink		
Faucets		
Electrical		
Towel racks		
Paint		
Other		

Figure 12–8. Interior Inspection Report Form

about 28 percent of the apartment building water usage. Traditional toilets use 5–7 gallons per flush (GPF). The new low-consumption toilets (called ULF) use only 1.6 GPF. These toilets cost between $100 and $200 with many local water companies offering rebates and allowances. The cost savings are about $100 per year, which means a short payback period. As of January 1, 1994, all residential toilets manufactured in or imported into the United States must be the new 1.6 ULF type according to Public Law 102 and 486.

Showerheads   Conventional showers use approximately 4.5 gallons per minute (GPM) while water-saving shower flow restrictors use only 2.5 GPM. This results in an approximate savings of 10,000 gallons per year for a unit with four people plus an additional $50 in hot water costs. Like toilets, all new manufactured showerheads as of January 1, 1994, must have a maximum flow of only 2.5 GPM. The Interim Inspection Form (Figure 12–8) can be used to identify water-saving facilities.

SELECTION OF MAINTENANCE PERSONNEL

The maintenance person must not only have competence, necessary skills, and preferably his or her own tools, but must also be trustworthy. A thorough background credit and reference check similar to that for a prospective tenant should be performed. The maintenance person has access to the apartment units and could possibly steal from or rape a tenant. The management company, as well as the owner, may incur liability from a maintenance person's actions. A pre-employment maintenance person skills test should be administered (Figure 12–9) to make sure the person has a basic understanding of maintenance.

ESTIMATING REPAIR COSTS

The property manager often needs estimates of repair costs for budgets, management plans, or specific projects. In some cases, bids by outside contractors are not readily available in a timely manner. Also, having a working knowledge of approximate costs allows the property manager to better interface and negotiate with contractors.

A helpful book is *Means Repair and Remodeling Cost Data for Commercial and Residential*. This book breaks down the unit price by description, crew, equipment cost, daily output, person hours, material, labor, and overhead and profit.

	Crew	Daily Output	Person Hours	Material	Labor	Total	Total O&P
Garbage disposal	L-1	10	1.6	$55.00	$38.00	$93.00	$120.00
Maximum				$190.00			$265.00

Source: *Means Repair and Remodeling Cost Data for Commercial and Residential.*

In the preceding table, you can see that the cost of an inexpensive garbage disposal (such as the Badger I) installed would be approximately $120. The maximum figure is $265 for a more expensive disposal. This book covers items ranging from site preparation to skylights, floor tile, plumbing, electrical, and concrete.

TOXIC WASTE
Superfund Law

Under the Superfund Law passed by Congress in 1980, the Environmental Protection Agency (EPA) has the authority to recover clean-up costs from the present owner or past owners who polluted the property. Strict liability interpretations include:

1. Present owners are liable even if they did not cause or know of the contamination.

YOU WILL BE GIVEN 15 MINUTES
TO COMPLETE THIS TEST.

Name: _____

Date: _____

PRE-EMPLOYMENT "MAINTENANCE" REPAIRPERSON
SKILLS TEST

CARPENTRY

1.   T   F   Roofing is started at the crown of the roof.

2.   T   F   Sticky locks should be loosened up by spraying WD-40
                in the locking mechanism.

3.   Give two uses for caulking - interior and exterior

      a. _____

      b. _____

4.   What are the four purposes of weatherstripping?

      a. _____   c. _____

      b. _____   d. _____

5.   What are the two common types of material used for patching holes
      in plaster or drywall?

      a. _____   b. _____

6.   List three commonly used materials for floor tiles.

      a. _____   b. _____

            c. _____

7.   What are glazier points and why should they be used when installing
      window glass?

      _____

      _____

8.   T   F   Lock parts from different manufacturers all have their
                own basic designs. They are not interchangeable.

PLUMBING

9.   When making any galvanized or black steel pipe repair, one should
      apply _____ to all joints.

Figure 12–9. Maintenance Test

10. What are the three important and necessary basic steps in making a sweat joint?

   a. _____

   b. _____

   c. _____

11. Anytime a water closet is pulled, it is always to change the
   _____ gasket.

12. T   F   A gas cock (valve) on a gas hot water heater should always
            be installed in the gas line before the union.

13. In replacing a nipple for a tub spout, you should use a:

   (check one)   ( ) black steel pipe nipple
                        ( ) galvanized steel pipe nipple

14. A rumbling or knocking noise in a gas hot water heater when the
   burner is on indicates:

   (check one)   ( ) excessive flame
                        ( ) excessive water pressure
                        ( ) excessive sediment or lime in tank
                        ( ) none of the above

ELECTRICITY

15. The purpose of a circuit breaker is that of a _____
   device.

16. Resistance is measured in _____.

17. This device can reduce or increase voltage. It has a primary and
   secondary coil. It is called a _____.

18. T   F   A high voltage test light is an accurate means of
            determining voltage.

19. When checking for continuity in an electrical circuit, one should
   have the circuit: (check one) ( ) ON   ( ) OFF

20. It is better, when replacing a defective circuit breaker and the
   proper size is unavailable, to install replacement breaker of:

   (check one)   ( ) larger size
                        ( ) smaller size

Why do you feel you would be a good maintenance repairperson?

   _____

   _____

   _____

Figure 12–9. Continued

2. Deep Pocket Rule means that if one party contributed only 5 percent of the pollution, and if other polluters have no assets, the financially solvent firm that contributed only 5 percent of the pollution could be held responsible for 100 percent of the clean-up cost.

The property manager should ask owners and tenants to inform him or her of any toxic activities or materials such as heavy metals, cyanides, PCBs, solvents, asbestos, or underground storage tanks. When purchasing property, the buyer should investigate previous usage of the property and have soil tests performed.

Refrigerant Management

The Federal Clean Air Act of 1990, Section 608, addresses chlorofluorocarbons (CFCs) and hydrochlorofluorocarbons (HCFCs), which are generally found in air-conditioning systems. The CFCs are R-11, R-12, R-500, R-502; the HCFCs are R-22. Some of the elements of this law include:

1. Covers systems that require 50 pounds or more of refrigerant.

2. Records of leak repairs must be maintained and the contractor must give written notice of leaks to the owner.

3. Effective November 1, 1994, all technicians must be EPA Section 608 certified and refrigerants will be sold only to certified contractors.

4. It is illegal to knowingly release refrigerants into the atmosphere. Fines of up to $25,000 may be assessed.

Lead-Based Paint

Congress passed the Residential Lead-Based Paint Hazard Reduction Act of 1992, called Title X for short. This act places a burden on owners of property constructed prior to 1978, the year lead paint was banned, to disclose lead paint presence prior to sale or rental of a residential building by giving a copy of the EPA/HUD brochure (Figure 12–10—16 pages) and signing a lead paint disclosure form (Figure 12–11). The effective date of regulation is September 6, 1996.

Lead poisoning in children can cause permanent damage to the nervous system, leading to behavioral disorders, and even death. Like asbestos, lead can create a serious hazard if the paint is improperly removed. In 1978, lead was banned from paint, so buildings built after that date probably will not contain lead paint. The federal allowable standard is 600 parts per million (PPM) in residential housing.

The most likely lead paint locations would be windows, door trim, stair trim and baseboards. The lead may be sealed under several layers of new paint and causes no harm unless there is chipping or peeling paint. Testing can de done with patches, X-ray machines, or laboratory analysis by the EPA or state certified testers. Abatement costs can run several thousand dollars per apartment. The removal is by chemical strippers, wet scraping, and the use of high-efficiency particle air (HEPA) pumps. Owners can also remove lead paint molding or cover lead areas with a long-lasting material such as plasterboard.

Environmental Reports

Preliminary Site Assessment   This report includes an executive summary, a statement of purpose, a site description, a site inspection, an area survey, a chain of title, and a regulatory review.

Phase I Assessment   This covers the same areas as the Preliminary Site Assessment (PSA) but includes testing of interior and exterior materials from the site. These may include ceiling tiles, water insulation, air quality, soil, piping, and so on.

Phase II Assessment   If contamination is found in PSA or Phase I, then a Phase II assessment is needed to investigate the problems identified.

1. Stage I consists of testing goals, test results, and executive summary.

2. Stage II consists of determining what course of action is needed and acceptable to local, state, and federal agencies. Approval of these agencies are needed before Phase III.

Protect Your Family From Lead In Your Home

United States
Environmental Protection
Agency

United States Consumer
Product Safety Commission

U.S. EPA Washington DC 20460
U.S. CPSC Washington DC 20207

EPA747-K-94-001
May 1995

Figure 12–10. EPA Brochure

IMPORTANT!

Lead From Paint, Dust, and Soil Can Be Dangerous If Not Managed Properly

FACT: Lead exposure can harm young children and babies even before they are born.

FACT: Even children that seem healthy can have high levels of lead in their bodies.

FACT: People can get lead in their bodies by breathing or swallowing lead dust, or by eating soil or paint chips with lead in them.

FACT: People have many options for reducing lead hazards. In most cases, lead-based paint that is in good condition is not a hazard.

FACT: Removing lead-based paint improperly can increase the danger to your family.

If you think your home might have lead hazards, read this pamphlet to learn some simple steps to protect your family.

Figure 12–10. Continued

(Continued)

Lead Gets in the Body in Many Ways

1 out of every 11 children in the United States has dangerous levels of lead in the blood-stream.

Even children who appear healthy can have dangerous levels of lead.

People can get lead in their body if they:

◆ Put their hands or other objects covered with lead dust in their mouths.

◆ Eat paint chips or soil that contain lead.

◆ Breathe in lead dust (especially during renovations that disturb painted surfaces).

Lead is even more dangerous to children than adults because:

◆ Babies and young children often put their hands and other objects in their mouths. These objects can have lead dust on them.

◆ Children's growing bodies absorb more lead.

◆ Children's brains and nervous systems are more sensitive to the damaging effects of lead.

②

Figure 12–10. Continued

Lead's Effects

If not detected early, children with lead in their bodies can suffer from:

◆ Damage to the brain and nervous system

◆ Behavior and learning problems (such as hyperactivity)

◆ Slowed growth

◆ Hearing problems

◆ Headaches

Lead is also harmful to adults. Adults can suffer from:

◆ Difficulties during pregnancy

◆ Other reproductive problems (in both men and women)

◆ High blood pressure

◆ Digestive problems

◆ Nerve disorders

◆ Memory and concentration problems

◆ Muscle and joint pain

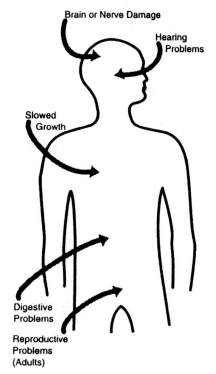

Lead affects the body in many ways.

Figure 12–10.   Continued

(Continued)

Checking Your Family for Lead

Get your children tested if you think your home has high levels of lead.

A simple blood test can detect high levels of lead. Blood tests are important for:

♦ Children who are 6 months to 1 year old (6 months if you live in an older building or home that might have lead in the paint).

♦ Family members that you think might have high levels of lead.

If your child is older than 1 year, talk to your doctor about whether your child needs testing.

Your doctor or health center can do blood tests. They are inexpensive and sometimes free. Your doctor will explain what the test results mean. *Treatment can range from changes in your diet to medication or a hospital stay.*

Where Lead-Based Paint Is Found

In general, the older your home, the more likely it has lead-based paint.

Many homes built before 1978 have lead-based paint. In 1978, the federal government banned lead-based paint from housing.

Lead can be found:

♦ In homes in the city, country, or suburbs.

♦ In apartments, single-family homes, and both private and public housing.

♦ Inside *and* outside of the house.

♦ In soil around a home. (Soil can pick up lead from exterior paint, or other sources such as past use of leaded gas in cars).

Figure 12–10.   Continued

Where Lead Is Likely To Be a Hazard

Lead-based paint that is in good condition is usually not a hazard.

Peeling, chipping, chalking, or cracking lead-based paint is a hazard and needs immediate attention.

Lead-based paint may also be a hazard when found on surfaces that children can chew or that get a lot of wear-and-tear. These areas include:

◆ Windows and window sills.

◆ Doors and door frames.

◆ Stairs, railings, and banisters.

◆ Porches and fences.

Lead dust can form when lead-based paint is dry scraped, dry sanded, or heated. Dust also forms when painted surfaces bump or rub together. Lead chips and dust can get on surfaces and objects that people touch. Settled lead dust can reenter the air when people vacuum, sweep, or walk through it.

Lead in soil can be a hazard when children play in bare soil or when people bring soil into the house on their shoes. Call your state agency (see page 12) to find out about soil testing for lead.

Lead from paint chips, which you can see, and lead dust, which you can't always see, can both be serious hazards.

Figure 12–10. Continued

(Continued)

Checking Your Home for Lead

Just knowing that a home has lead-based paint may not tell you if there is a hazard.

You can get your home checked for lead hazards in one of two ways, or both:

◆ A paint **inspection** tells you the lead content of every painted surface in your home. It won't tell you whether the paint is a hazard or how you should deal with it.

◆ A **risk assessment** tells you if there are any sources of serious lead exposure (such as peeling paint and lead dust). It also tells you what actions to take to address these hazards.

Have qualified professionals do the work. *The federal government is writing standards for inspectors and risk assessors. Some states might already have standards in place.* Call your state agency for help with locating qualified professionals in your area (see page 12).

Trained professionals use a range of methods when checking your home, including:

◆ Visual inspection of paint condition and location.

◆ Lab tests of paint samples.

◆ Surface dust tests.

◆ A portable x-ray fluorescence machine.

Home test kits for lead are available, but the federal government is still testing their reliability. These tests should not be the only method used before doing renovations or to assure safety.

⟨6⟩

Figure 12–10. Continued

What You Can Do Now To Protect Your Family

If you suspect that your house has lead hazards, you can take some immediate steps to reduce your family's risk:

- ◆ **If you rent, notify your landlord of peeling or chipping paint.**

- ◆ **Clean up paint chips immediately.**

- ◆ **Clean floors, window frames, window sills, and other surfaces weekly.** Use a mop or sponge with warm water and a general all-purpose cleaner or a cleaner made specifically for lead. REMEMBER: NEVER MIX AMMONIA AND BLEACH PRODUCTS TOGETHER SINCE THEY CAN FORM A DANGEROUS GAS.

- ◆ **Thoroughly rinse sponges and mop heads after cleaning dirty or dusty areas.**

- ◆ **Wash children's hands often, especially before they eat and before nap time and bed time.**

- ◆ **Keep play areas clean.** Wash bottles, pacifiers, toys, and stuffed animals regularly.

- ◆ **Keep children from chewing window sills or other painted surfaces.**

- ◆ **Clean or remove shoes before entering your home to avoid tracking in lead from soil.**

- ◆ **Make sure children eat nutritious, low-fat meals high in iron and calcium,** such as spinach and low-fat dairy products. Children with good diets absorb less lead.

Figure 12–10. Continued

(Continued)

How To Significantly Reduce Lead Hazards

Removing lead improperly can increase the hazard to your family by spreading even more lead dust around the house.

Always use a professional who is trained to remove lead hazards safely.

In addition to day-to-day cleaning and good nutrition:

♦ You can **temporarily** reduce lead hazards by taking actions like repairing damaged painted surfaces and planting grass to cover soil with high lead levels. These actions (called "interim controls") are not permanent solutions and will not eliminate all risks of exposure.

♦ To **permanently** remove lead hazards, you must hire a lead "abatement" contractor. Abatement (or permanent hazard elimination) methods include removing, sealing, or enclosing lead-based paint with special materials. Just painting over the hazard with regular paint is not enough.

Always hire a person with special training for correcting lead problems—someone who knows how to do this work safely and has the proper equipment to clean up thoroughly. If possible, hire a certified lead abatement contractor. Certified contractors will employ qualified workers and follow strict safety rules as set by their state or by the federal government.

Call your state agency (see page 12) for help with locating qualified contractors in your area and to see if financial assistance is available.

Figure 12–10. Continued

Remodeling or Renovating a Home With Lead-Based Paint

Take precautions before you begin remodeling or renovations that disturb painted surfaces (such as scraping off paint or tearing out walls):

◆ **Have the area tested for lead-based paint.**

◆ **Do not use a dry scraper, belt-sander, propane torch, or heat gun** to remove lead-based paint. These actions create large amounts of lead dust and fumes. Lead dust can remain in your home long after the work is done.

◆ **Temporarily move your family** (especially children and pregnant women) out of the apartment or house until the work is done and the area is properly cleaned. If you can't move your family, at least completely seal off the work area.

◆ **Follow other safety measures to reduce lead hazards.** You can find out about other safety measures by calling 1-800-424-LEAD. Ask for the brochure "Reducing Lead Hazards When Remodeling Your Home." This brochure explains what to do before, during, and after renovations.

If you have already completed renovations or remodeling that could have released lead-based paint or dust, get your young children tested and follow the steps outlined on page 7 of this brochure.

If not conducted properly, certain types of renovations can release lead from paint and dust into the air.

Figure 12–10. Continued

(Continued)

Other Sources of Lead

While paint, dust, and soil are the most common lead hazards, other lead sources also exist.

◆ **Drinking water.** Your home might have plumbing with lead or lead solder. Call your local health department or water supplier to find out about testing your water. You cannot see, smell, or taste lead, and boiling your water will not get rid of lead. If you think your plumbing might have lead in it:

- Use only cold water for drinking and cooking.

- Run water for 15 to 30 seconds before drinking it, especially if you have not used your water for a few hours.

◆ **The job.** If you work with lead, you could bring it home on your hands or clothes. Shower and change clothes before coming home. Launder your clothes separately from the rest of your family's.

◆ Old painted **toys** and **furniture.**

◆ Food and liquids stored in **lead crystal** or **lead-glazed pottery or porcelain.**

◆ **Lead smelters** or other industries that release lead into the air.

◆ **Hobbies** that use lead, such as making pottery or stained glass, or refinishing furniture.

◆ **Folk remedies** that contain lead, such as "greta" and "azarcon" used to treat an upset stomach.

Figure 12–10. Continued

For More Information

The National Lead Information Center

Call **1-800-LEAD-FYI** to learn how to protect children from lead poisoning.

For other information on lead hazards, call the center's clearinghouse at **1-800-424-LEAD.** For the hearing impaired, call, **TDD 1-800-526-5456.** (FAX: **202-659-1192,** Internet: **EHC@CAIS.COM**).

EPA's Safe Drinking Water Hotline

Call **1-800-426-4791** for information about lead in drinking water.

Consumer Product Safety Commission Hotline

To request information on lead in consumer products, or to report an unsafe consumer product or a product-related injury call **1-800-638-2772**. (Internet: info@cpsc.gov). For the hearing impaired, call **1-800-638-8270**.

Local Sources of Information

Figure 12-10. Continued

(*Continued*)

State Health and Environmental Agencies

Some cities and states have their own rules for lead-based paint activities. Check with your state agency (listed below) to see if state or local laws apply to you. Most state agencies can also provide information on finding a lead abatement firm in your area, and on possible sources of financial aid for reducing lead hazards.

State/Region	Phone Number	State/Region	Phone Number
Alabama	(205) 242-5661	Missouri	(314) 526-4911
Alaska	(907) 465-5152	Montana	(406) 444-3671
Arkansas	(501) 661-2534	Nebraska	(402) 471-2451
Arizona	(602) 542-7307	Nevada	(702) 687-6615
California	(510) 450-2424	New Hampshire	(603) 271-4507
Colorado	(303) 692-3012	New Jersey	(609) 633-2043
Connecticut	(203) 566-5808	New Mexico	(505) 841-8024
Washington, DC	(202) 727-9850	New York	(800) 458-1158
Delaware	(302) 739-4735	North Carolina	(919) 715-3293
Florida	(904) 488-3385	North Dakota	(701) 328-5188
Georgia	(404) 657-6514	Ohio	(614) 466-1450
Hawaii	(808) 832-5860	Oklahoma	(405) 271-5220
Idaho	(208) 332-5544	Oregon	(503) 248-5240
Illinois	(800) 545-2200	Pennsylvania	(717) 782-2884
Indiana	(317) 382-6662	Rhode Island	(401) 277-3424
Iowa	(800) 972-2026	South Carolina	(803) 935-7945
Kansas	(913) 296-0189	South Dakota	(605) 773-3153
Kentucky	(502) 564-2154	Tennessee	(615) 741-5683
Louisiana	(504) 765-0219	Texas	(512) 834-6600
Massachusetts	(800) 532-9571	Utah	(801) 536-4000
Maryland	(410) 631-3859	Vermont	(802) 863-7231
Maine	(207) 287-4311	Virginia	(800) 523-4019
Michigan	(517) 335-8885	Washington	(206) 753-2556
Minnesota	(612) 627-5498	West Virginia	(304) 558-2981
Mississippi	(601) 960-7463	Wisconsin	(608) 266-5885
		Wyoming	(307) 777-7391

Figure 12–10. Continued

EPA Regional Offices

Your Regional EPA office can provide further information regarding regulations and lead protection programs.

EPA Regional Offices

Region 1 (Connecticut, Massachusetts, Maine, New Hampshire, Rhode Island, Vermont)
John F. Kennedy Federal Building
One Congress Street
Boston, MA 02203
(617) 565-3420

Region 2 (New Jersey, New York, Puerto Rico, Virgin Islands)
Building 5
2890 Woodbridge Avenue
Edison, NJ 08837-3679
(908) 321-6671

Region 3 (Delaware, Washington DC, Maryland, Pennsylvania, Virginia, West Virginia)
841 Chestnut Building
Philadelphia, PA 19107
(215) 597-9800

Region 4 (Alabama, Florida, Georgia, Kentucky, Mississippi, North Carolina, South Carolina, Tennessee)
345 Courtland Street, NE
Atlanta, GA 30365
(404) 347-4727

Region 5 (Illinois, Indiana, Michigan, Minnesota, Ohio, Wisconsin)
77 West Jackson Boulevard
Chicago, IL 60604-3590
(312) 886-6003

Region 6 (Arkansas, Louisiana, New Mexico, Oklahoma, Texas)
First Interstate Bank Tower
1445 Ross Avenue, 12th Floor, Suite 1200
Dallas, TX 75202-2733
(214) 665-7244

Region 7 (Iowa, Kansas, Missouri, Nebraska)
726 Minnesota Avenue
Kansas City, KS 66101
(913) 551-7020

Region 8 (Colorado, Montana, North Dakota, South Dakota, Utah, Wyoming)
999 18th Street, Suite 500
Denver, CO 80202-2405
(303) 293-1603

Region 9 (Arizona, California, Hawaii, Nevada)
75 Hawthorne Street
San Francisco, CA 94105
(415) 744-1124

Region 10 (Idaho, Oregon, Washington, Alaska)
1200 Sixth Avenue
Seattle, WA 98101
(206) 553-1200

CPSC Regional Offices

Eastern Regional Center
6 World Trade Center
Vesey Street, Room 350
New York, NY 10048
(212) 466-1612

Central Regional Center
230 South Dearborn Street
Room 2944
Chicago, IL 60604-1601
(312) 353-8260

Western Regional Center
600 Harrison Street, Room 245
San Francisco, CA 94107
(415) 744-2966

Figure 12–10. Continued

(Continued)

Simple Steps To Protect Your Family From Lead Hazards

If you think your home has high levels of lead:

◆ Get your young children tested for lead, even if they seem healthy.

◆ Wash children's hands, bottles, pacifiers, and toys often.

◆ Make sure children eat healthy, low-fat foods.

◆ Get your home checked for lead hazards.

◆ Regularly clean floors, window sills, and other surfaces.

◆ Wipe soil off shoes before entering house.

◆ Talk to your landlord about fixing surfaces with peeling or chipping paint.

◆ Take precautions to avoid exposure to lead dust when remodeling or renovating (call 1-800-424-LEAD for guidelines).

◆ Don't use a belt-sander, propane torch, dry scraper, or dry sandpaper on painted surfaces that may contain lead.

◆ Don't try to remove lead-based paint yourself.

Recycled/Recyclable
Printed on paper that contains at least 20 percent postconsumer fiber

Figure 12–10. Continued

Are You Planning To Buy, Rent, or Renovate a Home Built Before 1978?

Many houses and apartments built before 1978 have paint that contains lead (called lead-based paint). Lead from paint, chips, and dust can pose serious health hazards if not taken care of properly.

By 1996, federal law will require that individuals receive certain information before renting, buying, or renovating pre-1978 housing:

LANDLORDS will have to disclose known information on lead-based paint hazards before leases take effect. Leases will include a federal form about lead-based paint.

SELLERS will have to disclose known information on lead-based paint hazards before selling a house. Sales contracts will include a federal form about lead-based paint in the building. Buyers will have up to 10 days to check for lead hazards.

RENOVATORS will have to give you this pamphlet before starting work.

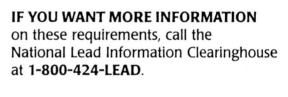

IF YOU WANT MORE INFORMATION on these requirements, call the National Lead Information Clearinghouse at **1-800-424-LEAD**.

This document is in the public domain. It may be reproduced by an individual or organization without permission. Information provided in this booklet is based upon current scientific and technical understanding of the issues presented and is reflective of the jurisdictional boundaries established by the statutes governing the co-authoring agencies. Following the advice given will not necessarily provide complete protection in all situations or against all health hazards that can be caused by lead exposure.

Figure 12–10. Continued

Disclosure of Information on Lead-Based Paint and/or Lead-Based Paint Hazards

Lead Warning Statement

Housing built before 1978 may contain lead-based paint. Lead from paint, paint chips, and dust can pose health hazards if not managed properly. Lead exposure is especially harmful to young children and pregnant women. Before renting pre-1978 housing, lessors must disclose the presence of known lead-based paint and/or lead-based paint hazards in the dwelling. Lessees must also receive a federally approved pamphlet on lead poisoning prevention.

Lessor's Disclosure

Presence of lead-based paint and/or lead-based paint hazards (check (a) or (b) below):

(a) _____ Known lead-based paint and/or lead-based paint hazards are present in the housing.
(explain):_____

(b) _____ Lessor has no knowledge of lead-based paint and/or lead based paint hazards in the housing.

Records and reports available to Lessor (check (c) or (d) below):

(c) _____ Lessor has provided the lessee with all available records and reports pertaining to lead-based paint and/or lead-based paint hazards in housing (list documents below.)
_____

(d) _____ Lessor has no reports or records pertaining to lead-based paint and/or lead-based paint hazards in the housing.

Lessee's Acknowledgment – Initial _____

(a) _____ Lessee has received copies of all information listed above.
(b) _____ Lessee has received the pamphlet entitled, *Protect Your Family from Lead in Your Home*.

Agent's Acknowledgment – Initial _____

(a) _____ Agent has informed the lessor of the lessor's obligations under 42 U.S.C. 485d and is aware of his/her responsibility to ensure compliance.

Certification of Accuracy

The following parties have reviewed the information above and certify, to the best of their knowledge, that the information they have provided is true and accurate.

_____	_____	_____	_____
Lessee	Date	Lessee	Date
_____	_____	_____	_____
Lessor	Date	Lessor	Date
_____	_____	_____	_____
Agent	Date	Agent	Date

JD Property Management, Inc.
PO Box 1230
Costa Mesa, CA 92628

JD PROPERTY
MANAGEMENT
INCORPORATED

**Equal
Housing
Opportunity**

Figure 12–11. Lead Disclosure Form

Phase III Program   In Phase III, the problem (such as asbestos or lead) has been identified and plans for remediation cleanup are implemented. The site may only require monitoring and not abatement.

The property manager should treat toxic waste like discrimination, as a legal minefield, to avoid potential liability to the owner and the agent.

Asbestos

An issue of increasing concern facing owners and property managers is how to discover and respond to the presence of asbestos in buildings. Asbestos has been routinely used in apartment and office buildings for the last 50 years for a variety of purposes, including fireproofing and thermal and acoustical insulation on pipes, ductwork, and boilers. An Environmental Protection Agency (EPA) survey has identified more than 750,000 buildings in the United States that contain asbestos. Over 20 percent of office buildings have been found to contain asbestos, which is a carcinogen that has been linked to cancer. It's estimated the cost of asbestos abatement could be as high as $250 billion over the next ten years.

The Federal Asbestos Hazard Abatement Act of 1987 set an exposure limit for workers in office buildings and tenants in rental buildings of ten or more units.

Asbestos is found in acoustic ceilings, floor tiles, roofing material, pipe wrap, and many other places. Buildings built after 1978 probably contain no asbestos in the acoustic (cottage cheese) ceiling as it was banned that year by the EPA. Buildings built before 1978 require a qualified testing service to test to see if asbestos is present. The Occupational Safety and Health Administration (OSHA) has set the exposure level at 0.1 fibers per cubic centimeter of air. A material containing more than that level is considered asbestos-containing material (ACM).

More information can be obtained by writing:

Consumer Product Safety Commission
Washington, DC 20207

or

EPA
Washington, DC 20207

SUMMARY

Many tenants view maintenance and management as the same entity. It is therefore important to have a good maintenance program for tenant (customer) satisfaction, thereby reducing turnover and increasing income. A second goal of a good maintenance program is to reduce or minimize cost. By reducing turnover and minimizing cost, the property manager increases the net operating income (NOI) and therefore the value of the property for the owner. The property manager, then, should be familiar with the terminology and maintenance operations, but need not be an expert.

The four basic types of maintenance are:

1. Service—emergencies, repairs

2. Routine—landscaping, janitorial

3. Preventive—regular repair tasks; e.g., air conditioning

4. Extraordinary—rehabilitation, replacement; e.g., roof

Plumbing is one of the most frequent problem areas in maintenance. Items of concern to the property manager include the location of shutoff valves, electrolysis, the insulation of hot water pipes, recirculating pumps, and hot water heaters.

Another major problem area, which is a habitability item, is heating. Temperature settings, airflow ventilation, heat exchangers, performance ratios, and Btus are some of the items to be considered. Electrical repairs should be done by licensed electricians and blueprints should be readily available on the property.

Selecting a good grade and color of carpeting can add marketing pizzazz as well as reduce replacement costs. Regularly scheduled pest control will prevent serious infestations and tenant unhappiness.

In addition to maintenance, the property manager is responsible for security, which to the tenant means peaceful enjoyment of the unit in a secure complex. Some preventive measures the property manager needs to address include

Hardware—locks, lighting, gates

Guards—employees or an outside service

Tenant participation —Neighborhood Watch program

Police—reduced rental rate for police officers who live in the complex

Smoke detectors—required by law

Energy management represents approximately 32 percent of office building and 25 percent of apartment building operating costs. Use of energy reduction measures such as caulking, photoelectric timers, recirculating pumps, separate metering of utilities, flow restrictions on showers and faucets, and so on, can reduce operating costs and increase NOI (net operating income) for the property.

Estimating cost of repairs is necessary for budgeting, management planning, and specific projects such as re-roofing. Bids from vendors and cost data books are helpful to the property manager.

The Super Fund Law of 1980 makes the property owner responsible for cleanup of toxic waste or waste runoff from the property. Toxic materials include refrigerants (CFCs), lead-based paint, and asbestos. Environmental reports include preliminary site assessment, Phase I, Phase II, and Phase III assessments.

PERSONALITY PROFILE

The property manager must not only increase the net operating income (NOI), but also protect the asset. Protection can be in the form of insurance coverage or security and safety programs and procedures. Glenn French of Raleigh, North Carolina, is a consultant who has written several articles, and a book and gives lectures around the country on protecting your assets from crime, drugs, and gang problems. He is a certified property manager (CPM) who had been successful managing troubled properties. He presently serves as a consultant for owners and manages in both the public and private sector.

Glenn has helped turn around some very difficult, drug-infested properties, such as Mayfair Mansions, a 569-unit complex in Washington, DC. Glenn's life has been threatened but he says, "I'm not afraid. I never have been. I've cleared out drug dealers from hallways and out of buildings so the residents know that someone cared and someone was against the dealers. In part, it gave me insight that people will have respect for authority if it is demanded."

Glenn is a proactive, hands-on property manager. Property management is not a stereotypical career, as many avenues and approaches can lead to success.

1. Service maintenance includes
   a. emergencies.
   b. repairs made within 24 hours.
   c. adding a new roof.
   d. both a and b
   e. both a and c

2. Routine maintenance includes
   a. landscaping.
   b. janitorial.
   c. replacing air-conditioners.
   d. both a and b
   e. none of the above

3. An example of preventive maintenance would be
   a. repairing a broken water main.
   b. replacing air-conditioning filters.
   c. putting in a new sprinkler system.
   d. replacing burned-out light bulbs.

4. Extraordinary maintenance involves:
   a. repairing a leaky faucet.
   b. installing a new hot water heater.
   c. installing a new garbage disposal.
   d. converting the master meter to individual meters.

5. The on-site manager should
   a. know the location of shutoff valves.
   b. be an expert plumber.
   c. be an expert electrician.
   d. be an expert carpenter.

6. Insulating pipes will result in
   a. a faster flow of water.
   b. energy savings.
   c. fewer stoppages.
   d. colder water.

7. Measures to prevent heat loss include
   a. utilizing high thermostat settings.
   b. installing fireplaces.
   c. installing low-flush toilets.
   d. insulating pipes.

8. Electrical work should be done by:
   a. the on-site manager.
   b. a licensed electrician.
   c. the property manager.
   d. a handyman.

9. Boric acid helps control
   a. cockroaches.
   b. flies.
   c. bugs.
   d. dogs.

10. Security measures include
    a. locks and gates.
    b. lighting.
    c. security guards.
    d. all of the above
    e. only a and c

11. Contractors are usually licensed by a
    a. federal agency.
    b. state agency.
    c. county agency.
    d. city agency.

12. Recirculating pumps are used to
    a. pump water faster.
    b. pump water higher.
    c. reduce energy costs.
    d. keep water clean.

13. What type of wiring is usually used in an office building?
    a. 120/240-volt, single-phase
    b. 120/208-volt, 3-phase
    c. 480/277-volt, 3-phase
    d. all of the above

14. Electrolysis refers to
    a. electrical.
    b. HVAC.
    c. carpeting.
    d. plumbing.

15. The EPA is a
    a. federal agency.
    b. state agency.
    c. county agency.
    d. city agency.

CASE STUDY PROBLEMS

Refer to the Case Study at the end of Chapter 5.

1. Would you recommend a preventive maintenance program for Civic Center Terrace? If so, why?

2. The present plumbing is copper. What type of plumbing should be used for repairs in order to prevent electrolysis?

3. You need to make some electrical repairs at the complex. What type of maintenance person would be preferable?

4. After a tenant moves out, and before re-renting, should you replace old, worn carpet?

5. Is the cheapest carpet always the best to install?

6. Should the manager purchase highly toxic chemicals and spray the interior of all tenant apartments every three months?

7. Civic Center Terrace has no outside lighting. Should you consider installation? Why or why not?

8. Should maintenance people be selected only for their competence?

9. Since there are deadbolts on all apartment doors, can Civic Center Terrace be advertised as a security complex?

10. List some specific measures to reduce energy consumption.

ADDITIONAL READING AND REFERENCES

Allen, Edward, *The Professional Handbook of Building Construction*, John Wiley & Sons, Somerset, NJ, 1985.

Asbestos Abatement Training Programs, PSI, 4820 W. 15th Street, Lawrence, KS 66049-3846.

Building Trade Services, *Tenant Improvement Price Guide*, San Diego, CA, 1987.

California Department of Housing and Community Development, *A New Horizon*, Sacramento, CA, 1985.

Institute of Real Estate Management, *No-Cost Low-Cost Energy Conservation Measures for Multi-Housing*, Chicago, IL, 1981.

International Conference of Building Officials, *Manual of Forms for Building Department Administration*, Whittier, CA, 1985.

Means Co., R.S., *Means Repair and Remodeling Cost Data Commercial and Residential*, Chicago, IL, 1988.

National Association of Homebuilders, *Building Construction Cost Data*, Washington, DC, 1984.

National Construction Estimator (Annual), Craftsman Book Company, 6058 Corte del Cedro, Carlsbad, CA 92008.

Shear, Mel, *Handbook of Building Maintenance*, Reston Publishing, Reston, VA, 1983.

Chapter 13

Administration and the Management Office

Key terms

Bank reconciliation	Fidelity bond	Pro forma budget
Check register	Hardware	Software
Co-insurance	Micro-computer	Umbrella policy
Deductible	Mini-computer	Workers'
Endorsements	Modem	compensation
FAX		

Food for thought

"Give someone a fish and they will eat for a day. Teach someone to fish and they will eat for a lifetime."

INTRODUCTION　Real estate management is comprised basically of four major groupings: "Ma and Pa" owners who manage for themselves; institutional investors (pension plans, insurance companies) who self-manage through a professional division within their company; local real estate offices managing either to secure or protect future listings; and professional "fee managers" who, without ownership interest, manage for several clients.

The goals and objectives of the management firm will differ depending on the grouping to which it belongs. For example, a fee manager will not want to keep a client who pays a low management fee that precludes making a profit. The local real estate office, although it may be running the property poorly due to inexperience, might be willing to suffer a loss in management fees hoping it will make a profit on the sale commission.

ESTABLISHING THE MANAGEMENT OFFICE
Types of Ownership

Property managers must decide on the legal form of ownership their company will take, such as sole proprietorship, partnership, or corporation. Each has legal and tax ramifications (refer to Figure 4-3). Consultation with a CPA or attorney is prudent.

Sole Proprietorship　This form of ownership exposes the owners to unlimited liability on the properties they manage and the employees that work for the company. Insurance may not cover acts of negligence, such as a resident manager shooting a tenant. This form of ownership appears on Schedule C of the owner's tax return.

General Partnership   A general partnership is exposed to unlimited liability like a sole proprietorship and is taxed directly to the taxpayer. The partnership will issue a K-1, which appears on Schedule E on the individual tax return (a sample of Schedule E is Figure 2–10).

Corporation   The management company can be either a regular C corporation or a Sub S corporation. The Sub S was created by Congress in 1958 to help smaller businesses limited to no more than 35 shareholders. It limits liability like a corporation but profits are taxed at the shareholder (taxpayer) level rather than at both the corporation and the taxpayer level as in a regular C corporation. The taxpayer would receive a K-1 that will appear on Schedule E of his or her return. One disadvantage is that only 30 percent of an owner's medical insurance premiums are deductible. The Sub S seems to be best suited for small management companies, but you should check with your CPA or attorney.

Office Location

Office location will depend on the type of clients, services offered, goals, and the geographic area of the property manager. The property manager should not work out of his or her home, but should have an office to reflect professionalism. Often, the property manager can negotiate with a client to rent space at a reduced rate in a building he or she manages. The owner benefits from the on-site proximity. Some offices are located in less-prestigious industrial areas. If your clients are professionals, such as doctors or attorneys, a suitable location is a must to portray the proper image. If you are dealing with residential tenants who bring rent to your office, the office should be centrally located, have easy access, be on the ground floor, and have ample parking. Consideration should also be given to expansion—how long is this space going to be large enough to serve your needs? Moving the office frequently is both expensive (moving costs, stationery, etc.) and confusing to clients and tenants.

Office Layout

A nice but small waiting room is necessary, separated by a partition from the work area but with a window so the receptionist can talk to tenants and clients. This gives a feeling of professionalism and keeps the tenants and/or visitors from wandering uninvited into the office where files, checks, or money may be accessible. The office should be cheerfully decorated with partitions and separate offices to reduce noise from copy machines, typewriters, and computer printers (Figure 13–1).

Equipment

The property manager provides a service, not a product. There is no inventory or large capital outlay for machinery. Every office, however, usually has typewriters, word processors, modem, computers, calculators, copy machines and FAX machines. The FAX (a contraction of "facsimile," meaning exact copy of an original) machines are transceivers and can send or receive messages over standard local and long-distance telephone lines. The message is transmitted on a sheet of paper into the FAX machine to be scanned and transmitted by electrical impulses to the receiving FAX machine, which copies it onto a sheet of paper, much like making a photocopy. The cost is low, only about $1.00 per page between Los Angeles and New York City, including phone costs and paper. The Group III FAX machine is the most desirable and fastest (12–15 seconds per page) and is compatible with the slower Group II and Group I FAX machines. Applications of FAX machine are many and varied for the property manager and include rent receipts, lease documents, proposals, blueprints, contracts, letters, and reports.

In smaller operations, posting of rents, posting of bills, and check writing are usually done by hand. In larger offices, many of these functions are done

Figure 13–1. Office Layout

with the assistance of a computer. Proper equipment increases productivity and reduces costs. Salary usually accounts for 40–50 percent of property management overhead. Profits can thus be increased significantly by increasing the volume of business and automating at the same time.

COMPUTERS If the management office portfolio exceeds 500 units, a computer is usually necessary in order to automate bookkeeping and generate timely financial reports. The three categories of computers (see Figure 13–2) are:

1. *Mainframe*—largest, fastest, and most expensive; usually not necessary for property management.

2. *Mini*—can be networked and has a memory to handle 20,000+ units, but at usually triple the cost of a micro.

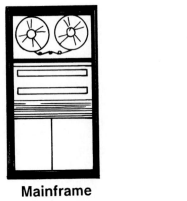
Mainframe

Mini

Micro

Figure 13–2. Computer Categories

3. *Micro*—the least expensive and has the smallest memory (the IBM PC is an example). It comes in both hard and floppy-disk drives and can handle several thousand units. Most management companies now use micros.

Key computer terms are explained in Figure 13–3.

HARDWARE	The actual physical computer system, including keyboard, printer, and display screen.
SOFTWARE	The programmed instructions used to run the computer; stored on disks or tapes.
	A. User friendly: cursor helps you input data.
	B. Canned program: purchase of property management program sold to many other users. There are over a hundred programs on the market ranging from $100-$20,000. (See list on following page.)
	C. Custom designed programs: expensive and written specifically for a firm and its hardware.
CRT	Cathode ray tube, a TV-like display terminal used to show information. i.e., monitor.
CP/M	Common operating system for microcomputer.
CPU	Central processing unit, the heart of the computer. It controls all operations and does the actual calculating.
DATABASE	Collection of data that can be retrieved by the computer, i.e., security deposit lists.
DISK	Storage device for data.
HARD COPY	The actual paper printout.
LINE PRINTER	High-speed printer as it prints a line at a time rather than one character at a time.
MODEM	A device that allows the computer to send and receive information over telephone lines. Can be internal or external.
RAM	Random Access Memory, the main type used in small computers, i.e., 8-16 Meg.
TERMINAL	Monitor and typewriter-like keyboard used for input.
WORD PROCESSING	A program used for typing correspondence, etc.

Figure 13–3.   Key Computer Terms

Figure 13–4.

COMPUTER SOFTWARE The Institute of Real Estate Management (IREM) has completed a list of software vendors who have certified compliance with IREM's minimum standards for property management accounting software. These minimum standards were recommended by an IREM software standards task force "to assist management firms in defining and locating acceptable software for property management accounting." The task force also provides software suppliers with a better understanding of the needs of management firms. In order to receive the certified compliance listing, software vendors must file an affidavit that their products comply in all respects with the IREM standards. IREM does not, however, evaluate the software to determine if these standards are met. Following is an annually updated list of firms that have complied. A complete list can be obtained by contacting IREM in Chicago.

Alternative Management Systems, Inc.
13831 NW Freeway, #550
Houston, TX 77040
(713) 690-2674

Maxwell Systems, Inc.
CIT
515 Cabrillo Park Dr., #160
Santa Ana, CA 92701
(714) 285-0501

Yardi Systems
819 Reddick St.
Santa Barbara, CA 93101
(805) 966-3666

CMS, Inc.
311B Maple Ave. West
Vienna, VA 22180
(800) 397-1499

Melson Technologies (Skyline Software)
707 Skokie Blvd.
Northbrook, IL 60062
(800) 445-7638

United Data Systems
432 S. Belair Rd.
Augusta, GA 30907
(716) 855-7016

Two computer reports shown later in this chapter are Figure 13–5, Bookkeeping Setup and Figure 13–6, New Property Information. Additional computer reports, not shown, but usually available, are check registers and tenant lists.

SELECTION OF A PROPERTY MANAGEMENT COMPANY

If an outside company is to be used for property management, the question is often asked, "How do we select that company?" The management firm will, after all, be entrusted with several thousand dollars in rent collections each month. It is prudent, therefore, to inquire about the management firm. Some questions which should be asked include:

1. What is the company's size?

2. How long has it been in business?

3. Is it bonded?

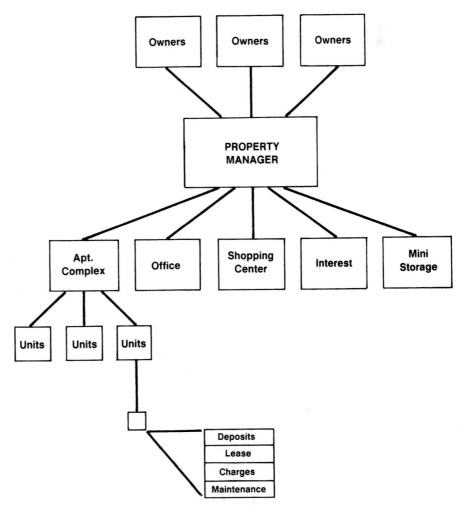

Figure 13–5. Bookkeeping Property Setup

4. Does it have a real estate license (a must in some states)?

5. Is it primarily in the property management business or in real estate sales?

6. Does it have a trust account?

Different types of properties require different management companies. For example, some management companies specialize in residential units and would be a poor choice to manage a medical building (see Figure 13–5). When selecting a management company, ask for a written proposal, which should include its fees, who has responsibility for hiring and training onsite resident managers, payment of bills, leasing proposals, inspection frequency, supervision criteria, a copy of the management agreement, references, and a history of the firm. Visit the management company's office and meet the people who will be in charge of your property. Do its executive managers have a CPM designation? Ask to see a sample of the monthly financial statement you will receive.

In summary, the property manager should bring diversified talents, experience, controls, and computer reporting systems all in one package to help the property perform to its maximum potential. The owner should benefit from the old cliché: Professional property management doesn't cost—it pays.

PURCHASING A PROPERTY MANAGEMENT COMPANY

Purchasing a property management company usually involves little in physical assets (computer, furniture, etc.) and is mostly the existing client accounts and goodwill. The present personnel may or may not stay with the new operation after purchase. It is, therefore, difficult to determine the purchase price due to these subjective and nebulous characteristics. One method is a lump-sum payment (3–6 months' present management fees) plus incentives at the end of each year, depending on the gross income. If income goes down (as it invariably will, due to sales and natural attrition), the seller would receive less. For example, if the gross management fees were $10,000 per month:

Down payment	—	3 mo. × $10,000	=	$30,000
End of 1st year	—	1 mo. × $ 8,000	=	$ 8,000
End of 2nd year	—	1 mo. × $ 7,000	=	$ 7,000
End of 3rd year	—	1 mo. × $ 5,000	=	$ 5,000
End of 4th year	—	1 mo. × $ 4,000	=	$ 4,000
End of 5th year	—	1 mo. × $ 2,000	=	$ 2,000
Total price paid				$56,000

Other methods of determining value include income capitalization, replacement cost, percentage of annual gross management fees, and net earning times a number of years.

INSURANCE FOR THE PROPERTY

The property manager, in addition to increasing the income stream, must also preserve and protect tenants and the property. This involves risk evaluation in dealing with possible liability and loss. Higher deductibles can reduce insurance costs, but the owner shares more of the risk.

Risk management

Retain risk—deductible or self-insurance

Avoid risk—fill in the swimming pool

> *Transfer risk*—insurance policy, required by lenders

> *Control risk*—install smoke alarms and safety systems

The property manager should seek the assistance of a good insurance broker for counsel on insurance needs. Adequate records and files should be kept, as well as a tickler file on expiration dates.

Types of Insurance

1. *All-peril, all-risk policy*—includes fire and extended coverage. Floods, earthquakes, and liability are usually excluded from coverage.

2. *Package policy*—covers both property and liability.

3. *Rent loss*—pays the owner for loss of rents if a unit is destroyed by fire.

4. *Surety bond*—an instrument providing monetary compensation should there be a failure to perform any specific acts within a certain period.

5. *Fidelity bond*—should cover all employees for losses from dishonest acts in the property manager's office or on property being managed.

6. *Non-owned auto*—covers the employer's liability for daily work by employees. It does not cover the employees.

7. *Umbrella policy*—additional liability coverage under existing underlying policy; relatively inexpensive.

8. *Workers' compensation*—covers medical and hospital payments for injuries sustained by employees on the job. Rates are set by the state and this policy is not transferable in the event of a sale. The property manager should make sure vendors have certificates of insurance or the property manager may be liable in the event of an accident. The management company may have a master policy or may arrange for each property to have a separate policy.

9. *Errors and omissions*—basically malpractice insurance. It covers legal fees and damages for liability less the deductible. It does not cover dishonest or fraudulent acts and is very expensive and difficult to obtain for a property manager.

10. *Co-insurance*—the owner accepts part of the risk and pays a lower premium. The property is insured for less than its value, usually 80 percent. The amount of loss collectible is dollar for dollar up to 80 percent of the value. Since buildings are seldom destroyed, the owner is "betting" his or her building will survive. For example, if a building worth $1,000,000 is insured for $800,000 and there is fire damage of $600,000, the property owner would receive the full amount ($600,000). If, however, the insurance policy is for only $500,000 , the owner would receive only 50 percent of the loss, or $300,000.

$$\text{Formula} = \frac{\text{amount of insurance carried}}{\text{value of building}} \text{ or } \frac{\$500,000}{\$1,000,000} = 50\% \text{ coverage}$$

It is important, therefore, to make sure the building is properly insured.

Endorsements

1. *Additional insured*—the management company should be listed as an additional insured on the owner's policy. The cost is usually nominal and it maintains the unity of interests of the owner, management company, and insurance company in the event of a lawsuit.

2. *Host liquor*—should be carried if liquor is served on the premises.

3. *Premises medical*—allows for a no-fault minimum on minor injuries.

Insurance Suggestions

1. Under new insurance regulations, claims will be covered only if they occur and were filed during the policy period. Notify the insurance company immediately if someone falls down an outside stairway.

2. Include instructions on how to handle losses such as fires or falls in your standard operating procedures manual.

3. The deductible should be at least $500 to eliminate nuisance claims. A higher deductible usually results in lower premiums.

4. Commercial properties should require tenants to carry contents and liability insurance coverage for inside their stores.

FILES AND RECORD KEEPING

Records and files should be kept in an efficient, organized manner so they can be easily retrieved. The legal retention period for the State Department of Real Estate is usually two to four years on most documents, but you may want to keep some records longer.

1. *Tenant files*—separate files should be kept for each unit, along with tenant information. They are set up when a new account is obtained (Figures 13–6 and 13–7). Rental and lease agreements, notices, and so forth, are kept in the files. Retain for three years.

2. *General correspondence files*—these can be kept either by date or by subject.

3. *Vendor files*—where bills, contracts, and bids are kept. Purchase orders (consecutively numbered) should also be retained.

4. *Check register*—usually kept on computer with each account reconciled monthly. Good accounting procedure dictates that a person other than the one who makes up or signs the checks should do the reconciliation. Also, checks over a certain amount (for example, $1,500) should require two signatures, and a daily balance should be maintained.

5. *Owner files*—management agreement, monthly statements, correspondence, insurance policies, tax bills, receipts. Most management companies do not keep the owner's bills (receipts), but instead mail them to the owner with the profit and loss statement.

6. *Eviction files*—usually kept on pending cases.

7. *Wage and hours files*—should be kept three years, including employment applications.

8. *Bank reconciliations*—trust accounts should be reconciled to bank statements on a monthly basis.

The use of the computer has been discussed previously, but in small offices a hand system of posting may be used. A similar system may be used in collecting rents. It consists of three parts.

1. Ledger sheet for the on-site manager

2. Ledger sheet for the management office

3. Individual receipt for the tenant

```
                    BOOKKEEPING PROPERTY SET UP

OWNER: _____  DATE TO START:_____
                                            SUPERVISION:_____

ADDRESS: _____

CITY,ZIP: _____

PHONE: (_____)_____(_____)_____
          HOME                          WORK


PROPERTY ADDRESS: _____ # UNITS: _____

CITY: _____


MANAGER: NAME _____
(if appropriate)
ADDRESS/PHONE: _____


                         INSURANCE CARRIER: _____

MANAGEMENT FEE: $_____  AGENT NAME/PHONE: _____

AREA MGR. FEE:  $_____  _____

RE-RENT FEE:    $_____  POLICY # _____

OTHERS:         $_____  CERTIFICATE ORDERED? ____ BY WHOM?_____


LENDER INFORMATION:

1st: AMOUNT: $_____ DUE: _____ DEL:_____

LENDER ADDRESS: _____

LOAN NUMBER: _____


2nd: AMOUNT: $_____ DUE: _____ DEL:_____

LENDER ADDRESS: _____

LOAN NUMBER: _____


ASSOCIATION DUES: DUE: _____ AMOUNT $_____

OTHER:           DUE: _____ AMOUNT $_____


Copyright 1996, J.D. Publications and Seminars, Inc.
permissions granted to publish in "Property Mgt"
```

Figure 13—6. New Property Information

DATE: _____

NEW PROPERTY INFORMATION

OWNER NAME: _____

ADDRESS/PHONE: _____

PROPERTY ADDRESS: _____

TENANT NAME & PHONE NO.	APT. #	UNIT TYPE	RENT	S.D.	PAID TO DATE	COMMENTS

BE SURE TO GET <u>ALL</u> KEYS - INCLUDING MAILBOX KEYS!

ATTACH RENTAL AGREEMENTS.

DISTRIBUTION: BOOKKEEPING, MAINTENANCE, RENTAL COORD., EXEC. ADMIN.

Figure 13–7. Flow Chart

MANAGEMENT COMPANY INCOME AND EXPENSES

The property manager must not only increase the net operating income (NOI) of the property by good management techniques, but also make a profit for the management company. In many instances, the management company bids too low, not knowing its costs, as we discussed in Chapter 4. Many small firms bid too low because the owner, who is also the property manager, does not take a monthly salary. This leads to reduced services, secret profit, or other illegal activities, or the management company goes out of business.

The management company should prepare a pro forma budget for itself, just as it does for the properties it manages. The budget is a road map to help the management company reach its goals. In Figure 13–8 we see that by categorizing monthly expenses and having an additional column for percentage of total expenses, the management company can review its progress on a monthly basis and make changes and corrections if necessary to stay on its intended course. The net profit as a percentage of income will vary, but the 5–10 percent range seems reasonable.

In order to complete Figure 13–8, a list of employees, salaries, cars, hours worked, and operating expenses is made. Subtracting expenses from revenues gives the monthly profit. By dividing expenses into total units managed, the cost of management per apartment ($15–25) is obtained. This gives a rule of thumb to use in bidding. All units do not require the same intensity of management, so individual complexes' costs will vary from the average. The Institute of Real Estate Management publishes a yearly study, *Income and Expense Analysis: Office Buildings*, which gives average costs in the different office expense areas and can be a useful tool for the management company when doing its own budgeting (Figure 13–9). A sample management company profit and loss statement is shown in Figure 13–10.

Consulting Fees

When dealing with a client in the real estate industry, traditionally, the agent gets paid only if the deal is consummated. An example would be a property manager who does a comprehensive inspection and market survey for an owner who is contemplating purchasing an apartment building. The owner promises to give management to the property manager if the building is purchased. If, however, the building is not purchased, the property manager gets zero for services rendered and time spent. It is hard to believe that because the property manager found serious plumbing problems in the proposed building, saving the buyer from financial disaster, the property manager will not be paid for expert professional advice. It is nice to be paid for advice, and even nicer to be paid whether or not that advice is followed. Landauer and Associates recently represented NBC, which was considering moving its corporate headquarters. Landauer received a nice fee even though NBC decided to stay at Rockefeller Center.

If the client requests additional services, consultation should be charged on either an hourly or set-fee basis. Such consultation areas include:

1. Refinancing the property

2. In-depth management plan

3. Appraisals

4. Rehabilitation

5. Zone or use changes

6. Sale or exchange of property

7. Property tax reassessment

8. Special bookkeeping or accounting

9. Leasing

INCOME	1st Mo.	%	6th Mo.	%	12th Mo.	%
Multi-unit fees	_____	___	_____	___	_____	___
Commercial fees	_____	___	_____	___	_____	___
Leasing fees	_____	___	_____	___	_____	___
Miscellaneous	_____	___	_____	___	_____	___
TOTAL INCOME	_____	___	_____	___	_____	___

OPERATING EXPENSES						
Advertising/promotion	_____	___	_____	___	_____	___
Auto expenses	_____	___	_____	___	_____	___
Computer expenses	_____	___	_____	___	_____	___
Dues/subscriptions	_____	___	_____	___	_____	___
Insurance	_____	___	_____	___	_____	___
Legal/accounting fees	_____	___	_____	___	_____	___
Licenses	_____	___	_____	___	_____	___
Miscellaneous	_____	___	_____	___	_____	___
Office expenses	_____	___	_____	___	_____	___
Payroll taxes	_____	___	_____	___	_____	___
Repairs/maintenance	_____	___	_____	___	_____	___
Referral fees/leasing splits	_____	___	_____	___	_____	___
Rent	_____	___	_____	___	_____	___
Salaries	_____	___	_____	___	_____	___
Executive	_____	___	_____	___	_____	___
Accounting/clerical	_____	___	_____	___	_____	___
Property supervisors	_____	___	_____	___	_____	___
Bonuses	_____	___	_____	___	_____	___
Telephone	_____	___	_____	___	_____	___
Taxes	_____	___	_____	___	_____	___
Utilities	_____	___	_____	___	_____	___
TOTAL EXPENSES	_____	___	_____	___	_____	___

NET PROFIT OR LOSS	_____	___	_____	___	_____	___

NO. OF UNITS MANAGED _____ DIVIDED BY EXPENSES _____ = COST PER UNIT_____

Figure 13–8. Management Company Budget

Suburban Office Buildings: Metropolitan Miami, Florida

Chart of Accounts	$/Gross Area of Entire Bldg. Bldgs (10,000)	Sq. Ft. Med.	$ Range Low	$ Range High	$/Gross Rentable Office Area Bldgs (10,000)	Sq. Ft. Med.	$ Range Low	$ Range High	$/Net Rentable Office Area Bldgs (10,000)	Sq. Ft. Med.	$ Range Low	$ Range High
Income												
Offices	17	215	12.58	8.22	16.07	9	111	8.22		16	180	15.11	8.57	17.15
Retail												
Parking	5	111	.12	.08	.12	2	45	.22		5	104	.13	.08	.13
Pass-Throughs	16	212	.99	.47	1.57	8	108	.49		15	177	.86	.37	1.63
Retail % Income												
Misc. Income	16	211	.08	.05	.14	8	107	.16		15	175	.08	.04	.12
Vacancy/Delin. Rents	17	215	.46	.00	.79	9	111	.00		16	180	.82	.00	.85
Total Collections	17	215	13.28	9.50	16.17	9	111	9.90		16	180	15.17	9.50	17.26
Expenses												
Electricity	8	75	.12	.09	1.00	7	69	.12		8	71	.12	.09	1.14
Water	16	189	.06	.04	.09	9	111	.10		15	155	.06	.03	.07
Sewer	9	83	.03	.03	.04	3	17	.05		9	76	.04	.03	.05
HVAC Fuel												
Gas	1	25	.01	.01	.01	1	21	.02		1	23	.01	.01	.01
Fuel Oil	2	29	.00	.00	.00	2	29	.00		2	27	.00	.00	.00
Electricity	1	4	.24	.24	.24	1	3	.28		1	3	.29	.29	.29
Steam												
Other												
Combination Electric	10	147	1.64	1.45	1.66	2	43	1.66		9	115	1.71	1.55	1.81
Total Energy Plant												
Subtotal Utilities	17	215	1.45	1.11	1.65	9	111	1.11		16	180	1.58	1.26	1.76
Janitorial												
Payroll/Contract	17	215	.58	.43	.76	9	111	.43		16	180	.63	.49	.81
Cleaning Supplies	14	194	.05	.01	.06	6	90	.05		13	158	.05	.01	.07
Miscellaneous	8	121	.02	.01	.02	5	60	.02		8	114	.02	.02	.03
Maintenance & Repair												
Payroll	17	215	.25	.21	.28	9	111	.27		16	180	.27	.23	.27
Supplies	16	190	.06	.04	.09	8	90	.04		15	156	.07	.04	.09
Htg/Ven & AC Repairs	16	212	.16	.09	.25	8	108	.13		15	177	.14	.10	.26
Electric Repairs	16	211	.03	.01	.04	8	107	.03		15	175	.03	.01	.05

(Continued)

Figure 13–9. Sample Monthly Statement (Annual Report)
© Institute of Real Estate Management,
430 N. Michigan, Chicago, IL 60611.

Chart of Accounts	$/Gross Area of Entire Blg. Bldgs	Sq. Ft. (10,000) Med.	$ Range Low	High	$/Gross Rentable Office Area Bldgs	Sq. Ft. (10,000) Med.	$ Range Low	High	$/Net Rentable Office Area Bldgs	Sq. Ft. (10,000) Med.	$ Range Low	High
Plumbing Repairs	15	207	.02	.01	.02	7	103	.01			14	171	.02	.01	.03
Elev Repr/Mainten.	13	191	.10	.09	.11	5	87	.11			12	155	.11	.10	.13
Exterior Repairs	13	152	.01	.01	.02	5	55	.02			13	144	.01	.01	.02
Roof Repairs	9	140	.01	.00	.05	8	108	.02			8	110	.02	.00	.05
Parking Lot Repairs	9	153	.02	.01	.03	7	104	.02			8	122	.02	.01	.03
Decorating—Tenant	6	102	.01	.01	.04	3	36	.04			6	94	.01	.01	.04
Decorating—Public	7	123	.01	.00	.01	5	78	.01			6	94	.01	.01	.01
Misc. Repairs	13	131	.01	.00	.02	8	90	.02			13	122	.01	.00	.02
Subtotal Jan/Maint/Rpr	17	215	1.35	1.09	1.59	9	111	1.11			16	180	1.54	1.19	1.69
Administrative															
Payroll—Administ.	16	211	.38	.34	.43	8	107	.43			15	175	.40	.29	.43
Advertising	7	110	.06	.03	.10	4	47	.12			6	81	.08	.03	.11
Management Fee	15	187	.48	.05	.57	7	83	.05			14	152	.55	.05	.66
Other Administrative	17	215	.15	.10	.17	9	111	.12			16	180	.17	.11	.18
Other Payroll Costs															
Payroll Taxes	10	127	.11	.09	.11	2	24	.11			10	118	.12	.10	.12
Employee Benefits	4	65	.05	.01	.05	1	3	.10			4	60	.06	.01	.06
Subtotal Admin/Payrl	17	215	1.09	.61	1.19	9	111	.69			16	180	1.17	.63	1.31
Insurance	17	215	.13	.13	.18	9	111	.17			16	180	.16	.14	.19
Services															
Landscape	17	215	.21	.15	.25	9	111	.15			16	180	.23	.18	.26
Trash Removal	16	203	.12	.10	.14	8	99	.11			15	167	.12	.10	.15
Security—Payroll	2	49	.21	.07	.21	2	43	.23			1	23	.07	.07	.07
Security—Contracted	16	212	.22	.05	.32	8	108	.29			15	177	.23	.06	.33
Window Washing	9	123	.03	.03	.04	1	21	.02			9	115	.03	.03	.04
Snow Removal															
Miscellaneous	15	188	.08	.02	.14	7	85	.02			15	175	.09	.02	.15
Subtotal Insur/Srvcs	17	215	.71	.60	1.08	9	111	.65			16	180	.82	.69	1.08
Net Operating Costs	17	215	5.00	3.26	5.28	9	111	3.26			16	180	5.40	3.72	5.67
Real Estate Taxes	17	215	1.77	1.14	1.89	9	111	1.36			16	180	1.98	1.24	2.00
Other Tax/Fee/Permit	6	114	.01	.00	.01	3	46	.01			5	84	.01	.01	.01
Total Operatng Costs	17	215	6.70	4.31	7.14	9	111	4.58			16	180	7.38	5.14	7.63

Occupancy Level 94%
Vacancy Level 6%

E/I Ratio (NOC/TAC) .34
Cleang Services (% Yes) 100%

Tenants   3-Year   (3) $12.50
Alteratns   5-Year   (10) $21.50

Figure 13–9. Continued

Published annually by the Institute of Real Estate Management, 430 N. Michigan Ave., Chicago, IL 60611.

ABC Property Management Company

Income	$ Amount	%
Multi-unit fees	$25,000	55.00%
Commercial fees	12,000	27.00%
Leasing fees	3,000	7.00%
Broker commissions	5,000	11.00%
Miscellaneous		
Total income	$45,000	100.00%
Operating Expenses		
Advertising and promotion	810	1.80%
Automobile expense	1,710	3.80%
Computer expense	2,250	5.00%
Dues and subscriptions	450	1.00%
Insurance	1,350	3.00%
Legal and accounting	675	1.50%
Licenses	225	.05%
Miscellaneous	900	2.00%
Office expense	2,925	6.50%
Payroll expense	1,350	3.00%
Repairs and maintenance	1,080	2.40%
Referral fees	900	2.00%
Rent	1,800	4.00%
Salaries:		
Executive	5,850	13.00%
Accounting and Clerical	7,650	17.00%
Property supervisors	6,300	14.00%
Bonuses	900	2.00%
Telephone	1,440	3.20%
Travel and entertainment	1,350	3.00%
Utilities	1,170	2.60%
Total operating expenses	41,085	91.30%
Net profit or loss (before taxes)	$ 3,915	8.70%

Figure 13–10. Office Expense Areas

SUMMARY

The goals and objectives of a property management company will differ depending on the type of company:

1. Ma and Pa owner

2. Institutional investor (in-house)

3. Local real estate office

4. Professional fee manager

The location of the property manager's office should reflect professionalism, but need not be in an exclusive area or lavishly decorated. The layout and color scheme should be cheerful and have partitions and separate offices to reduce noise and provide privacy. Since the property manager offers a service, not a product, no machinery is needed except computers and office equipment. The three kinds of computers (hardware) are mainframe, mini, and micro (PC). A good software program is crucial; the main question to be answered is, What specific tasks need to be accomplished?

The selection of a property management company is based on several criteria, some of which includes the size and length of time in business, bonding, and whether employees have real estate licenses or professional designations such as certified property manager (CPM).

The property manager handles the insurance on the property, which involves risk evaluation such as retaining, avoiding, transferring, and controlling risk. The different types of policies include all-peril, all-risk; rent loss; surety bond; fidelity bond; umbrella policies; workers' compensation; and co-insurance.

The property management office may purchase errors and omissions insurance for its own protection as well as being covered as additionally insured under the owner's policy for each property. Records and files should be kept for income tax and Department of Real Estate purposes for two to four years.

The management company should, like other well-run professional companies, prepare an annual budget and produce monthly profit and loss statements. The management company should also charge the client for additional services such as refinancing the property, appraisals, management plans, rehabilitation, zone changes, sale or exchange of the property, special reports, and leasing.

PERSONALITY PROFILE

Running a successful property management company requires business and leadership skills well beyond those required for a knowledgeable and seasoned property manager. John Bennett, president of Tomlinson Black Management, Inc., of Spokane, Washington, is an individual who has been successful at this endeavor.

Following studies at Washington State University, John entered the property management field in 1975. A second-generation property manager, John had the benefit of growing up in and around the business. His father Jerry, CPM® Emeritus, retired in 1987 after 37 years in the industry.

John Bennett earned the certified property manager (CPM®) designation from the Institute of Real Estate Management (IREM) in 1982. He credits educational, leadership development, and networking resources connected with IREM as major factors in his professional development and corporate achievements.

John has developed special expertise in the merger and acquisition of property management companies, using this method to grow the business, enhance operating economies of scale, and, on occasion, sell off accounts that did not fit the company's strategic plan. John's company, Tomlinson Black, is the largest full-service real estate company in a 1.5-million-resident, geographically wide-ranging market. Tomlinson Black's property management division interfaces with the company's commercial and residential brokers. The commercial brokerage is comprised of approximately 30 brokers, leasing and selling all commercial property types.

John's company's scope of services is wide ranging. Rather than looking at the organization as having a generalist outlook, John calls the company a "department store of real estate specialists." The company manages over 200 investment properties, large and small, commercial and residential. The demands of specialization and portfolio diversification make administration and control both time consuming and demanding. John trains and counsels his property managers and support teams to focus on asset management considerations, keying in on value enhancement and ownership objectives for each asset as a unique business enterprise.

REVIEW QUESTIONS

1. A type of ownership for a fee property management office is a
   a. sole proprietorship.
   b. REIT.
   c. corporation.
   d. both a and c
   e. both a and b

2. Property management offices should
   a. always be located in a bank building.
   b. always be located in a major city.
   c. be cheerfully and tastefully decorated.
   d. be lavishly and expensively decorated.

3. The goal of using the computer in property management is to
   a. replace all people.
   b. reduce redundant tasks and improve efficiency.
   c. calculate the management fee faster.
   d. reduce typing costs.

4. Categories of computers include
   a. micro (PC).
   b. mini.
   c. both a and b
   d. neither a nor b

5. Word processing is primarily for
   a. calculating vacancy reports.
   b. typing letters.
   c. calculating cash flow statements.
   d. calculating delinquency reports.

6. The function of the disk is to
   a. store data.
   b. display data.
   c. print data.
   d. send information.

7. Computer hardware includes
   a. the keyboard.
   b. the printer.
   c. both a and b
   d. neither a nor b

8. Software is used to:
   a. repair the computer.
   b. run the computer program.
   c. turn the computer on and off.
   d. reduce emergency requirements of the computer.

9. The management company specializes in certain properties based on
   a. size.
   b. type—medical, apartments, etc.
   c. both a and b
   d. neither a nor b

10. The purpose of insurance is to
    a. avoid lawsuits.
    b. transfer risk.
    c. control risk.
    d. both b and c
    e. both a and b

11. Which type of ownership minimizes liability?
    a. sole proprietorship
    b. partnership
    c. corporation
    d. all of the above

12. Sub S corporation profits are taxed at the
    a. corporation level.
    b. partnership level.
    c. individual taxpayer level.
    d. both a and c

13. Which category of computer hardware is most commonly used by property management companies?
   a. mainframe
   b. mini
   c. micro (PC)

14. What type of insurance covers dishonest acts?
   a. surety bond
   b. errors and omissions
   c. workers' compensation
   d. fidelity bond

15. What type of insurance would be called malpractice insurance?
   a. co-insurance
   b. errors and omissions
   c. non-owned auto
   d. fidelity bond

CASE STUDY PROBLEMS

Refer to the Case Study at the end of Chapter 5.

1. Should the insurance policy have a rent loss clause?

2. The present maintenance is done by "Ben the Handyman," who works out of his house and is not licensed or covered under workers' compensation. What changes would you make?

3. The liability on the present policy is $200,000. Should this amount be increased?

4. If you, as a management company, were to bid on managing Civic Center Terrace, how much would you bid?

5. If the owners wanted you to do refinancing paperwork on the property, would you charge over and above the management fee?

ADDITIONAL READING AND REFERENCES

Boykin, James H., *Real Estate Counseling*, American Society of Real Estate Counselors, Chicago, IL, 1984.

California Real Estate (Monthly), California Association of Realtors, 525 S. Virgil Ave., Los Angeles, CA 90020.

Downs, James Jr., CPM, *Principles of Real Estate Management*, Institute of Real Estate Management, Chicago, IL, 1991.

Hansen, James H., *Guide to Buying or Selling a Business*, Prentice-Hall, Englewood Cliffs, NJ, 1975.

Mehr, Robert I., *Fundamentals of Insurance*, Richard Irwin, Inc., Homewood, IL, 1983.

Real Estate Today, National Association of Realtors, 430 N. Michigan Ave., Chicago, IL 60611.

Walters, William Jr., CPM, *The Practice of Real Estate Management*, Institute of Real Estate Management, Chicago, IL, 1983.

Chapter 14

Landlord/Tenant Law

Key terms

Actual eviction
ADA Law
Amendment Act
Constitution

Constructive eviction
Habitability
Notice to pay rent
Repair and deduct

Retaliation
Unlawful detainer
Writ

Food for thought

"Some people bring happiness wherever they go. Some people only bring happiness whenever they go."

Oscar Wilde

SOURCES OF PROPERTY MANAGEMENT LAW

In order to understand fully the nature of landlord/tenant laws, it is important to see how these laws interface with our legal system. Figure 14–1 illustrates the principal sources of law. The significance of these sources is in ranking, starting with the U.S. Constitution, which is the source and comparison for all laws. If any federal, state, or local law or regulation is contrary to the Constitution, as determined by the courts, it is ruled unconstitutional and therefore void.

In order to better explain these sources, we use rent control as an example. Rent-control laws are passed by local governments (city or county). These laws can be preempted by state law or federal law. Through an administrative ruling, the Department of Housing and Urban Development (HUD) can decree that those cities having rent control would have federal housing subsidies cut off unless the rent-control laws are repealed. The landlords also can challenge in court the fact that rent control is an uncompensated taking of property which may be unconstitutional.

Local, state, and federal laws and regulations are interwoven. The property manager should note the pecking order, however, as federal laws and regulations supersede both state and local laws as contained in Figure 14–1. Court decisions are ranked last as sources of law, as they interpret the laws and regulations and then will move up the ladder depending on the court and its jurisdiction (i.e., federal court takes precedence over state, which takes precedence over local).

COMMERCIAL VERSUS RESIDENTIAL LAWS

In many instances, the state laws governing commercial and residential management are similar, but not exactly the same. For example, the period for giving the disposition and return of a security deposit is usually shorter in residential than in commercial. In residential, the law often mandates a max-

1. U.S. Constitution (e.g., 14th Amendment)

2. Treaties (e.g., Treaty of Guadalupe Hidalgo)

3. Laws of Congress (e.g., 1968 Civil Rights Act)

4. Federal regulations (e.g., HUD)

5. State Constitution (e.g., discrimination)

6. State laws (e.g., disclosure)

7. State regulations (e.g., real estate licensing)

8. Local ordinances (e.g., rent control)

9. Court decisions (e.g., *Pennell v. City of San Jose*

Figure 14–1. Sources of Law

imum security deposit that can be collected. Usually, the last month's rent, if collected, is treated as if it were a deposit. In most states, no maximum exists on commercial security deposits. Property managers should consult a local real estate attorney to be familiar and up to date on landlord/tenant laws.

The courts often will look differently on commercial and residential tenants. The commercial tenant is viewed on a parity with the landlord, as two Roman gladiators, each with a sword and shield, battling it out in a coliseum. However, the court views residential tenants as unsophisticated underdogs in comparison to landlords, or like the Christians facing the lions.

Residential versus Commercial Leases

Leases for real property are traditionally construed as conveyances, as opposed to contracts. The fundamental difference is that conveyances are interpreted by real property law, which provides that the covenants are independently (as opposed to dependently) construed. Commercial leases are generally still interpreted under real property law, with the covenant to pay rent looked on as independent from the other covenants of the lease. Thus, if a toilet overflows or the roof leaks in a commercial property, the tenant still has to pay rent. Conversely, for residential leases, many states chose to apply the provisions of contract law which provide that failure by the landlord to comply with the implied covenant of habitability allows a tenant not to pay rent. This comes very close to converting residential leases from conveyances to contracts.

LANDLORD RESPONSIBILITIES

The property manager, acting as an agent for the owner, must understand and obey the legal duties of the landlord. Many courts are holding on-site managers and property managers, as well as owners, legally responsible.

Habitability

Maintaining habitability in residential property is one of the most important responsibilities of the property manager. Figure 14–2 contains some typical provisions in many states; the property manager needs to obtain specific provisions for his/her state.

Many state laws set forth conditions constituting a substandard building, such as lack of working toilet facilities or kitchen sinks, pest infestation, improper maintenance, and so on. Courts have ruled that every residential lease

Habitability provisions

1. Waterproofing and weatherproofing

2. Doors and windows reasonably secure

3. Hot and cold water (plumbing)

4. Heating system in good working order

5. Electrical system in safe working order

6. Building in good repair (stairs and railings)

7. Trash and garbage removal

8. Free from pests

9. Smoke detectors installed and working

Figure 14–2. Habitability

has an implied warranty of habitability which the tenant cannot waive. If the premises have breaches of habitability, the tenant may reduce or withhold rent accordingly.

The warranty of habitability is not waivable by the tenant, even if the lease or rental agreement excludes habitability provisions.

Discrimination In renting or leasing residential or commercial space, the landlord or property manager cannot discriminate against a prospective tenant on the listed bases shown in Figure 14–3. The property manager must be diligent in efforts to have the on-site manager know and observe these laws.

	Fed. Fair Housing Acts	ADA Law	State Laws	Local Laws*
Race	X		X	
Religion	X		X	
Color	X		X	
National origin	X		X	
Sex	X		X	
Familial status	X		X	
Handicap	X	X	X	
Rent control			X	X

*May also include all the seven protected categories.

Figure 14–3. Discrimination Chart

Unlawful Discrimination

It is unlawful to discriminate in the rental or sale of residential or commercial properties, based on the seven protected categories under the Civil Rights Act of 1968 and subsequent amendments. This act is also referred to as the Fair Housing Act, which is the term we will use in this book.

1. *Race*—e.g., Asian, Hispanic, etc.
2. *Religion*—e.g., Catholic, Jewish, etc.
3. *National origin*—e.g., Vietnam, Cuba, etc.
4. *Color*—e.g., Brown, Black, White, etc.
5. *Sex*—e.g., male, female
6. *Familial status*—e.g., children, elderly, etc.
7. *Handicap*—autistic, blind, etc.

In addition, once the prospects become tenants they must be treated equally. For example, maintenance requests from a Japanese tenant cannot be ignored because he or she is of Japanese origin.

Lawful Discrimination

The owner/manager is permitted to differentiate among tenants in the three following areas:

1. *Income and ability to pay rent*—The owner or manager can establish reasonable guidelines for prospective tenant selection. If the applicant's income is below the guidelines, he or she can be denied residency. For example, if the rent is $550 per month and the guideline is that rent shall not exceed 30 percent of the gross monthly income, the gross monthly income of the applicant needs to be a minimum of $1,830 per month in order to qualify. The higher the income, such as $2,000 per month, the better. Some managers use a qualifying form which deducts monthly payments such as cars or other items. This is more accurate but more difficult to figure and administer. Owners or managers should ask to see a pay stub or other verification of income.

2. *Poor credit history*—If the applicant's credit history shows late payments, collections, bankruptcy, or prior evictions, this would be a reason to deny residency. Computerized credit checks (see Chapter 7) should be run on each applicant.

3. *History of violence or destructiveness*—If the applicant's former landlord reports that he or she was evicted or arrested for drunkenness at his or her prior residency, this would be a legitimate reason for denying residency.

Any of these rental guidelines must be applied uniformly to all applicants and not used on a selective basis. State or local laws may also limit the landlord's authority to use these rental guidelines.

FAIR HOUSING LAWS
Federal Laws

1. *Civil Rights Act of 1866*—prohibits any type of discrimination based on race. Guarantees all citizens equal rights under the law.

2. *Jones v. Mayer* (1964)—U.S. Supreme Court decision upheld the Civil Rights Act of 1866 which prohibits racial discrimination.

3. *Fair Housing Act of 1968 (Title VIII of Civil Rights Act of 1968)*—makes it unlawful to discriminate on the basis of race, religion, or color in leasing residential property.

4. *Fair Housing Act Amendment (1972)*—mandates that a real estate agent (property manager) must display the equal opportunity poster (Figure 14–4). Failure to do so is evidence of discrimination.

5. *Fair Housing Amendment Act (1988)*—effective March 12, 1989, on a national basis, prohibits discrimination against families with children and handicapped persons in rental housing.

EQUAL HOUSING OPPORTUNITY

We Do Business in Accordance With the Federal Fair Housing Law

(Title VIII of the Civil Rights Act of 1968, as Amended by the Housing and Community Development Act of 1974)

IT IS ILLEGAL TO DISCRIMINATE AGAINST ANY PERSON BECAUSE OF RACE, COLOR, RELIGION, SEX, OR NATIONAL ORIGIN

- In the sale or rental of housing or residential lots
- In advertising the sale or rental of housing
- In the financing of housing
- In the provision of real estate brokerage services

Blockbusting is also illegal

An aggrieved person may file a complaint of a housing discrimination act with the:

U.S. DEPARTMENT OF HOUSING AND URBAN DEVELOPMENT

Assistant Regional Administrator for Fair Housing and Equal Opportunity
450 Golden Gate Ave. P.O. Box 36003
San Francisco, CA 94102

HUD-928.1 (7-75) Previous editions are obsolete

☆ U.S. GOVERNMENT PRINTING OFFICE 1982-587-033 359

Figure 14–4. HUD Poster

6. *Americans with Disabilities Act (1992)*—the definition of handicap under the ADA includes both physical and mental impairments which substantially limit one or more of a person's life activities. Disabilities can also include perceived disabilities such as physical disfigurement or obesity. This is a broad and confusing definition as a current drug user is not considered handicapped, but a reformed drug addict would be covered under the act. How does the manager determine if an applicant is a current or a reformed addict? If you deny a drug addict, he or she may sue both you and the owner under the federal law for discrimination.

   a) *Reasonable accommodation*—the law requires the owner/manager to apply rules, practices, policies, and services so that the disabled have equal housing opportunity. For example, a no-pets policy would not apply to a blind person's seeing eye dog. If a handicapped person needs a parking space close to his or her unit, this would be a reasonable request. The recreation room and manager's office are public places and also must be made accessible, with ramps, wide doors, and so forth.

      (1) *Cost of accommodation*—if the accommodation would cause an undue hardship on the owner, it is not required. Factors considered for undue hardship include:

      (*a*) Nature and total cost

      (*b*) Financial resources of owner and effect on operating expenses

      (*c*) Type and size of building

In other words, wealthy owners may be held to a higher standard than poorer or financially strapped owners under the ADA law.

   b) *Reasonable modification*—the law defines modifications as physical changes to the property, when readily achievable, that allow the handicapped person full use of the premises. For example, a special lift for a second story apartment unit to accommodate a disabled person would not be a reasonable modification. If, however, the disabled person agreed to pay for the costs and remove it upon leaving, it would be a reasonable modification.

      (1) *Removal of barriers*—public accommodations (offices, lobbies, recreation room, stores) must remove architectural and communication barriers in existing facilities when readily achievable.

      (*a*) *Physical barriers*—furniture, office equipment, and so on. A manager may install ramps or curb cuts on sidewalks, or widen doors. Some low-cost methods include installing paper cup dispensers at existing inaccessible water fountains, repositioning paper towel dispensers in bathrooms, or repositioning furniture in offices to make wheelchair access feasible.

      (2) *Readily achievable*—this is defined as being able to be carried out without much difficulty or expense. A determination would include the circumstances, the building, and the financial position of the owner. The term "readily achievable" is however, less demanding than "undue hardship" that is used in reasonable accommodation.

      (3) *Penalties for violations*—the attorney general or private parties may file suit under the ADA. The penalties and legal remedies include:

      (*a*) Actual and punitive damages

      (*b*) Equitable relief (injunction)

      (*c*) Attorney's fees

      (*d*) Civil penalties

         i) up to $50,000 for first violation

         ii) up to $100,000 for subsequent violations

In summary, the ADA law does take economic cost into consideration for reasonable accommodation and modification, which is balanced against benefits to the handicapped. The purpose is to bring disabled persons into the mainstream so they can lead useful and productive lives. More than 15 percent of the U.S. population is currently regarded as disabled.

Exemptions to Federal Fair Housing Laws

Three basic exemptions to fair housing laws exist: religious organizations and clubs, housing for the elderly, and small owner-occupied properties.

1. *Religious organizations and clubs*—these organizations may limit to their members rentals, occupancy, or sale of housing owned and operated for other than commercial purpose. Retail and office managers cannot discriminate.

2. *Housing for the elderly*—if the property can qualify for one of the two following exemptions, you may discriminate against tenants with children. These exemptions are for senior citizen buildings:
   a) Housing intended solely for and occupied solely by those over the age of 62.
   b) Housing in which 80 percent of the units are occupied by persons over the age of 55. Recent legislation, December 29, 1995, eliminated the provision that senior citizen housing projects needed to have significant facilities and services for senior care before children could be banned.

3. *Individuals' exemptions* (no real estate agent can be involved in rental or sale)
   a) Persons who own four single-family houses or fewer are exempt for one transaction in any two-year period.
   b) Persons may rent rooms or units in a dwelling containing four units or fewer—if they live in the dwelling without regard to federal fair housing laws.

Enforcement of Federal Fair Housing Laws

Suits against individuals or entities who discriminate can be brought by:

1. The Department of Housing and Urban Affairs (HUD), who will also investigate the charge

2. U.S. Attorney General

3. Private parties

4. State agencies when the case has been turned over to them by HUD

Choice of Administrative Proceedings

Any person who feels he or she is a victim of housing discrimination may file an administrative complaint with HUD, or file suit, or both (Figures 14–5, 14–6 and 14–7). If the plaintiff files complaint with HUD, an investigation will commence. If evidence of discrimination is found, the charge will be tried before an administrative law judge (ALJ) unless the plaintiff or defendant elects to have the case tried in federal court or the Justice Department decides to pursue the complaint. A complaint must be filed by the aggrieved party within two years of the discriminatory act. Statute requires HUD to complete the investigation within 100 days unless it is impractical to do so. (See HUD complaint form, Figure 14–6, and HUD regional offices, Figure 14–7).

State Laws

In addition to federal laws such as the Amendments Act and the Americans with Disabilities Act (ADA), many states have similar and often more restrictive laws. Usually the most restrictive (either federal or state) will prevail. Most states have amended their fair housing laws to meet substantial equiva-

Fair Housing Practices Benefit Everyone

Federal and State Fair Housing Laws Prohibit Discrimination in the Sale, Rental, or Advertisement of Housing on the basis of:

RACE

RELIGION

COLOR

NATIONAL ORIGIN

SEX

AGE

MARITAL STATUS

DISABILITY

PRESENCE OF CHILDREN

These prohibitions apply to all housing except owner-occupied buildings with two or fewer units. However, it is always illegal to discriminate on the basis of race.

The **Fair Housing Council** of Central New York, Inc. is an organization dedicated to the promotion of Fair Housing Opportunities in Central New York. Activities of the Council are currently conducted by a volunteer board of directors who are committed to eliminating illegal housing discrimination in our community.

The **Fair Housing Council** works in conjunction with The Fair Housing Enforcement Project at Legal Services of Central New York to:

- protect the rights of persons who have been illegally discriminated against by filing cases with HUD, or in federal or state court

- investigate claims of housing discrimination

- educate the community on fair housing practices

- counsel individuals about their rights under state and federal fair housing regulations

If you suspect you have experienced housing discrimination, contact the Fair Housing Enforcement Project at 475-3127.

Join the Fight Against Housing Discrimination

— I would like more information about fair housing. Please telephone me.

— I would like a speaker about fair housing. Please telephone me.

— **I would like to become a member of the Fair Housing Council.** Enclosed is:

    ___ $100 Sponsor
    ___ $50 Organizational Member
    ___ $15 Individual/Family
    ___ $3 Low Income

I would like to support the Fair Housing Council with a contribution of:

___ $25 ___ $35 ___ $50 ___ $100 ___ Other

Name _____

Organization _____

Address _____ ZIP _____

Phone (Home): _____

    (Work): _____

FAIR HOUSING COUNCIL
OF CENTRAL NEW YORK, INC.
P.O. Box 6051 • Syracuse, New York 13217

Figure 14–5. Fair Housing Council

Housing Discrimination Complaint

U.S. Department of Housing and Urban Development
Office of Fair Housing and Equal Opportunity

OMB Approval No. 2529-0011 (Exp. 09/30/95)

Please type or print this form - Do not write in shaded area

Public Reporting Burden for this collection of information is estimated to average 1.0 hours per response, including the time for reviewing instructions, searching existing data sources, gathering and maintaining the data needed, and completing and reviewing the collection of information. Send comments regarding this burden estimate or any other aspect of this collection of information, including suggestions for reducing this burden, to the Reports Management Officer, Office of Information Policies and Systems, U.S. Department of Housing and Urban Development, Washington, D.C. 20410-3600 and to the Office of Management and Budget, Paperwork Reduction Project (2529-0011), Washington, D.C. 20503. Do not send this completed form to either of these addresses.

Instructions: Read this form and the instructions on reverse carefully before completing. All questions should be answered. However, if you do not know the answer or if a question is not applicable, leave the question unanswered and fill out as much of the form as you can. Your complaint should be signed and dated. Where more than one individual or organization is filing the same complaint, and all information is the same, each additional individual or organization should complete boxes 1 and 7 of a separate complaint form and attach it to the original form. Complaints may be presented in persons or mailed to the Regional Office covering the State where the complaint arose (see list on back of form), any local HUD Field Office, or to the Office of Fair Housing and Equal Opportunity, U.S. Department of HUD, Washington, D.C. 20410.

This section is for HUD use only.

Number: _____

Filing Date: _____

(Check ✓ applicable box):
☐ Referral and Agency (specify)
☐ Systemic ☐ Military Referral

Jurisdiction:
☐ Yes ☐ No
☐ Additional Info

Signature of HUD personnel who established Jurisdiction:

1. Name of aggrieved person or organization (last name, first name, middle initial) (Mr.,Mrs.,Miss,Ms.)
   Home Phone: (   )   Business Phone: (   )

   Street Address (city, county, State and zip code)

2. Against whom is this complaint being filed? Name (last name, first name, middle initial)
   Phone Number: (   )

   Street Address (city, county, State and zip code)

Check the applicable box or boxes which describe(s) the party named above
☐ Builder ☐ Owner ☐ Broker ☐ Salesperson ☐ Supt. or Manager ☐ Bank or Other Lender ☐ Other

If you named an individual above who appeared to be acting for a company in this case, check ✓ this box ☐ and write the name and address of the company in this space:

Name: _____   Address: _____

Name and identify others (if any) you believe violated the law in this case

3. What did the person you are complaining against do? Check ✓ all that apply and give the most recent date these act(s) occurred in block No. 6a below.
☐ Refuse to rent, sell, or deal with you
☐ Discriminate in the conditions or terms of sale, rental occupancy, or in services or facilities
☐ Other (explain)
☐ Falsely deny housing was available
☐ Advertise in a discriminatory way
☐ Engage in blockbusting
☐ Discriminate in financing
☐ Discriminate in broker's services
☐ Intimidated, interfered, or coerced you to keep you from the full benefit of the Federal Fair Housing Law

4. Do you believe that you were discriminated against because of your race, color, religion, sex, handicap, the presence of children under 18, or a pregnant female in the family or your national origin? Check ✓ all that apply:

☐ Race or Color
  ☐ Black
  ☐ White
  ☐ Other
☐ Religion
  (specify)
☐ Sex
  ☐ Male
  ☐ Female
☐ Handicap
  ☐ Physical
  ☐ Mental
☐ Familial Status
  ☐ Presence of children under 18 in the family
  ☐ Pregnant female
☐ National Origin
  ☐ Hispanic
  ☐ Asian or Pacific Islander
  ☐ American Indian or Alaskan Native
  ☐ Other (specify)

5. What kind of house or property was involved?
☐ Single-family house
☐ A house or building for 2, 3, or 4 families
☐ A building for 5 families or more
☐ Other, including vacant land held for residential use (explain)

Did the owner live there?
☐ Yes
☐ No
☐ Unknown

Is the house or property:
☐ Being sold?
☐ Being rented?

What is the address of the house or property? (street, city, county, State and zip code)

6. Summarize in your own words what happened. Use this space for a brief and concise statement of the facts. Additional details may be submitted on an attachment. **Note:** HUD will furnish a copy of the complaint to the person or organization against whom the complaint is made.

6a. When did the act(s) checked in Item 3 occur? (Include the most recent date if several dates are involved)

7. I declare under penalty of perjury that I have read this complaint (including any attachments) and that it is true and correct.

Signature and Date:

Previous edition, dated, 11/92, **may not** be used; other editions may be used until stock is exhausted.

form **HUD-903** (1/93)
ref Handbook 8020.1

Figure 14–6. HUD Complaint Form

What Does the Fair Housing Amendments Act of 1988 Provide?

The Fair Housing Act declares that it is national policy to provide fair housing throughout the United States and prohibits eight specific kinds of discriminatory acts regarding housing if the discrimination is based on race, color, religion, sex, handicap, familial status or national origin.

1. Refusal to sell or rent or otherwise deal with a person.

2. Discriminating in the conditions or terms of sale, rental, or occupancy.

3. Falsely denying housing is available.

4. "Blockbusting"—causing person(s) to sell or rent by telling them that members of a minority group are moving into the area.

6. Discrimination in financing housing by a bank, savings and loan association, or other business.

7. Denial of membership or participation in brokerage, multiple listing, or other real estate services.

8. Interference, coercion, threats or intimidation to keep a person from obtaining the full benefits of the Federal Fair Housing Law and/or filing a complaint.

What Does the Law Exempt?

The first three acts listed above do not apply (1) to any single family house where the owner in certain circumstances does not seek to rent or sell it through the use of a broker or through discriminatory advertising, nor (2) to units in houses for two-to-four families if the owner lives in one of the units.

What Can You Do About Violations of the Law?

Remember, the Fair Housing Act applies to discrimination based on race, color, religion, sex, handicap, familial status, or national origin. If you believe you have been or are about to be, discriminated against or otherwise harmed by the kinds of discriminatory acts which are prohibited by law, you have a right, within 1 year after the discrimination occurred to:

1. **Complain to the Secretary of HUD** by filing this form by mail or in person. HUD will investigate. If it finds the complaint is covered by the law and is justified, it will try to end the discrimination by conciliation. If conciliation fails, other steps will be taken to enforce the law. In cases where State or local laws give the same rights as the Federal Fair Housing Law, HUD must first ask the State or local agency to try to resolve the problem.

2. **Go directly to Court** even if you have not filed a complaint with the Secretary. The Court may sometimes be able to give quicker, more effective, relief than conciliation can provide and may also, in certain cases, appoint an attorney for you (without cost).

   You Should Also Report All Information about violations of the Fair Housing Act to HUD even though you don't intend to complain or go to court yourself.

   Additional Details. If you wish to explain in detail in an attachment what happened, you should consider the following:

   1. If you fee that others were treated differently from you, please explain the facts and circumstances.

   2. If there were witnesses or others who know what happened, give their names, addresses, and telephone numbers.

   3. If you have made this complaint to other government agencies or to the courts, state when and where and explain what happened.

Racial/Ethnic Categories

1. **White (Non Hispanic)**—A person having origins in any of the original peoples of Europe, North Africa, or the Middle East.

2. **Black (Non Hispanic)**—A person having origins in any of the black racial groups of Africa.

3. **Hispanic**—A person of Mexican, Puerto Rican, Cuban, Central or South American or other Spanish Culture or origin, regardless of race.

4. **American Indian or Alaskan Native**—A person having origins in any of the original peoples of North America, and who maintains, cultural identification through tribal affiliation or community recognition.

5. **Asian or Pacific Islander**—A person having origins in any of the original peoples of the Far East, Southeast Asia, the Indian Subcontinent, or the Pacific Islands. This area includes, for example, China, Japan, Korea, the Philippine Islands, and Samoa.

You can obtain assistance (a) in learning about the Fair Housing Act, or (b) in filing a complaint at the HUD Regional Offices listed below:

Region I – Boston (Connecticut, Maine, Massachusetts, New Hampshire, Rhode Island, Vermont)
HUD - Fair Housing and Equal Opportunity (FHEO)
Boston Federal Office Building, 10 Causeway Street
Boston, Massachusetts 02222-1092

Region II – New York (New Jersey, New York)
HUD - Fair Housing and Equal Opportunity (FHEO)
26 Federal Plaza
New York, New York 10278-0068

Region III – Philadelphia (Delaware, District of Columbia, Maryland, Pennsylvania, Virginia, West Virginia)
HUD - Fair Housing and Equal Opportunity (FHEO)
Liberty Square Building, 105 S. 7th Street
Philadelphia, Pennsylvania 19106-3392

Region IV – Atlanta (Alabama, Florida, Georgia, Kentucky, Mississippi, North Carolina, South Carolina, Tennessee, Puerto Rico, Virgin Islands)
HUD - Fair Housing and Equal Opportunity (FHEO)
Richard B. Russell Federal Building, 75 Spring Street, S.W.
Atlanta, Georgia 30303-3388

Region V – Chicago (Illinois, Indiana, Michigan, Minnesota, Ohio, Wisconsin)
HUD - Fair Housing and Equal Opportunity (FHEO)
Ralph H. Metcalfe Federal Building, 77 West Jackson Blvd.
Chicago, Illinois 60604-3507

Region VI – Fort Worth (Arkansas, Louisiana, New Mexico, Oklahoma, Texas)
HUD - Fair Housing and Equal Opportunity (FHEO)
1600 Throckmorton, P.O. Box 2905
Forth Worth, Texas 76113-2905

Region VII – Kansas City (Iowa, Kansas, Missouri, Nebraska)
HUD - Fair Housing and Equal Opportunity (FHEO)
Gateway Tower II, 400 State Avenue
Kansas City, Kansas 66101-2406

Region VIII – Denver (Colorado, Montana, North Dakota, South Dakota, Utah, Wyoming)
HUD - Fair Housing and Equal Opportunity (FHEO)
Executive Tower Building, 1405 Curtis Street
Denver, Colorado 80202-2349

Region IX – San Francisco (Arizona, California, Hawaii, Nevada, Guam, American Samoa)
HUD - Fair Housing and Equal Opportunity (FHEO)
450 Golden Gate Avenue
San Francisco, California 94102-3448

Region X – Seattle (Alaska, Idaho, Oregon, Washington)
HUD - Fair Housing and Equal Opportunity (FHEO)
Suite 200 Seattle Federal Building, 909 1st Ave.
Seattle, Washington 98104-1000

Privacy Act of 1974 (P.L. 93-579)

Authority: Title VIII of the Civil Rights Act of 1968, as amended by the Fair Housing Amendments Act of 1988, (P.L. 100-430).

Purpose: The information requested on this form is to be used to investigate and to process housing discrimination complaints.

Use: The information may be disclosed to the United States Department of Justice for its use in the filing of pattern or practice suits of housing discrimination or the prosecution of the person who committed the discrimination where violence is involved; and to state or local fair housing agencies which administer substantially equivalent fair housing laws for complaint processing.

Penalty: Failure to provide some or all of the requested information will result in delay or denial of HUD assistance.

Disclosure of this information is voluntary.

For further information call the Toll-free Fair Housing Complaint Hotline 1-800-669-9777.
Hearing Impaired persons may call (TDD) 1-800-927-9275.

form **HUD-903**

Figure 14–7. HUD Regional Offices

lency with federal law which reduces the confusion of disparate housing laws for the manager. Property managers should consult with a local real estate attorney or join local real estate trade organizations, such as apartment associations, IREM, BOMA, and so on.

1. *AIDS*—many states now have laws regulating when and how licensees must disclose to an applicant or buyer that the former tenant or owner died of AIDS in the apartment, unit, or house. In some states, the agent has no duty to disclose an AIDS death and is prohibited from doing so unless directly asked.

2. *Waterbeds*—some states allow the manager to refuse to rent to a tenant with a waterbed, or to demand that the tenant purchase waterbed insurance before renting.

3. *Telephone jacks*—some states require the owner to install and maintain a telephone jack in each residential unit.

4. *Smoking ban*—some states prohibit smoking in restaurants, office buildings, schools, and so forth.

5. *Occupancy standards*—this is an area in which HUD and state laws many times overlap and may conflict. The Fair Housing Act allows housing providers to adhere to reasonable local, state, and federal restrictions regarding the number of persons that can occupy a dwelling unit. The law also allows managers to develop and implement their own reasonable occupancy standards. HUD and advocacy groups mistakenly assume that the managers have made and will make occupancy standards to discriminate against renters with children. The old "safe harbor" rule endorsed by HUD was two people per bedroom. In other words, if a manager observed the guideline of at least two people per bedroom, for example, a two-bedroom unit housing four people, HUD would not file suit on grounds of familial status discrimination.

HUD may now require other considerations such as the size of the unit, the type of building, state building codes, and Building Owners Code Administrator (BOCA) standards (see Figure 14–8) for occupancy requirements.

State Agencies Each state has departments and commissions that duplicate and parallel federal agencies. Areas covered include discrimination, wages, and regulations of rental and leasing agents.

1. *State Department of Housing.* This agency could have many names and may not be a separate agency in some states. Its purpose is to administer housing and discrimination laws, e.g., occupancy guidelines.

Space	1 Person	2 Persons	3–5 Persons	6 or More
Total square feet	150	250	250–550	650
Living room	N/A	N/A	120	150
Dining room	N/A	N/A	80	100
Kitchen	50	50	50	60
Bedrooms	70	100	150–250	300+

Figure 14–8. BOCA Square Feet Requirements

2. *Department of Real Estate.* This agency supervises real estate licensees, including rental agents. They audit the broker's trust accounts and investigate complaints including misrepresentation and fraud, e.g., missing security deposits.

3. *Department of Labor.* This agency administers the labor code in relation to on-site (resident) managers, e.g., they must be paid at least minimum wage.

4. *State courts.* Names of state courts differ from justice court to municipal court to superior court. The hierarchy usually ends up at the state supreme court or court of appeals, which has the final decision on state cases.

Penalties for Fair Housing Violations

1. *Actual damages*—out-of-pocket costs, higher rents for alternative housing; may also include emotional distress, humiliation, mental anguish, etc.

2. *Civil penalties*—range from $10,000 for the first violation to $50,000 for the third violation.

3. *Punitive damages*—these are monetary awards designed to deter the defendant from future misconduct. These awards have no limits and can be in the millions of dollars.

4. *Injunctions*—prohibit the wrongdoer from performing a specific act; may require corrective action such as advertising or renting to minorities.

5. *Attorney's fees*—under fair housing laws, attorney fees may be awarded to the prevailing party.

Testing for Discrimination

HUD and private nonprofit advocacy groups organize "sting operations" to entrap unsuspecting owners in discriminatory acts. In some areas, these special-interest groups might photograph rental signs that contain phrases such as "adults only," "prefer adults," and "no kids." They then contact the owner to negotiate a settlement in lieu of filing a complaint with HUD. The terms of the settlement vary but could include a $10,000 donation to the nonprofit advocacy organization, removal of the sign, an agreement to rent a certain percentage of future vacancies to households with children, and so on.

Testing is an investigative technique to identify whether the manager is discriminating in any of the seven protected areas. An example would be two persons, one white and one black, posing to rent the one-bedroom apartment advertised as available. Each tester applies separately and provides identical credit information and references. Each tester notes the treatment and units shown. They then try to isolate one variable, in this case, race, as the reason for rejection or unequal treatment. For example, the black person might be told that the space has been rented. A white tester who applies 30 minutes later might then be told that the space is still available. In other cases, using different rent criteria (such as rents cannot exceed 20 percent of income for Hispanics, but can be 30 percent for blacks) could be interpreted as discrimination.

Both of these cases are grounds for a discrimination suit even though the testers were not actually seeking housing and were lying. The U.S. Supreme Court has upheld information from testers as admissible in housing discrimination cases even though it was obtained under false pretenses.

The best defense for the manager is to treat each applicant as a tester and treat everyone equally. Having forms for documentation such as the prospect form (Figure 14–9) and the apartment availability form (Figure 14–10) are necessary for an affirmative defense. Also, a tenant application (Figure 7–8) should be given to every applicant to fill out.

Today's Date_____

Name_____

Current address_____

City/State/Zip_____Home phone_____

Employer & occupation_____Work phone_____

```
┌─────────────────────────────────────────────────────────────┐
│                    Apartment Desired                        │
│   ☐   Studio                                                │
│   ☐   1 Bedroom                    ☐   Furnished            │
│   ☐   2 Bedroom/1 Bath             ☐   Unfurnished          │
│   ☐   2 Bedroom/2 Bath                                      │
│   ☐   3 Bedroom                                             │
└─────────────────────────────────────────────────────────────┘
```

Pets? (yes or no)_____Type and size?_____

Desired move-in date?_____Number of occupants?_____

How did you hear about us?_____

_____

_____

Office Use Only

☐   Walk-in   ☐   Telephone call

Apartment(s) shown_____Shown by_____

Comments made by prospect about apartments shown_____

_____

Application made?_____Apartment applied for?_____

If no application, was reason given?_____

Figure 14–9. Prospect Form

Community:_____   **Date**_____

Summary: Units currently occupied   _____
                 + Units with leases pending   _____
                 + Units vacant/not available   _____
                 + Units vacant/available   _____
                 = Total units   _____

Vacant Unit Detail:

Currently Available

Bldg/unit number	Location in bldg	Apt. size & layout	Date vacated	Date made available
1.				
2.				
3.				
4.				
5.				

Not Currently Available

Bldg/unit number	Location in bldg	Apt. size & layout	Date vacated	Date made available
1.				
Work still to be completed				
2.				
Work still to be completed				
3.				
Work still to be completed				

Figure 14–10. Apartment Availability Form

TENANT RESPONSIBILITIES

1. Pay rent on time. Most rental agreements state that rent must be paid on the first of the month. A common-sense approach to rent collection is that if a tenant moves in during the month, rent is prorated during the second month as the property manager should always strive to collect the first month's rent plus a deposit (cashier's check, money order, or cash) before allowing a tenant to move in. Personal checks are not usually desirable for the first month as they may be returned NSF (nonsufficient funds)—a typical ploy of the professional rent skipper.

2. Maintain the rented premises in clean, sanitary, and undamaged condition, excluding normal wear and tear.

3. Give proper legal notice in writing (the property manager should not accept verbal notice). For example, moving notice is usually 30 days with a month-to-month tenancy.

4. Allow other tenants quiet enjoyment of their units (e.g., do not play the stereo too loudly).

5. Abide by reasonable rules and regulations of the landlord (e.g., no skateboard riding on the complex sidewalks, designated parking areas) pet policy, etc. (Figure 14–11).

6. Comply with local laws such as overcrowding provisions in rent-control laws.

7. Do not commit crimes against property, such as vandalism.

LANDLORD REMEDIES

In residential management, the court system usually favors the tenant, so the property manager must be diligent in documenting a case with facts, pictures, and so forth, as the burden of proof is usually on the landlord. Legal notices vary according to local and state laws. For example, in California, the following are requirements.

1. *Notice to Pay Rent or Quit*—can be served by anyone over 18 years of age, including the property manager or owner, to the tenant for delinquent rent. The amount can include only actual rent, not damage charges, late payment fees, etc. (See Figure 14–12.)

2. *Notice to Correct Breach of Covenant or Quit (3-Day)*—used when the tenant seriously violates the terms of the rental agreement, house rules, or breaks local ordinances. Again, anyone may serve this notice. In residential property, this notice should proceed to court only on the advice of an attorney as many judges view the three-day period as insufficient time to require anyone to terminate tenancy except in cases of very serious magnitude (see Figure 14–13).

3. *Notice to Quit (30-Day)*—this notice, also called a 30-Day Notice of Termination of Tenancy, is given to the tenant who is on a month-to-month tenancy. No reason need be given except if required in areas of rent control (check local ordinances), but the notice cannot be used for retaliatory or discriminatory reasons. Anyone may serve. (See Figure 14–14.)

4. *Notice of Belief of Abandonment*—provides the owner with a procedure to recover the premises after the tenant has not paid rent for 14 days and there is reasonable belief the tenant has vacated and will not return. The tenant has to respond within 18 days. Service may be by mail.

5. *Notice of Right to Reclaim Abandoned Personal Property*—used when the tenant leaves personal property (e.g., furniture, clothing, etc.). The property manager should make a complete and accurate inventory with an esti-

This agreement is an addendum to the lease dated _____ between

_____ (Owner/Agent) and

_____ (Tenant) for the property located at

_____ .

1. The resident desires to keep the following pet identified as:

    Type (dog, cat): _____ Breed (beagle, Persian): _____

    Weight: _____ Length of time owned:_____

    Age: _____

2. An additional security deposit of $ _____ will be paid by the tenant.

3. An additional monthly rental amount of $ _____ will be paid by the tenant each month that the pet is kept in the unit.

4. Tenant agrees to comply with all health, safety, and government laws and regulations regarding this pet.

5. Tenant represents that the pet is housebroken and will not cause damage to the unit or common areas and will not harm or annoy other tenants. If violation occurs, written notice will be given by Owner/Agent to Tenant for the first violation. If a second violation occurs, Tenant agrees to remove the pet.

6. Tenant shall be liable to Owner for all damages or expense incurred by or in connection with said pet, and shall hold Owner harmless for any and all damages or costs in connection with said pet.

_____   _____
Signature   Owner/Manager   Signature   Tenant

_____   _____
Printed Name   Printed Name

_____   _____
Date   Date

Figure 14–11. Pet Agreement

mate of value. The property manager must store the personal property for 18 days after mailing a notice to the last known address of the tenant. By paying reasonable storage costs, the tenant can take possession of the goods even if back rent is owed. If unclaimed and under a specific value, the owner may dispose of the goods in any manner desired. If the value is over the limit, a public sale notice must be published in the newspaper and the items auctioned. After deducting reasonable storage and sale costs, the proceeds must be returned to the tenant or turned over to the county to be held for the tenant. If the tenant does not claim the proceeds within five years, they revert to the state. (See Figure 14–15.)

TO: _____

AND ALL OTHERS IN POSSESSION:

WITHIN THREE (3) DAYS after service upon you of this Notice, you are hereby required to pay to the undersigned, or to _____ as owner/authorized agent, the rent of the premises hereinafter described, of which you now hold possession amounting to the sum of:

_____($ _____)

enumerated as follows:

$ Due From   to
$ Due From   to
$ Due From   to
$ Due From   to

OR QUIT AND DELIVER UP POSSESSION OF THE PREMISES:

The premises herein referred to are situated in the City of _____ , County of _____ , State of _____ , and designated by the street and number as: _____ .

WITHIN THREE DAYS after receipt of this Notice on you, you are required to pay said rent in full or to deliver up possession of said premises to the undersigned or your landlord, or legal proceedings will be commenced against you to recover all rents, damages (including treble damages), costs, and attorneys' fees for the unlawful detention of said premises.

YOU ARE FURTHER notified that in the event of your failure to pay said rent as hereinabove set forth, it is the intention of your landlord to obtain possession of the demised premises and to attempt to relet same without terminating your liability under said lease and to take such other actions as may be provided in said lease. The undersigned hereby elects at this time to declare a forfeiture of the tenancy under which you occupy said premises in the event you fail to pay the rent in full. A partial payment of rent by you shall not waive the landlord's election of forfeiture.

FURTHER NOTICE IS GIVEN that in the event that any partial payments of rent, expenses, or other charges are tendered and accepted by the undersigned after service of this Notice on you and/or after the filing of the Complaint for Unlawful Detainer, acceptance shall be without a waiver of any of the rights of the landlord, including the right to recover possession of the premises hereinabove described and the balance of the rent, expenses, and other charges due under this Notice and/or the lease.

_____   _____
Date   Owner/Agent

Figure 14–12.   Notice to Pay Rent or Quit

_____

You are hereby notified that you are in Breach of Covenant of your lease covering

_____

City of _____

County of _____

Within three days after the service of this notice, you are hereby required to correct said Breach, to wit:

OR QUIT AND DELIVER UP THE POSSESSION OF THE PREMISES.

YOU ARE FURTHER NOTIFIED THAT the undersigned does not hereby elect to declare the forfeiture of your lease or rental agreement under which you hold possession of the above-described premises and Lessor will institute legal proceedings to recover rent and possession of said premises which could result in a judgment against you including costs and necessary disbursements together with treble damages as allowed by law for such unlawful detention.

_____   _____

Date   Owner/Agent

                                       J.D. Property Management, Inc.
                                       3520 Cadillac Ave., Suite B
                                       Costa Mesa, CA 92626 (714)

Figure 14–13. Notice to Correct Breach of Covenant or Quit

6. _Change of Terms Notice_—must be given before increasing the rent or changing the terms of the agreement (such as allowing pets). The notice time on a month-to-month tenancy is 30 days. (See Figure 14–16.)

7. _Transfer of Security Deposit_—upon sale of the property, the rents are usually prorated and security deposits are transferred. Notice telling of disposition of deposits must be sent out to the tenants within 14 days. This notice should also include the amount of the deposit and the name and address of the new property manager. (See Figure 14–17.)

8. Eviction
   a) _Retaliatory eviction_—The landlord cannot retaliate against a tenant who exercises the right to complain about habitability. The property man-

```
TO: _____


PLEASE TAKE NOTICE THAT THE TENANCY UNDER WHICH YOU OCCUPY THE

PREMISES KNOWN AS _____

CITY OF _____ COUNTY OF _____

STATE OF _____ IS HEREBY TERMINATED ON THE _____ DAY OF

_____ , 199__ .


AND YOU ARE HEREBY REQUIRED TO QUIT AND SURRENDER TO ME POSSESSION
OF THE PREMISES ON SAID DAY.


THIS IS INTENDED AS LEGAL NOTICE FOR THE PURPOSE OF TERMINATING YOUR
TENANCY.


SERVED THIS DAY _____ OF _____ , 199__ .



_____
SIGNATURE—OPERATOR/AGENT


_____
PRINT NAME AND TITLE
```

Figure 14–14. Notice to Quit

ager cannot evict or increase the rent for a specific amount of time if
the reason for that eviction or rent increase is a result of the tenant exercising the right to complain about habitability. If the tenant is
evicted, the landlord or property manager must stand prepared to
prove that the action was not retaliatory (e.g., proof of nonpayment of
rent, severe breach of contract, etc.).

b) *Constructive eviction*—Eviction is considered constructive if the landlord
turns off the utilities, changes locks, removes the tenant's personal
property, removes the front door, etc. These actions are prohibited
and carry mandatory penalties.

c) *Actual eviction*—If the tenant has not paid the rent, the landlord must
go to court using an "unlawful detainer action" to remove the tenant
and collect unpaid rent. Small claims court is inexpensive, but time
consuming (75–90 days), so most property managers use the municipal court. Legal counsel should be obtained from an attorney who
specializes in evictions. The main goal is to regain possession and re-

To:_____

Address:_____

_____

When you vacated the premises at:_____

the following personal property remained:_____

_____

_____

You may claim this property at:_____

Unless you pay the reasonable cost of storage for all the above-described property, and take possession of the property which you claim, not later than_____this property may be disposed of pursuant to the law.

If you fail to reclaim the property, it will be sold at a public sale after notice of the sale has been given by publication. You have the right to bid on the property at this sale. After the property is sold and the cost of storage, advertising, and sale is deducted, the remaining money will be turned over to the county. You may claim the remaining money at any time within (1) one year after the county receives the money.

Dated:_____   _____

                                          _____

                                          _____

Figure 14–15. Notice of Right to Reclaim Abandoned Property

rent the property to a paying tenant as soon as possible. Often, the money judgments obtained are worthless as the tenant is unemployed, on welfare, or leaves the area. Even the self-managing owner who may represent himself "in pro per" will find using an attorney prudent as procedural guidelines must be followed exactly or the case will be dismissed and the landlord will have to start again from the beginning with a Notice to Pay Rent or Quit (Figure 14–12).

To:_____

(List all persons in possession)

and to all others in possession of the premises commonly known and designated by number and

street as_____

_____, apartment #_____

in the City of _____, County of _____State of _____

You are hereby notified, in accordance with your rental agreement that (30) thirty days after

service upon you of this notice, or _____, whichever is later, your tenancy of the

above designated premises will be changed as follows:

1.   The monthly rent, which is payable in advance on or before the _____ day of each

      month will be the sum of $ _____, instead of $ _____, the

      current monthly rent.

2.   Other changes:_____

      _____

      _____

      _____

Except as herein provided, all other terms of your tenancy shall remain in full force and effect.

Dated this _____ day of _____ 19_____

_____   _____
              (Agent)   (Owner)

Figure 14–16. Notice of Change of Terms of Tenancy

TO: Resident(s) _____

effective _____ , 19__ , we will no longer manage/own the unit in

which you reside, located at _____ .

You are being informed that your security deposit, in the amount of $ _____ , has

been:

[_____]   TRANSFERRED TO: _____

                _____

                _____

[_____]   RETURNED TO YOU. _____
                                        Date

YOUR PRESENT RENTAL AGREEMENT/LEASE WILL REMAIN IN EFFECT. FOR
MORE INFORMATION ABOUT YOUR NEW OWNER/AGENT, CONTACT:

Name _____

Address _____

City _____ State _____ Zip _____

Phone #_____ Fax # _____

On _____ , 19__ , this Notice was:

[_____]   mailed to you by certified mail.

[_____]   personally delivered to you

Dated _____   _____
                                                Owner/Agent

Figure 14–17. Transfer of Security Deposit

CALIFORNIA COURT SYSTEM

SMALL CLAIMS COURT

1. Maximum limit is $5,000.

2. Low cost -- filing fee

3. No attorney representation.

4. Limitations on usage.

    a. Slow and time-consuming, may take 75-90 days.

5. Appeal -- only defendant can appeal; 20 days to appeal if he shows, 35 days if he doesn't appear in court.

6. Cannot file for eviction in Small Claims Court.

MUNICIPAL COURT

1. Maximum limit is $1,500 per month rent for commercial unlawful detainer, no limit per month for residential, $25,000 maximum.

2. Probably need attorney, but can file "in pro per." Agent cannot act as attorney.

3. Quickest eviction -- 25-35 days (priority for fast trial, CC 1179A).

4. Limitations on usage:

    a. Back rent.

    b. Writ of Possession.

SUPERIOR COURT

1. Higher attorney costs.

2. Must be utilized if rent for commercial properties is over $1,500 per month or total due is over $25,000.

APPELLATE COURT

1. An appeals court that hears cases on appeal.

CALIFORNIA SUPREME COURT

1. Final decision on state laws and the state Constitution.

Figure 14-18. California Court System

The actual unlawful detainer processes varies among municipalities and states, but follows similar steps. We will illustrate the California system, Figure 14–18, which goes through the steps and procedures. If the tenant has no assets or job, he or she is "judgment proof" and it is not usually worthwhile spending a great deal of time and money trying to collect the judgment. The judgment should be recorded in case the tenant wins the lottery or comes into a huge inheritance.

Certified versus Registered Mail

Some notices such as a three-day notice may be sent by regular mail. According to the U.S. Postal Service, registered mail should be used when you are mailing something of monetary value that can be insured, such as money or jewelry. A declared value is made at the time of mailing and, if lost, reimbursement will be made by the postal service. Certified mail should be used when the item to be mailed has no intrinsic value, such as a letter or notice, and therefore does not require insurance. Certified mail is approximately 40 percent cheaper than registered mail. In most instances, a letter sent certified mail, return receipt requested, is adequate to meet notice requirements, even if the lease says registered mail. Property managers should verify their state laws regarding services.

TENANT PROTECTION

The tenant is protected by law from abuses by the landlord. The property manager, by following the Golden Rule of "Do unto others as you would have them do unto you," will avoid many hassles and pitfalls. As we discussed in Chapter 4, in addition to avoiding costly legal action for the owner, the property manager is usually paid a percentage of rents collected and will not make a profit if time is consumed in tenant disputes.

Refer to Figure 14–19.

1. *Repair and deduct*—The tenant may, after a "reasonable" time and after either written or, in some states, oral notice to the landlord of conditions making the unit uninhabitable, make the repairs himself or have the repairs completed by others. His or her costs may then be deducted from rent owed.

2. *Nonwaiver of tenant's rights*—As discussed earlier in this chapter, the tenant cannot waive rights of habitability.

3. *Entry of tenant's unit*—The tenant must be allowed quiet enjoyment of the dwelling. Many states' code sections spell out the four reasons for which a landlord may enter:
   a) Emergency (e.g., water or gas leak).
   b) To make necessary or agreed-on repairs, provide service, show the unit to prospective tenants or buyers, or normal inspection. Twenty-four hour written notice usually must be given and entry must be during reasonable hours.
   c) Abandoned or surrendered premises.
   d) Pursuant to court order.

   If the property manager uses tact, reasonableness, and understanding, entry is not usually a problem. (See Figure 14–20.)

4. *Forcible entry*—Defined as the breaking of windows or doors or threats of violence or terror to gain entry. It is strictly illegal.

5. *Soldiers and Sailors Civil Relief Act of 1940*—Protects the rights of persons in the service by providing special methods for serving notices and seizing or holding personal property.

Uncontested Unlawful Detainer Steps
1. Service Notice to Pay Rent or Quit (anyone may serve).
2. File Summons and Complaint.
3. Service of Summons and Complaint by disinterested party (best to use marshal or a process server).
4. Tenant, if personally served, has five days to answer, and 15 days if by substitute service.
5. If tenant doesn't respond, file "Request to Enter Default" with clerk. In some jurisdictions you need to go to court for a "prove-up" to get a judgment.
6. After receiving a judgment, file for a "Writ of Possession."
7. File the "Writ of Possession" with the marshal's office for service.
8. Marshal serves "Eviction Notice" and tenant has five days to vacate.
9. Marshal will, after five days, physically evict tenant and turn apartment over to property manager who may immediately change the locks.
10. File declaration to obtain "money judgment" for unpaid rent.

Contested Cases
1. Follow Steps 1–4 above.
2. Tenant files answer to complaint and a "Memorandum to Set Civil Case for Trial" or "Request for Trial" with clerk. A trial date will then be set by the court.
3. When owner wins judgment at trial, he should proceed with Steps 6–10 above.

Proper Service of Notices
1. Attempt must be made for "personal service."
   a. If unable to personally serve, notice may be posted on door with copy mailed first class except for 30-day notices, which should be sent by certified or registered mail.
   b. Summons and Complaint may be filed on the fourth day after personal service of Notice to Pay Rent or Quit, or Breach of Covenant, 31st day for Notice to Vacate.

2. Substituted Service (to occupant other than tenant) or "Post Substituted and Mail."
   a. Pay Rent or Quit or Breach of Covenant must be served three days prior to filing, not counting day of service.

3. Change in Terms or Rent Increase
   a. Served as above or by certified mail.

What is Personal Service?
If you hand the notice to the tenant (or tenants) named on the notice, this is considered personal service. If you hand the notice to anyone else in the unit, who in turn is to give it to the named tenant, this is considered "substituted service." Service must be on an adult, in any case, rather than a child.

Figure 14–19. Sample Eviction Process (California)

6. *Credit reporting*—The tenant is protected by the Federal Fair Credit Reporting Act if credit is denied. The reason must be given in writing. When a credit reporting agency has been used, the property manager should refer tenant requests for information to that agency (e.g., "You were turned down because of information received from Landlord/Tenant Credit.") and not deal in specifics with the tenant. In some states the manager must give written notice of bad credit when rejecting a tenant.

7. *Seizing personal property*—The landlord or property manager may not usually seize personal property without a court order in most states.

8. *Removal of vehicles*—The property manager must have the property properly posted to conform with local ordinances. A towing service, licensed to operate in the specific local area, should be used to avoid illegal towing claims by tenants and other persons.

TENANT ABUSES The pendulum has swung in favor of tenant rights with little regard for those remaining landlord rights. This legal environment makes it difficult and time consuming for the property manager when dealing with evictions. For exam-

Owner/Manager hereby gives notice to: _____

_____ , and all

persons in occupancy of the premises located at:

_____

that owner, owner's agent or owner's employees will enter said premises on or about the

_____ day of _____ , 19__ , during normal

business hours _____ for the reason set forth in the

checked [✔] numbered item below:

_____   1.   To make necessary or agreed-on repairs

_____   2.   Pest control

_____   3.   Alterations or improvements

_____   4.   Supply necessary or agreed-on services

_____   5.   To show the dwelling unit

Dated _____ , 19___ .   _____
                                                         Owner/Agent

Figure 14–20.   Notice to Enter Dwelling

ple, Figure 14–21 shows a flyer from a paralegal clinic posted on a tenant's door after an unlawful detainer was served. These clinics search the court records daily and either mail or post notices on the tenant doors telling them that, for a fee, eviction can be delayed.

An evicting owner wins only a hollow victory as many evicted residential tenants are "judgment-proof" (no assets or job), so monies awarded are not collectable. In turn, this leads to higher rent for the rest of the good tenants as owners have to make up their loss. The phrase "caveat feofatus," owner beware, is appropriate.

RENT CONTROL   Rent-control laws are at local and state levels, there is no federal rent-control law. Each municipality that has rent control usually is unique and will take time and study on the part of the property manager to understand. The most famous local rent control is probably in New York City.

The Emergency Price Control Act froze rental rates as of March 1, 1943. This law, although modified, is still in force. In 1969, the rent stabilization program went into effect which allowed decontrol if the original tenant or family vacated. Units under rent control are rented at only a fraction of their true mar-

"We Can Help"

CALIFORNIA PARALEGAL CLINIC

Dear Tenant:

An "EVICTION LAWSUIT" has been filed against you by your landlord. The
purpose of this action is to EVICT you from the premises you now occupy.

You will notice that you have been given five (5) CALENDAR DAYS in which to
file an ANSWER to this SUMMONS. If you fail to answer within this time period,
your landlord will win a Judgment by Default and have the Marshal post a Five
Day Notice to Move (vacate the property) on your residence within a few days.

We can assist you in STOPPING THE EVICTION. Helping tenants faced with an
eviction problem can result in the TENANT retaining possession of the premises
or obtaining the necessary TIME to move in an orderly and dignified fashion.

We can assist you. WE CAN HELP prevent or prolong the abrupt disruption of
your home life.

"YOU MUST ACT QUICKLY"

ACT RIGHT NOW because your time is very short. Call our office for an
appointment, or come in IMMEDIATELY!!!! Bring this letter along with any
other papers you have received.

Sincerely,

CALIFORNIA PARALEGAL CLINIC

O U R   T O T A L   F E E: $55.00

Figure 14–21. Stopping Eviction

ket value. This has led to a deterioration of the private housing stock in New York City as owners cannot maintain the property on the income received.

Rent-Control Rules

1. *Demolition*—In some areas, such as Santa Monica, California, the landlord was prohibited from tearing down his or her building and going out of business and was forced to absorb annual losses. A special law (the Ellis Act) was passed by state legislature to allow landlords to choose to go out of business by superseding the local ordinance.

2. *Annual increases*—These rules differ according to locale, but often are tied to the Consumer Price Index (CPI). For example, a landlord can raise rent three-fourths of CPI increases over the last 12 months. If the CPI increase was 4 percent, rent could be raised 3 percent.

3. *Vacancy decontrol*—In some locales, when the tenant voluntarily moves, the landlord may raise rent to current market rate. In some areas, a maximum increase upon vacancy, such as 15 percent, is only allowed.

4. *Evictions*—Usually need just cause such as nonpayment of rent.

United States Supreme Court— *Pennell v. City of San Jose*

In *Pennell v. the City of San Jose* (Rent-Control Ordinance) (1986), the California Supreme Court declared that an owner may be entitled to less than a "fair return" depending on the income of the tenant.

In 1988 the case was appealed to the federal level. The U.S. Supreme Court, in a 6–2 majority opinion, said: "We have long recognized that a legitimate and rational goal of price or rate regulation is the protection of consumer welfare." The ordinance "represents a rational attempt to accommodate the conflicting interests of protecting tenants from burdensome rent increases while at the same time ensuring that landlords are guaranteed a fair return of their investment."

The dissenting opinion by Justice Scalia best describes the landlord's predicament in this case:

> The San Jose Rent Control Law is no different from a requirement that a grocer charge poor shoppers less than wealthier ones. Rather than putting the social burden on all citizens, the San Jose rent law works to establish a welfare program privately funded by those landlords who happen to have hardship tenants.

This case has been described as a "Robin Hood law" that steals from the rich (landlords) to pay the poor (tenants).

The Future of Rent Control

A politician once told me that he voted in favor of rent control because there are more renters than landlords. Many cities have vacancy rates approaching 10 percent yet still have rent control in force. The U.S. Supreme Court has upheld the local government's ability to create rent control. The future format of rent control will probably change as demographic figures have shown that rent control discriminates against minorities. New and revised rent-control laws will mandate income limitations on tenants who live in rent-control units, which may lead to more ghetto and barrio areas in rent-control communities. Most investors and developers do not want to own or build in rent-control areas, which lessens the supply of units. Many existing owners do not have positive cash flows or cannot refinance their buildings under rent control and are deferring maintenance and will eventually abandon their properties.

SUMMARY

It is essential that the property manager be familiar with federal, state, and local regulations and laws in order to properly manage and protect the property from lawsuits. The highest source of law is the Constitution, so any local law in conflict with federal or state law will be void. Local laws such as rent control vary from municipality to municipality. Commercial tenants are viewed as equal to landlords in most courts and are not given the protections (such as rent control) granted to residential tenants.

The owner/manager has a responsibility to maintain a habitable dwelling unit. The definition of habitability includes: weatherproofing; security; plumbing, heating, and electrical systems in good working order; timely repairs, trash removal, freedom from pests, and smoke detectors. The courts and legislation have said that the owner/manager cannot discriminate on the basis of race, religion, color, national origin, age, handicap, or sex. There are laws at the federal, state, and local levels as well as the Department of Real Estate Commission's regulation.

The tenant has responsibilities, including paying rent on time, maintaining a clean and sanitary unit, giving proper notice, respecting the rights of other tenants, abiding by reasonable rules and regulations, and complying with laws. Landlord remedies against the tenant include 3-day, and 30-day notices, Notice of Belief of Abandonment, Notice of Change of Terms, and eviction. There are two kinds of evictions: actual (court ordered) and constructive (turning off utilities). Tenant protection includes laws against retaliatory eviction, allowing repairs and deduction for repairs by the tenant, nonwaiver of tenant rights, notice before entry to unit, and so on.

Court cases have set precedents over the years which established landlord/tenant laws. When considering rent control, the latest U.S. Supreme Court case, *Pennell v. the City of San Jose*, upheld the right of the city to limit rent increases to poor tenants.

The property manager constantly must be updating and learning about changes and new landlord/tenant laws. A relationship with a good eviction attorney should be established, as a nonpaying tenant is worse than a vacancy. The key in landlord/tenant relationships is treating the other person as you yourself would want to be treated.

PERSONALITY PROFILE

The real estate agent and property manager learn in their basic courses not to give legal advice. Often a client will ask the property manager, "How should I hold title to the apartment building my wife and I are purchasing?" The answer, of course, is for the client to consult their attorney and CPA. Some real estate brokers, such as Gene Trowbridge, CCIM and National Faculty Member of the Commercial Investment Real Estate Institute, decide to combine the practice of real estate with the practice of law. Gene went to law school and passed the California State Bar Association's exam and is now an attorney specializing in real estate law. Using his knowledge as a broker in the real estate industry, he is able to counsel clients in how to make the deal work or how to constructively restructure a proposed deal.

Gene was able to combine interests in law and real estate into a unique area of specialization to help his clients and the clients of other brokers and property managers.

REVIEW QUESTIONS

1. The highest source of law is
   a. Congress.
   b. the president.
   c. the Constitution
   d. local government.

2. In a conflict of authority between state and federal government, which usually prevails?
   a. state
   b. federal
   c. local
   d. city

3. It is lawful to discriminate on the basis of
   a. credit.   c. religion.
   b. race.   d. sex.

4. Reasonable accommodation and modifications is covered in which law?
   a. Fair Housing Act of 1988   c. Civic Rights Act of 1866
   b. ADA Law   d. Fair Housing Act of 1968

5. Rent control does not usually involve
   a. federal law.   c. state law.
   b. local law.

6. Habitability includes
   a. payment of rent on time by the tenant.
   b. always charging market rent.
   c. hot and cold running water in good working condition.
   d. both a and b
   e. both b and c

7. Tenant responsibilities include
   a. paying rent on time.   d. both a and b
   b. maintaining a clean unit.   e. both b and c
   c. paying market rent.

8. Eviction for nonpayment of rent starts with a
   a. 30-day notice.   c. summons and complaint.
   b. Notice to Pay Rent or Quit.   d. writ of possession.

9. Which is an example of reasonable accommodation?
   a. curb cut   c. elevator
   b. ramps   d. allowing seeing eye dog

10. The penalty for a first fair housing violation could be
    a. a million-dollar fine.   d. both a and b
    b. actual and punitive damages.   e. both b and c
    c. a fine of $500,000.

11. Housing complaints must be filed within how many years after occur-
    rence?
    a. 1 year   c. 3 years
    b. 2 years   d. 4 years

12. Who is exempt from fair housing laws?
    a. the property managers   c. the corporations
    b. the agent   d. the owner of a single fourplex

13. In order for a building to be a senior citizen complex, what percentage of
    occupants must be over 55 years old?
    a. 50 percent   c. 75 percent
    b. 60 percent   d. 80 percent

14. Testing for discrimination against prospective applicants by trying to en-
    trap the manager is:
    a. illegal by state law.   c. legal by federal law.
    b. legal by state law.   d. illegal by federal law.

15. Evicting a tenant because he or she filed a health complaint against the
    property may be
    a. retaliatory eviction.   c. constructive eviction.
    b. actual eviction.   d. court-ordered eviction.

CASE STUDY PROBLEMS

Refer to the Case Study at the end of Chapter 5.

1. Civic Center Terrace has some roof leaks that two tenants complained about six months ago. What should be done?

2. In determining the tenant mix for the apartment complex, the owner says he doesn't want to rent one-bedroom units to applicants with children due to the small size of the units. What should you, as the property manager, tell him?

3. A blind applicant wants to rent an apartment on the second floor and asks you (the property manager) to install an elevator. Do you legally have to install an elevator?

4. What rent-collection procedures would you implement to reduce delinquencies at Civic Center Terrace?

5. The previous manager started eviction proceedings (gave 30 days' notice) to a tenant she did not like because he complained about plumbing leaks. What should you do?

6. Would you handle the evictions differently from going to small claims court? Why or why not?

7. Who would you have serve Pay Rent or Quit Notices?

8. The previous manager used to change the locks when tenants did not pay after three months. What would be your policy?

9. The previous manager used her pass key to enter tenant apartments for repairs, to see if they had extra pets, and so on. Would you revise that policy?

10. The owner is worried about being sued and wants to include a clause in the rental agreement that prohibits tenants from suing the owner. What should you tell the owner?

ADDITIONAL READING AND REFERENCES

Brown, David, and Ralph Warner, *The Landlord's Law Book*, Nolo Press, Berkeley, CA, 1986.

California Apartment Association, *California Rental Housing Reference Book*, Sacramento, CA, 1985.

Casale, William, *Property Management*, California Association of Realtors, Los Angeles, CA, 1983.

DeCarlo, Joseph W., *Essential Facts: Real Estate Management*, Warren, Gorham, and Lamont, Boston, MA, 1996.

DeCarlo, Joseph W., *Property Management in California*, JD Seminars and Publications Inc., Costa Mesa, CA, 1996.

DeCarlo, Joseph W., *Real Estate Adventures, Principles and Practices*, JD Seminars and Publications Inc., Costa Mesa, CA, 1993.

The Fair Housing Advisor (Quarterly), The Fair Housing Institute, P.O. Box 920520, Norcross, GA 30092.

Gordon, Theodore H., *California Real Estate Law*, Prentice-Hall, Englewood Cliffs, NJ, 1985.

Real Estate Law Journal (Quarterly), Warren, Gorham, and Lamont, Inc., 31 St., James St., Boston, MA 02116.

Real Property Law Reporter (Monthly), University of California, Department CEB, 2300 Shattuck Avenue, Berkeley, CA 94704.

Chapter 15

Human Relations in Property Management

Key terms

1099 forms	Fair Employment	Overtime
Business plan	Independent	Planning
Controlling	contractor	Staffing
Directing	Minimum wage	Task traits
Employment contract	Notices	Withholding
Eviction of manager	Organization	

Food for thought

> "Education is a social process . . . Education is growth . . . Education is not preparation for life: Education is life itself."
>
> *John Dewey*
> *American philosopher/educator*

INTRODUCTION

In previous chapters we have examined the mechanics and systems of property management. In this chapter we will examine how the interaction of these systems is successfully coordinated by the CPM, sometimes referred to as a certified property "magician" rather than the certified property manager. As illustrated by one's own body, in which the heart, lungs, brain, and kidneys all must work in harmony to enjoy a healthy life, maintenance, rent collection, tenant selection, and accounting also must be in harmony to run a successful building. The property manager, on-site manager, staff, vendors, and tenants must work symbiotically even though their personalities, behavior patterns, approaches, and goals may be dissimilar.

THE MANAGEMENT FUNCTION

The property manager's function is to deliver a service while dealing with the quality, quantity, cost-effectiveness, and efficiency of the building in the marketplace. The management function is dynamic and constantly changing. In the early 1900s, engineer Fredrich Taylor developed a scientific theory of management and many of his principles are still followed. Property management relies on six steps.

1. *Planning*—develop a management plan to achieve goals and objectives.
2. *Organizing*—define jobs; e.g., on-site manager.

3. *Staffing*—hire and train people to fill positions, such as that of maintenance foreman.

4. *Directing*—lead and motivate the staff, such as by developing goals and offering rewards for their fulfillment (bonuses, etc.).

5. *Controlling*—measure performance and identify problem areas. Such a measurement may be the monthly profit and loss statement.

6. *Feedback*—test to see if assumptions are valid. Monthly vacancy reports will verify whether the 5 percent projected vacancy assumption was valid.

STAFFING THE MANAGEMENT OFFICE

Since the property manager provides a service and not a product, people are the most important asset. Firm sizes range from small (only the property manager and a secretary) to a large office consisting of several layers of personnel (see Figure 15–1). The management company should prepare a business plan (for a discussion of budgets see Chapter 13) to use as a guide for when to hire additional employees (see Figure 13–8).

Job Descriptions

In a research project commissioned by the Institute of Real Estate Management (IREM) Foundation, Potential Unlimited, Inc. (San Rafael, CA, 1986), a firm specializing in employment behavioral analysis and research, concluded that there was no "perfect property manager." No one behavior or trait closely correlated with success in the majority of property manager/supervisor positions.

The very nature of property management involves an unusually demanding and conflicting mix of behavioral requirements. One position might require a dynamic "self-starting" salesperson, able to deal with the multiple personalities of tenants, vendors, and owners alike, while another might focus on the pyramid of details and paperwork inherent in lease administration. Thus, when the executive manager looks at a job candidate, a definition of the position's priorities through a job description is essential.

1. Who will the applicant be dealing with? Residential tenants? Outside owners? In-house staff only?

2. What will be the primary functions of the job? Leasing? Property supervision? Lease administration? New account solicitation?

3. What technical knowledge is required? Experience with sophisticated building systems? Commercial lease clause familiarity? Accounting?

From an adequately prepared job description, behavioral traits can be matched to job requirements.

Each employee must be trained in the company's operations and procedures. This task is made easier if the company has a policy and procedures guide for employees to read, review, and keep for future reference. The future education and professional growth of the employee should also be a company goal. For example, employees should be encouraged to become candidates to achieve the certified property manager designation. William Walters, Jr., CPM, in *The Practice of Real Estate Management for the Experienced Property Manager* (Chicago: Institute of Real Estate Management, 1979) discussed in depth the staffing of the management office.

PAYMENT OF EMPLOYEES

Persons working permanently on the complex are employees, whether they receive wages or just a rental allowance. As such, state and federal employment laws must be followed.

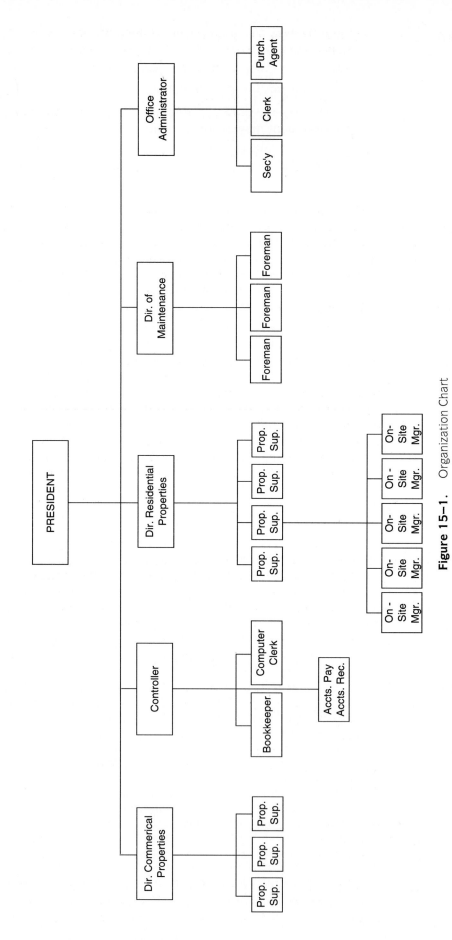

Figure 15-1. Organization Chart

Resident Managers

The Federal minimum wage increased to $4.75 effective October 1, 1996 and $5.15 effective September 1, 1997. State law may vary. Usually, the employer pays the higher of federal or state minimum wage.

8 hrs. @ $5.15 per hr.	$41.20/day
4 hrs. @ $7.73 per hr.	$30.90/day
12 hrs. @ $10.30 per hr.	$123.60/day
Total for 24 hours	$195.70/day
30 days	$5,871.00/month
365 days	$71,430.50/year

Resident managers may, in some states, have State Disability Insurance (SDI) and lodging deducted from their gross wages. The salary range depends on the size of the property, experience, the number of employees supervised, training, and the region of the country. The accredited resident manager (AMO) designee (see Chapter 1) made salary and wages of $26,400, according to a 1993 Institute of Real Estate Management profile. If bonus monies and free rent are calculated, the figure climbs to $31,100. They are considered employees by IRS guidelines and should be covered under workers' compensation insurance.

Property Managers

Property managers usually manage several properties and in many instances work for more than one owner. They may need a real estate license and/or a separate license for management of rental property. The salary range for certified property managers (CPMs), according to the Institute of Real Estate Management (IREM) profile survey in 1993, varied according to region, education, size of portfolio and experience. The median compensation ranged from $66,500 in western states to a low of $58,000 in the Southwest. CPMs with graduate degrees were at the top at $105,000. A property manager is usually an independent contractor to a landlord, but may be an employee of a management company.

Personality Tests

Several personality tests have been developed to help determine behavior traits. Among the best is the Myers-Briggs test of psychological types which breaks personalities down to 16 basic groups. Thus, if the job description calls for the empirical, objective thinking of a senior executive manager responsible for the overall goals and objectives of the management company, results of the Myers-Briggs test would indicate hiring an "ENTJ" (extroverted, intuitive, thinking, judgmental) type. In turn, a job description heavy in the detailed administrative behavior of commercial lease administration might favor an "ISTJ" (introverted, sensing, thinking, judgmental) type.

For a thorough discussion of these behavioral types and their characteristics, read *Please Understand Me* by David Keirsey and Marilyn Bates (Promotions Nemesis Book Co., Del Mar, CA, 1984), which also contains an abbreviated version of the test and an answer grid.

An individual considering property management as a career could also take this test to help select the areas in the industry most appropriate for his or her personality.

Overtime

Overtime must usually be paid for any time worked over 40 hours per week. Payment must be at time and a half for the first four hours of overtime each day beyond the initial eight hours, and double time after 12 hours. Check your state law.

Time cards should be kept along with the resident manager agreement since the on-site manager works odd hours (emergency calls). Without time cards, a disgruntled former manager can claim to the Labor Board that he worked 24 hours per day, 7 days per week, for the entire year. As evidenced by the example below, this has disastrous potential.

8 hrs. @ $4.25 per hr.	$34.00/day
4 hrs. @ $6.38 per hr.	$25.50/day
12 hrs. @ $8.50 per hr.	$102.00/day
Total for 24 hours	$161.50/day
30 days	$4,845/month
365 days	$58,947.50/year

Taxability of Manager's Apartment

If lodging (an apartment) is provided on the employer's premises, for the owner's convenience and as a condition of employment, and the rental value is used to meet minimum wage requirements, then the following conditions apply:

- No Federal income tax is withheld.

- No Social Security (FICA) tax is withheld.

- No state income tax is withheld in some states.

- SDI is withheld on part of the rental value, not to exceed a maximum deduction.

- SUI and ETT are paid by the employer on part of the rental value, not to exceed a maximum deduction; check with state law.

Is the On-site Manager an Employee or an Independent Contractor?

IRS revenue ruling 87-41 lists 20 factors that determine if a person is an employee or independent contractor for federal tax purposes. Each factor that can be answered yes supports the arrangement to be considered an employee.

1. *Instructions*—control of how, where, and when work is to be done.

2. *Training*—outside sources, licenses, designations.

3. *Integration*—continuing service.

4. *Personal services*—Can person have another person on the job?

5. *Hire, supervise*—Does worker hire other workers for employer?

6. *Continuing relationship*—Are duties routine?

7. *Hours of work*—set hours

8. *Time required*—full or part-time?

9. *Workplace*—one location for work.

10. *Scheduling*—established work schedule.

11. *Reports*—submission of regular reports.

12. *Payment*—Does worker receive regular compensation at fixed intervals?

13. *Expense reimbursement*—travel and entertainment.

14. *Tools*—Are tools furnished by employee?

15. *Investment*—Has worker invested in his or her own office or building?

16. *Profits*—Can worker suffer a loss or gain?

17. *Number of firms*—Can worker work for more than one employer in the same field?

18. *General public*—Are services available to the public?

19. *Right to discharge*—Can worker be fired?

20. *Right to quit*—Can worker quit without liability?

Federal guidelines say that if a business grosses over $250,000 per year, it is covered under federal law. Most property management companies collect rents in excess of this amount on their combined properties. The on-site manager is, then, for all practical purposes, an employee by both state and federal law (see Figure 15–2, Assignment of Duties).

Payment When Firing the On-site Manager

Payment will differ among states, but typically:

1. Wages must be paid immediately.

2. If the manager quits, he or she must be paid within 48 hours if he or she has a contract.

3. If the manager quits and does not have a contract, he or she must be paid within 72 hours.

Eviction of the On-site Manager

Many on-site manager contracts contain a clause stating that residency is part of the job and that the manager must leave within 72 hours of termination. As yet not fully tested in courts, this clause, as well as the entire manager employment contract, should be reviewed by legal counsel.

If the manager is a tenant, he or she may have to be evicted in the normal manner.

Employment Contract

The employment contract with the on-site manager should be in writing and set forth duties, responsibilities, hours, and remuneration (see Figure 15–3).

Payroll

The employer must establish at least twice-monthly pay periods and give the employee a pay stub with all basic payroll information on it; that is, number of hours, pay period, taxes, and so on.

Records

The company must keep accurate payroll records for three years showing total daily hours. W-2 forms must be given by January 31 to all employees. All documentation relating to hiring, performance, and firing also should be kept for three years.

Withholding from Employees' Pay

1. Social Security

2. Federal and state income tax

3. State disability

4. Medicare tax

Employer Contributions

1. Federal and state unemployment insurance

2. Workers' compensation insurance (7–10 percent of wages)

3. Social Security

OSHA

State OSHA (Occupational Safety Hazards Act) covers the safety of employees relative to unsafe work areas and practices.

Resident Manager Duties

The duties of a Resident Manager of a rental property are to generally oversee the property and perform the following services:

1. Laundry room maintenance
   a) Keep clean.
   b) Call laundry company when necessary.

2. Ground care
   a) Pick up litter.
   b) Water lawns and plants.
   c) Make sure trash area is kept organized and clear of clutter.
   d) Make sure tenants are responsible for their trash.

3. Call in any vacancies to office.
   a) Put out "For Rent" sign immediately.

4. Replace common area light bulbs.

5. Handle all minor maintenance, examples:
   a) Change washers.
   b) Un-jam garbage disposals.
   c) Snake clogged toilets.

6. Schedule major maintenance through office.
   a) Work orders of maintenance workers are to be signed when workers arrive and when they are through.

7. Perform walk-throughs with vacating tenants to determine security deposit refunds and evaluate what needs to be done to turn around.

8. Call office or area manager for name of vendors to use for turnaround or any other repair and maintenance.

9. Collect rents.

10. Serve three-day notices on the third of each month (no exceptions).

11. If resident pays partial payment, give him or her a new three-day notice for the balance with his or her receipt.

12. Check rental application to make sure all necessary information is completed.

13. Call for credit check or have area manager call.

14. Fill out rental agreement completely and sign.

15. Give new tenant move-in/move-out sheet and have them return it as soon as possible.

16. Fill out key form and have tenant sign for all keys; keep with rental agreement and move-in/move-out sheet.

17. Absolutely no cash is to be accepted except at the management company's main office.

18. When taking an application the first time, do not take a personal check. Only a money order or cashier's check should be accepted the first month. This includes credit check money, rent, and security deposit.

19. When you need an ad placed, call the office and let the person in charge of advertising know when you would like the ad placed. Also remember to call that person back as soon as the apartment is rented.

Figure 15–2. Assignment of Duties

20. If your building allows pets:
   a) An additional security deposit of $200 is required.
   b) There will also be an additional $20 per month for the pet.
   c) The additional security deposit will be refunded if the pet does no damage. If the prospective tenant is not willing to pay extra deposit and rent for a pet, then the pet cannot be accepted in the building.

21. Communicate and coordinate with the area manager, if any.

22. Handle tenant complaints as much as possible.

23. Call emergency services.

Manager Name _____

Agent _____

Manager Signature _____

Agent Signature _____

Date _____

Date _____

Figure 15–2. Continued

Fair Employment

Notices of fair employment hours and working conditions must be posted.

1099 Form

Form 1099 on services of $600 or more per year must be sent to nonemployee vendors and filed with the Internal Revenue Service by January 31 each year. The vendor is exempt if he or she is incorporated. Noncorporate vendors must supply you with a Social Security or federal I.D. number. If this number is not given to you, 20 percent of future payments must be withheld and forwarded to the IRS on a regular basis. Failure to file 1099s can result in penalties to the management company of $50 for failure to send to the IRS, $50 for failure to send to the vendor, or 10 percent of the amount of the services rendered, whichever is greater (See Figure 15–4). The management company should request a taxpayer identification number (TIN) form, which is called a W-9 (Figure 15–5).

STAFF SELECTION

Behavioral assessment reports have been developed to assist in personnel selection. A leader in this field is Phil Herman of Potential Unlimited, Inc., of San Rafael, California. The personal, interpersonal, and work traits of a bookkeeper are different from those of a property manager or leasing agent. For example, under task (work) traits, a prospective property manager who is seldom decisive, orderly, detailed, objective, or persistent would have little likelihood of success. During the employment interview, the candidate's traits should be compared to the task traits of successful property managers (Figure 15–6). Using this structured system and open-ended interview questions, you can increase the probability of hiring successful applicants.

Open-ended questions elicit more than a yes or no answer. For example, "Tell me about your family and education." "What are your strengths?" "How do you motivate yourself?" "How do you learn best?" Using a four-page format, Career Potential Analysis (CPA) usually can prepare written reports on a job applicant for the management company in less than ten days.

This Employment Agreement, entered into this _____ day of _____ , 19__ , between _____ , hereinafter referred to as "employer," and

_____ ,

hereinafter referred to as "employee," is for employment as the resident manager of the property

known as _____ ,

located at _____ ,

California, _____ units.

Compensation shall be as follows:

$ _____ Salary

$ _____ Apartment Value

$ _____ Apt. Phone, Utility Value

$ _____ TOTAL VALUE

Manager shall pay rent of $ _____ per month while acting as resident manager. In the event resident manager's employment is terminated for any reason, the employee will vacate the apartment within seven (7) days. The employee agrees to pay rent at the prevailing market rate per day on the apartment commencing the day following termination of employment.

The hours per month for the duties listed on the attached sheet shall not exceed _____ hours per month, and shall not exceed eight (8) hours per day nor forty (40) hours per week, and shall not exceed six days of work in any one week. If for any reason the hours shall be inadequate to perform the management responsibilities assigned, then:

A. Employee shall notify the employer prior to performing such services and obtain consent therefor.
B. Any additional hours that are necessary to be worked in emergencies shall be reported to the employer at once and not later than forty-eight (48) hours.

The employee shall record hours worked daily on a time sheet, which he or she shall sign as verification of accuracy and submit to the employer at a designated time each month.

The employee shall not discriminate as to race, sex, color, religious creed, ancestry, or national origin in the selection of residents for this property.

This agreement may be terminated by either party at any time without liability for compensation, except such as may have been earned at the date of such termination.

If an action is brought for the recovery of rent or other monies due, or to become due under this Agreement, or by reason of a breach of any covenant herein, or for the recovery of the possession of said premises, or to recover for damage to said property, the employee agrees to pay all costs in connection therewith, including, but not limited to, reasonable attorney's fees, whether or not the action proceeds to judgment.

Figure 15–3.   Resident Manager's Employment Agreement

It is further agreed that there are no other or further agreements between the parties not contained in this instrument.

EMPLOYER: DATE:

_____   _____

(Employer's Agent)

_____   _____

(Agent's Title)

EMPLOYEE: DATE:

_____   _____

(Please Print Name)

EMPLOYEE: DATE:

_____   _____

(Please Print Name)

Figure 15–3. Continued

Selection of a Resident Manager

In many instances, a couple is preferred for resident management, which makes the selection process more difficult. One person usually has to be good in maintenance and the other in leasing and bookkeeping. Unless the apartment community is large, over 150 units, it is difficult to pay wages sufficient to attract high-caliber on-site managers. For example, a 20-unit building with a gross collected income of $10,000 per month may pay only 5 percent or $500, or just give a free apartment. The managers must have another job or other source of income in order to live. In smaller complexes, this author prefers to find a person good in leasing and dealing with people and have the maintenance done by outside contractors. In some states, if a complex has more than 16 units, you are required to have an on-site manager.

In all cases, the prospective manager should be carefully screened. A credit check should be run just as on a regular tenant and references should be thoroughly checked. A personal interview is also a must; a resident manager pre-employment test (Figure 15–7) is desirable. Frequently, the most appro-

9595 ☐ VOID ☐ CORRECTED For Official Use Only

Type or macnine print PAYER'S name, street address, city, state, and ZIP code		1 Rents $	OMB No. 1545-0115	Miscellaneous Income
		2 Royalties $	19 Statement for Recipients of	
PAYER'S Federal identification number	RECIPIENT'S identification number	3 Prizes and awards $	4 Federal income tax withheld $	Copy A For Internal Revenue Service Center
Type or machine print RECIPIENT'S name (first, middle, last)		5 Fishing boat proceeds $	6 Medical and health care payments $	For Paperwork Reduction Act Notice and instructions for completing this form, see Instructions for Forms 1099, 1098, 5498, 1096, and W-2G.
Street address		7 Nonemployee compensation $	8 Substitute payments in lieu of dividends or interest $	
City, state, and ZIP code		9 Payer made direct sales of $5,000 or more of consumer products to a buyer (recipient) for resale . . . . . ▶ ☐		
Account number (optional)		10 The amount in Box 7 is crop insurance proceeds . . ▶ ☐		

Form **1099-MISC** 95-2830662 **Do NOT Cut or Separate Forms on This Page** Department of the Treasury - Internal Revenue Service

Figure 15–4. 1099 Form

Form **W-9**
(Rev. July 1984)
Department of the Treasury
Internal Revenue Service

Payer's Request for Taxpayer Identification Number and Certification

Give This Form to the Payer, Middleman, Broker, or Barter Exchange

Please print or type

Name as shown on account (If joint account, list first and circle the name of the person or entity whose number you enter in Part I below.)

Address

City, State, and ZIP code

List account number(s) here ▶

Part I **Taxpayer Identification Number—For All Accounts**

Enter your taxpayer identification number in the appropriate box. For most individuals, this is your social security number. If you do not have a number, see *How to Obtain a TIN.*

Note: *If the account is in more than one name, see the chart on page 2 for guidelines on which number to give the payer.*

Social security number

OR

Employer identification number

Part II **For Payees Exempt From Backup Withholding (See Instructions)**

Certification.—Under penalties of perjury, I certify that:

(1) The number shown on this form is my correct Taxpayer Identification Number (or I am waiting for a number to be issued to me), **and**

(2) I am not subject to backup withholding either because I have not been notified by the Internal Revenue Service (IRS) that I am subject to backup withholding as a result of a failure to report all interest or dividends, or the IRS has notified me that I am no longer subject to backup withholding.

Certification Instructions.—You must cross out item (2) above if you have been notified by IRS that you are subject to backup withholding because of underreporting interest or dividends on your tax return. However, if after being notified by IRS that you were subject to backup withholding you received another notification from IRS that you are no longer subject to backup withholding, do not cross out item (2). (Also see *Certification* under *Specific Instructions.*)

Please Sign Here **Signature ▶** **Date ▶**

Figure 15–5. W-9 Form

EXPLORATORY INTERVIEW WORKSHEET

CANDIDATE _____ DATE _____

POSITION _____ INTERVIEWER _____

RAPPORT/PURPOSE

LIFE EXPERIENCE QUESTIONS
WORK:
EDUCATION:
FAMILY:
INTERESTS:
GOALS

PERSONAL TRAITS	PERSON L M H	JOB L M H
AMBITIOUS		
CONFIDENT		
ENERGETIC		
COMPETITIVE		
FLEXIBLE		
INDEPENDENT		

INTER— PERSONAL TRAITS	PERSON L M H	JOB L M H
EMPATHETIC		
OUTGOING		
TACTFUL		
PERSUASIVE		
ASSERTIVE		
DOMINANT		

WORK TRAITS	PERSON L M H	JOB L M H
DECISIVE		
ORDERLY		
DETAILED		
OBJECTIVE		
PERSISTENT		
ANALYTICAL		
COMPLIANT		

Decision: ☐ Continue ☐ Stop

Company/Job Sell

Selection System Sell

Administer Forms/CPA

Potential Unlimited, Incorporated

Figure 15–6. Interview Worksheet

RESIDENT MANAGER PRE-EMPLOYMENT TEST

You will be given thirty minutes to answer these questions. Please circle the best answer for the multiple choice questions.

1. The resident from apartment #107 comes into the office to tell you that a sudden leak of water from apartment #207 has formed a pool of water in her kitchen. You should:

    a. Call the police so you can enter apartment #207. Have a maintenance person or plumber repair the leak with the police there.
    b. Call the resident of apartment #207 and have them come home so you can fix the leak.
    c. Enter apartment #207, have maintenance or plumber fix the leak and leave everything just the way you found it so the resident doesn't know you were there.
    d. Enter apartment #207, have maintenance or plumber fix the leak and leave a notice to let the resident know you were in the apartment and why.

2. A family with two children wants to rent an apartment. There is only a one bedroom available. You may:

    a. Tell them you don't rent to people with children.
    b. Tell them that children of the opposite sex may not share a bedroom.
    c. Tell them the policy of the property will not permit four people to share a one bedroom unit.
    d. None of the above.

3. Pro-rate the following, assuming that the apartment rents for $300 per month, and the resident moves in on the dates shown. Using a 30 day month, calculate the amount of rent that is prorated and due on the first of the following month:

Move In Date	Pro-rated Amount
1st of month	_____
5th of month	_____
15th of month	_____

4. If a prospective tenant enters the office while you are busy, you should:

    a. Finish what you are working on and greet the person.
    b. Tell the person to sit down and have some coffee.
    c. Stop what you are doing and greet the person immediately.
    d. Ignore the person until they say what they want.

Figure 15–7. Resident Manager Test

5. What can be deducted from a tenant's security deposit after move out?

    a. Any back rent.
    b. Any damage to the apartment beyond normal wear and tear.
    c. A carpet which has become discolored by the sun.
    d. Both a and b.

6. The appearance of the rental office is:

    a. A reflection on the property.
    b. A reflection on the manager and employees.
    c. One of the first impressions a potential resident has of the property.
    d. All of the above.

7. When you are showing an apartment, you would:

    a. Take the fastest route to the apartment and the scenic route back.
    b. Take the scenic route to the apartment and the fastest route back.
    c. Take the fastest route to the apartment and back.
    d. Take the scenic route to the apartment and back.

8. In qualifying a prospective resident for an apartment, you ask:

    a. How many people will be living in the apartment.
    b. The move-in date needed.
    c. Where they work.
    d. If they can put down a deposit.
    e. All of the above.

9. A resident named May Smith lives in your building. She has decided to let John Adams move in, and has come to the office to let you know. You would:

    a. Refuse to let them live together.
    b. Take a rental application from John, verify employment and credit, and have a new rental agreement signed by both residents.
    c. Take a rental application from John. You trust May, so there is no reason to check further.
    d. None of the above.

10. May Smith moves out, leaving John Adams in the apartment in question #9, and without giving you notice. She wants her security deposit back.

    a. You advise her to get her share from John and get a statement from her that John now has full right to the security deposit you hold.
    b. Tell her she doesn't get anything back anyway because she didn't give notice.
    c. Ask your property supervisor what to do.

Figure 15–7. Continued

(Continued)

11. You have five vacancies. Three of the apartments have been vacant for three weeks. An ad has been running in a newspaper for several weeks and you are displaying signs and banners. Name three things you could also try to increase the traffic and rent those units:

_____

_____

_____

12. You don't like a resident. He acts funny toward you and other residents. You would like to evict him. You may legally do so:

    a. Only if he doesn't pay his rent on time.
    b. By calling the police immediately.
    c. Only if he breaks the terms of his rental agreement.
    d. Either a or c.

13. A tenant meets you in the laundry room and tells you verbally that he will be moving soon. You should:

    a. Prepare a written 30 day notice and take it to him to sign.
    b. Forget about it. If he wants his security deposit back, it's his obligation to comply with the rules.
    c. Call your supervisor and tell her you have a verbal notice.

14. A resident manager may not discriminate against people based on their:

    a. _____
    b. _____
    c. _____
    d. _____
    e. _____
    f. _____

15. A couple who are black want to rent an apartment. You should:

    a. Tell them they really won't be happy living at the property as there are no other black families.
    b. Take their application, show them an apartment just as you would any other prospective resident.
    c. Tell them you have no vacancies and there is a long waiting list.
    d. Add another $300 to the security deposit and charge them more rent.

16. Every morning you should:

    a. Walk the property to be sure everything is clean.
    b. Dust the rent ready apartments or models.
    c. Clean the rental office.
    d. All of the above.

Figure 15–7. Continued

17. Complete the following math problems:

$375.00	What is 75%	$374.95	1,879.99
485.00	of 110?	316.39	8,798.13
+ 620.00		333.33	5,455.92
		+ 498.88	+ 8,122.25

18. A resident has moved out on the 15th of the month. You should prepare a Security Deposit Refund Statement form so the main office can process their deposit refund:

    a. As soon as possible. By law the deposit refund must be give to the resident in 14 days.

    b. At the end of the month. By law the deposit refund must be given to the resident in 30 days.

    c. As soon as possible. By law, the deposit refund must be given to the resident immediately at move out.

    d. At the end of the month if the resident doesn't have a refund. As soon as possible if they have a refund.

19. If the electricity is not working in a tenant's apartment, you should:

    a. Tell the tenant the maintenance person will be by next week to look at the problem.

    b. Tell the tenant to buy some candles.

    c. Consider it an emergency and get it repaired immediately.

20. Please explain briefly why you feel you are qualified for this position, and what knowledge and experience you possess that would make you an asset to this company.

_____

_____

_____

_____

_____

_____

_____

_____

_____

_____

_____

_____

_____

_____

Figure 15–7. Continued

priate place to conduct the interview is at the prospective manager's present home where you can gain insights into his or her housekeeping standards.

Motivation

The property supervisor should reinforce the behavior expected of employees. Dr. Michael Le Boeuf, in his book *The Greatest Management Principles in the World*, states that "things that get rewarded are things that get done." If you want to reduce vacancy, the manager's compensation should be structured so that fewer vacancies mean more money each month.

In *The One-Minute Manager* (Berkeley Books, N.Y., 1984), authors Ken Blanchard and Spencer Johnson state that the manager should:

- Set one-minute goals

- Give one-minute praisings

- Give one-minute reprimands

- Encourage people

- Speak the truth

- Laugh

- Enjoy work

The property supervisor needs to be aware of his or her own actions and how they affect employees in order to encourage their best performance.

COMPENSATION AND REWARDS

In a recent study conducted by the *Personnel Journal*, job satisfaction is ranked the number one worker concern. In second place was job security, followed by money. Company benefits were in fourth place, followed by challenges and then promotional opportunities.

In today's society, employees are expecting more from their jobs than traditional wages and employee benefits. They are turning to their work as a source of personal fulfillment, social relationships, and community responsibilities.

If the management company has a history of hassling tenants in returning security deposits, and the company develops a poor reputation, employees cannot be proud of the company and are often subjected to verbal and sometimes physical abuse. The key to a successful management company is stability. If a firm is always replacing and retraining its best personnel, it usually indicates a problem with the management company.

EFFECTIVE COMMUNICATION

In order to motivate, the property supervisor must establish effective communication with personnel. Are your plans for managing the apartment building (see Figure 15–8):

1. *Being comprehended?* "Clean the sidewalks every day."

2. *Being accepted?* "No broom, so we couldn't sweep today."

3. *Being understood?* "Clean sidewalks lead to better curb appeal and lower vacancy."

4. *Are you understanding your employees?* "We can't find our broom because we want to buy a motorized sweeper."

Kinds of Communication

1. *Formal*—written notices, letters.

2. *Informal*—custom, the way it has always been done.

"WHAT DID THE BOSS HAVE TO SAY?"

Figure 15–8.   Motivation

3. *Official*—standard operating procedure (SOP).

4. *Grapevine*—how others perceive you and the formal system.

5. *Verbal*—not what we say, but how we say it; i.e., tone of voice.

6. *Nonverbal*—includes body language such as smiling when saying "Thank you."

Abraham Maslow, noted psychologist, developed a hierarchy of needs (Figure 15–9) that managers should be aware of when supervising and motivating employees. When an employee is only making minimum wage and doesn't have a place to live or enough food to feed his or her family, trying to motivate through self-actualization such as using creativity, curiosity, or independence will probably be futile. This individual still has basic needs (food, shelter, clothing) that first must be met. Exploring how this individual can earn more money would be a successful approach. On the other hand, a certified property manager (CPM) whose salary adequately covers basic needs would be more amenable to creativity and independence as target motivators.

SUMMARY

The property manager must coordinate operations in various areas such as rent collection, maintenance, tenant selection, and accounting in order for the building to operate harmoniously. Different personalities, behavior patterns, approaches, and goals must be channeled in the right direction. Property management relies on six steps: planning, organization, staffing, directing, control-

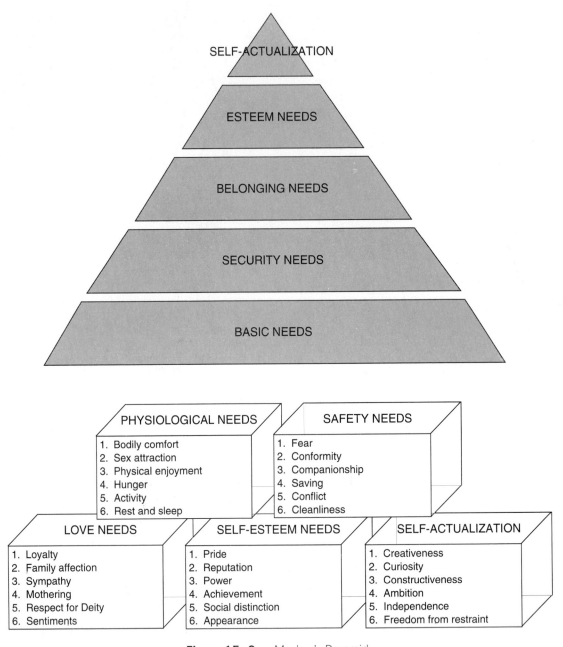

MASLOW'S PYRAMID OF NEEDS
PREPONENT — STRONGER NEEDS ARE MET FIRST

SELF-ACTUALIZATION

ESTEEM NEEDS

BELONGING NEEDS

SECURITY NEEDS

BASIC NEEDS

PHYSIOLOGICAL NEEDS
1. Bodily comfort
2. Sex attraction
3. Physical enjoyment
4. Hunger
5. Activity
6. Rest and sleep

SAFETY NEEDS
1. Fear
2. Conformity
3. Companionship
4. Saving
5. Conflict
6. Cleanliness

LOVE NEEDS
1. Loyalty
2. Family affection
3. Sympathy
4. Mothering
5. Respect for Deity
6. Sentiments

SELF-ESTEEM NEEDS
1. Pride
2. Reputation
3. Power
4. Achievement
5. Social distinction
6. Appearance

SELF-ACTUALIZATION
1. Creativeness
2. Curiosity
3. Constructiveness
4. Ambition
5. Independence
6. Freedom from restraint

Figure 15—9. Maslow's Pyramid

ling, and feedback. When staffing the management office, an organizational chart can help to delineate the chain of command in the organization.

Payment of employees according to local, state, and federal guidelines can be complex and difficult, as state and federal minimum wage rates may differ. Some compensation for the on-site manager is exempt from withholding taxes. The on-site manager should sign a manager's contract and be given an assignment of duties and responsibilities. The number of hours worked should equate to at least the minimum wage. The on-site manager is considered an employee, not an independent contractor. Records such as time sheets and wages paid should be kept, as well as a W-2 form issued by January 31 each year. For vendors who are not corporations, a 1099 form must be prepared and sent for any labor amounts over $600 (see Figure 15–4).

Personnel behavior assessment reports are available from outside consulting firms to help the property manager select personnel. Incentives should be based on performance, with bonuses or rewards offered for the things you want accomplished. To motivate and communicate, the property manager must be aware of the six types of communication: formal, informal, official, grapevine, verbal, and nonverbal.

The future of property management looks bright as investors are looking at properties as businesses that need to be run professionally in order to increase cash flow and appreciation. This means that the demand for competent, experienced, and knowledgeable, and certified property managers (CPMs) will increase. As the demand for these professionals grows faster than the supply, salaries will escalate and compensation will be greater for those who are the real achievers and producers.

<table>
<tr><td>

PERSONALITY PROFILE

</td><td>

Shortly after graduating from Brigham Young University in Utah, Judy Jenks and her then husband, after some coaxing from her sister, moved to Southern California in 1980. Because of their college backgrounds and her husband's maintenance skills, they gained enough experience while being assistant resident managers on a small property to move on and become full-fledged resident managers of a 123-unit apartment complex. Judy was fortunate enough to work for a company that allowed her to have her newborn child with her during her day.

</td></tr>
</table>

Her employer was impressed enough with her skills to promote her to manager of 48 town homes. This would be a new experience for Judy as this property was clearly in need of new managers and because the current situation had a low occupancy factor and several evictions in progress. Not only would Judy have to upgrade her marketing skills to attract more desirable tenants, but she also would be required to attend meetings and work with the homeowners association.

After three years in this position and a divorce, Judy was ready for a change. She was asked to open a 60-unit apartment complex. Her duties were expanded once again to deal more heavily in customer service, staff, utility companies, and so on. Judy said, "It was very exciting setting up a model and opening a new complex."

In 1986, Judy was asked to open a brand new 254-unit complex. Judy says this was the most challenging opportunity she had ever been given. She had to set up a leasing staff, along with working with the city and the affordable housing program. She also dealt with construction, building, and safety crews. Judy remains at this property, but admits she looks forward to the doors that will be opened to her upon achieving the prestigious CPM designation.

REVIEW QUESTIONS

1. The management function includes
   a. market surveys.
   b. organizing.
   c. staffing.
   d. both a and c
   e. both b and c

2. Controlling is
   a. hiring and training personnel.
   b. developing goals and objectives.
   c. measuring performance and identifying problem areas.
   d. defining jobs.

3. The property manager provides
   a. goods.   c. a service.
   b. products.   d. none of the above

4. All employees should be paid at least
   a. minimum wage.   c. poverty wage.
   b. the highest wage.   d. comparable wage.

5. The on-site manager is
   a. an independent contractor.   c. a casual laborer.
   b. an employee.   d. on commission only.

6. A fired employee should be paid
   a. within 24 hours.   c. within 72 hours.
   b. within 48 hours.   d. immediately.

7. A prudent property manager would have
   a. the highest management fee.   c. the lowest-cost employees.
   b. a written resident manager   d. the highest-cost employees.
      agreement.

8. The property manager should post
   a. HUD discrimination posters.   d. both a and c
   b. Playboy posters.   e. both a and b
   c. fair employment posters.

9. Use of behavior assessment reports considers the
   a. sex of the applicant.   d. both a and c
   b. personal and work traits of   e. both b and c
      the applicant.
   c. color of the applicant.

10. Laws in property management
    a. are constantly changing.   c. never change.
    b. change only every ten years.   d. are the same nationwide.

11. The property management company should have
    a. luxury offices.   d. both a and b
    b. an organizational chart.   e. both b and c
    c. an annual budget.

12. The "perfect property manager" is
    a. a CPA.   c. a developer.
    b. an attorney.   d. unable to identify.

13. The employee should receive by the end of January from the employer
    a. a W-2 form.   c. a K-1 form.
    b. a 1099 form.   d. a 1040 form.

14. Employees' number one concern according to recent studies is
    a. wages.   c. job satisfaction.
    b. challenges.   d. long lunch hours.

15. Written notices would be what kind of communication?
    a. verbal   c. informal
    b. nonverbal   d. formal

CASE STUDY PROBLEMS

Refer to the Case Study at the end of Chapter 5.

1. How much will you pay the new manager at Civic Center Terrace? Does this amount meet minimum wage requirements?

2. Will your new manager be an employee or an independent contractor?

3. How will you fire and evict the present manager?

4. Will the new manager have an employment contract?

5. Should you run extensive credit and background checks on the new manager before hiring?

For students who want to do extra work, here are additional case study problems.

6. Prepare a management plan as outlined in Chapter 3. The plan should include rent increases, rehabilitation costs, and increased NOI projections for five years (use your own cost assumptions).

7. What is the new value using the same cap rate of 9 with the increased NOI?

8. Prepare an operating budget (for one month) to show the owner a pro forma projection.

9. Make recommendations on obtaining new financing.

10. Write up a proposal to manage Civic Center Terrace.

ADDITIONAL READING AND REFERENCES

Blanchard, Ken, and Spencer Johnson, *The One-Minute Manager*, Berkeley Books, New York, NY, 1984.

Boykin, James H., *Real Estate Counseling*, American Society of Real Estate Counselors, Chicago, IL, 1984.

Carnegie, Dale, *How to Win Friend and Influence People*, Simon and Schuster, New York, NY, 1977.

Covey, Stephen R., *The 7 Habits of Highly Effective People*, Simon and Schuster, New York, NY, 1989.

DeCarlo, Joseph W., *Essential Facts: Real Estate Management*, Warren, Gorham & Lamont, Boston, MA, 1996.

DeCarlo, Joseph W., *Property Management in California*, JD Seminars and Publications, Costa Mesa, CA, 1996.

DeCarlo, Joseph W., *Real Estate Adventures, Principles, and Practices*, JD Seminars and Publications, Costa Mesa, CA, 1993.

Keirsey, David, and Marilyn Bates, *Please Understand Me*, Prometheus Nemesis, Del Mar, CA, 1984.

Nierenberg, Gerald, *The Art of Negotiating*, Simon and Schuster, New York, NY, 1981.

Urban Land Institute, *Dollars and Cents of Shopping Centers*, Washington, D.C., 1995.

Waitley, Denis, *The Psychology of Winning*, Nightingale-Conant, Chicago, IL, 1979.

Appendix A

Glossary of Real Estate Terms

Acceleration Clause: Lease clause that calls for specified rental increases at specific times.

Accredited Management Organization (AMO): Professional designation awarded to property management firms by the Institute of Real Estate Management (IREM).

Accredited Resident Manager (ARM): A professional designation awarded by IREM to resident managers who have completed certain experience and education requirements.

Actual Eviction: Forcible ouster of a tenant from a rental property, pursuant to a court order (writ of execution).

Agency: The relationship between principal and agent by which the agent is employed to act for the principal.

Agent: One who acts and represents another from whom he or she has derived legal authority.

Anchor Tenant: The major (key) tenant that will attract other businesses and customers.

Appraisal: An estimate of value as of a certain date.

Assessment (Condo): A monthly fee paid by homeowners to cover the operation and maintenance of common areas.

Assignee: One to whom the property shall be transferred.

Assignment: The transfer of an existing tenant's rental rights in a property to a third party: for example, a lease assignment.

Assignor: One who assigns or transfers property.

Automatic Extension Clause: A lease covenant providing that a lease can be renewed unless one party gives notice to terminate.

Beneficiary: The lender on the security of a note and deed of trust.

British Thermal Unit (Btu): The quantity of heat required to raise the temperature of one pound of water one degree Fahrenheit.

Building Code: Regulations adopted by local, county, and state agencies to regulate construction of buildings.

Building Owners and Managers Association (BOMA): An international organization that fosters industry standards through educational programs and publications.

Bylaws: Rules and regulations adopted by associations.

Capitalization Rate: The rate of return considering interest and risk which an investor desires to achieve; used to determine the value of a property based on net operating income.

Cash Flow: Net income after expenses and debt financing, but before depreciation.

CBD: Central business district.

Certified Commercial Investment Member (CCIM): A designation bestowed by the National Association of Realtors.

Certified Property Manager (CPM): A professional designation conferred by IREM on property managers who have met stringent educational and experience requirements.

Certified Shopping Center Manager (CSM): A professional designation conferred by the International Council of Shopping Centers (ICSC) after education requirements are completed.

Community Association Institute (CAI): A professional organization for condominium and cooperative owners and managers.

Condemnation: The taking of a property by government agencies.

Condominium: A system whereby the owner holds title to an individual unit plus an undivided fee-simple interest in the common areas.

Constructive Eviction: Illegal eviction by a landlord through methods that render the unit unusable by the tenant; for example, changing locks, removing doors, and so on.

Covenants, Conditions, and Restrictions (CC&Rs): Usually refers to condominium management and the powers and duties of its governing entity.

Curable Depreciation: Physical deterioration and/or functional obsolescence which can be repaired or replaced.

Deep Pockets: A term used to refer to a defendant in a lawsuit who has little liability, but more assets than other defendants with more liability in the case.

Deferred Maintenance: Needed but postponed repairs.

Department of Housing and Urban Development (HUD): A government agency that provides financial assistance and construction of housing for low-income tenants.

Depreciation: Loss of value due to physical deterioration or economic or functional obsolescence.

Economic Life: The useful period over which the property will yield a return on the investment.

Economic Obsolescence: Loss of value due to factors other than the building, for example, neighborhood deterioration.

Economic Rent: The expected or predicted scheduled rent (not actual rent).

Eminent Domain: The right of the government to acquire property for public use by condemnation.

Environmental Protection Agency (EPA): The federal agency responsible for planning and enforcing air quality improvements.

Escalation Clause: A lease clause providing for upward or downward adjustment of the rental rate at certain times (usually tied to the Consumer Price Index).

Estate for Years: A leasehold interest that continues for a specific period of time.

Estoppel: A doctrine of law that prevents the assertion of rights that are inconsistent with a previous position or representation.

Eviction: The removal of a tenant from property pursuant to a court judgment.

Eviction Notice: A legal notice given to a tenant when he or she defaults under the terms of his or her lease or rental agreement.

Experience Exchange Report: A publication by IREM of operating costs for apartments, office buildings, and condominiums.

Facade: The front of a building.

Fair Housing Act: A federal law prohibiting housing discrimination based on race, religion, color, creed, national origin, family status, or sex.

Federal Deposit Insurance Corporation (FDIC): A government agency that insures bank deposits.

Fee: Payment for services.

Fidelity Bond: An employer's insurance against loss of money or property caused by an employee.

Fiduciary: The relationship of trust and confidence between the principal and the property manager.

Fixed Expense: A property expense that does not fluctuate with rental income, for example, a loan payment.

Flat Fee: A management fee expressed as a dollar amount, usually per month.

Foreclosure: When property pledged as security for a debt is sold to pay the debt if payments haven't been made.

Forfeiture: The giving up of rights such as in the forfeiture of a lease.

Functional Obsolescence: The loss of property value due to adverse building features; for example, small elevators, out-of-date electrical wiring, low ceilings.

Graduate Realtor Institute (GRI): A designation bestowed by the National Association of Realtors (NAR).

Graduated Lease: A lease that provides for varying rent, for example, a 5 percent increase every year.

Highest and Best Use: The most productive use a property can be put to in order to produce the highest economic gain.

Holdover Tenant: A tenant who remains after the expiration of a lease.

House Rules: The building rules and regulations under which a tenant will operate, usually in a residential building.

Hundred Percent Location: The best retail location in a geographic area.

HVAC: Heating, ventilation, and air-conditioning equipment.

Hypothecate: To pledge an item as security without giving up possession.

Impounding: An act by lenders of accumulating funds in an account to pay taxes and insurance on properties on which they loaned money.

Income Approach: A process of estimating value by capitalizing the annual net operating income.

Industrial Park: A subdivision that accommodates light manufacturing and distribution uses.

Inflation: When the money supply increases faster than goods and services; results in increased wages and decreased purchasing power.

Injunction: A writ or court order restraining a party's action.

Institute of Real Estate Management (IREM): The professional organization of property managers that is part of the National Association of Realtors (NAR).

International Council of Shopping Centers (ICSC): The professional organization of shopping center managers and owners which provides information exchange and education for its members.

Key Tenant: A major tenant in an office building or shopping center; also referred to as the **Anchor Tenant**.

Kiosk: Free-standing counter shops located in shopping center malls.

Landlord: The owner of the property.

Lease: A contract given by a landlord to a tenant setting forth conditions, terms, and length of occupancy.

Leasing Agent: The person (agent) who rents the space to another.

Lessee: One who rents property (tenant).

Lessor: The owner or landlord.

Life Support Systems: The safety and security procedures of a complex.

Limited Partnership: Allows investors to reduce risks, usually by being only "at risk for the amount of investment."

Lis Pendens: Constructive notice of a pending lawsuit.

Loss Factor: The ratio of rentable space to usable space.

Maintenance Contract: A contract that assigns vendors specific duties, usually on a monthly basis; for example, an HVAC landscape contract.

Management Agreement: A written contract signed by the owner and agent outlining the duties, obligations, responsibilities, and terms under which a property will be managed.

Management Fee: The cost charged by the management company, usually on a monthly basis, to manage a particular property.

Management Plan: The financial and operational strategy for the management of a property to attain the owner's goals.

Market Analysis: Studies of economic, demographic, sales, and leasing information to evaluate the supply and demand and market price and rate for a specific building.

Mechanic's Lien: A lien against the property by a vendor who supplied labor and materials for improvements.

Member of Appraisal Institute (MAI): The designation of a professional appraiser.

Merchants Association: An organization of merchants of a shopping center to promote joint advertising, promotions, and decorations to enhance their businesses.

Mini-warehouse: A facility that provides smaller space rentals to individuals and businesses.

Minor: Any person under 18 years of age.

Mixed-Use Project: A planned development that incorporates several uses such as residential, office, and retail.

Modernization: The updating of existing space or equipment to enhance the value.

Mortgagee: The person who lends the money, for instance, a bank or savings and loan.

Mortgagor: The borrower who pledges the property as security.

National Association of Realtors: The umbrella or organization of all the specialized real estate organizations such as the Institute of Property Management (IREM).

Neighborhood Analysis: Used in management plans to determine the characteristics of the population in a small geographic area.

Neighborhood Center: A smaller retail center (25,000 to 100,000 square feet) catering to convenience shopping.

Net Lease: A lease in which the tenant usually pays base rent plus extra expenses such as taxes, insurance, and maintenance.

Net Operating Income (NOI): Gross collected income minus operating expenses; doesn't include debt service or depreciation expense.

Nominal Interest Rate: The interest rate stated in the loan documents.

Noncompetition Clause: A lease clause giving one tenant the exclusive right to operate a particular business in a shopping center, for example, a florist shop.

Noncontrollable Expenses: Items the property manager has little or no control over, for instance, taxes and utility rates.

Normal Wear and Tear: Normal maintenance on a residential unit for which tenants are not held responsible, for example, painting of apartments after one year.

Notary Public: An officer who has authority to acknowledge documents and affix a seal.

Notice of Responsibility: A notice to relieve the owner of responsibility of cost of work being done; must be recorded and posted.

Notice to Quit: A legal notice to a tenant to vacate a rented space.

Novation: The substitution of a new party or agreement for an existing one.

Nuisance Rent Increase: A small (usually $10 or less) rent increase that the tenant will pay to avoid the cost of moving.

Pass-Through Costs: Certain cost increases (taxes, insurance, etc.) passed from the owner to the tenant.

Percentage Fee: The management fee expressed as a percentage of collected income.

Percentage Lease: A lease based on a percentage of gross sales for retail stores; usually contains a base, or minimum, monthly rent.

Physical Life: The length of useful time the building is expected to be functional.

Police Power: The right of the government to enact laws for health, safety, and general public welfare.

Power of Attorney: An instrument authorizing a person to act as an agent of the principal; can be general or specific.

Preventive Maintenance: A program of regularly scheduled inspections and maintenance that allows potential problems to be prevented or repaired less expensively than if left to turn into major repairs, for example, monthly changing of filters.

Principal: The property owner to whom the property manager (agent) is responsible.

Procuring Cause: The results from an agent's employment in the sale or leasing of property, finding a buyer or tenant.

Profit and Loss Statement: A monthly report of the income and expenses of a property, which is sent to the owner.

Property Management: The operation and supervision of a property by an agent to increase the net operating income (NOI) and enhance the value of the property.

Property Supervisor (Manager): The person who usually supervises several on-site (resident) managers.

Proprietary Lease: The right of a shareholder to occupy a specific unit in a building under certain conditions.

Proration: The adjustment of rent, taxes, insurance, interest, and so forth, on the proportional time in use.

Quiet Enjoyment: The right of the owner or tenant to use the property without interference.

Quit Claim Deed: The relinquishing of a right or claim, if any, one may have had in the property.

Radius Clause: A lease term in which a retailer agrees not to own or operate a similar business within a specific distance of the leased store.

Real Estate Cycle: The pattern of real estate experience over a long period of time in response to the economy and changing conditions.

Real Estate Investment Trust (REIT): A tax entity trust that purchases property and passes at least 90 percent of its income to its shareholders.

Real Property Administrator (RPA): A property management designation bestowed by the Building Owners and Managers Association.

Realtor: A real estate broker who is a dues-paying member in good standing in a Board of Realtors associated with the National Association of Realtors.

Recapture Clause: A clause in percentage leases that allows the owner to terminate the lease if a merchant's sales have not reached a specified level.

Recycling: Changing the use and modernization of a building, for example, converting an old warehouse into a restaurant.

Referral: Obtaining new business from reference of existing clients or associates.

Regional Center: A large shopping center (500,000 to 900,000 square feet) that has at least two anchor tenants, merchandises a wide variety of goods, and has a large geographic radius of customer attraction.

Reminder Notice: A notice sent to a tenant who is late in paying rent.

Rent: The periodic payment to the owner or agent by the tenant for space used.

Rent Control: Local government regulations governing increases in rents and evictions.

Rentable Space: The floor area minus stairs, elevator shafts, ducts, and areas not available to the tenant according to BOMA standards.

Rental Schedule: The total amount of rent if all units are rented.

Repair and Deduct: When the tenant makes repairs necessary for habitability. If the landlord doesn't respond within a reasonable time, the cost of the repairs are then deducted from rent owed.

Replacement Cost: The cost of replacing an existing structure with an equivalent building, but with modern materials, design, and layout.

Rescission: The repealing of a contract by mutual consent of the parties to the contract.

Resident Manager (On-site): One who is directly responsible for the rental, maintenance, and personnel of a building.

Retaliatory Eviction: An illegal action based on a reprisal against a tenant by a landlord.

Return on Investment: The owner measure of profitability; calculated by dividing the cost into the existing or projected profits and then multiplying by 100.

Rules and Regulations: Set guidelines, usually in an apartment building. Set forth guidelines such as pool hours, behavior (no skateboards), and so on.

Sale-Leaseback: The owner sells property, but retains occupancy by leasing from the buyer.

Sandwich Lease: A leasehold interest that lies between the primary lease and the operating lease.

Section 8: Housing assistance from HUD through local housing agencies that send payments directly to the owner for part of the qualified tenant rent. The tenant pays the balance to the owner.

Security Deposit: Money held by the owner or agent until the tenant moves, to cover damage, cleaning, lost keys, and/or unpaid rent.

Sheriff Deed: A deed given by the court to satisfy a judgment.

Sherman Anti-Trust Act: A federal law that prohibits price-fixing or collusion in the fixing of management fees among competitors.

Sign-Restriction Clause: A lease clause that regulates tenant signs and displays.

Society of Industrial Realtors (SIR): An organization of industrial Realtors.

Special Purpose Property: A building designed for a particular use, for example, a hotel or church.

Specialty Center: A small retail center (less than 250,000 square feet) that specializes in unique merchandise; usually located near resorts or large centers.

Statute of Frauds: Provision of this statute states that contracts of real property longer than one year must be in writing in order to be enforceable.

Step-Up Clause: A lease clause allowing for rental increases at specified times.

Straight-Line Depreciation: A conservative method of calculating tax depreciation based on equal increments for the life of the building.

Strip Center: A small convenience center with stores configured in a straight line.

Super-Regional Center: The largest form of shopping center (750,000+ square feet), attracting customers from a large radius.

Technical Storage: A market condition that occurs when supply (units) is exceeded by demand (tenants).

Tenancy at Sufferance: When the tenant continues to occupy the premises without the consent of the owner after the lease has expired.

Tenancy at Will: The tenant has the right of possession of the property for an indefinite period of time or until either party gives a termination notice.

Tenancy in Common: Ownership by two or more persons who hold individual interest without the right of survivorship.

Tenant: One who pays the rent; also called the **Lessee**.

Tenant Improvement Allowance (TI): An allowance for the cost of alterations needed to make the space suitable for the tenant's business.

Tenant Mix: The combination of tenants that occupy a building. Thought and careful consideration should be given to compatibility.

Tenants Organization: A tenant union usually formed to control rent increases or to enforce specified actions on the owner.

Time Is of the Essence: A contract provision specifying punctual performance.

Trade Fixtures: Personal property affixed to real property that is removable by the owner.

Trading Area: The geographic area in which customers reside or work.

Trust Account: A separate account maintained by the property manager (broker) for the deposit and distribution of owner (client) funds.

Trust Deed: A legal document in which the borrower (trustor) pledges his or her property as security to pay off the note of the beneficiary (lender).

Trustee: The person or entity holding naked title under a trust deed for the beneficiary.

Trustor: The person who holds the deed, but owes money to the lender (beneficiary) under a trust deed.

Uniform Residential Landlord/Tenant Act: A model law drafted by the National Conference of Commissions on Uniform State Laws (1972) to standardize resident landlord/tenant relationships among different local and state governments.

Urban Land Institute (ULI): An industry association that provides education and research for its members and the public.

Urban Renewal: A program to rehabilitate and redevelop slum residential properties.

U.S. Housing Act of 1968: Prohibits discrimination based on race, religion, color, creed, national origin, or sex.

Use Clause: A lease provision that states the type of business to be conducted on the leased premises (shopping center).

Usury: Charging interest rates greater than permitted by law.

Utilities: Services provided by public utilities, for example, gas, water, electricity.

Valuation: An estimation of the value or worth of a property.

Value: The worth of goods or services in the marketplace.

Variable Expenses: Costs that increase or decrease with the occupancy level of the property, for example, the water bill.

Vendee: The purchaser (buyer).

Vendor: The seller.

Void: Unenforceable.

Voidable: Enforceable unless action is taken to void, for example, a contract with a person under 18 years of age (minor).

Waive: To relinquish or abandon one's right to enforce.

Waiver: The giving up of specified rights or responsibilities.

Wall Shops: Retail shops that break up long, bland walls in a large shopping center; usually very narrow in depth.

Yield: A return earned on money or investment.

Zoning: Restrictions on the type of use or building in certain areas.

Appendix B

Answers to Review Questions

Chapter 1	Chapter 2	Chapter 3	Chapter 4	Chapter 5	Chapter 6	Chapter 7	Chapter 8
1. c	1. c	1. a	1. a	1. d	1. a	1. c	1. b
2. c	2. c	2. b	2. b	2. a	2. c	2. e	2. c
3. a	3. a	3. a	3. a	3. d	3. a	3. a	3. c
4. c	4. a	4. c	4. c	4. b	4. c	4. b	4. a
5. d	5. e	5. c	5. b	5. c	5. c	5. a	5. a
6. b	6. e	6. b	6. c	6. b	6. b	6. a	6. c
7. a	7. a	7. a	7. b	7. d	7. c	7. d	7. b
8. b	8. c	8. a	8. a	8. b	8. d	8. b	8. d
9. c	9. a	9. c	9. b	9. c	9. d	9. c	9. a
10. a	10. c	10. c	10. a	10. d	10. c	10. d	10. a
11. b	11. b	11. b	11. d	11. c	11. c	11. b	11. b
12. c	12. b	12. d	12. a	12. d	12. b	12. c	12. c
13. d	13. d	13. b	13. b	13. c	13. c	13. a	13. a
14. c	14. b	14. b	14. d	14. b	14. d	14. b	14. d
15. b	15. c	15. c	15. d	15. d	15. a	15. c	15. c

Chapter 9	Chapter 10	Chapter 11	Chapter 12	Chapter 13	Chapter 14	Chapter 15
1. a	1. b	1. d	1. d	1. d	1. c	1. e
2. e	2. c	2. a	2. d	2. c	2. b	2. c
3. a	3. a	3. c	3. b	3. b	3. a	3. c
4. e	4. c	4. c	4. d	4. c	4. b	4. a
5. b	5. a	5. b	5. a	5. b	5. a	5. b
6. c	6. b	6. d	6. b	6. a	6. c	6. d
7. e	7. c	7. c	7. d	7. c	7. d	7. b
8. c	8. d	8. b	8. b	8. b	8. b	8. d
9. e	9. b	9. a	9. a	9. c	9. d	9. b
10. b	10. b	10. b	10. d	10. d	10. b	10. a
11. a	11. d	11. a	11. b	11. c	11. b	11. e
12. b	12. b	12. d	12. c	12. c	12. d	12. d
13. c	13. c	13. c	13. b	13. c	13. d	13. a
14. b	14. d	14. d	14. d	14. d	14. c	14. c
15. d	15. c	15. c	15. a	15. b	15. a	15. d

Appendix C

Answers to Case Study Problems

Chapter 3 (while these questions are introduced in Chapter 5, much of the information addressed in these questions is in Chapter 3).

1. Yes. The high employment rate, the growing population, and the increase in service-related industries indicate an influx of tenants who can pay higher rents for a newly rehabbed complex.

2. Yes. The civic center is an excellent source employed tenants. There are good public services, nice neighbors, and the Catholic Church. The comparable buildings in the area are in good condition.

3. Whiskey Manor excels in location and it has a play area. However, it lacks a pool, garage, and spa.

4. The curb appeal—like the landscaping—appears to be nonexistent. Only at night when the red light shines above Big Bertha's apartment does the curb appear to have any appeal.

5. Good management doesn't cost; it pays. Any cost will quickly be recaptured with an applied management plan.

Chapter 7

1. No. In a 20-unit building there frequently will be times of 100 percent occupancy. A model apartment unnecessarily drains the property cash flow. The manager can make arrangements with the vacating tenant to show his or her unit, or use the manager's apartment to show.

2. Landscaping is the cheapest and quickest method to improve curb appeal. How about a new wormwood facade to decry the building's age?

3. A new name means a new identity. Whiskey Manor has long been identified with Big Bertha. A new name will help prospects forget the nefarious past.

4. Let's identify with the positive aspects of the area. We'll rename the complex "Civic Center Terrace." Now, not only does the property have identification of location, but also a new image. ("Whiskey Manor," indeed!)

5. Yes. Signage is the cheapest form of advertising.

6. | CIVIC CENTER TERRACE
1–2 bdrm. apts.
$500–$600
Just east of the Civic Center
12042 Civic Center Plaza
Westminster, CA 92683
(714) 751-2787
"A nice place to live"

7. Big Bertha will be retired to the Old Bordello Workers' Retirement Home where she'll eventually be laid to rest. (FIRE HER!)

8. With as high a vacancy factor as you will have after evicting the delinquent tenants and undesirables, you would benefit from hiring a professional apartment manager training company to train your new manager in the art of salesmanship.

9. Easily, with a bit of maintenance and praying, the rents can go up.

10. Read the book! (A comparison grid can be found in Chapter 7 and a fact sheet in Chapter 5.)

11. What security deposit procedure? They are collecting rent. You could forget last month's rent and charge slightly less than one month's rent as a security deposit (slightly less so the prospective tenant won't confuse it with rent). From the security deposit you can then deduct damages, lost keys, cleaning, unpaid rent, etc. (see Chapter 7).

12. Yes. A written rental agreement allows attorney's fees to be charged to the tenant if the owner wins in court.

Chapter 12

1. Yes. It prevents minor problems from turning into major ones.

2. Repair with copper pipe.

3. A licensed electrician.

4. Yes. The apartment will show better and can get higher rent.

5. No. Also, you should always use a pad.

6. Never do this. Use a licensed pest control vendor.

7. Reduce liability.

8. No. He must also be trustworthy and honest.

9. No. It could lead to a lawsuit.

10. Caulk outside cracks, joints, holes, etc. Install a hot water recirculating pump, separate or submeter, flow restrictors on shower heads, solar heating of hot water, and other improvements.

Chapter 13

1. Yes. However, you would still have to pay mortgage payments.

2. Hire a licensed contractor covered by workers' compensation, or cover Ben yourself.

3. Increase to at least $1,000,000.

4. Refer to Figure 4–5, Bid Sheet.

5. Yes, either hourly or as points on the loan.

Chapter 14

1. Fix immediately as this is a habitability problem.

2. Tell the owner that this would be illegal (Amendment Act 1988).

3. No. You can't discriminate, but you don't have to remodel.

4. Presently it is hit and miss. Serve the 3-Day Notices to Pay or Quit by the fifth of the month and then take legal action. You could also give a $20 rebate off the rent if they pay by the first.

5. Drop eviction as this would be retaliatory eviction, and then fix the plumbing problems.

6. Yes. Forget small claims court and hire an attorney who specializes in eviction (25–35 days, usually).

7. The on-site manager.

8. Discontinue. This is illegal.

9. Yes. It is unlawful entry.

10. Tenants can't waive their rights.

Chapter 15

1. You must pay the new manager at least minimum wage and apartment rental can't exceed maximum deduction in some states.

2. Employee.

3. You must pay the present manager immediately and give him or her a 30-Day Notice to Vacate the apartment.

4. Yes (written).

5. Yes, including credit report.

6.–10. are questions for additional exercises. The answers will vary according to the interpretation and direction of the reader.

Index

Certified Shopping Center Manager (CSM), 3, 163, 350
Change of use, 49
Check register, 79
Co-insurance, 281
Commingling, 68
Common area maintenance, 102, 159, 209
Community Association Institute (CAA), 192, 350
Community center, 148
Comparison grid, 131–132
Comparison worksheet, 46, 176
Compensation, 327–331, 342
Computer hardware, 276–277
Condominium, 182
Constructive eviction, 312
Consulting fees, 68, 285
Cooperative, 182
Corporations, 59, 275
Court system, 316
CPI Index, 97, 115
Credit applications, 118, 133, 134
Curb appeal, 40, 76, 126

D

Deferred maintenance, 24, 40, 237, 350
Delinquency, 80, 82
Demand, 16, 166
Demographics, 37, 151–154
Depreciation, 24
Discrimination, 135, 296, 302, 305
Display ad, 129
Diversification, 62
Dun & Bradstreet (D&B), 173

E

Economic indicators, 17
Economic obsolescence, 24
Effective tax rates, 44
Elderly housing, 224–227
Electrical, 240–41
Electrolysis, 239
Employment contract, 331
Employment forecast, 18
Employment test, 338
Energy management, 76, 243–245
Environmental reports, 221, 251–253
Errors and Omissions, 281
Estate at sufferance, 93
Estate at will, 94
Estate for years, 93, 351
Estate from period, 94
Ethics, 70
Eviction, 282, 318
Exclusive use, 101
Extraordinary maintenance, 239

F

Facsimile machine (FAX), 275
Fair housing laws, 297–300, 305, 351
Family formations, 19
Fee management, 62, 68, 91–92
FIABCI-USA, 5
Fidelity bond, 281

Files, 282
Flat Fee, 68, 351
Forms of ownership, 58
Functional obsolescence, 24, 351

G

Garden apartments, 123
General partnership, 58
Government policies, 15, 17, 221, 225
Gross leasable area, 168
Gross lease, 94, 210
Gross multiplier, 24
Gross sales, 94, 150

H

Habitability, 295–96
Handicapped, 299
High rise, 124, 167
Holdover tenant, 93, 351
House rules, 118, 351
HP12C calculator, 50
HP19B calculator, 50
HUD management, 225–233, 298, 302, 350
HVAC, 240, 351
Hypermart, 149

I

ICSC, 3, 39, 352
Income approach, 21
Income report, 78
Independent contractor, 330–331
Industrial parks, 208, 352
Inflation, 14–16, 352
Infrastructure, 39
Insurance, 100, 189, 280–282
IREM, 3, 39, 192, 329, 352
IRR, 49, 52
IRV formula, 21–23

J

Job descriptions, 327

K

Keenagers, 224
Key money, 224
Key tenant, 224, 352
Kiosk, 157

L

Landlord remedies, 308
Last month's rent, 136
Late charges, 118, 189
Lead-based paint, 251–269
Lease(s), 95–112, 209, 352
Leasing technique, 174–176
Leverage, 61
Licensed contractor, 239
Limited Liability Company (LLC), 60
Limited partnership, 59, 352